FBP

℮ FEDERAL BUREAU OF PHYSICS

VOLUME 1
THE PARADIGM SHIFT

Simon Oliver Writer
Robbi Rodriguez Artist
Rico Renzi Colorist
Steve Wands Jared K. Fletcher Letterers
Nathan Fox Cover Artist
FBP created by Oliver & Rodriguez

FBP: FEDERAL BUREAU OF PHYSICS VOLUME 1: THE PARADIGM SHIFT

Published by DC Comics. Copyright © 2014 Simon Oliver and Robbi Rodriguez.
All Rights Reserved.

Originally published in single magazine form as FBP: FEDERAL BUREAU OF
PHYSICS 1-7 © 2013 Simon Oliver and Robbi Rodriquez. All Rights Reserved.
All characters, their distinctive likenesses and related elements featured in
this publication are trademarks of DC Comics. VERTIGO is a trademark of
DC Comics. The stories, characters and incidents featured in this publication
are entirely fictional. DC Comics does not read or accept unsolicited ideas,
stories or artwork.

DC Comics, 1700 Broadway, New York, NY 10019
A Warner Bros. Entertainment Company.
Printed by RR Donnelley, Salem, VA, USA. 1/17/14. First Printing.
ISBN: 978-1-4012-4510-8

Library of Congress Cataloging-in-Publication Data

Oliver, Simon.
 FBP : Federal Bureau of Physics. Vol. 1, The Paradigm Shift / Simon
Oliver ; [illustrated by] Robbi Rodriguez.
    pages cm
 Summary: "Wormholes in your kitchen. Gravity failures at
school. Quantum tornadoes tearing through the midwest. As with
all natural disasters, people do what they always do: They adapt
and survive. And if things get really bad, the Federal Bureau of
Physics (FBP) is only a call away. FBP: Federal Bureau of Physics
is the story of Adam Hardy: Young, brash and smart, he's a rising
star at the FBP, but when a gravity failure leads to the creation of
an alternate dimension known as a "BubbleVerse," Adam is sent on
a rescue mission and finds his skills and abilities pushed to their
limits when he discovers his partner has a different agenda.."—
Provided by publisher.
 ISBN 978-1-4012-4510-8 (pbk.)
 1. Graphic novels. I. Title. II. Title: Paradigm Shift.
PN6727.O5F37 2014
 741.5'973—dc23
                                    2013045685

Physics is broken. Gravity failures, entropy loops and wandering wormholes are the norm. But it's no longer front-page news, and Federal Bureau of Physics' resident slacker, Agent ADAM HARDY, is about to get a harsh reminder of why he joined the bureau.

"Prevent and protect" is the FBP motto, because if only one thing's for certain in this upside-down world, it's that "the impossible is always possible."

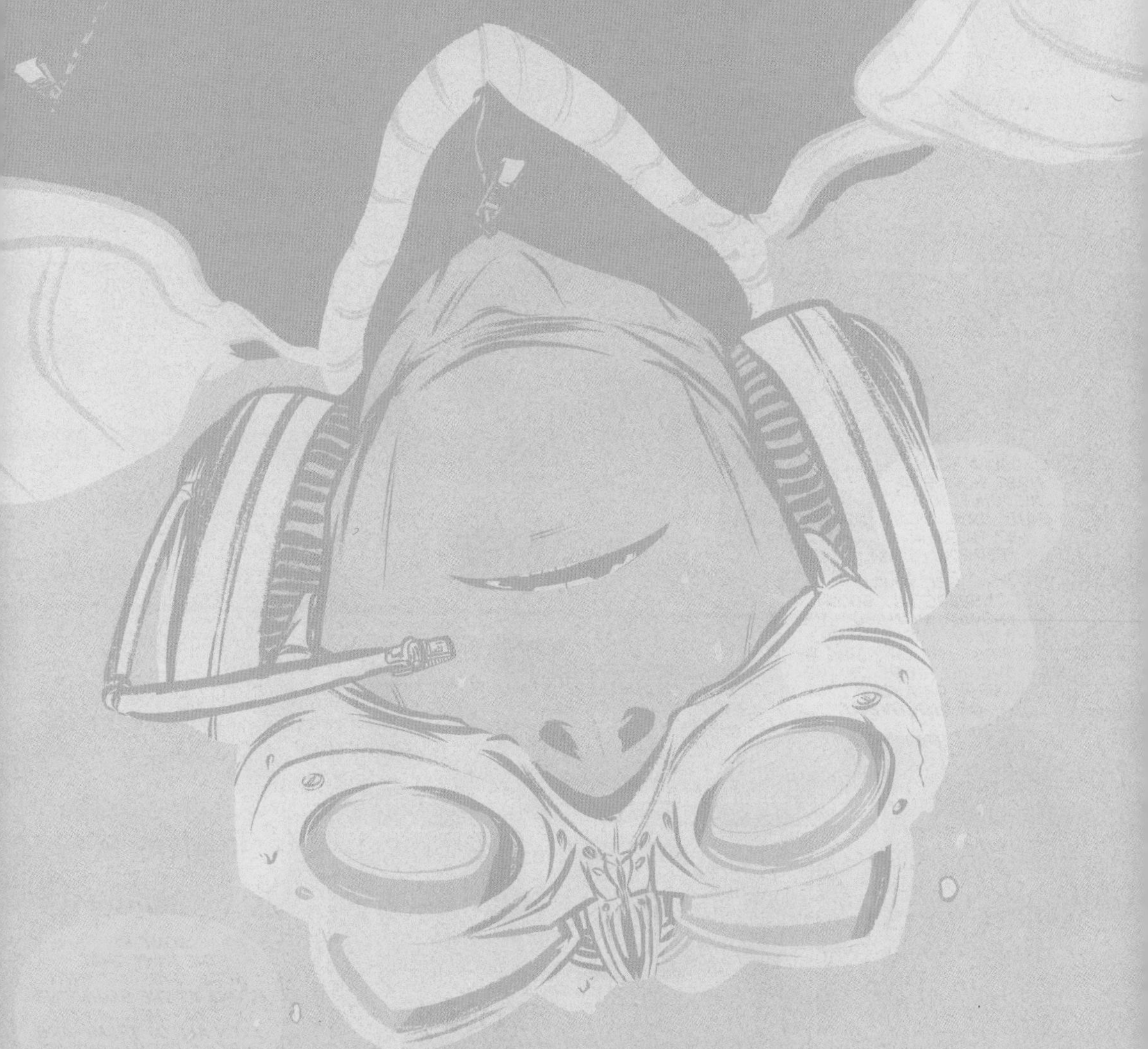

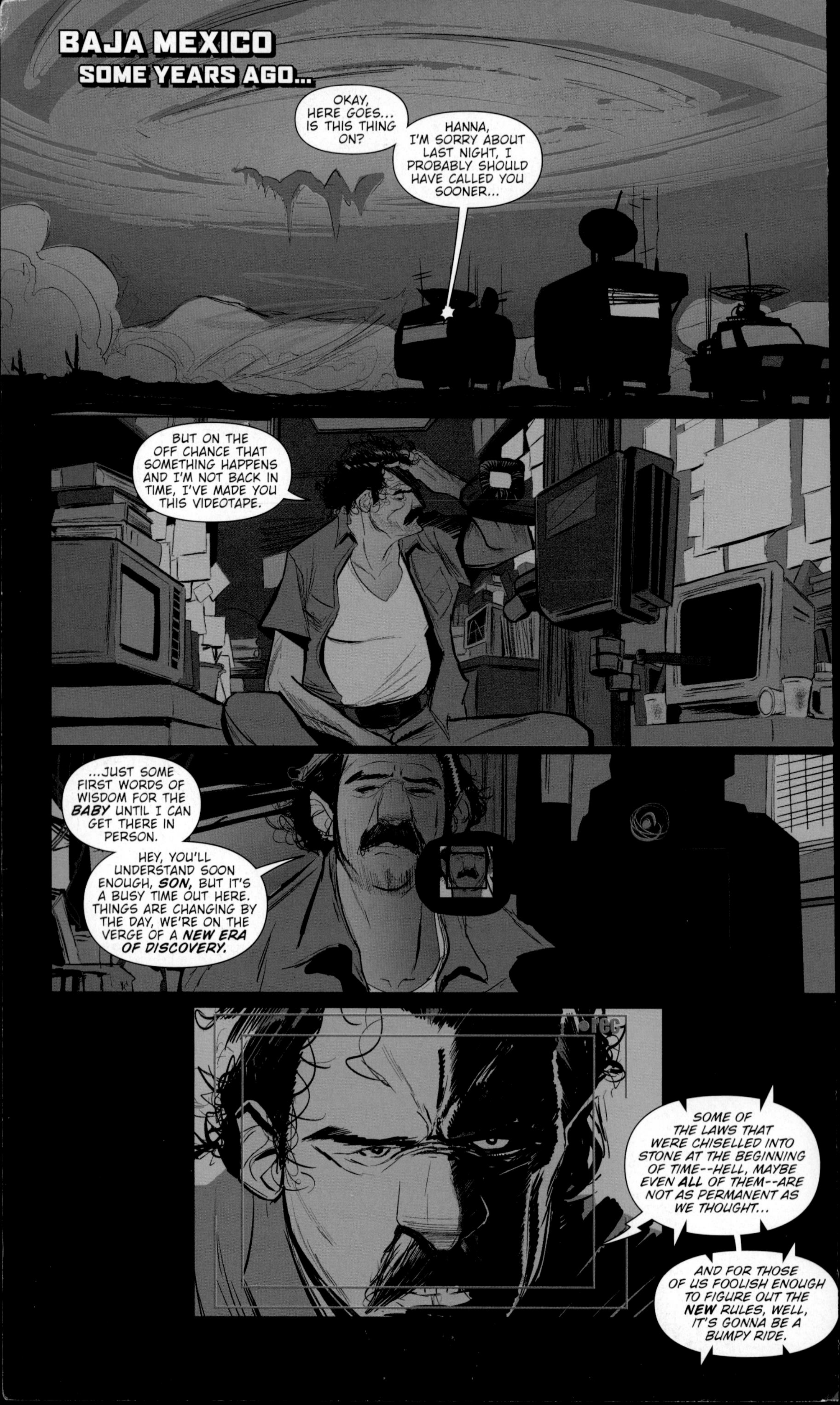
BAJA MEXICO
SOME YEARS AGO...
OKAY, HERE GOES... IS THIS THING ON?
HANNA, I'M SORRY ABOUT LAST NIGHT, I PROBABLY SHOULD HAVE CALLED YOU SOONER...
BUT ON THE OFF CHANCE THAT SOMETHING HAPPENS AND I'M NOT BACK IN TIME, I'VE MADE YOU THIS VIDEOTAPE.
...JUST SOME FIRST WORDS OF WISDOM FOR THE BABY UNTIL I CAN GET THERE IN PERSON.
HEY, YOU'LL UNDERSTAND SOON ENOUGH, SON, BUT IT'S A BUSY TIME OUT HERE. THINGS ARE CHANGING BY THE DAY, WE'RE ON THE VERGE OF A NEW ERA OF DISCOVERY.
rec
SOME OF THE LAWS THAT WERE CHISELLED INTO STONE AT THE BEGINNING OF TIME--HELL, MAYBE EVEN ALL OF THEM--ARE NOT AS PERMANENT AS WE THOUGHT...
AND FOR THOSE OF US FOOLISH ENOUGH TO FIGURE OUT THE NEW RULES, WELL, IT'S GONNA BE A BUMPY RIDE.

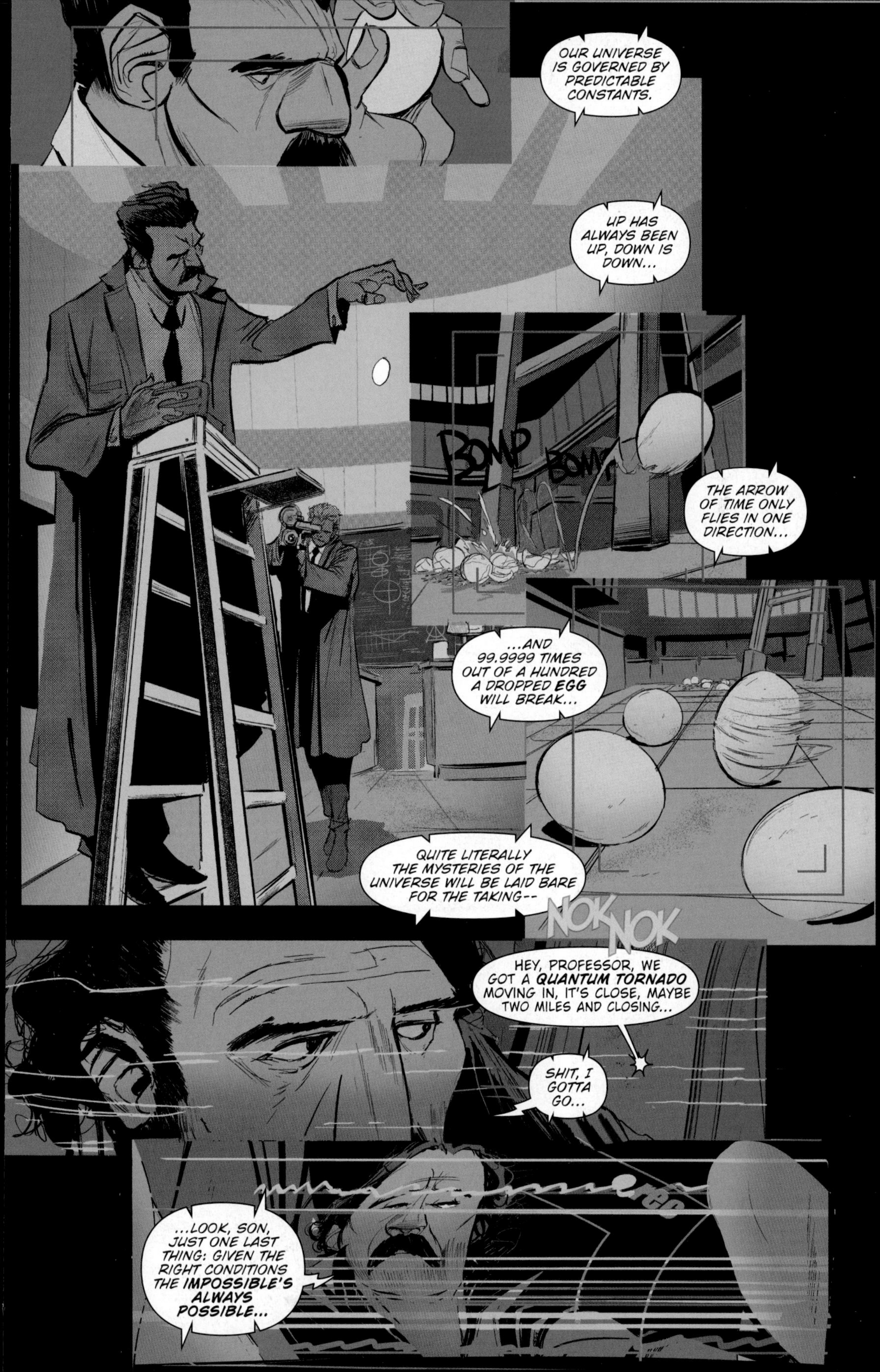
OUR UNIVERSE IS GOVERNED BY PREDICTABLE CONSTANTS.
UP HAS ALWAYS BEEN UP, DOWN IS DOWN...
BOMP BOMP
THE ARROW OF TIME ONLY FLIES IN ONE DIRECTION...
...AND 99.9999 TIMES OUT OF A HUNDRED A DROPPED EGG WILL BREAK...
QUITE LITERALLY THE MYSTERIES OF THE UNIVERSE WILL BE LAID BARE FOR THE TAKING--
NOK NOK
HEY, PROFESSOR, WE GOT A QUANTUM TORNADO MOVING IN, IT'S CLOSE, MAYBE TWO MILES AND CLOSING...
SHIT, I GOTTA GO...
...LOOK, SON, JUST ONE LAST THING: GIVEN THE RIGHT CONDITIONS THE IMPOSSIBLE'S ALWAYS POSSIBLE...

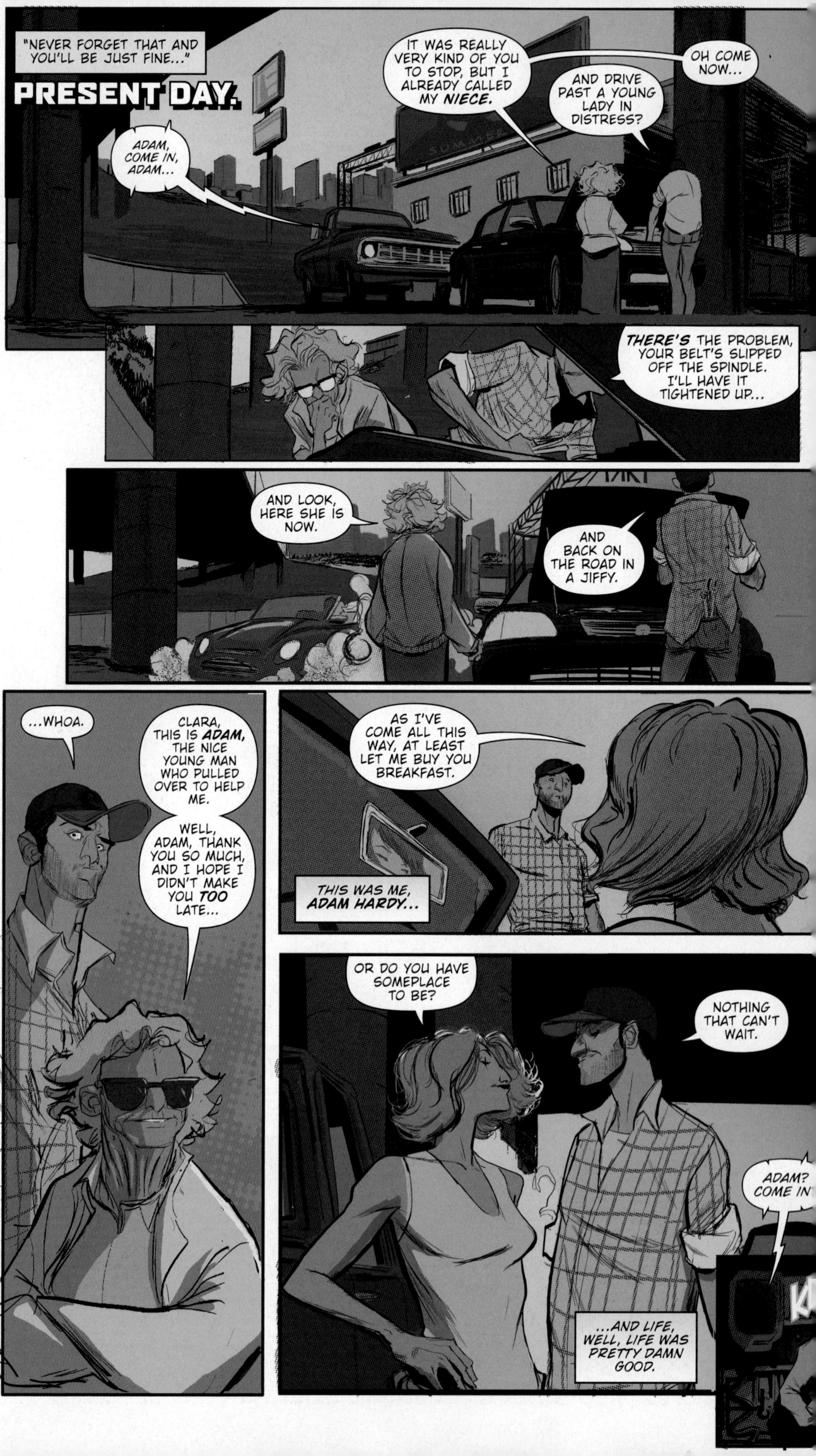
"NEVER FORGET THAT AND YOU'LL BE JUST FINE..."
PRESENT DAY.
ADAM, COME IN, ADAM...
IT WAS REALLY VERY KIND OF YOU TO STOP, BUT I ALREADY CALLED MY NIECE.
OH COME NOW...
AND DRIVE PAST A YOUNG LADY IN DISTRESS?
THERE'S THE PROBLEM, YOUR BELT'S SLIPPED OFF THE SPINDLE. I'LL HAVE IT TIGHTENED UP...
AND LOOK, HERE SHE IS NOW.
AND BACK ON THE ROAD IN A JIFFY.
...WHOA.
CLARA, THIS IS ADAM, THE NICE YOUNG MAN WHO PULLED OVER TO HELP ME.
WELL, ADAM, THANK YOU SO MUCH, AND I HOPE I DIDN'T MAKE YOU TOO LATE...
AS I'VE COME ALL THIS WAY, AT LEAST LET ME BUY YOU BREAKFAST.
THIS WAS ME, ADAM HARDY...
OR DO YOU HAVE SOMEPLACE TO BE?
NOTHING THAT CAN'T WAIT.
ADAM? COME IN
...AND LIFE, WELL, LIFE WAS PRETTY DAMN GOOD.

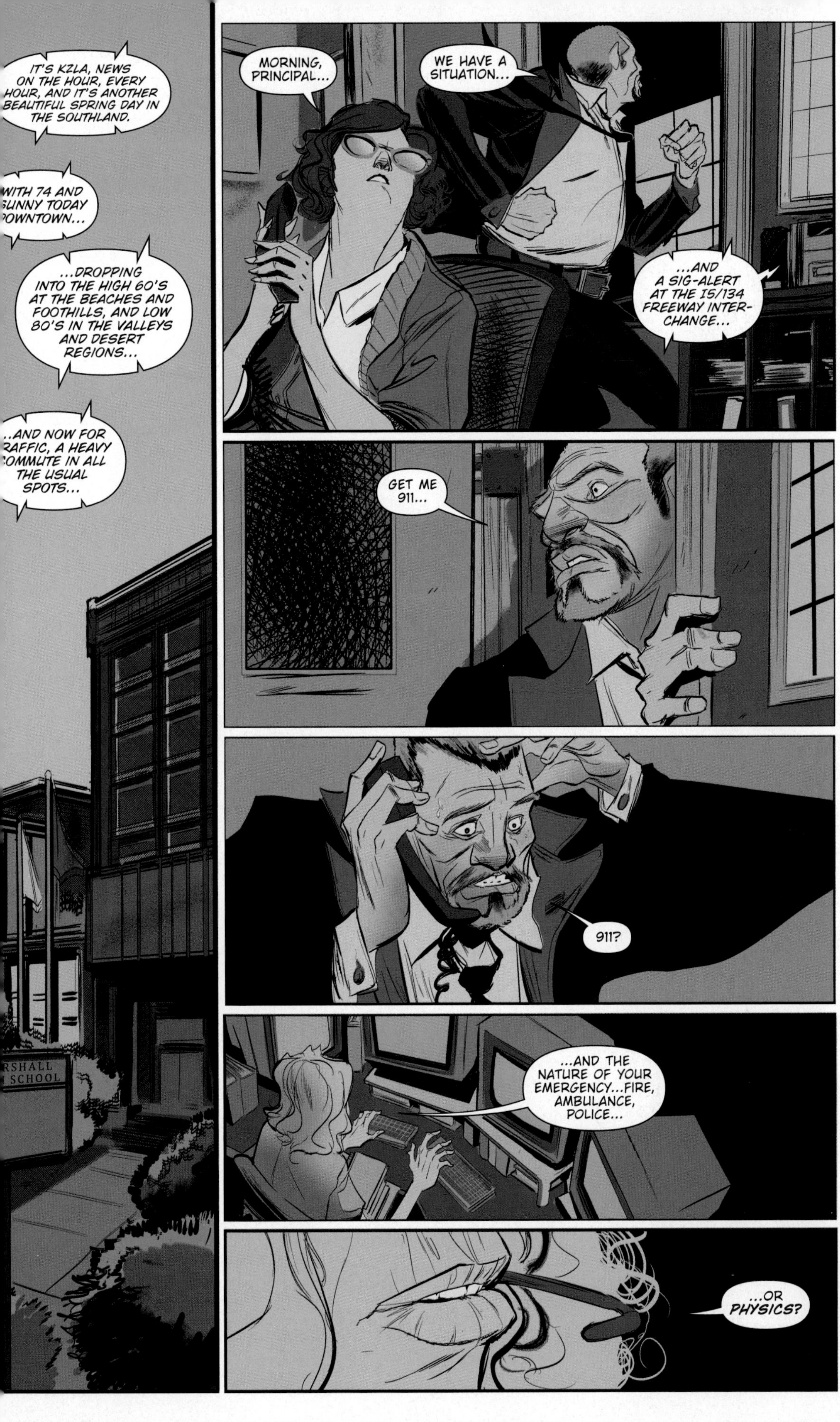
IT'S KZLA, NEWS ON THE HOUR, EVERY HOUR, AND IT'S ANOTHER BEAUTIFUL SPRING DAY IN THE SOUTHLAND.
WITH 74 AND SUNNY TODAY DOWNTOWN...
...DROPPING INTO THE HIGH 60'S AT THE BEACHES AND FOOTHILLS, AND LOW 80'S IN THE VALLEYS AND DESERT REGIONS...
...AND NOW FOR RAFFIC, A HEAVY COMMUTE IN ALL THE USUAL SPOTS...
RSHALL
SCHOOL
MORNING, PRINCIPAL...
WE HAVE A SITUATION...
...AND A SIG-ALERT AT THE I5/134 FREEWAY INTER-CHANGE...
GET ME 911...
911?
...AND THE NATURE OF YOUR EMERGENCY...FIRE, AMBULANCE, POLICE...
...OR PHYSICS?

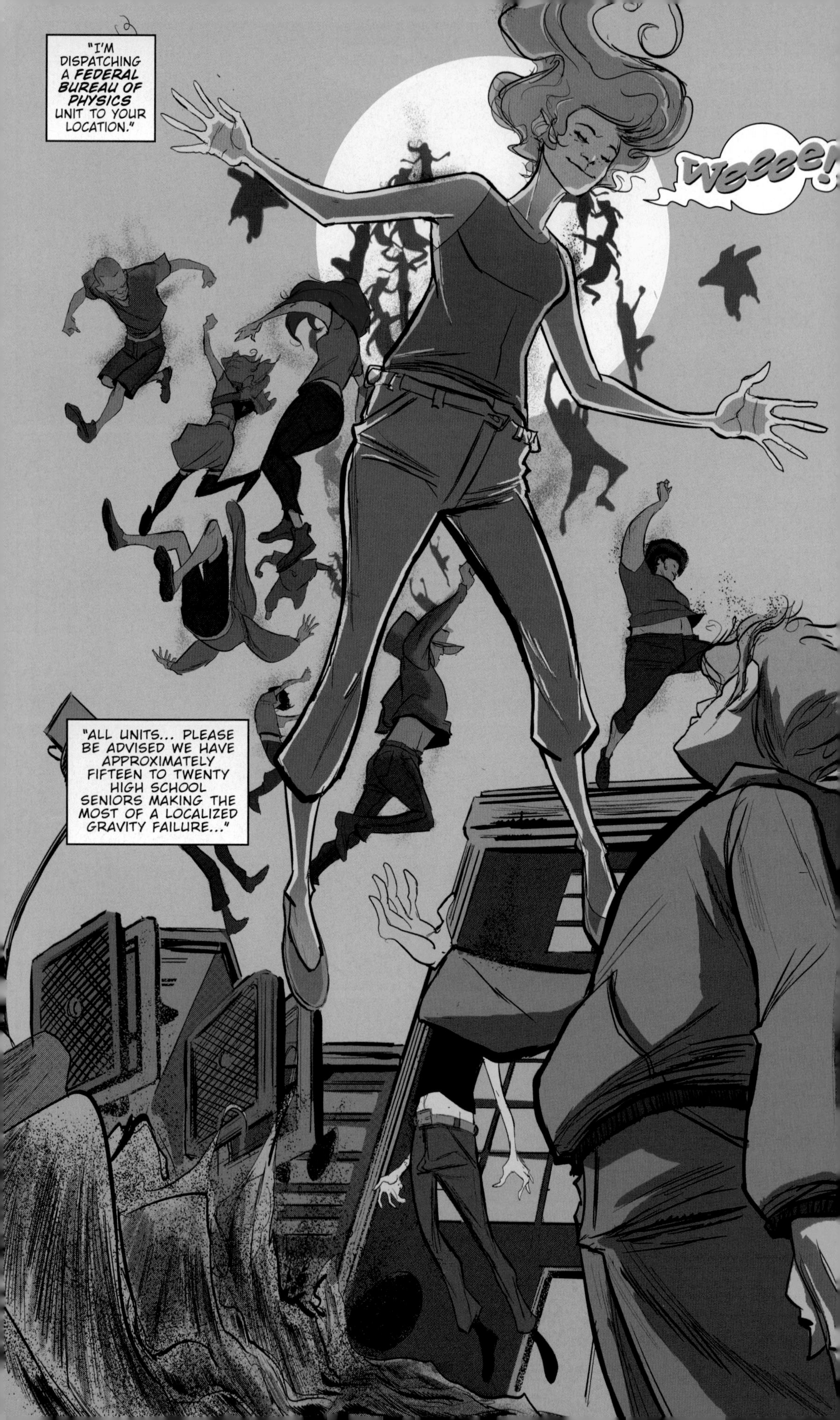
"I'M DISPATCHING A FEDERAL BUREAU OF PHYSICS UNIT TO YOUR LOCATION."
Weeeee!
"ALL UNITS... PLEASE BE ADVISED WE HAVE APPROXIMATELY FIFTEEN TO TWENTY HIGH SCHOOL SENIORS MAKING THE MOST OF A LOCALIZED GRAVITY FAILURE..."

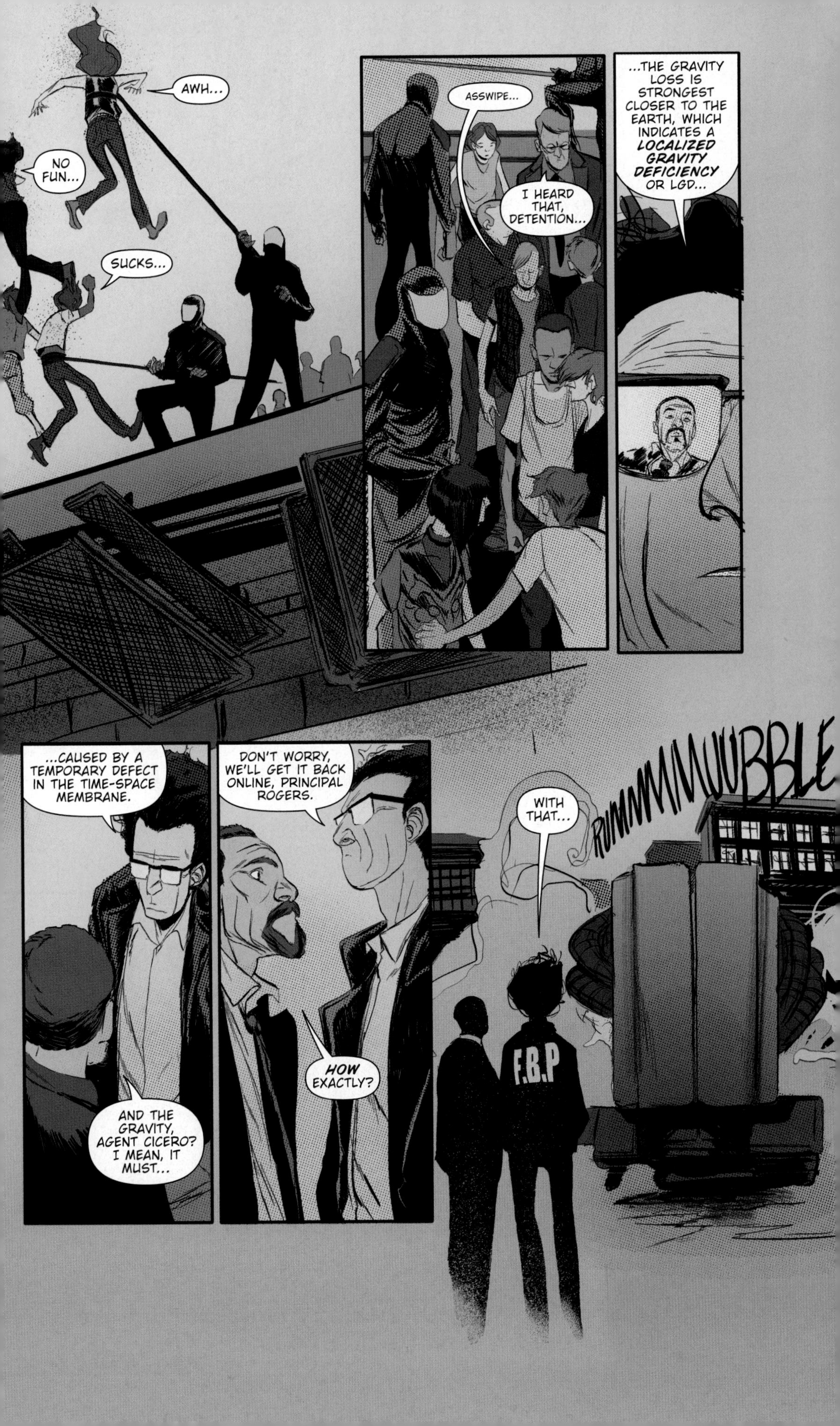
AWH...
NO FUN...
SUCKS...
ASSWIPE...
I HEARD THAT, DETENTION...
...THE GRAVITY LOSS IS STRONGEST CLOSER TO THE EARTH, WHICH INDICATES A LOCALIZED GRAVITY DEFICIENCY OR LGD...
...CAUSED BY A TEMPORARY DEFECT IN THE TIME-SPACE MEMBRANE.
AND THE GRAVITY, AGENT CICERO? I MEAN, IT MUST...
DON'T WORRY, WE'LL GET IT BACK ONLINE, PRINCIPAL ROGERS.
HOW EXACTLY?
WITH THAT...
RUMMMMUUBBLE
F.B.P

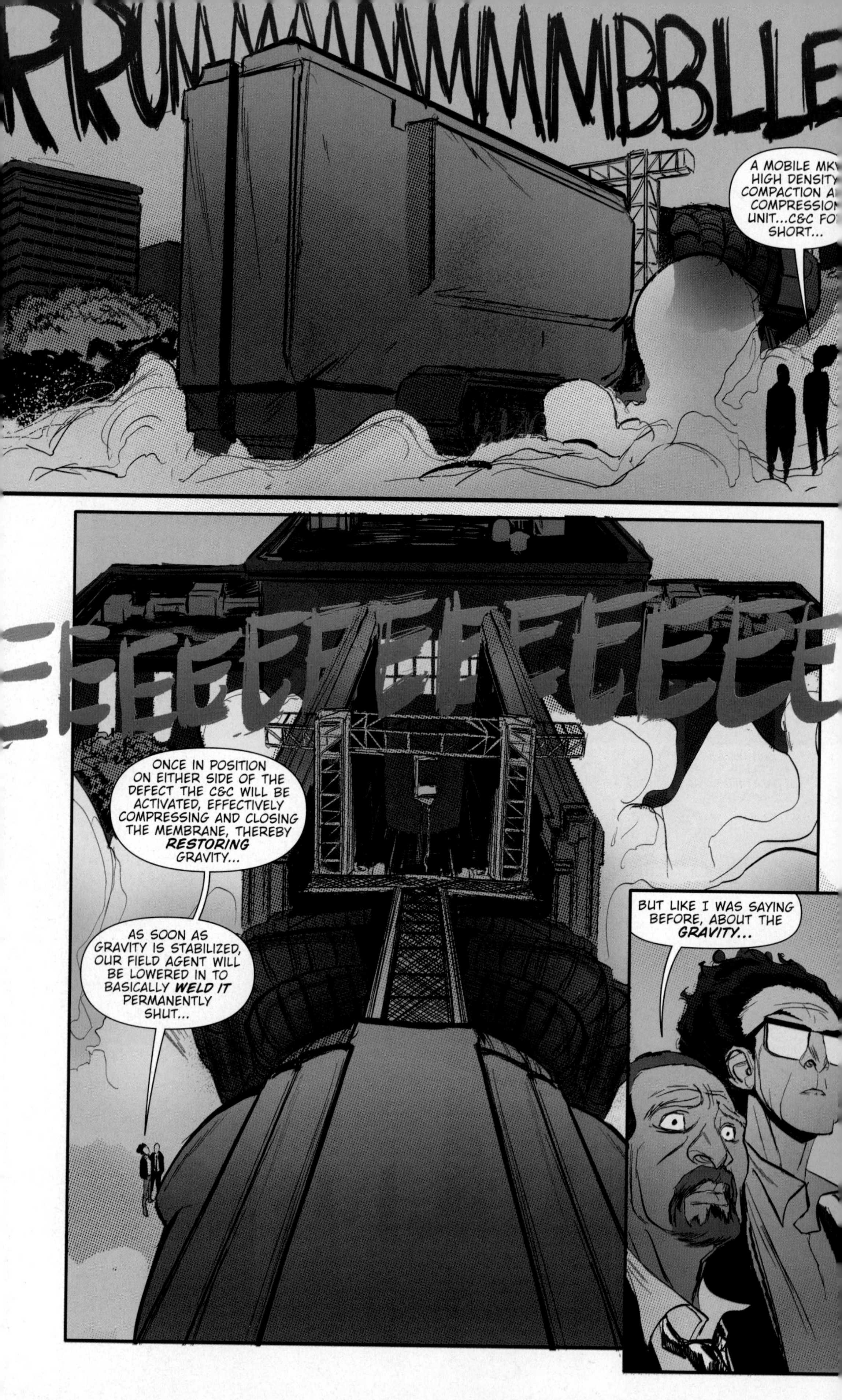
RRUMMMMMMMMBBLLE
A MOBILE MKV HIGH DENSITY COMPACTION AND COMPRESSION UNIT...C&C FOR SHORT...
EEEEEEEEEEEEE
ONCE IN POSITION ON EITHER SIDE OF THE DEFECT THE C&C WILL BE ACTIVATED, EFFECTIVELY COMPRESSING AND CLOSING THE MEMBRANE, THEREBY **RESTORING** GRAVITY...
AS SOON AS GRAVITY IS STABILIZED, OUR FIELD AGENT WILL BE LOWERED IN TO BASICALLY **WELD IT** PERMANENTLY SHUT...
BUT LIKE I WAS SAYING BEFORE, ABOUT THE **GRAVITY...**

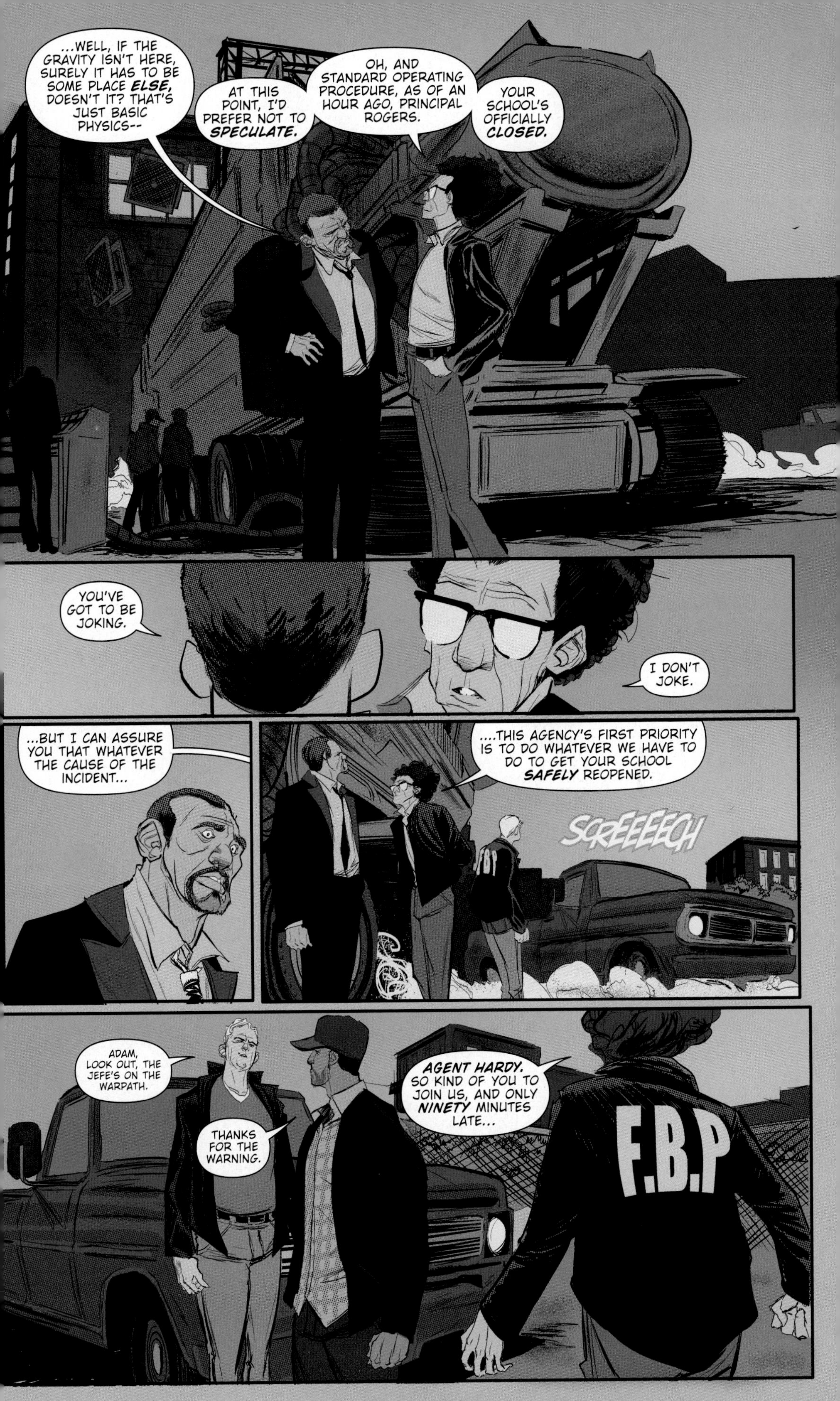
...WELL, IF THE GRAVITY ISN'T HERE, SURELY IT HAS TO BE SOME PLACE ELSE, DOESN'T IT? THAT'S JUST BASIC PHYSICS--
AT THIS POINT, I'D PREFER NOT TO SPECULATE.
OH, AND STANDARD OPERATING PROCEDURE, AS OF AN HOUR AGO, PRINCIPAL ROGERS.
YOUR SCHOOL'S OFFICIALLY CLOSED.
YOU'VE GOT TO BE JOKING.
I DON'T JOKE.
...BUT I CAN ASSURE YOU THAT WHATEVER THE CAUSE OF THE INCIDENT...
....THIS AGENCY'S FIRST PRIORITY IS TO DO WHATEVER WE HAVE TO DO TO GET YOUR SCHOOL SAFELY REOPENED.
SCREEEEECH
ADAM, LOOK OUT, THE JEFE'S ON THE WARPATH.
THANKS FOR THE WARNING.
AGENT HARDY. SO KIND OF YOU TO JOIN US, AND ONLY NINETY MINUTES LATE...
F.B.P

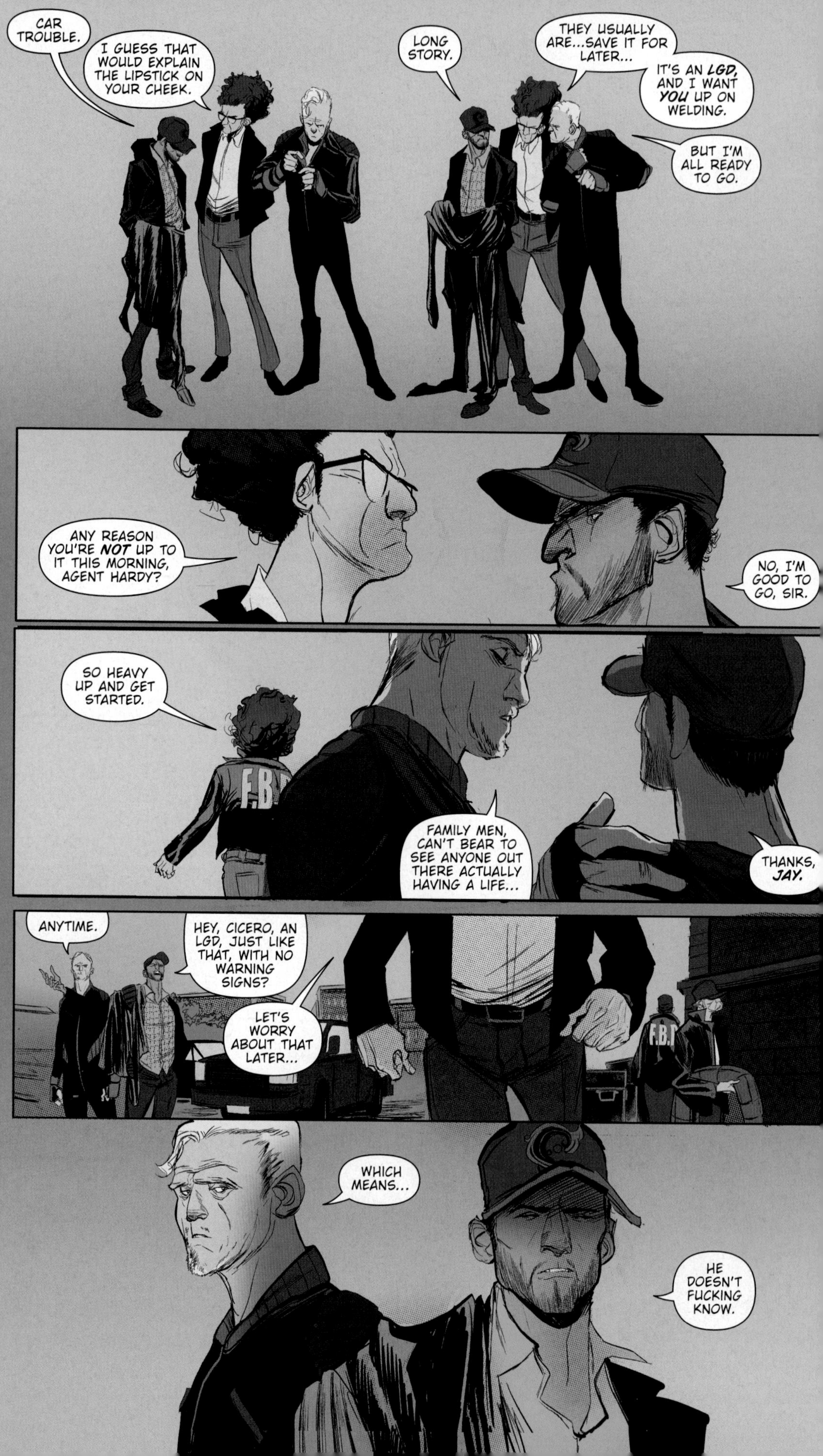

CAR TROUBLE.
I GUESS THAT WOULD EXPLAIN THE LIPSTICK ON YOUR CHEEK.
LONG STORY.
THEY USUALLY ARE...SAVE IT FOR LATER...
IT'S AN LGD, AND I WANT YOU UP ON WELDING.
BUT I'M ALL READY TO GO.
ANY REASON YOU'RE NOT UP TO IT THIS MORNING, AGENT HARDY?
NO, I'M GOOD TO GO, SIR.
SO HEAVY UP AND GET STARTED.
FAMILY MEN, CAN'T BEAR TO SEE ANYONE OUT THERE ACTUALLY HAVING A LIFE...
THANKS, JAY.
ANYTIME.
HEY, CICERO, AN LGD, JUST LIKE THAT, WITH NO WARNING SIGNS?
LET'S WORRY ABOUT THAT LATER...
WHICH MEANS...
HE DOESN'T FUCKING KNOW.

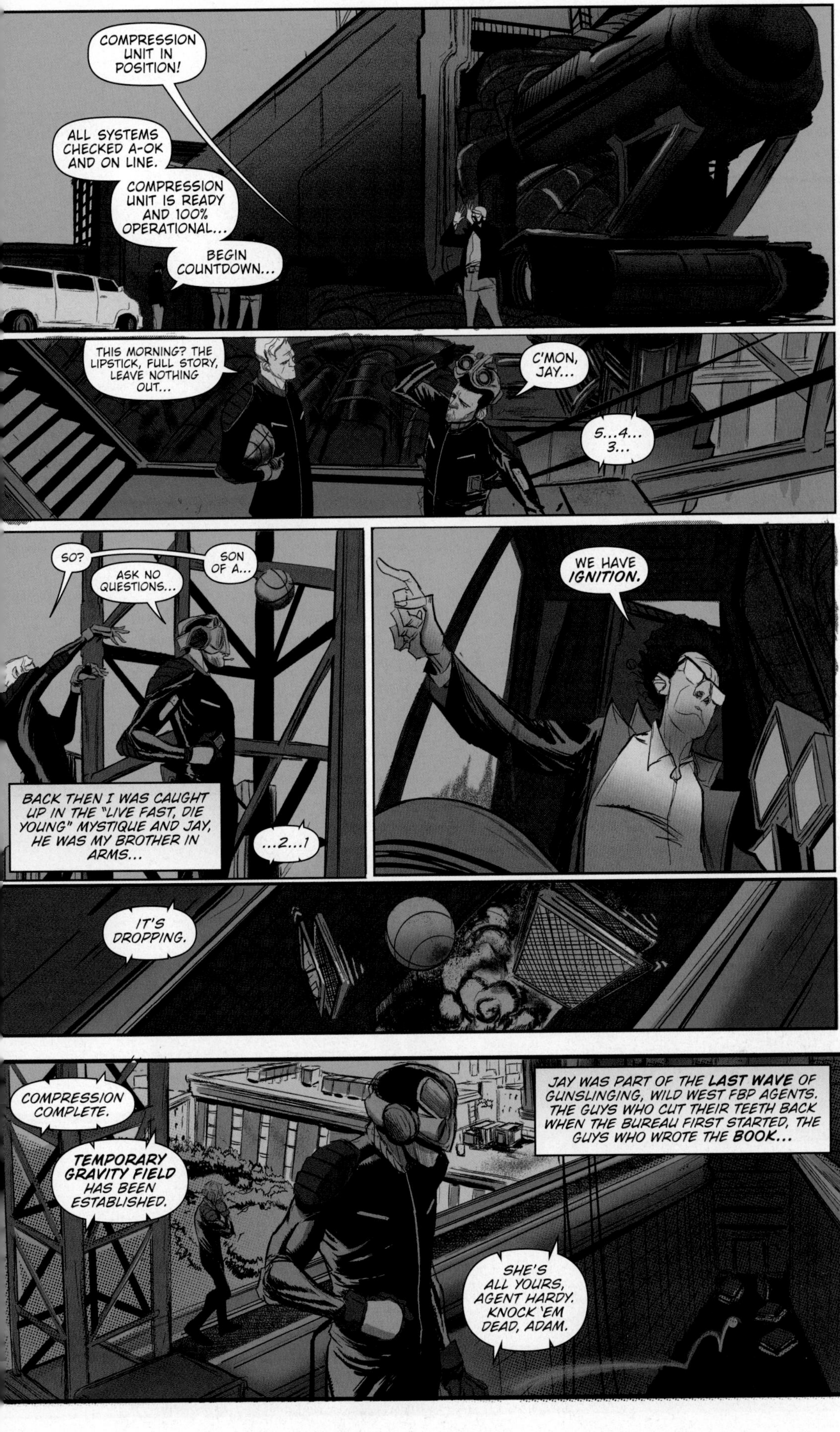
COMPRESSION UNIT IN POSITION!
ALL SYSTEMS CHECKED A-OK AND ON LINE.
COMPRESSION UNIT IS READY AND 100% OPERATIONAL...
BEGIN COUNTDOWN...
THIS MORNING? THE LIPSTICK, FULL STORY, LEAVE NOTHING OUT...
C'MON, JAY...
5...4... 3...
SO?
SON OF A...
ASK NO QUESTIONS...
BACK THEN I WAS CAUGHT UP IN THE "LIVE FAST, DIE YOUNG" MYSTIQUE AND JAY, HE WAS MY BROTHER IN ARMS...
...2...1
WE HAVE IGNITION.
IT'S DROPPING.
COMPRESSION COMPLETE.
TEMPORARY GRAVITY FIELD HAS BEEN ESTABLISHED.
JAY WAS PART OF THE LAST WAVE OF GUNSLINGING, WILD WEST FBP AGENTS. THE GUYS WHO CUT THEIR TEETH BACK WHEN THE BUREAU FIRST STARTED, THE GUYS WHO WROTE THE BOOK...
SHE'S ALL YOURS, AGENT HARDY. KNOCK 'EM DEAD, ADAM.

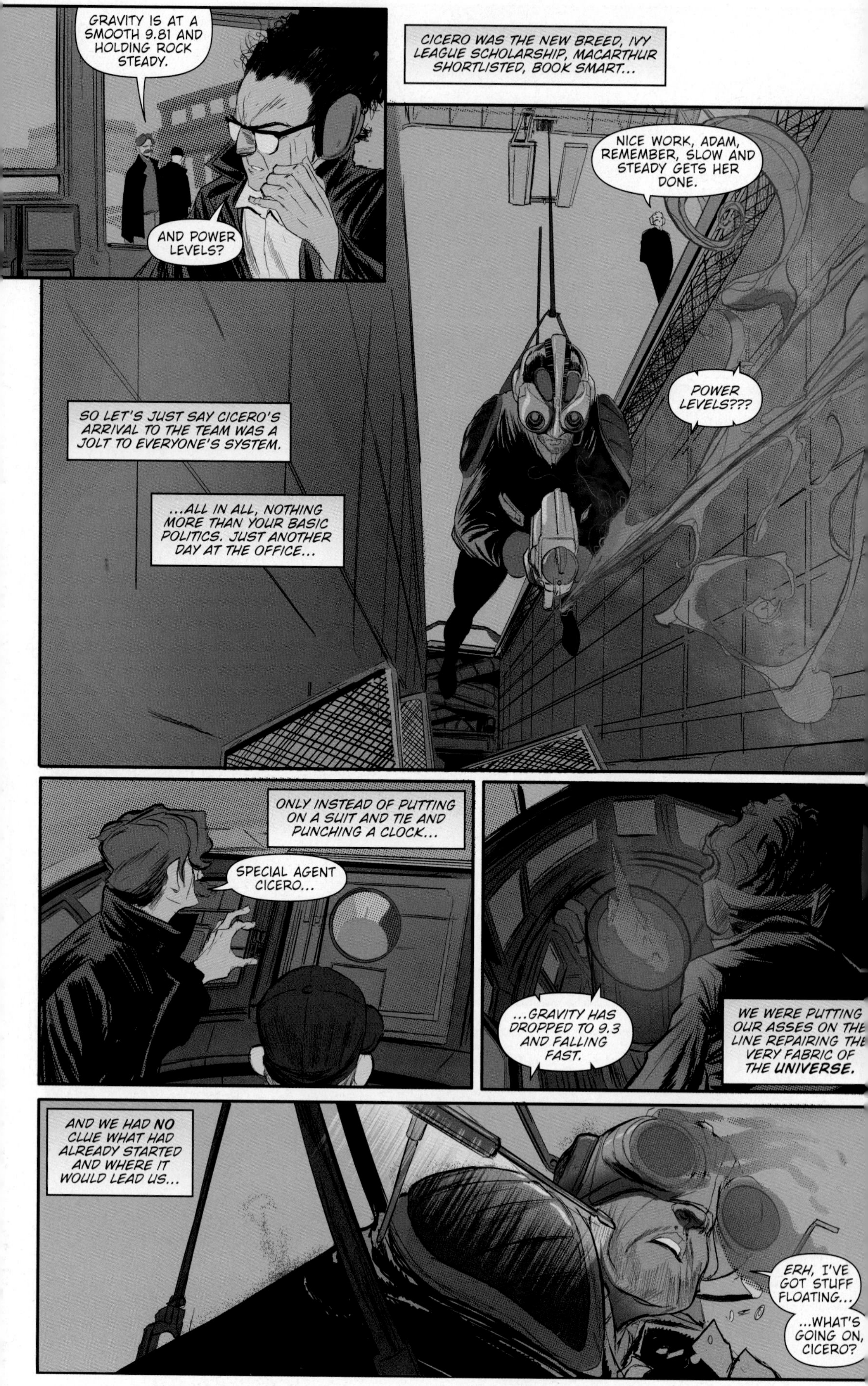
GRAVITY IS AT A SMOOTH 9.81 AND HOLDING ROCK STEADY.
AND POWER LEVELS?
CICERO WAS THE NEW BREED, IVY LEAGUE SCHOLARSHIP, MACARTHUR SHORTLISTED, BOOK SMART...
NICE WORK, ADAM, REMEMBER, SLOW AND STEADY GETS HER DONE.
SO LET'S JUST SAY CICERO'S ARRIVAL TO THE TEAM WAS A JOLT TO EVERYONE'S SYSTEM.
POWER LEVELS???
...ALL IN ALL, NOTHING MORE THAN YOUR BASIC POLITICS. JUST ANOTHER DAY AT THE OFFICE...
ONLY INSTEAD OF PUTTING ON A SUIT AND TIE AND PUNCHING A CLOCK...
SPECIAL AGENT CICERO...
...GRAVITY HAS DROPPED TO 9.3 AND FALLING FAST.
WE WERE PUTTING OUR ASSES ON THE LINE REPAIRING THE VERY FABRIC OF THE UNIVERSE.
AND WE HAD NO CLUE WHAT HAD ALREADY STARTED AND WHERE IT WOULD LEAD US...
ERH, I'VE GOT STUFF FLOATING...
...WHAT'S GOING ON, CICERO?

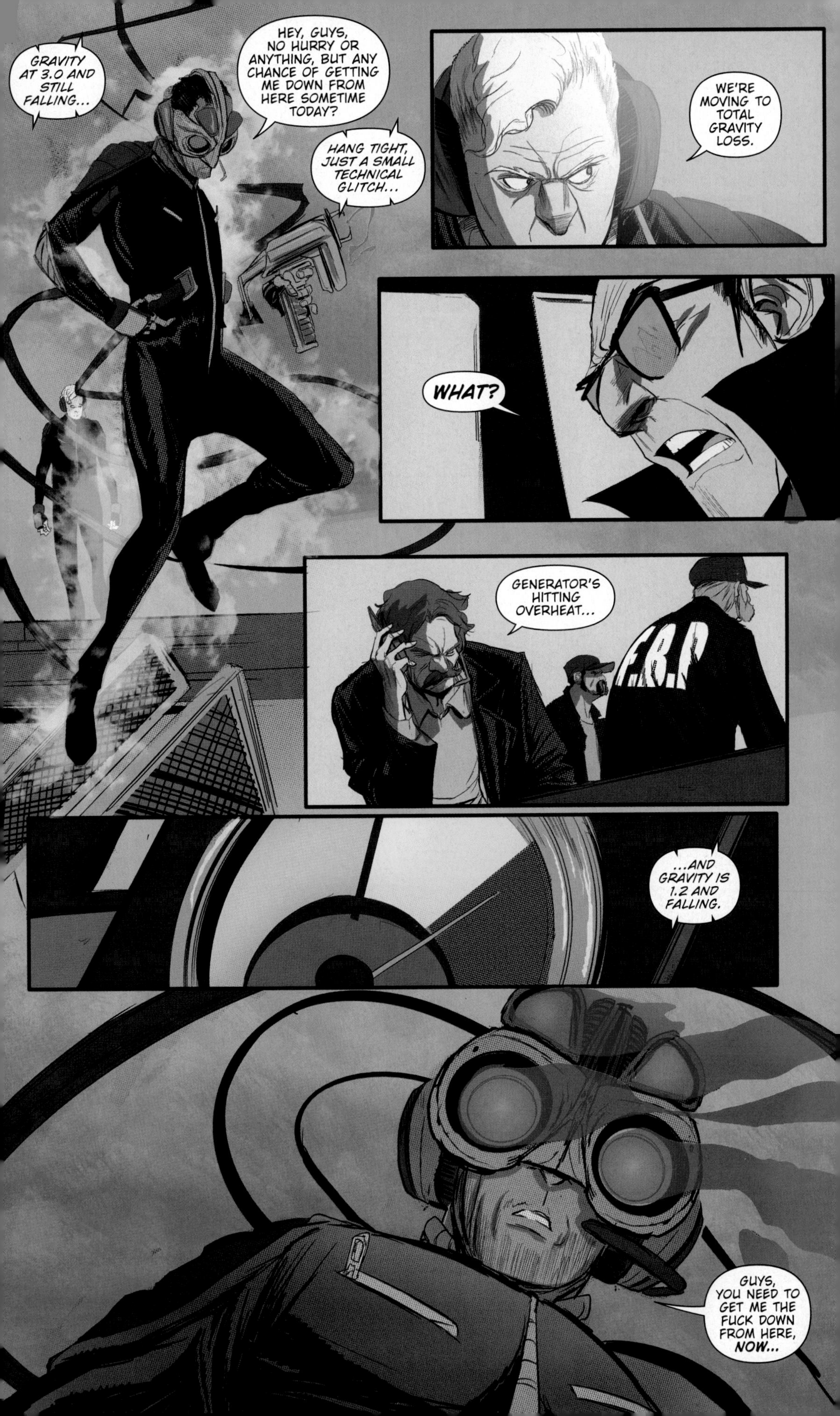
GRAVITY AT 3.0 AND STILL FALLING...
HEY, GUYS, NO HURRY OR ANYTHING, BUT ANY CHANCE OF GETTING ME DOWN FROM HERE SOMETIME TODAY?
HANG TIGHT, JUST A SMALL TECHNICAL GLITCH...
WE'RE MOVING TO TOTAL GRAVITY LOSS.
WHAT?
GENERATOR'S HITTING OVERHEAT...
...AND GRAVITY IS 1.2 AND FALLING.
GUYS, YOU NEED TO GET ME THE FUCK DOWN FROM HERE, NOW...

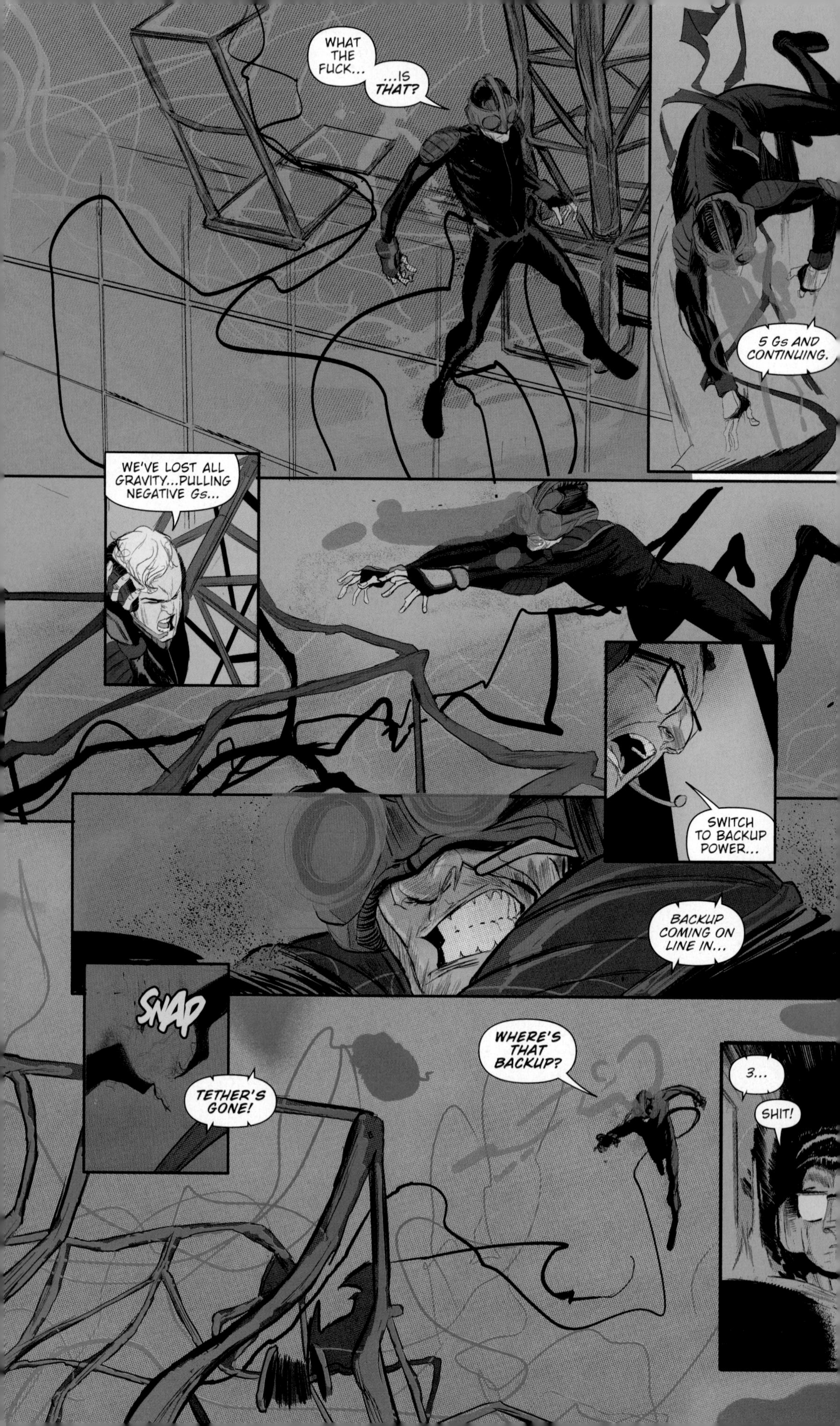
WHAT THE FUCK...
...IS THAT?
5 Gs AND CONTINUING.
WE'VE LOST ALL GRAVITY...PULLING NEGATIVE Gs...
SWITCH TO BACKUP POWER...
BACKUP COMING ON LINE IN...
SNAP
TETHER'S GONE!
WHERE'S THAT BACKUP?
3...
SHIT!

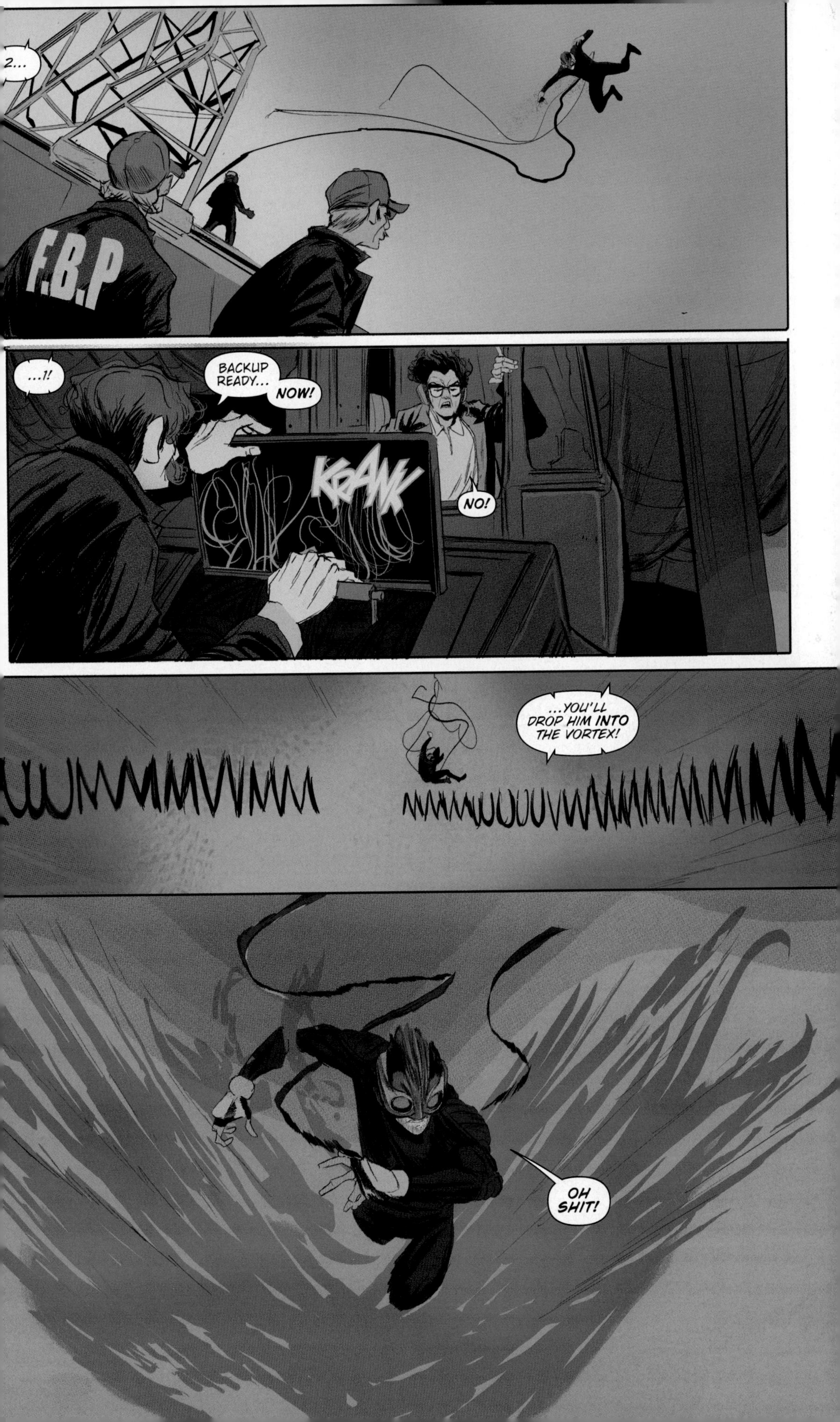
2...
F.B.P
...1!
BACKUP READY... NOW!
KRANK
NO!
...YOU'LL DROP HIM INTO THE VORTEX!
OH SHIT!

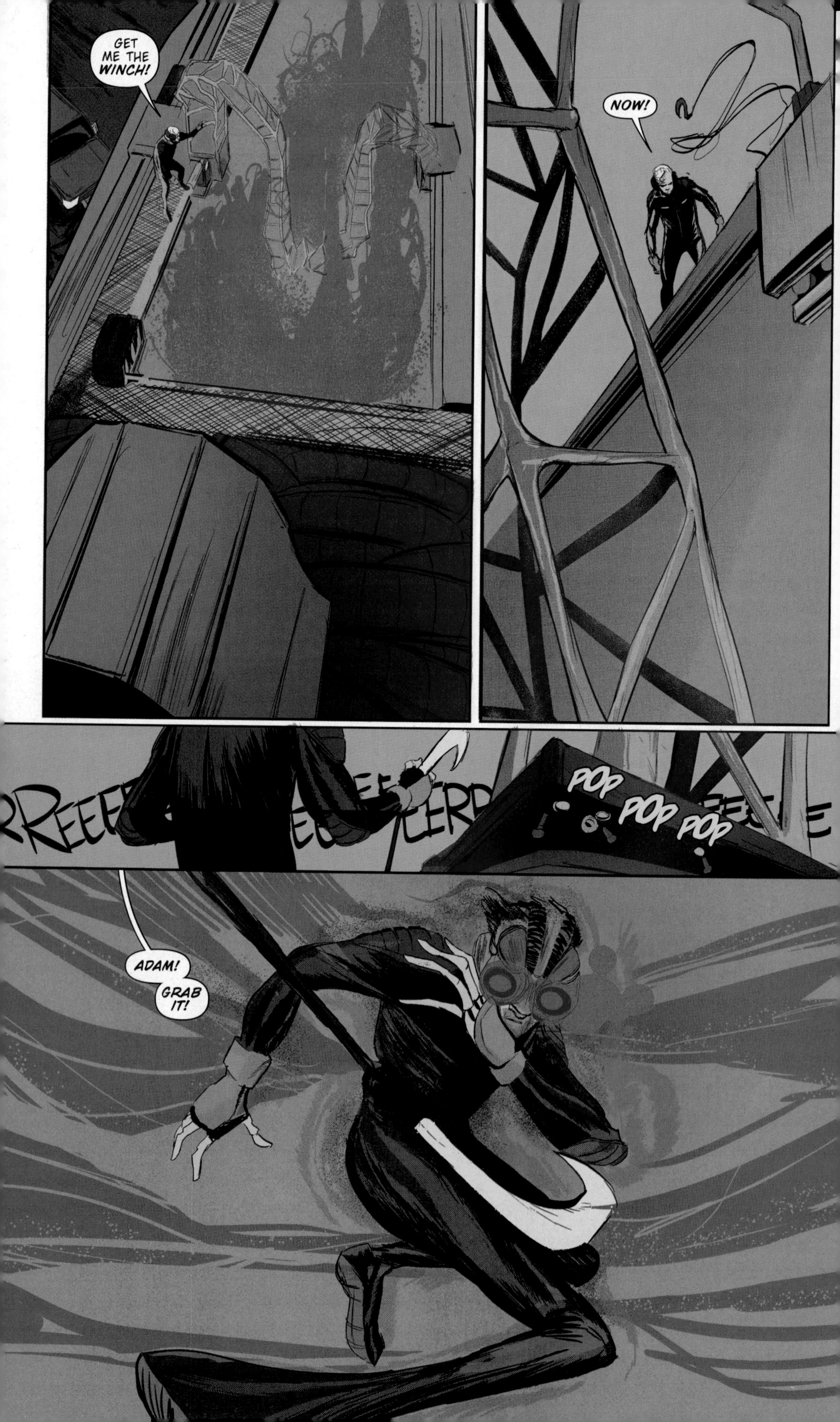
GET ME THE WINCH!
NOW!
POP
POP
POP
ADAM! GRAB IT!

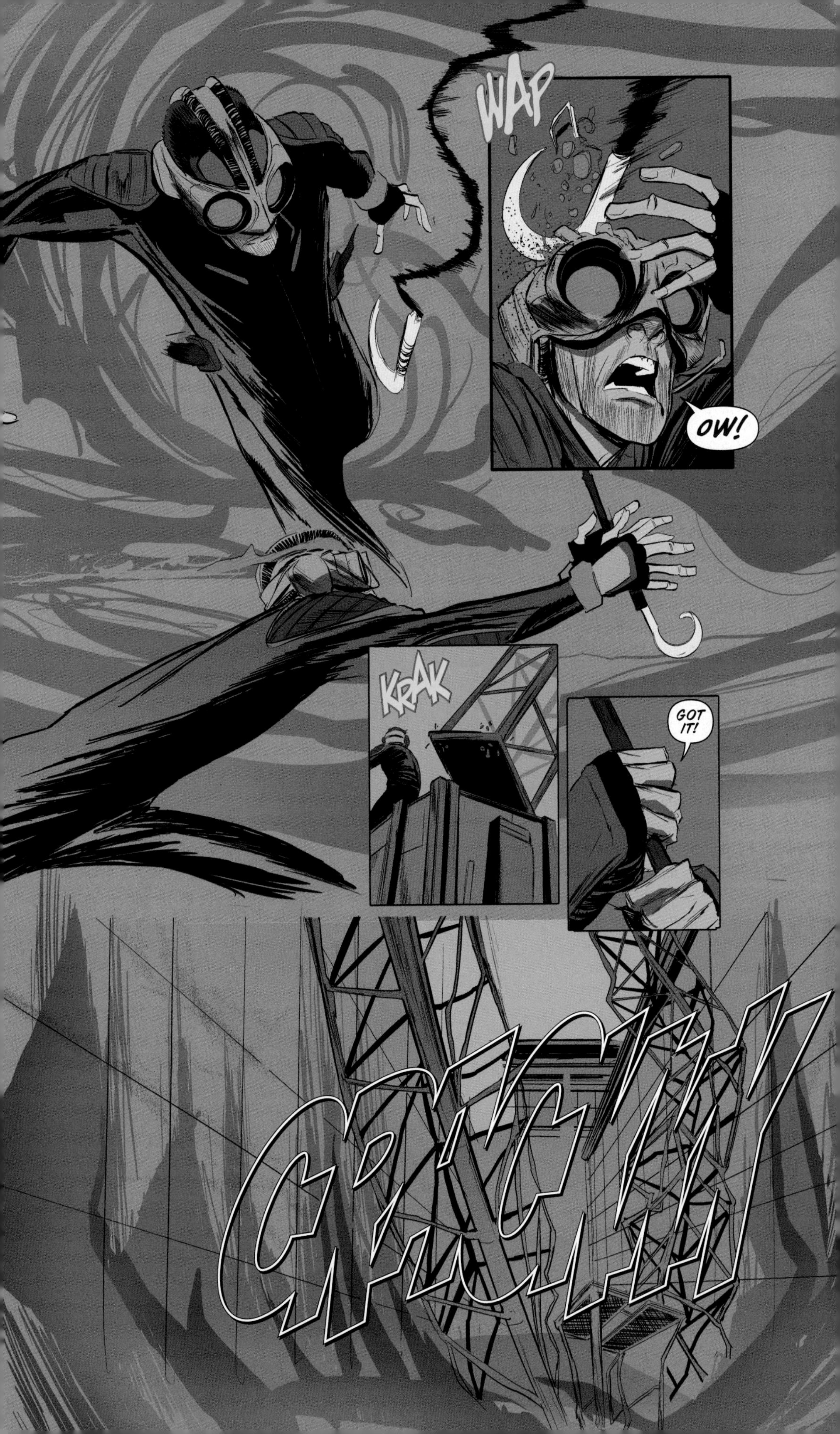
WAP
OW!
KRAK
GOT IT!

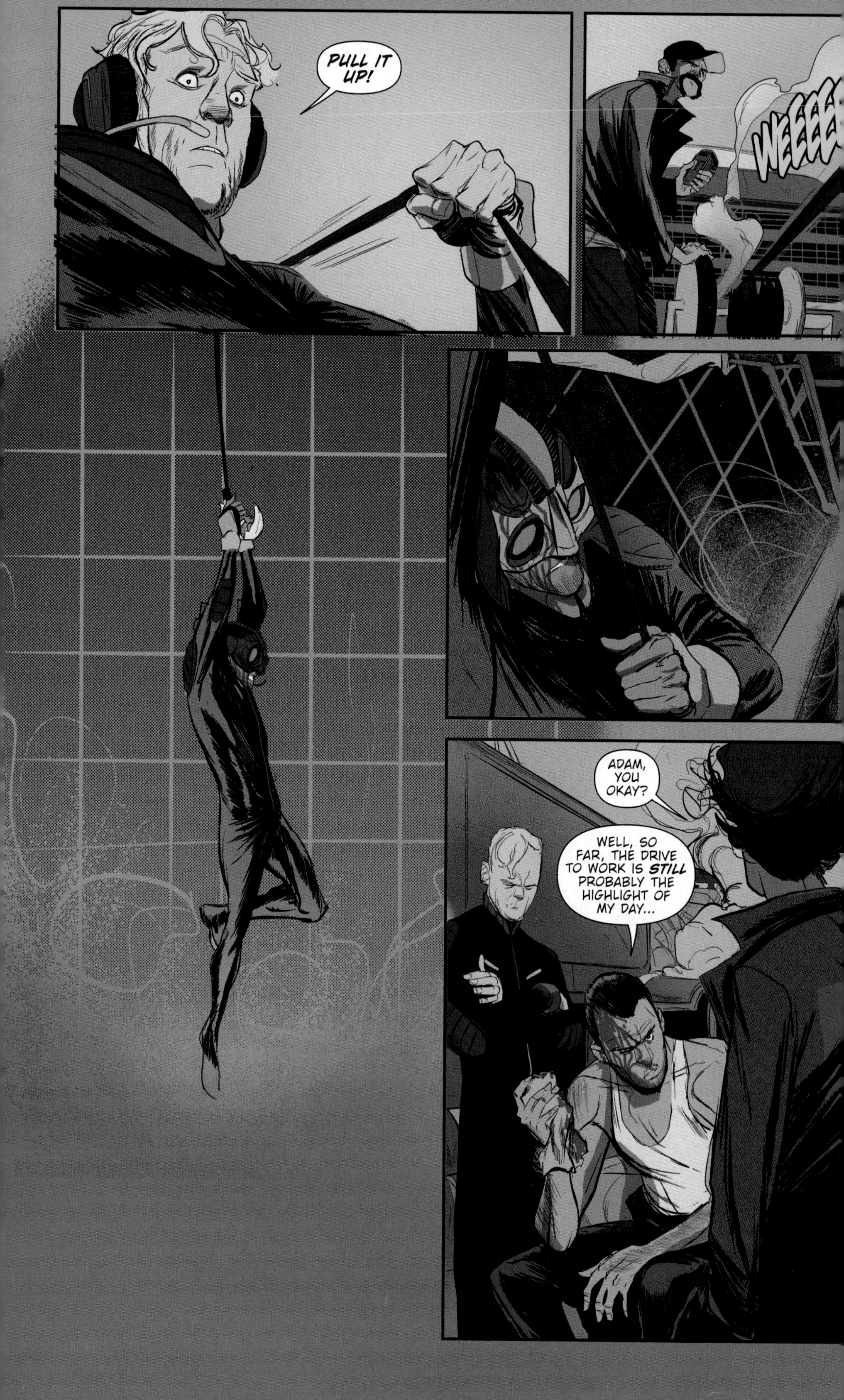
PULL IT UP!
WEEEEE
ADAM, YOU OKAY?
WELL, SO FAR, THE DRIVE TO WORK IS STILL PROBABLY THE HIGHLIGHT OF MY DAY...

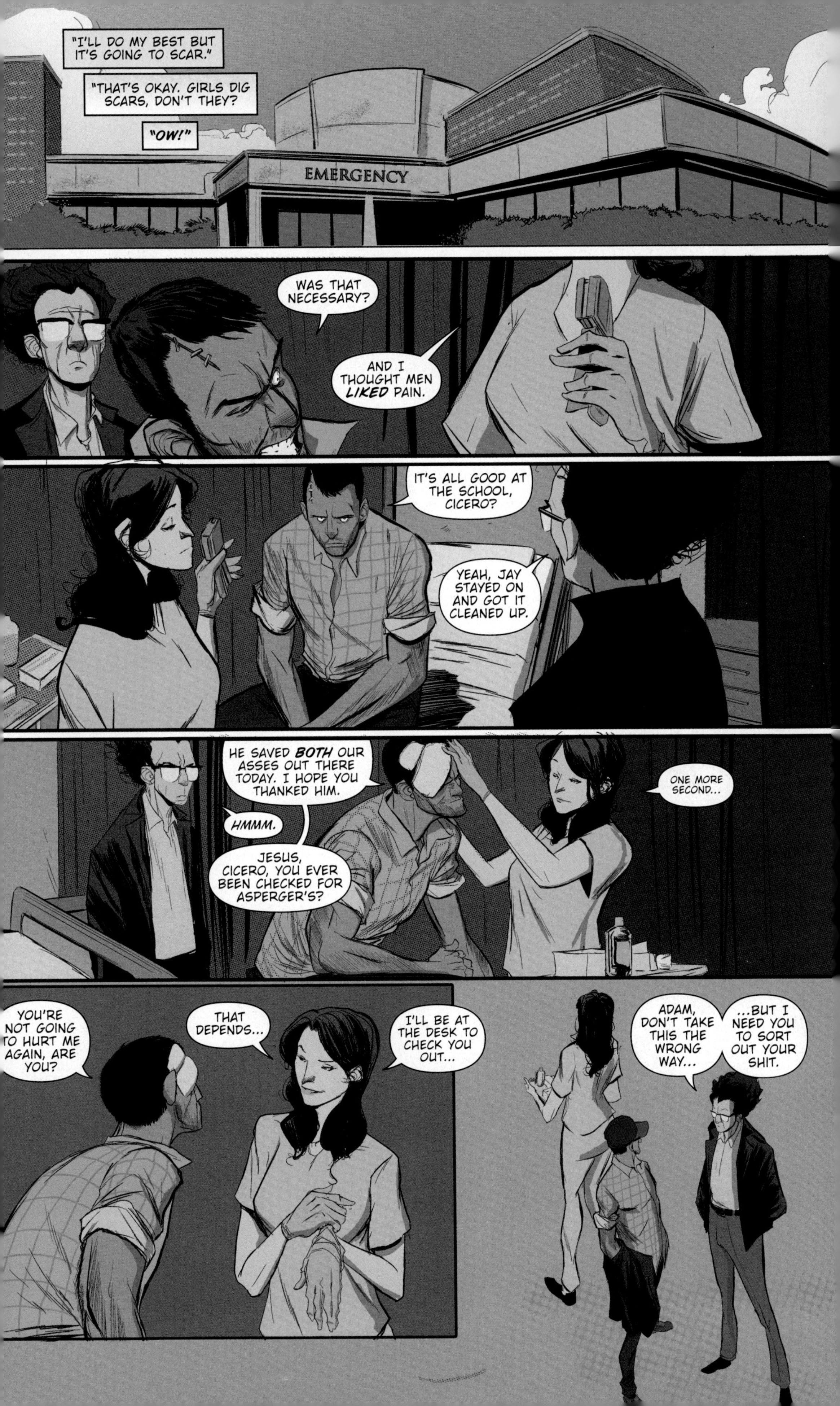
"I'LL DO MY BEST BUT IT'S GOING TO SCAR."
"THAT'S OKAY. GIRLS DIG SCARS, DON'T THEY?
"OW!"
EMERGENCY
WAS THAT NECESSARY?
AND I THOUGHT MEN LIKED PAIN.
IT'S ALL GOOD AT THE SCHOOL, CICERO?
YEAH, JAY STAYED ON AND GOT IT CLEANED UP.
HE SAVED BOTH OUR ASSES OUT THERE TODAY. I HOPE YOU THANKED HIM.
HMMM.
JESUS, CICERO, YOU EVER BEEN CHECKED FOR ASPERGER'S?
ONE MORE SECOND...
YOU'RE NOT GOING TO HURT ME AGAIN, ARE YOU?
THAT DEPENDS...
I'LL BE AT THE DESK TO CHECK YOU OUT...
ADAM, DON'T TAKE THIS THE WRONG WAY...
...BUT I NEED YOU TO SORT OUT YOUR SHIT.

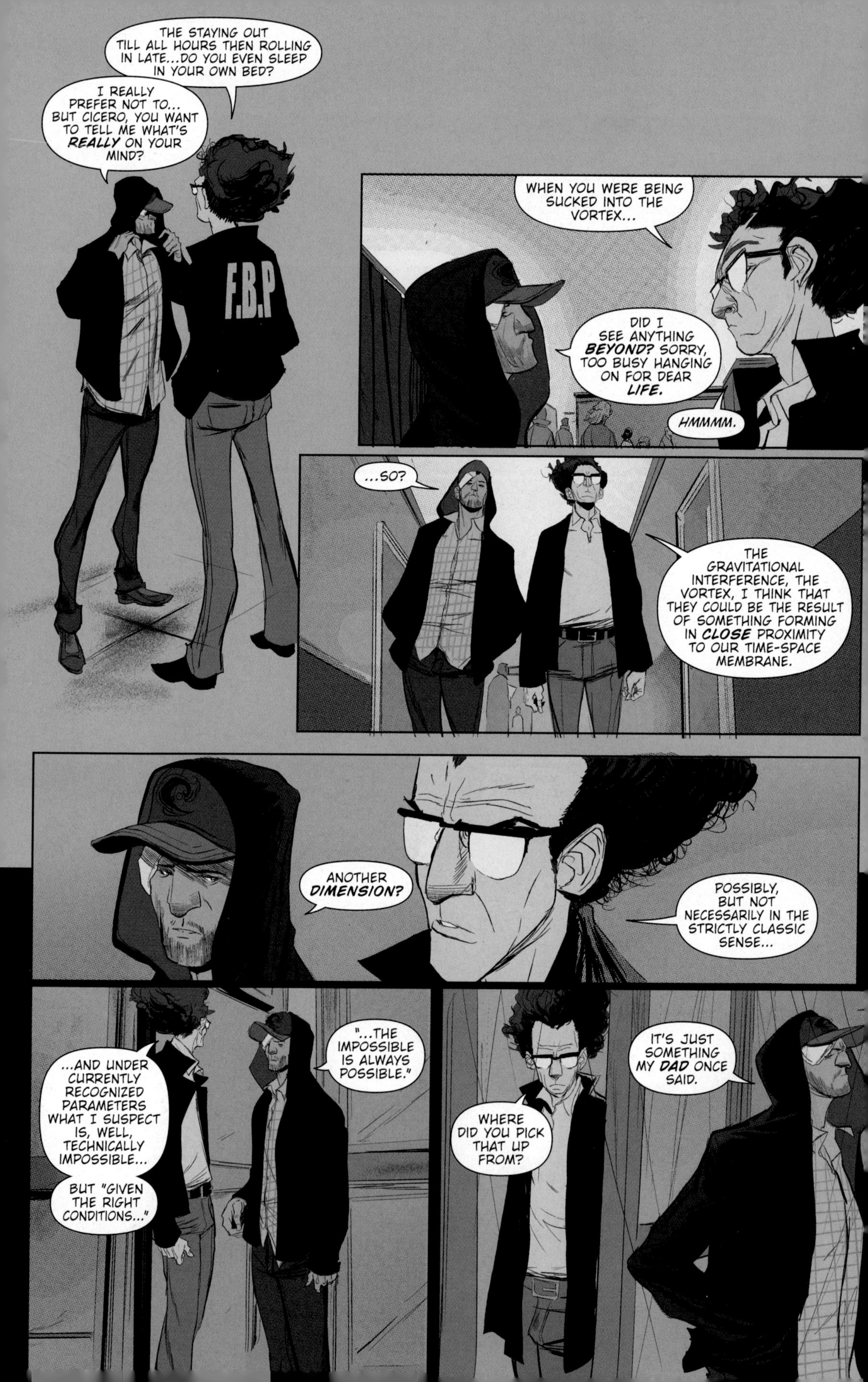
THE STAYING OUT TILL ALL HOURS THEN ROLLING IN LATE...DO YOU EVEN SLEEP IN YOUR OWN BED?
I REALLY PREFER NOT TO... BUT CICERO, YOU WANT TO TELL ME WHAT'S REALLY ON YOUR MIND?
F.B.P
WHEN YOU WERE BEING SUCKED INTO THE VORTEX...
DID I SEE ANYTHING BEYOND? SORRY, TOO BUSY HANGING ON FOR DEAR LIFE.
HMMMM.
...SO?
THE GRAVITATIONAL INTERFERENCE, THE VORTEX, I THINK THAT THEY COULD BE THE RESULT OF SOMETHING FORMING IN CLOSE PROXIMITY TO OUR TIME-SPACE MEMBRANE.
ANOTHER DIMENSION?
POSSIBLY, BUT NOT NECESSARILY IN THE STRICTLY CLASSIC SENSE...
...AND UNDER CURRENTLY RECOGNIZED PARAMETERS WHAT I SUSPECT IS, WELL, TECHNICALLY IMPOSSIBLE...
BUT "GIVEN THE RIGHT CONDITIONS..."
"...THE IMPOSSIBLE IS ALWAYS POSSIBLE."
WHERE DID YOU PICK THAT UP FROM?
IT'S JUST SOMETHING MY DAD ONCE SAID.

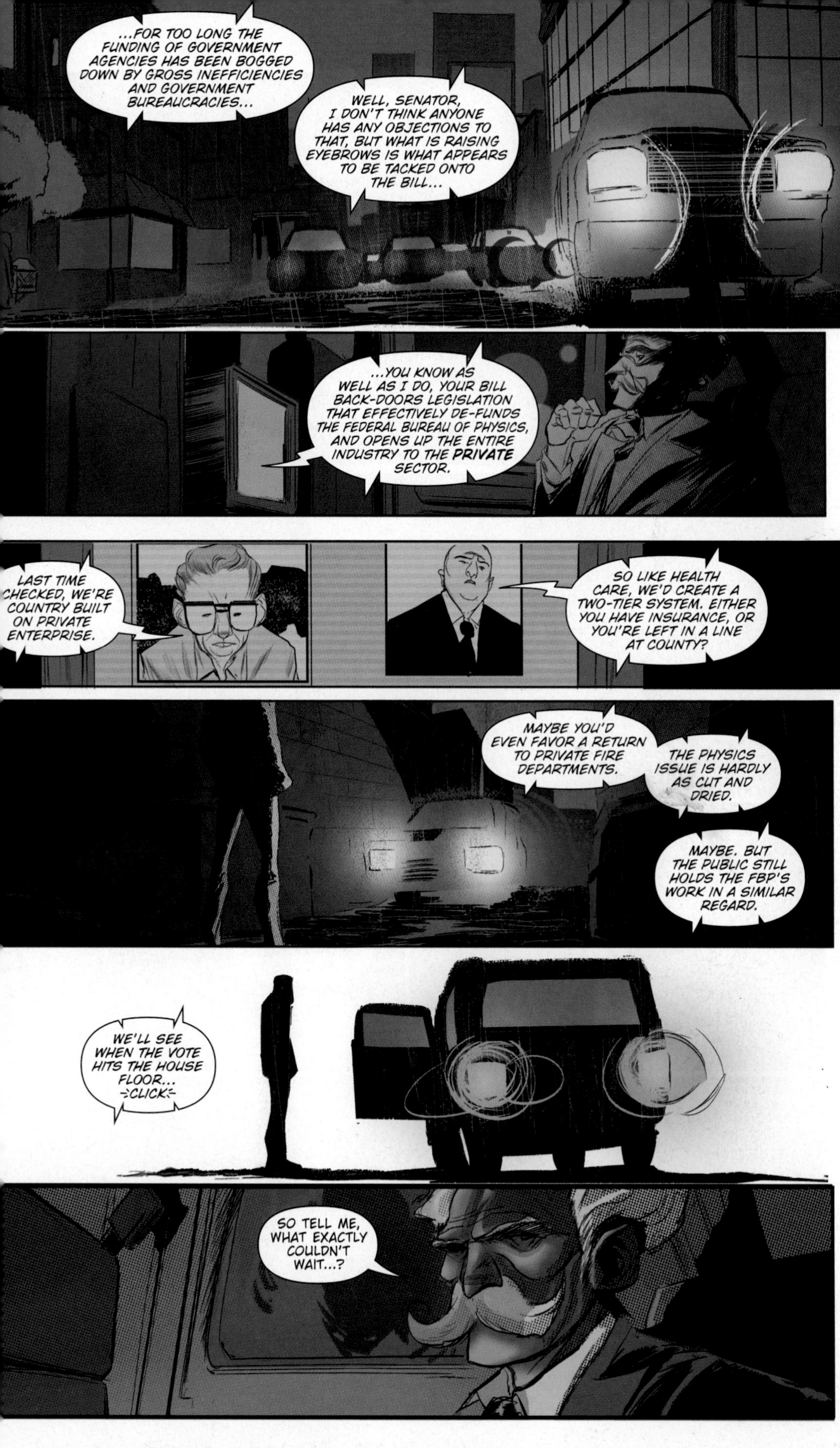
...FOR TOO LONG THE FUNDING OF GOVERNMENT AGENCIES HAS BEEN BOGGED DOWN BY GROSS INEFFICIENCIES AND GOVERNMENT BUREAUCRACIES...
WELL, SENATOR, I DON'T THINK ANYONE HAS ANY OBJECTIONS TO THAT, BUT WHAT IS RAISING EYEBROWS IS WHAT APPEARS TO BE TACKED ONTO THE BILL...
...YOU KNOW AS WELL AS I DO, YOUR BILL BACK-DOORS LEGISLATION THAT EFFECTIVELY DE-FUNDS THE FEDERAL BUREAU OF PHYSICS, AND OPENS UP THE ENTIRE INDUSTRY TO THE **PRIVATE** SECTOR.
LAST TIME CHECKED, WE'RE COUNTRY BUILT ON PRIVATE ENTERPRISE.
SO LIKE HEALTH CARE, WE'D CREATE A TWO-TIER SYSTEM. EITHER YOU HAVE INSURANCE, OR YOU'RE LEFT IN A LINE AT COUNTY?
MAYBE YOU'D EVEN FAVOR A RETURN TO PRIVATE FIRE DEPARTMENTS.
THE PHYSICS ISSUE IS HARDLY AS CUT AND DRIED.
MAYBE. BUT THE PUBLIC STILL HOLDS THE FBP'S WORK IN A SIMILAR REGARD.
WE'LL SEE WHEN THE VOTE HITS THE HOUSE FLOOR...
CLICK
SO TELL ME, WHAT EXACTLY COULDN'T WAIT...?

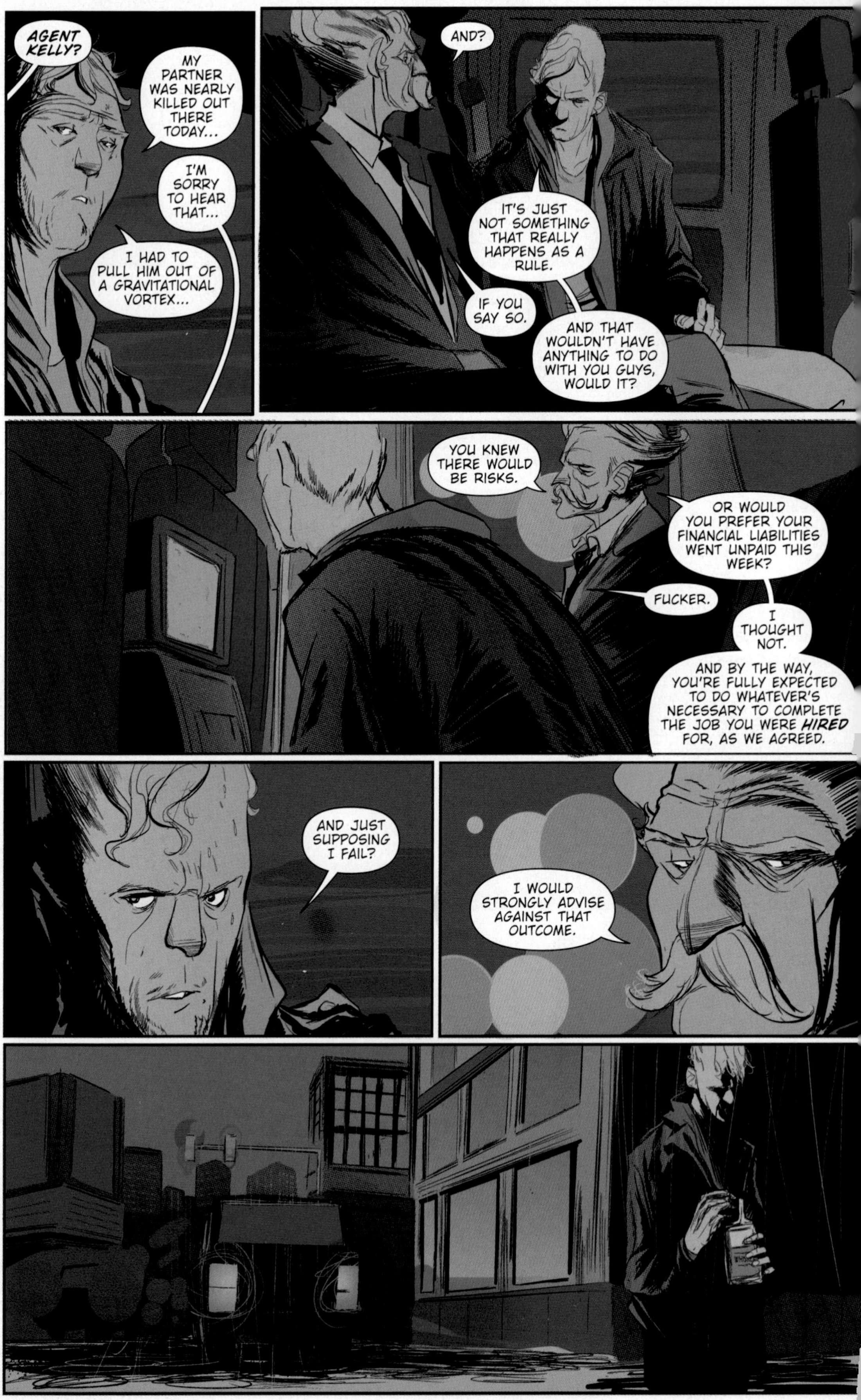
AGENT KELLY?
MY PARTNER WAS NEARLY KILLED OUT THERE TODAY...
I'M SORRY TO HEAR THAT...
I HAD TO PULL HIM OUT OF A GRAVITATIONAL VORTEX...
AND?
IT'S JUST NOT SOMETHING THAT REALLY HAPPENS AS A RULE.
IF YOU SAY SO.
AND THAT WOULDN'T HAVE ANYTHING TO DO WITH YOU GUYS, WOULD IT?
YOU KNEW THERE WOULD BE RISKS.
OR WOULD YOU PREFER YOUR FINANCIAL LIABILITIES WENT UNPAID THIS WEEK?
FUCKER.
I THOUGHT NOT.
AND BY THE WAY, YOU'RE FULLY EXPECTED TO DO WHATEVER'S NECESSARY TO COMPLETE THE JOB YOU WERE *HIRED* FOR, AS WE AGREED.
AND JUST SUPPOSING I FAIL?
I WOULD STRONGLY ADVISE AGAINST THAT OUTCOME.

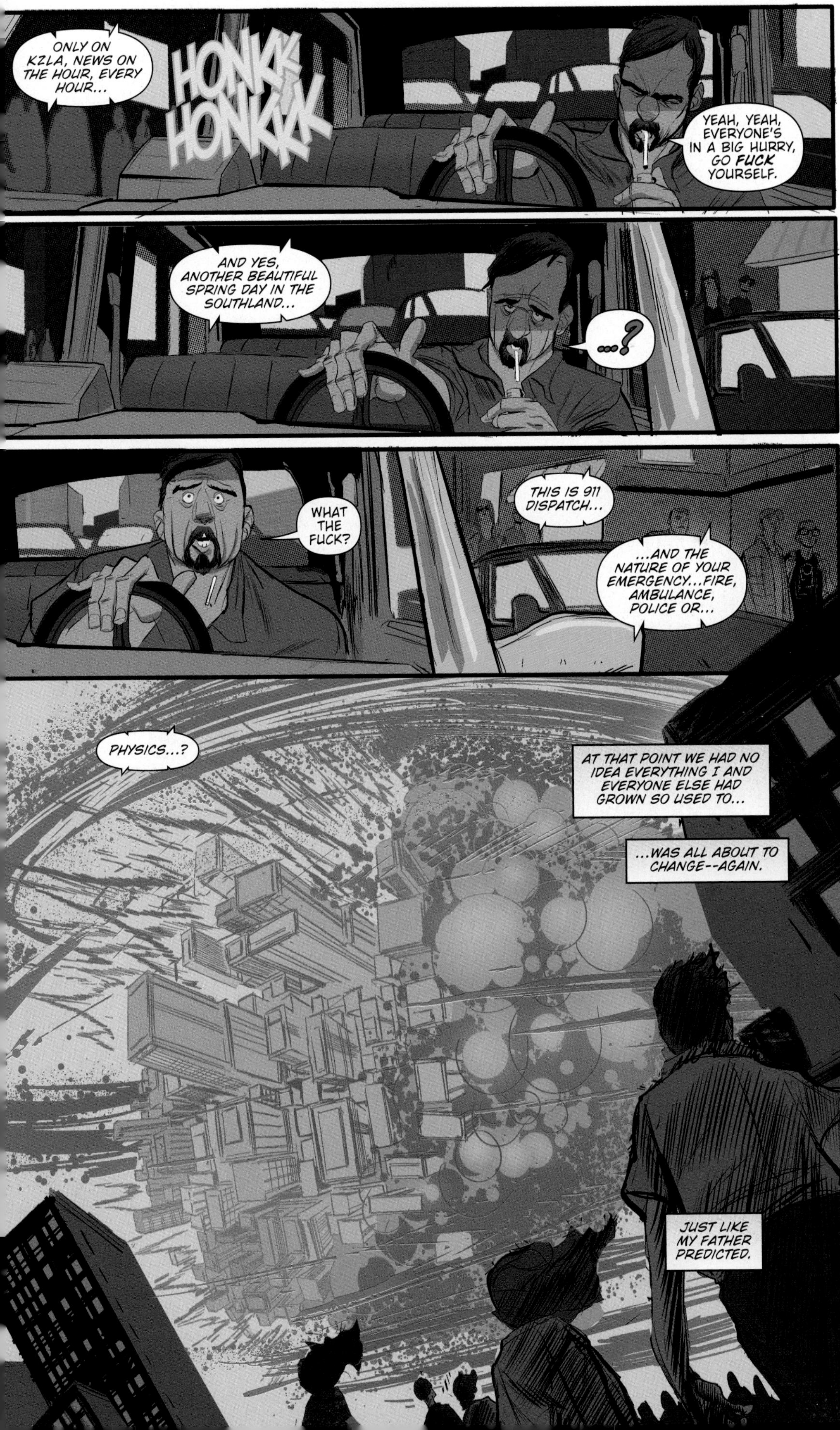
ONLY ON KZLA, NEWS ON THE HOUR, EVERY HOUR...
HONKK HONKKK
YEAH, YEAH, EVERYONE'S IN A BIG HURRY, GO FUCK YOURSELF.
AND YES, ANOTHER BEAUTIFUL SPRING DAY IN THE SOUTHLAND...
...?
WHAT THE FUCK?
THIS IS 911 DISPATCH...
...AND THE NATURE OF YOUR EMERGENCY...FIRE, AMBULANCE, POLICE OR...
PHYSICS...?
AT THAT POINT WE HAD NO IDEA EVERYTHING I AND EVERYONE ELSE HAD GROWN SO USED TO...
...WAS ALL ABOUT TO CHANGE--AGAIN.
JUST LIKE MY FATHER PREDICTED.

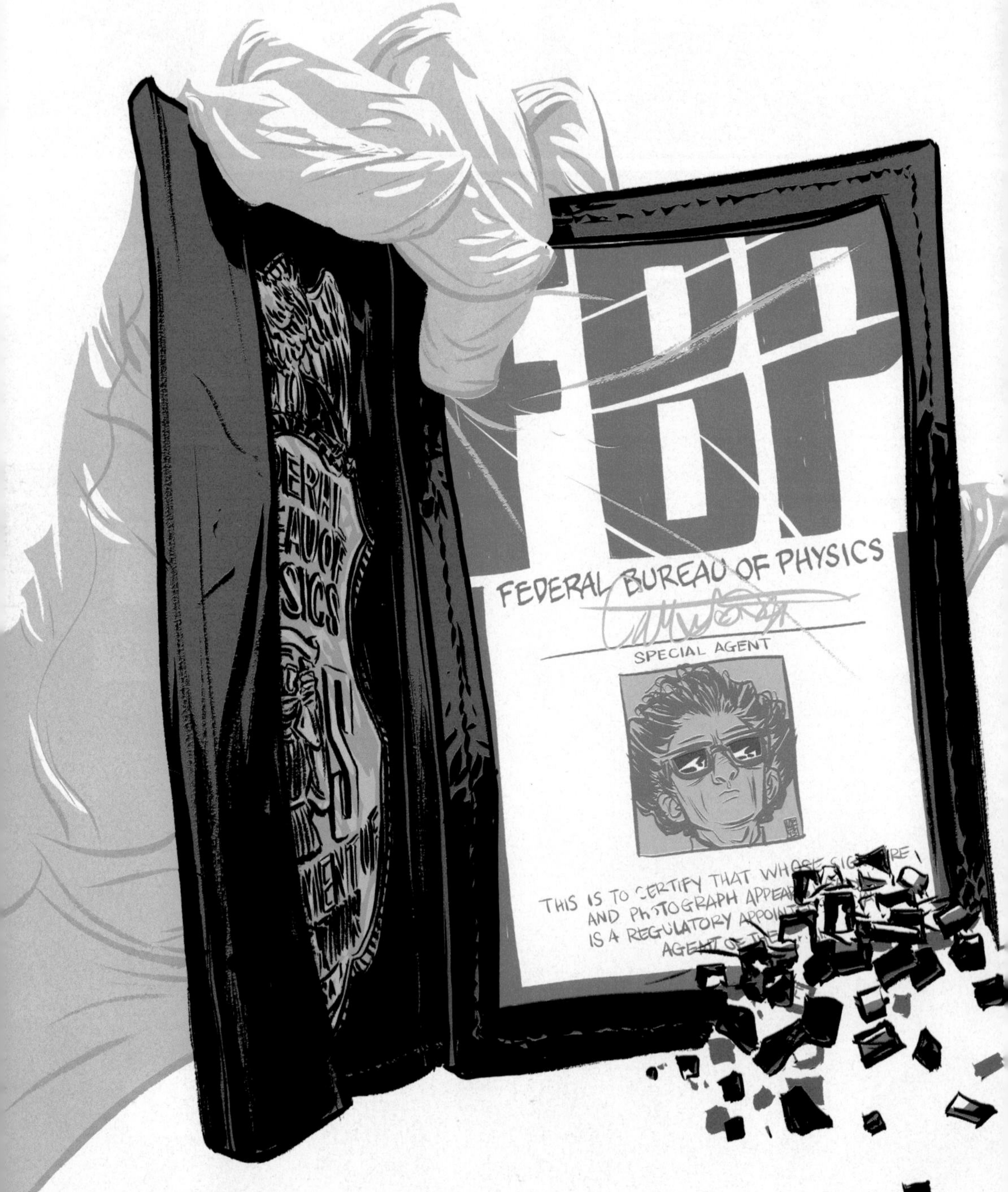
FBP
FEDERAL BUREAU OF PHYSICS
SPECIAL AGENT

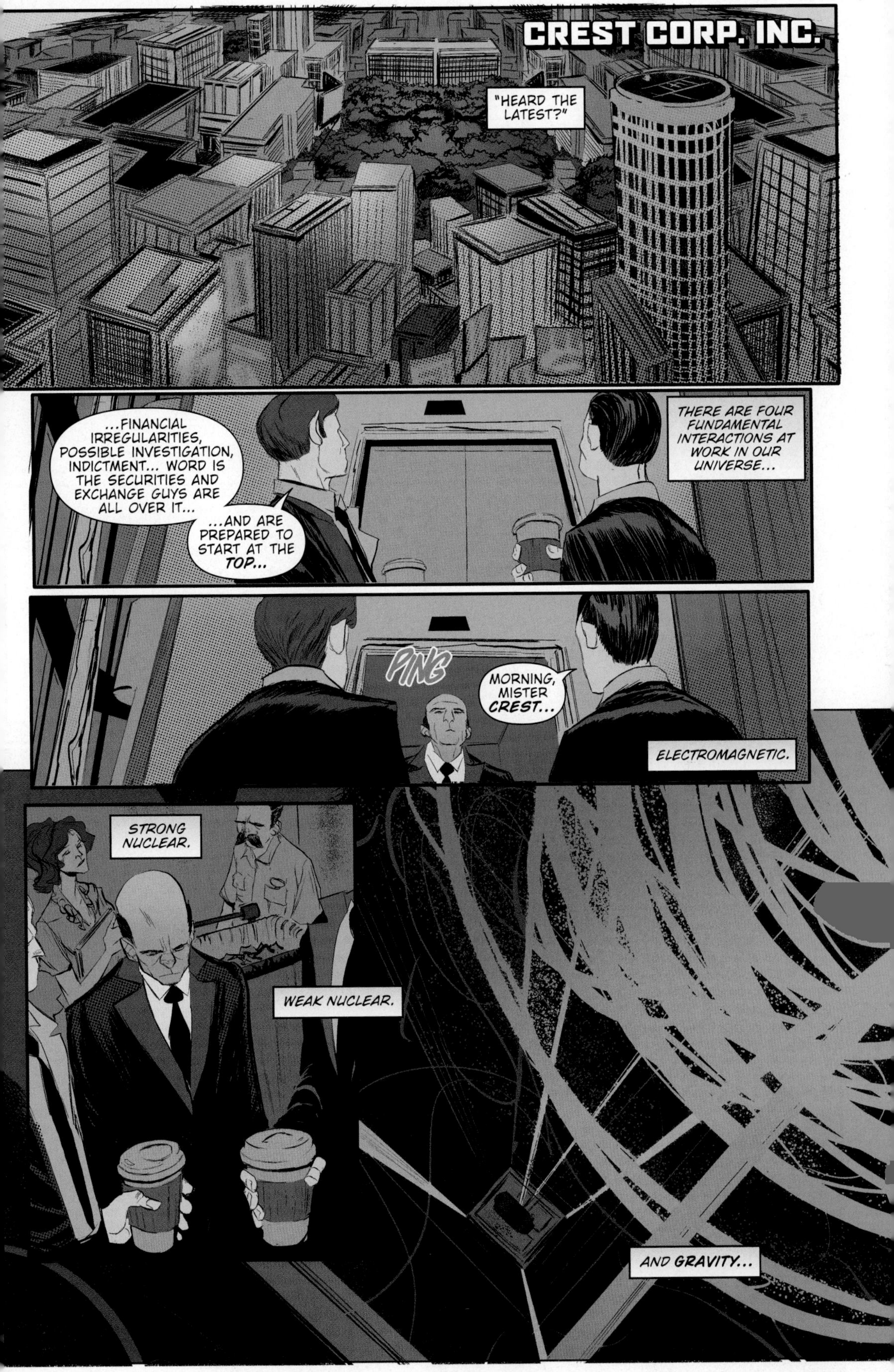
CREST CORP. INC.
"HEARD THE LATEST?"
...FINANCIAL IRREGULARITIES, POSSIBLE INVESTIGATION, INDICTMENT... WORD IS THE SECURITIES AND EXCHANGE GUYS ARE ALL OVER IT...
...AND ARE PREPARED TO START AT THE TOP...
THERE ARE FOUR FUNDAMENTAL INTERACTIONS AT WORK IN OUR UNIVERSE...
PING
MORNING, MISTER CREST...
ELECTROMAGNETIC.
STRONG NUCLEAR.
WEAK NUCLEAR.
AND GRAVITY...

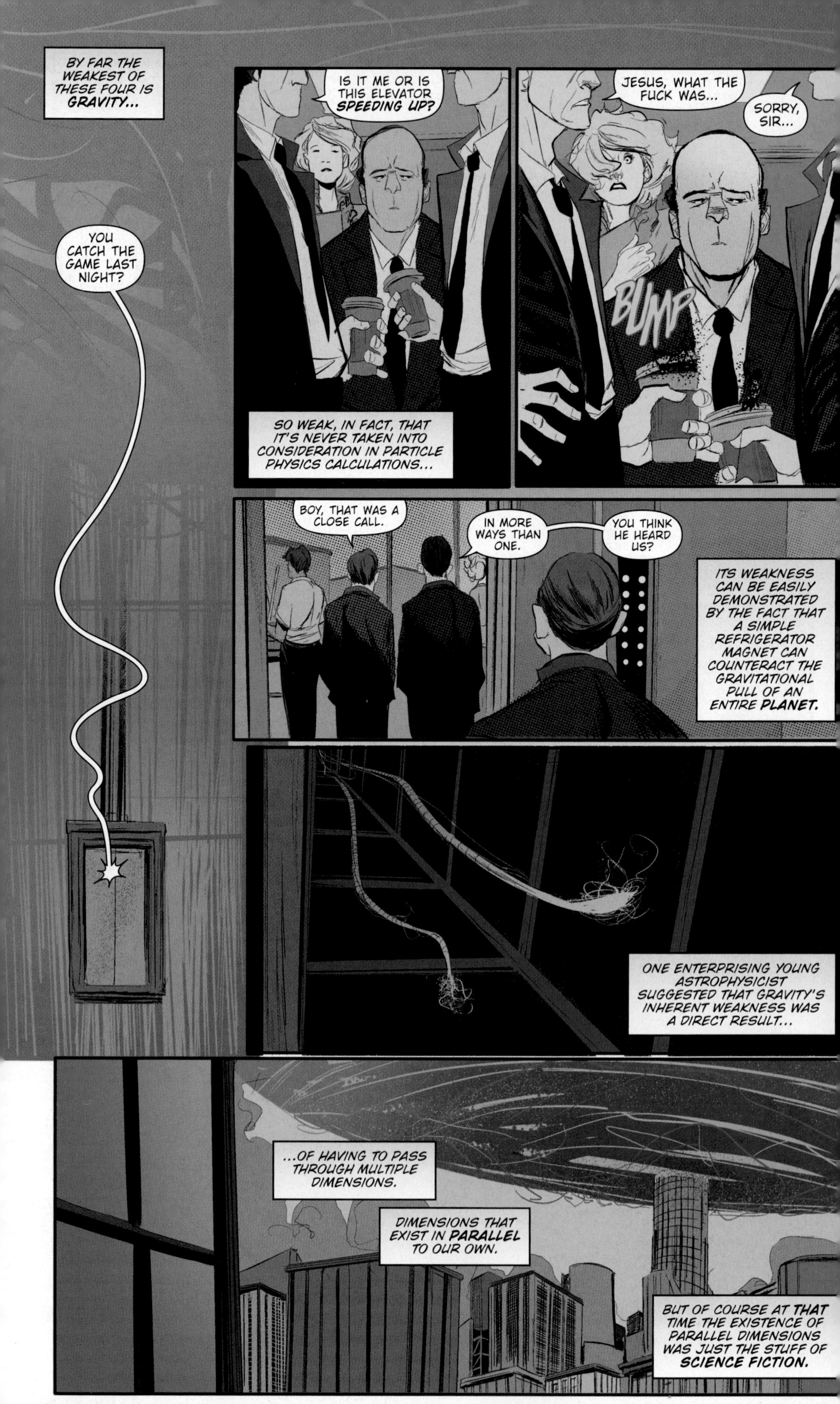
BY FAR THE WEAKEST OF THESE FOUR IS GRAVITY...
IS IT ME OR IS THIS ELEVATOR SPEEDING UP?
YOU CATCH THE GAME LAST NIGHT?
SO WEAK, IN FACT, THAT IT'S NEVER TAKEN INTO CONSIDERATION IN PARTICLE PHYSICS CALCULATIONS...
JESUS, WHAT THE FUCK WAS...
SORRY, SIR...
BUMP
BOY, THAT WAS A CLOSE CALL.
IN MORE WAYS THAN ONE.
YOU THINK HE HEARD US?
ITS WEAKNESS CAN BE EASILY DEMONSTRATED BY THE FACT THAT A SIMPLE REFRIGERATOR MAGNET CAN COUNTERACT THE GRAVITATIONAL PULL OF AN ENTIRE PLANET.
ONE ENTERPRISING YOUNG ASTROPHYSICIST SUGGESTED THAT GRAVITY'S INHERENT WEAKNESS WAS A DIRECT RESULT...
...OF HAVING TO PASS THROUGH MULTIPLE DIMENSIONS.
DIMENSIONS THAT EXIST IN PARALLEL TO OUR OWN.
BUT OF COURSE AT THAT TIME THE EXISTENCE OF PARALLEL DIMENSIONS WAS JUST THE STUFF OF SCIENCE FICTION.

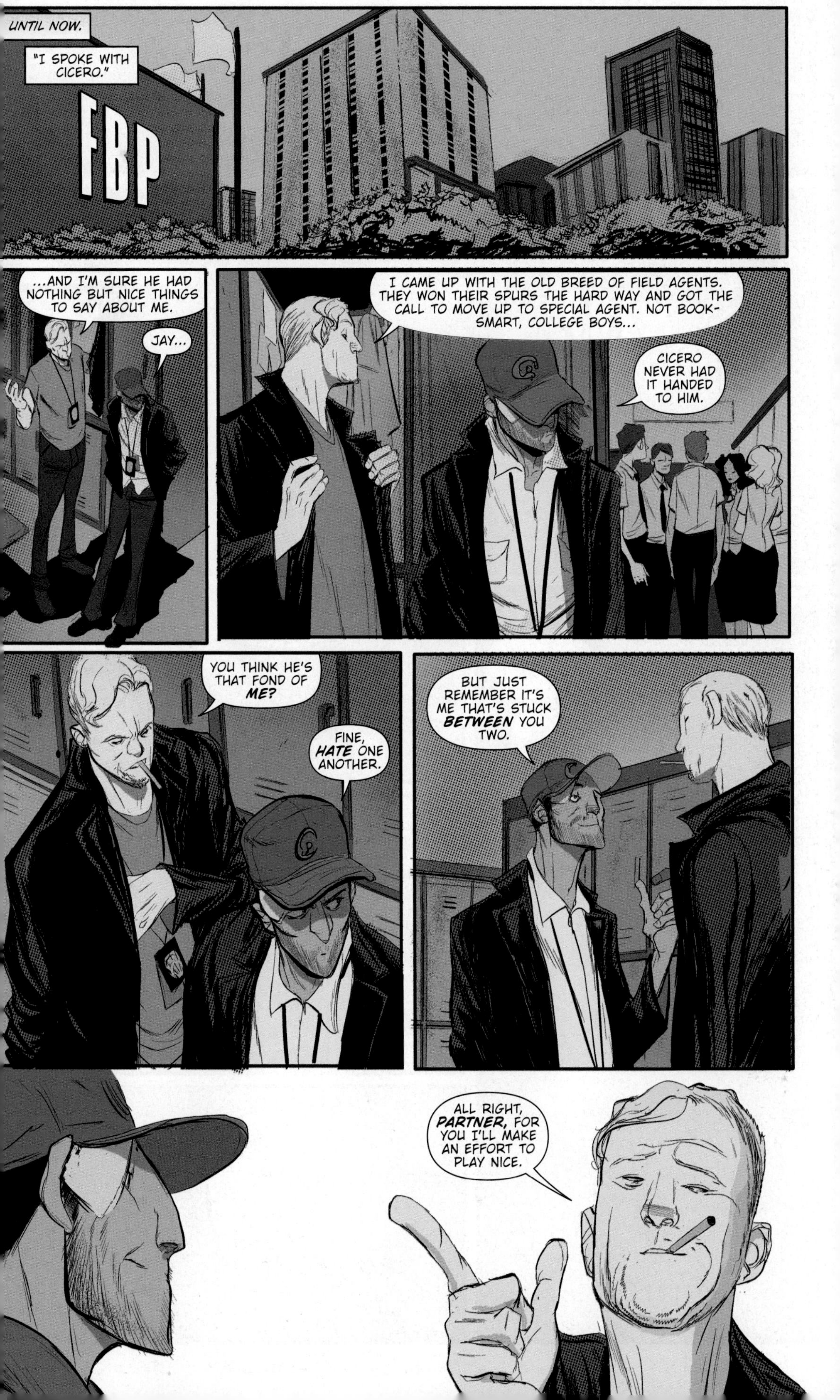

UNTIL NOW.
"I SPOKE WITH CICERO."
FBP
...AND I'M SURE HE HAD NOTHING BUT NICE THINGS TO SAY ABOUT ME.
JAY...
I CAME UP WITH THE OLD BREED OF FIELD AGENTS. THEY WON THEIR SPURS THE HARD WAY AND GOT THE CALL TO MOVE UP TO SPECIAL AGENT. NOT BOOK-SMART, COLLEGE BOYS...
CICERO NEVER HAD IT HANDED TO HIM.
YOU THINK HE'S THAT FOND OF ME?
FINE, HATE ONE ANOTHER.
BUT JUST REMEMBER IT'S ME THAT'S STUCK BETWEEN YOU TWO.
ALL RIGHT, PARTNER, FOR YOU I'LL MAKE AN EFFORT TO PLAY NICE.

4 YEARS AGO...

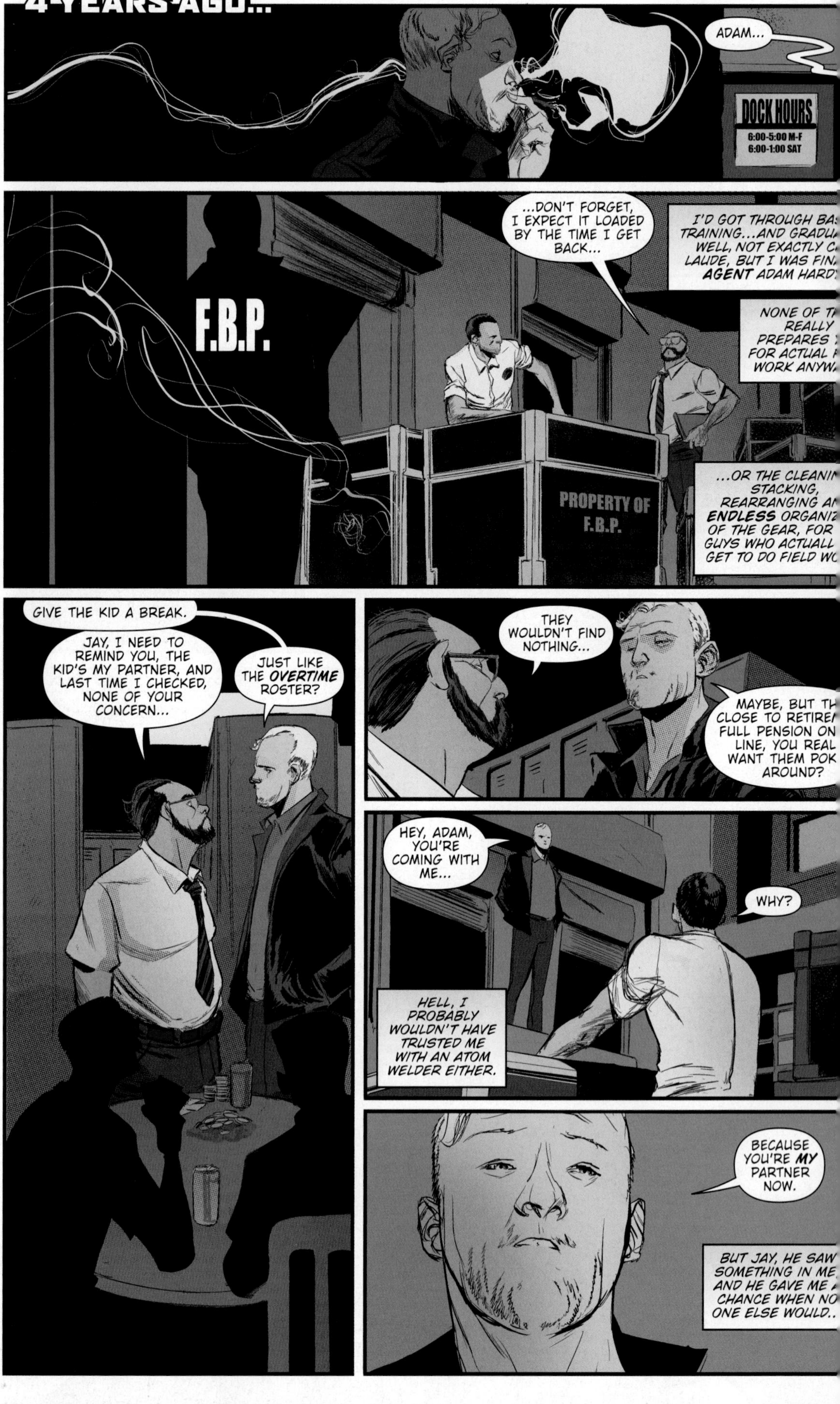
ADAM...
DOCK HOURS
6:00-5:00 M-F
6:00-1:00 SAT
F.B.P.
...DON'T FORGET, I EXPECT IT LOADED BY THE TIME I GET BACK...
I'D GOT THROUGH BAS TRAINING...AND GRADU WELL, NOT EXACTLY C LAUDE, BUT I WAS FIN AGENT ADAM HARD
NONE OF T REALLY PREPARES FOR ACTUAL WORK ANYW
PROPERTY OF F.B.P.
...OR THE CLEANI STACKING, REARRANGING A ENDLESS ORGANIZ OF THE GEAR, FOR GUYS WHO ACTUALL GET TO DO FIELD W
GIVE THE KID A BREAK.
JAY, I NEED TO REMIND YOU, THE KID'S MY PARTNER, AND LAST TIME I CHECKED, NONE OF YOUR CONCERN...
JUST LIKE THE OVERTIME ROSTER?
THEY WOULDN'T FIND NOTHING...
MAYBE, BUT T CLOSE TO RETIRE FULL PENSION O LINE, YOU REA WANT THEM PO AROUND?
HEY, ADAM, YOU'RE COMING WITH ME...
WHY?
HELL, I PROBABLY WOULDN'T HAVE TRUSTED ME WITH AN ATOM WELDER EITHER.
BECAUSE YOU'RE MY PARTNER NOW.
BUT JAY, HE SAW SOMETHING IN ME AND HE GAVE ME CHANCE WHEN N ONE ELSE WOULD..

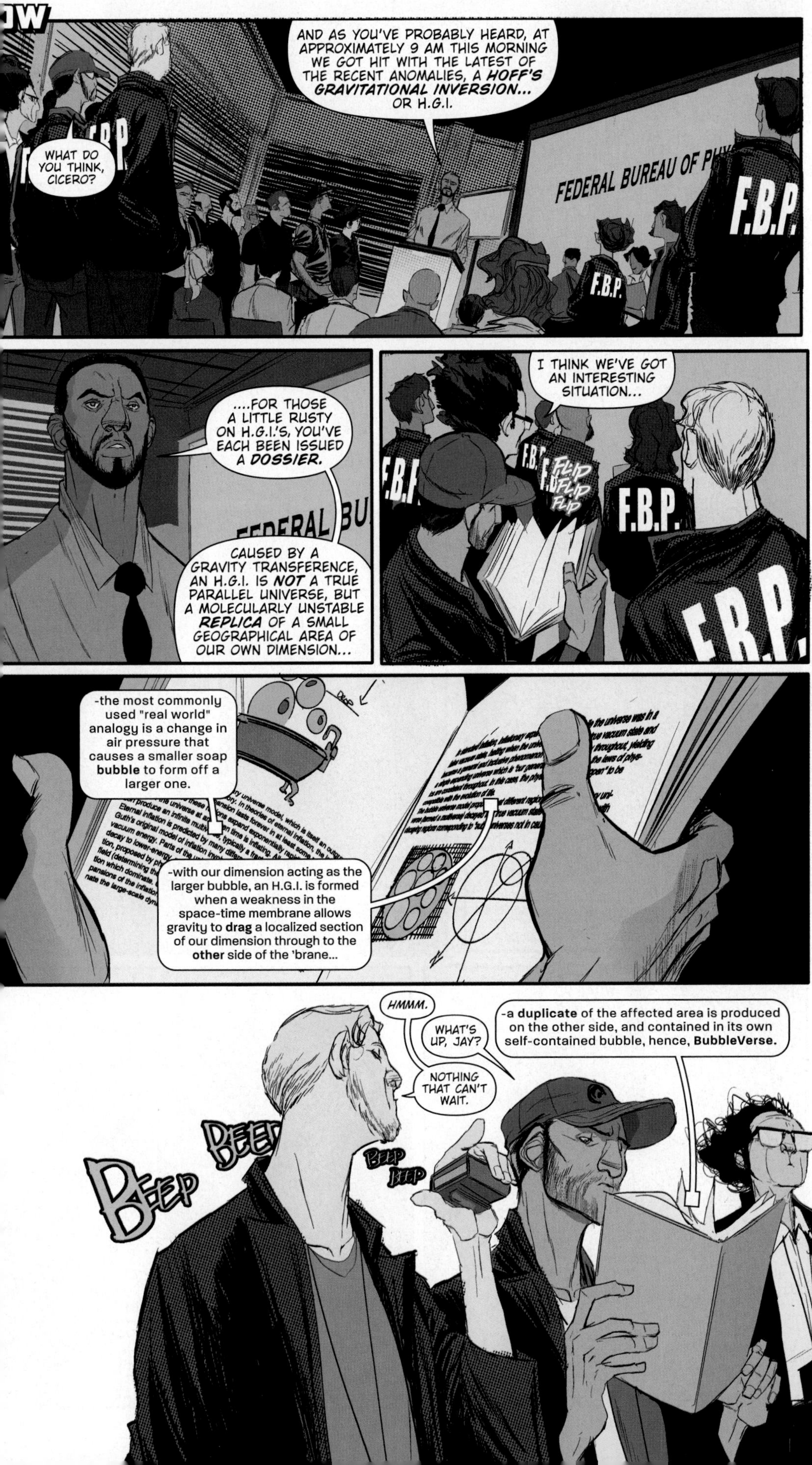
AND AS YOU'VE PROBABLY HEARD, AT APPROXIMATELY 9 AM THIS MORNING WE GOT HIT WITH THE LATEST OF THE RECENT ANOMALIES, A HOFF'S GRAVITATIONAL INVERSION... OR H.G.I.
WHAT DO YOU THINK, CICERO?
FEDERAL BUREAU OF PHY
F.B.P.
F.B.P.
....FOR THOSE A LITTLE RUSTY ON H.G.I.'S, YOU'VE EACH BEEN ISSUED A DOSSIER.
CAUSED BY A GRAVITY TRANSFERENCE, AN H.G.I. IS NOT A TRUE PARALLEL UNIVERSE, BUT A MOLECULARLY UNSTABLE REPLICA OF A SMALL GEOGRAPHICAL AREA OF OUR OWN DIMENSION...
FEDERAL BU
I THINK WE'VE GOT AN INTERESTING SITUATION...
FLIP FLIP FLIP
F.B.P.
F.B.P.
-the most commonly used "real world" analogy is a change in air pressure that causes a smaller soap bubble to form off a larger one.
-with our dimension acting as the larger bubble, an H.G.I. is formed when a weakness in the space-time membrane allows gravity to drag a localized section of our dimension through to the other side of the 'brane...
HMMM.
WHAT'S UP, JAY?
NOTHING THAT CAN'T WAIT.
-a duplicate of the affected area is produced on the other side, and contained in its own self-contained bubble, hence, BubbleVerse.
BEEP BEEP BEEP BEEP

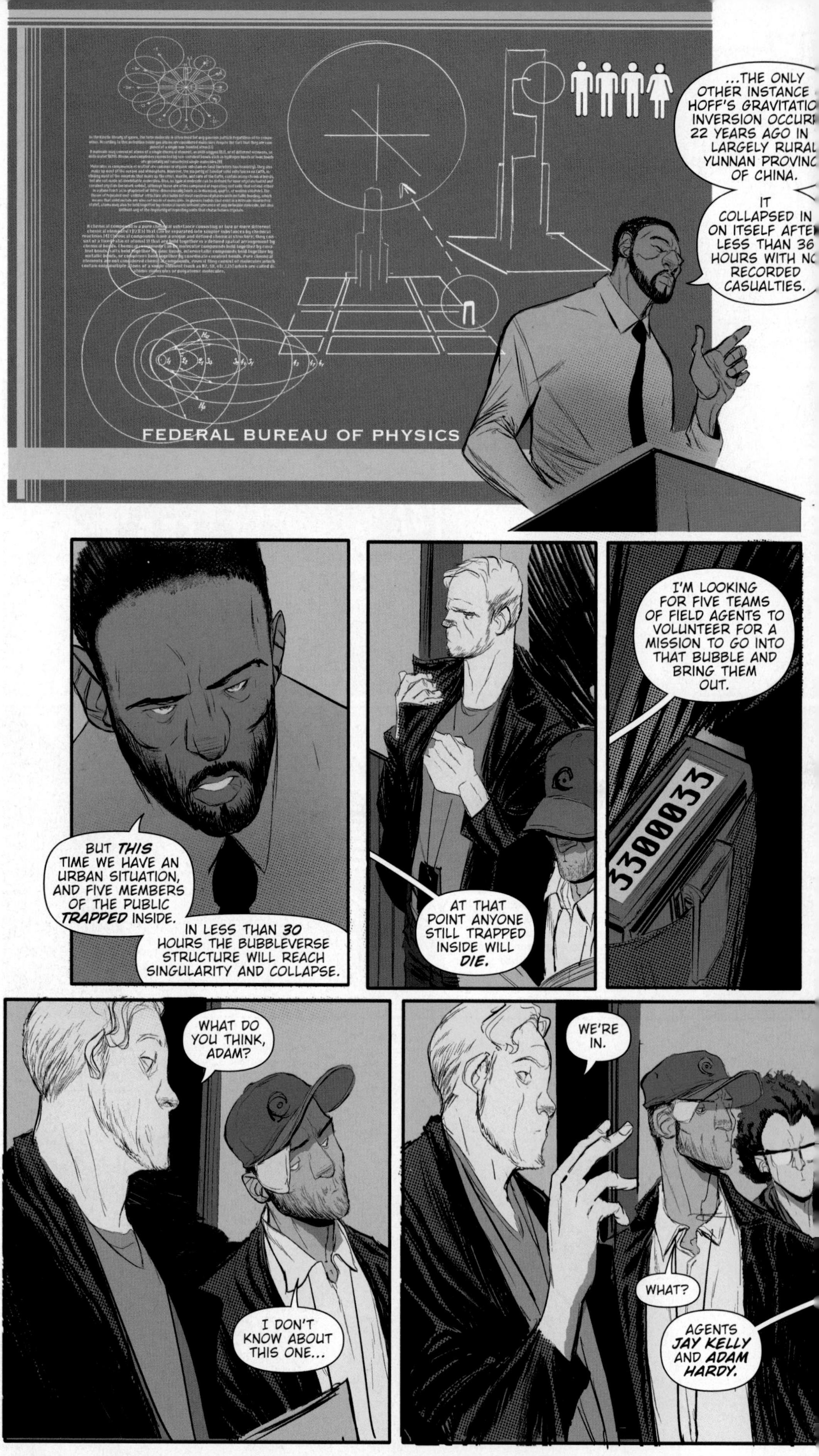
FEDERAL BUREAU OF PHYSICS
...THE ONLY OTHER INSTANCE HOFF'S GRAVITATIO INVERSION OCCUR 22 YEARS AGO IN LARGELY RURAL YUNNAN PROVINC OF CHINA.
IT COLLAPSED IN ON ITSELF AFTE LESS THAN 36 HOURS WITH NO RECORDED CASUALTIES.
BUT THIS TIME WE HAVE AN URBAN SITUATION, AND FIVE MEMBERS OF THE PUBLIC TRAPPED INSIDE.
IN LESS THAN 30 HOURS THE BUBBLEVERSE STRUCTURE WILL REACH SINGULARITY AND COLLAPSE.
AT THAT POINT ANYONE STILL TRAPPED INSIDE WILL DIE.
I'M LOOKING FOR FIVE TEAMS OF FIELD AGENTS TO VOLUNTEER FOR A MISSION TO GO INTO THAT BUBBLE AND BRING THEM OUT.
3300033
WHAT DO YOU THINK, ADAM?
I DON'T KNOW ABOUT THIS ONE...
WE'RE IN.
WHAT?
AGENTS JAY KELLY AND ADAM HARDY.

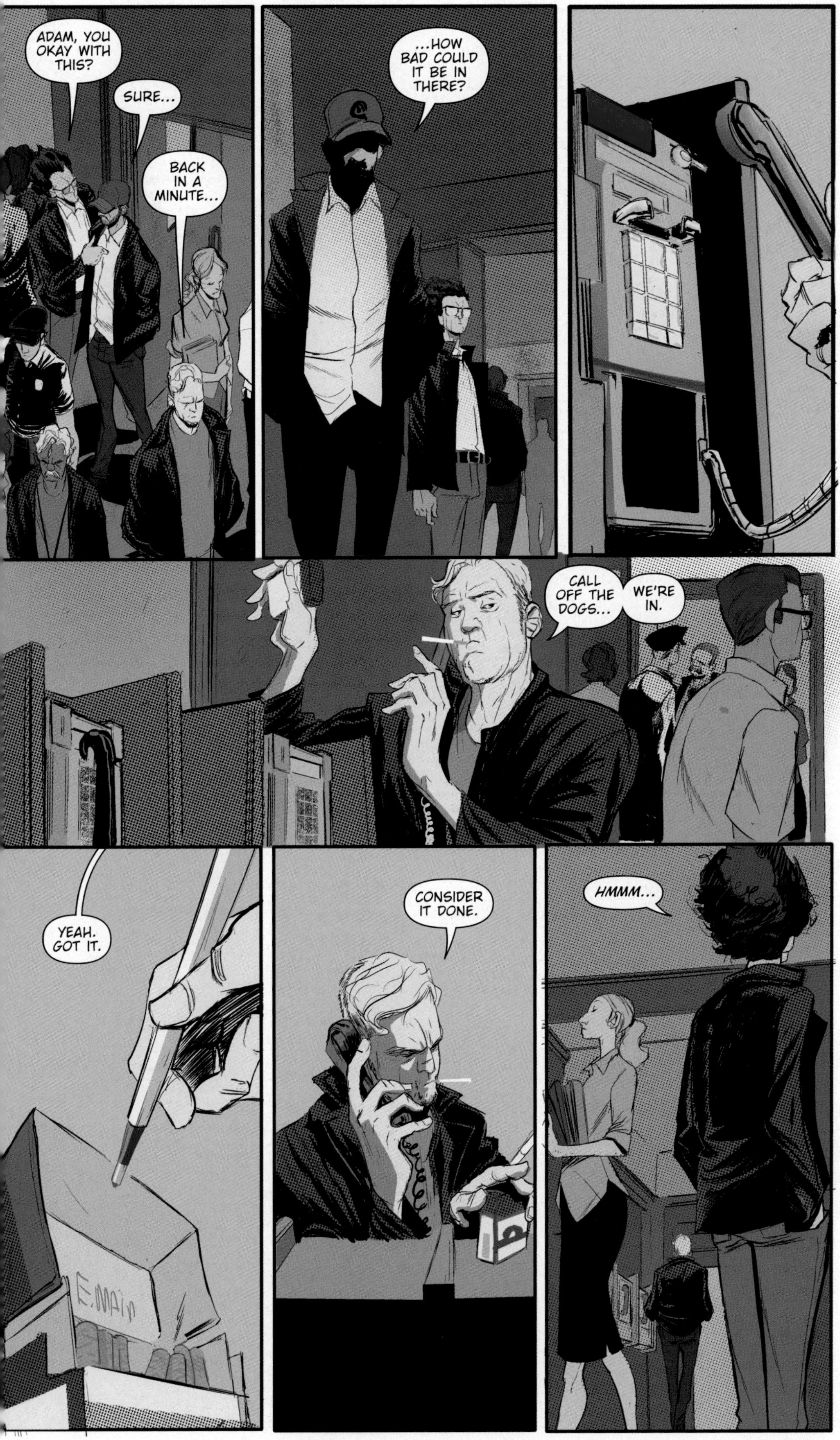
ADAM, YOU OKAY WITH THIS?
SURE...
BACK IN A MINUTE...
...HOW BAD COULD IT BE IN THERE?
CALL OFF THE DOGS...
WE'RE IN.
YEAH. GOT IT.
CONSIDER IT DONE.
HMMM...

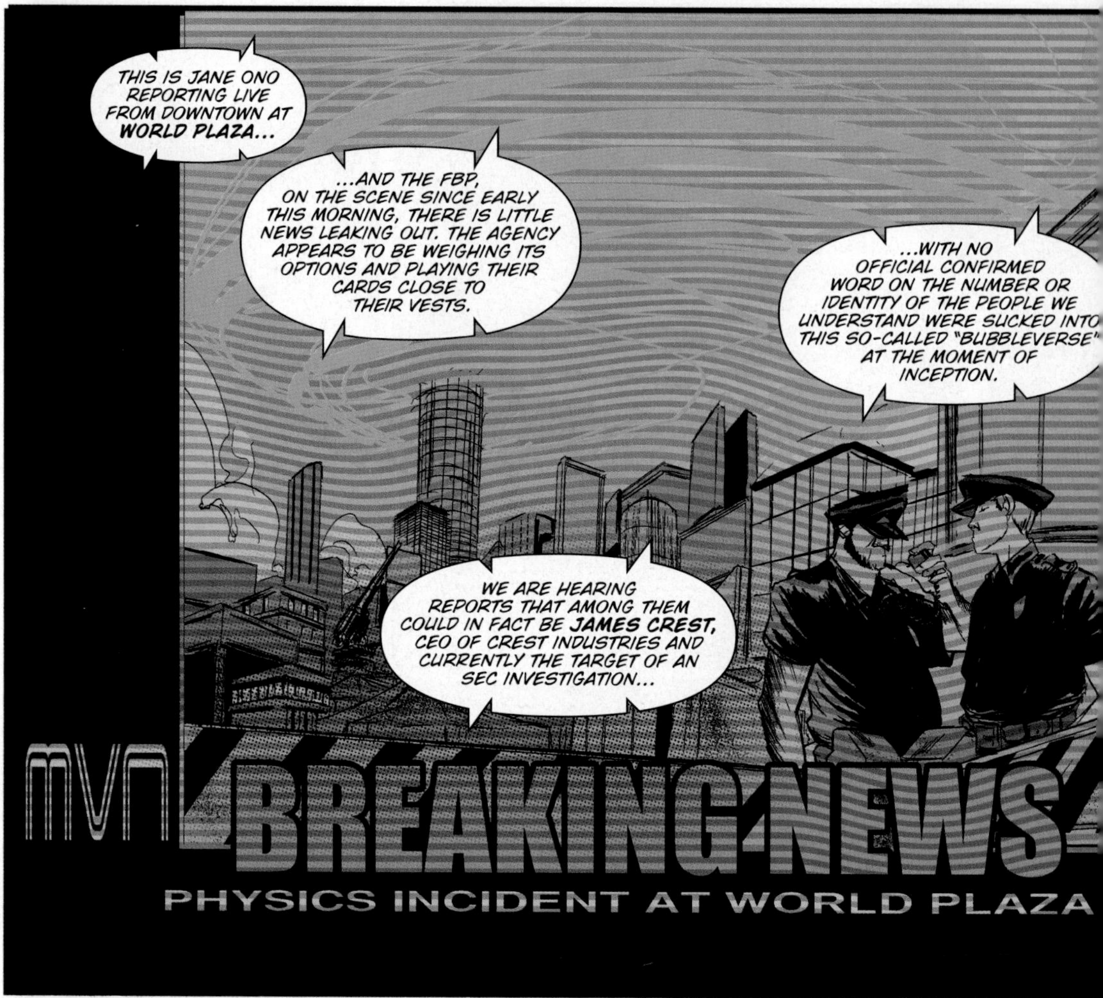
THIS IS JANE ONO REPORTING LIVE FROM DOWNTOWN AT WORLD PLAZA...
...AND THE FBP, ON THE SCENE SINCE EARLY THIS MORNING, THERE IS LITTLE NEWS LEAKING OUT. THE AGENCY APPEARS TO BE WEIGHING ITS OPTIONS AND PLAYING THEIR CARDS CLOSE TO THEIR VESTS.
...WITH NO OFFICIAL CONFIRMED WORD ON THE NUMBER OR IDENTITY OF THE PEOPLE WE UNDERSTAND WERE SUCKED INTO THIS SO-CALLED "BUBBLEVERSE" AT THE MOMENT OF INCEPTION.
WE ARE HEARING REPORTS THAT AMONG THEM COULD IN FACT BE JAMES CREST, CEO OF CREST INDUSTRIES AND CURRENTLY THE TARGET OF AN SEC INVESTIGATION...
MVN
BREAKING NEWS
PHYSICS INCIDENT AT WORLD PLAZA

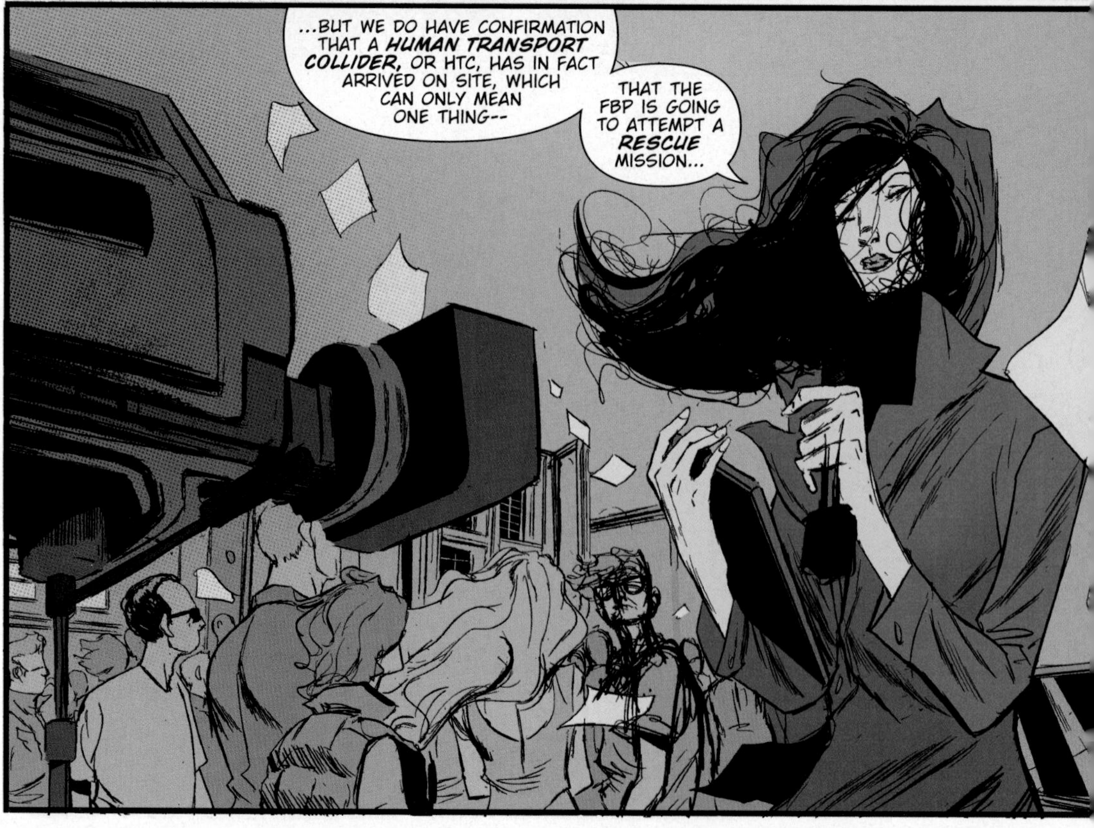
...BUT WE DO HAVE CONFIRMATION THAT A HUMAN TRANSPORT COLLIDER, OR HTC, HAS IN FACT ARRIVED ON SITE, WHICH CAN ONLY MEAN ONE THING--
THAT THE FBP IS GOING TO ATTEMPT A RESCUE MISSION...

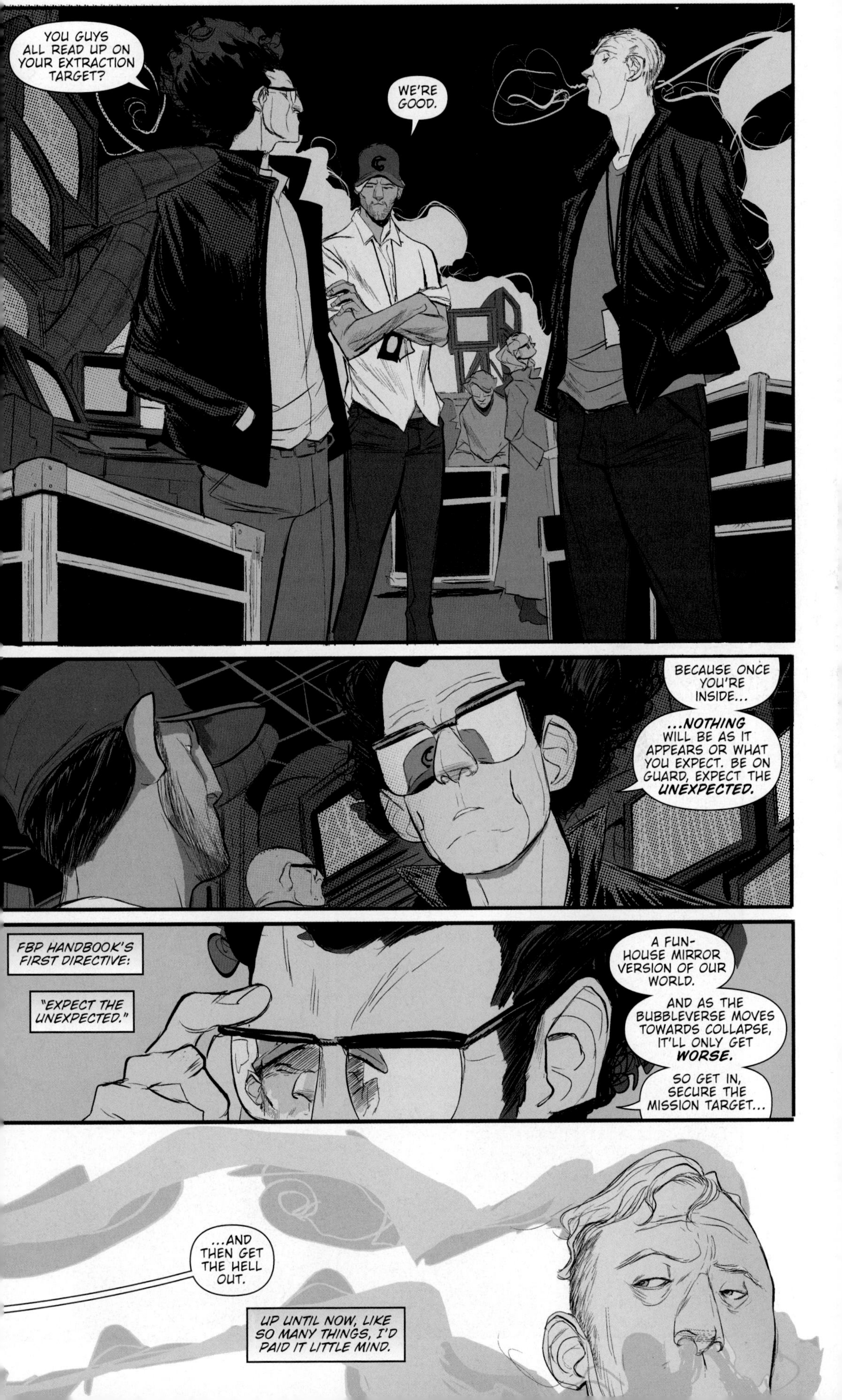
YOU GUYS ALL READ UP ON YOUR EXTRACTION TARGET?
WE'RE GOOD.
BECAUSE ONCE YOU'RE INSIDE...
...NOTHING WILL BE AS IT APPEARS OR WHAT YOU EXPECT. BE ON GUARD, EXPECT THE UNEXPECTED.
FBP HANDBOOK'S FIRST DIRECTIVE:
"EXPECT THE UNEXPECTED."
A FUN-HOUSE MIRROR VERSION OF OUR WORLD.
AND AS THE BUBBLEVERSE MOVES TOWARDS COLLAPSE, IT'LL ONLY GET WORSE.
SO GET IN, SECURE THE MISSION TARGET...
...AND THEN GET THE HELL OUT.
UP UNTIL NOW, LIKE SO MANY THINGS, I'D PAID IT LITTLE MIND.

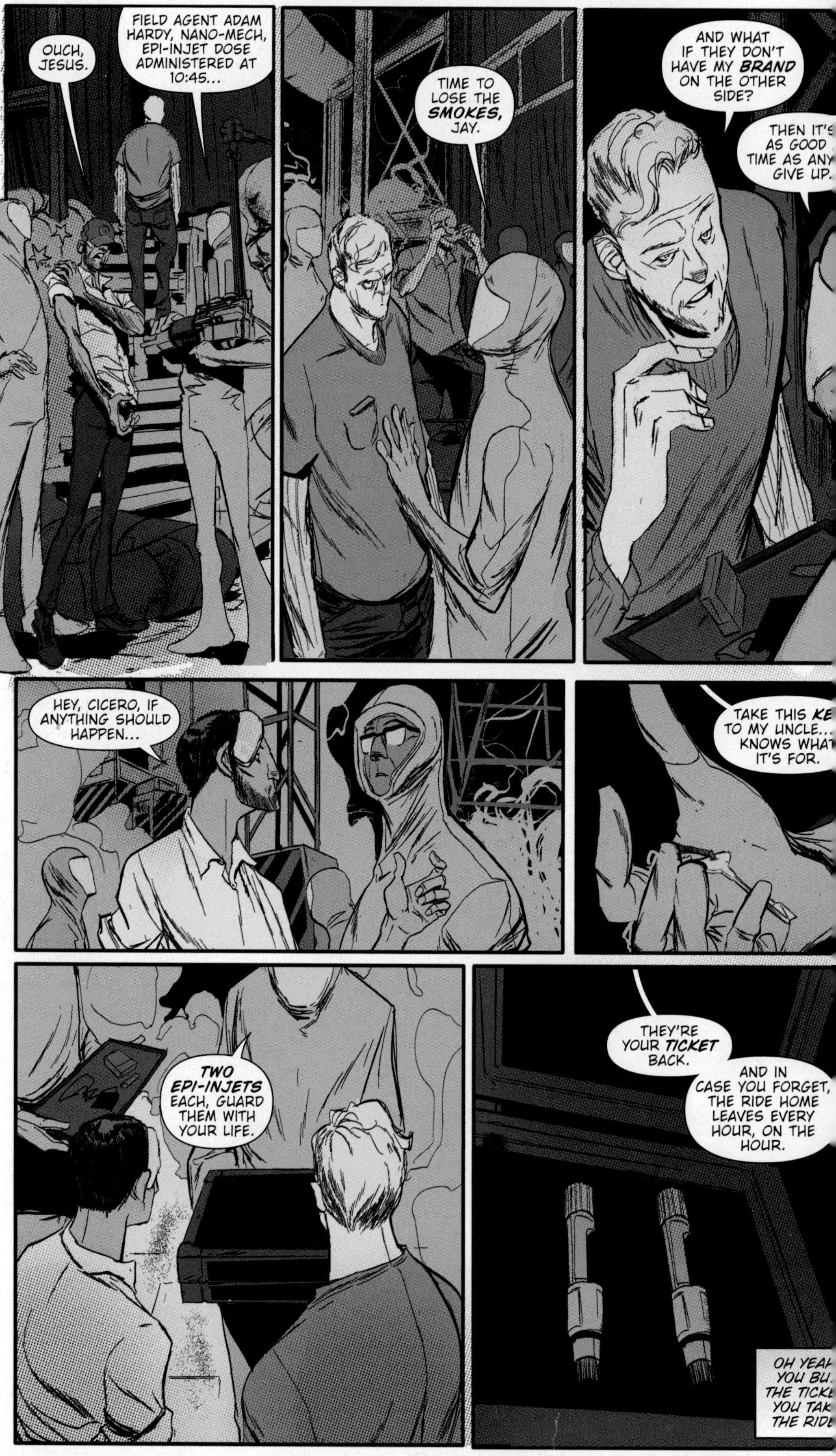
OUCH, JESUS.
FIELD AGENT ADAM HARDY, NANO-MECH, EPI-INJET DOSE ADMINISTERED AT 10:45...
TIME TO LOSE THE SMOKES, JAY.
AND WHAT IF THEY DON'T HAVE MY BRAND ON THE OTHER SIDE?
THEN IT'S AS GOOD TIME AS ANY GIVE UP.
HEY, CICERO, IF ANYTHING SHOULD HAPPEN...
TAKE THIS KE TO MY UNCLE... KNOWS WHAT IT'S FOR.
TWO EPI-INJETS EACH, GUARD THEM WITH YOUR LIFE.
THEY'RE YOUR TICKET BACK.
AND IN CASE YOU FORGET, THE RIDE HOME LEAVES EVERY HOUR, ON THE HOUR.
OH YEA YOU BU THE TICK YOU TAK THE RID

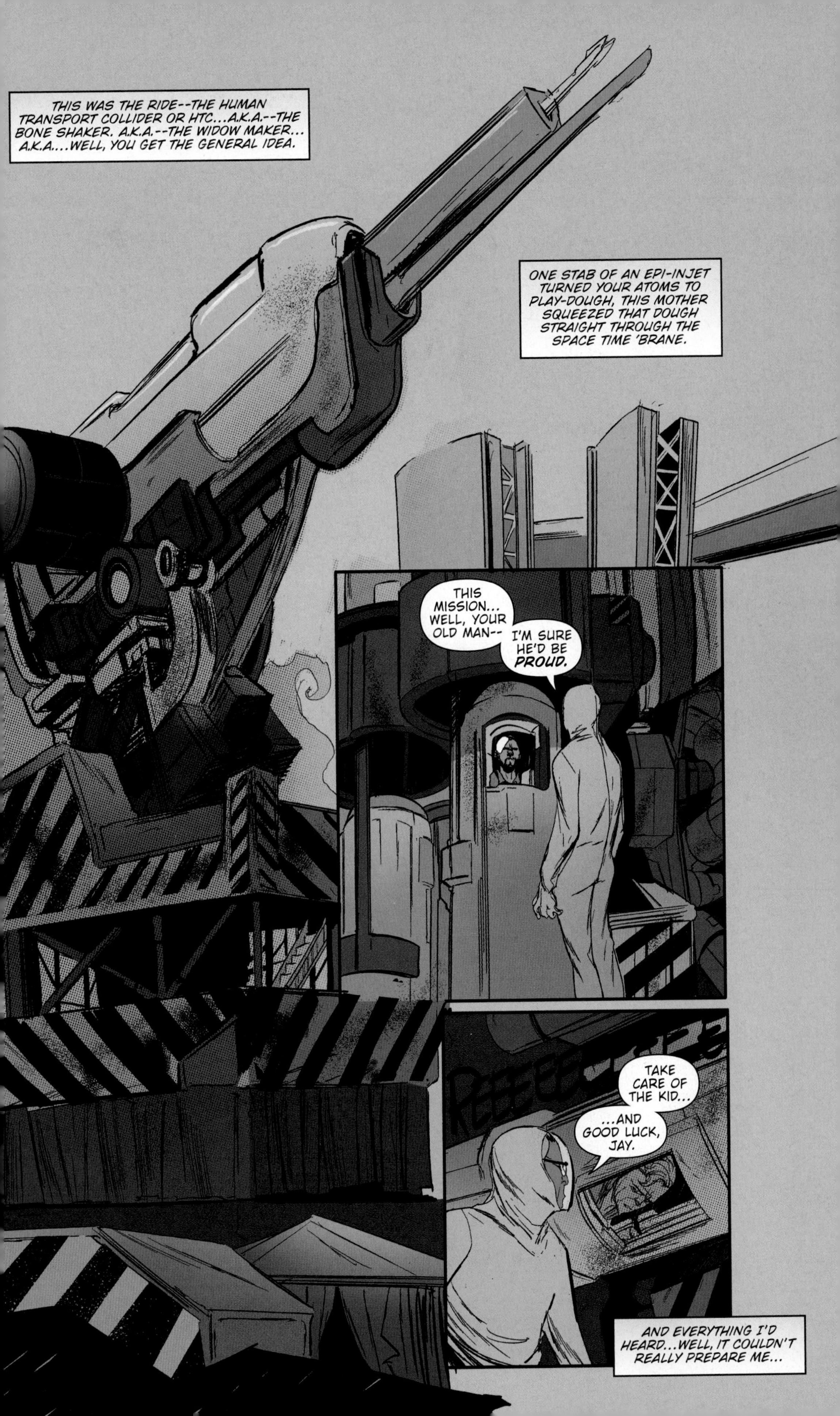
THIS WAS THE RIDE--THE HUMAN TRANSPORT COLLIDER OR HTC...A.K.A.--THE BONE SHAKER. A.K.A.--THE WIDOW MAKER... A.K.A....WELL, YOU GET THE GENERAL IDEA.
ONE STAB OF AN EPI-INJET TURNED YOUR ATOMS TO PLAY-DOUGH, THIS MOTHER SQUEEZED THAT DOUGH STRAIGHT THROUGH THE SPACE TIME 'BRANE.
THIS MISSION... WELL, YOUR OLD MAN--
I'M SURE HE'D BE **PROUD.**
TAKE CARE OF THE KID...
...AND GOOD LUCK, JAY.
AND EVERYTHING I'D HEARD...WELL, IT COULDN'T REALLY PREPARE ME...

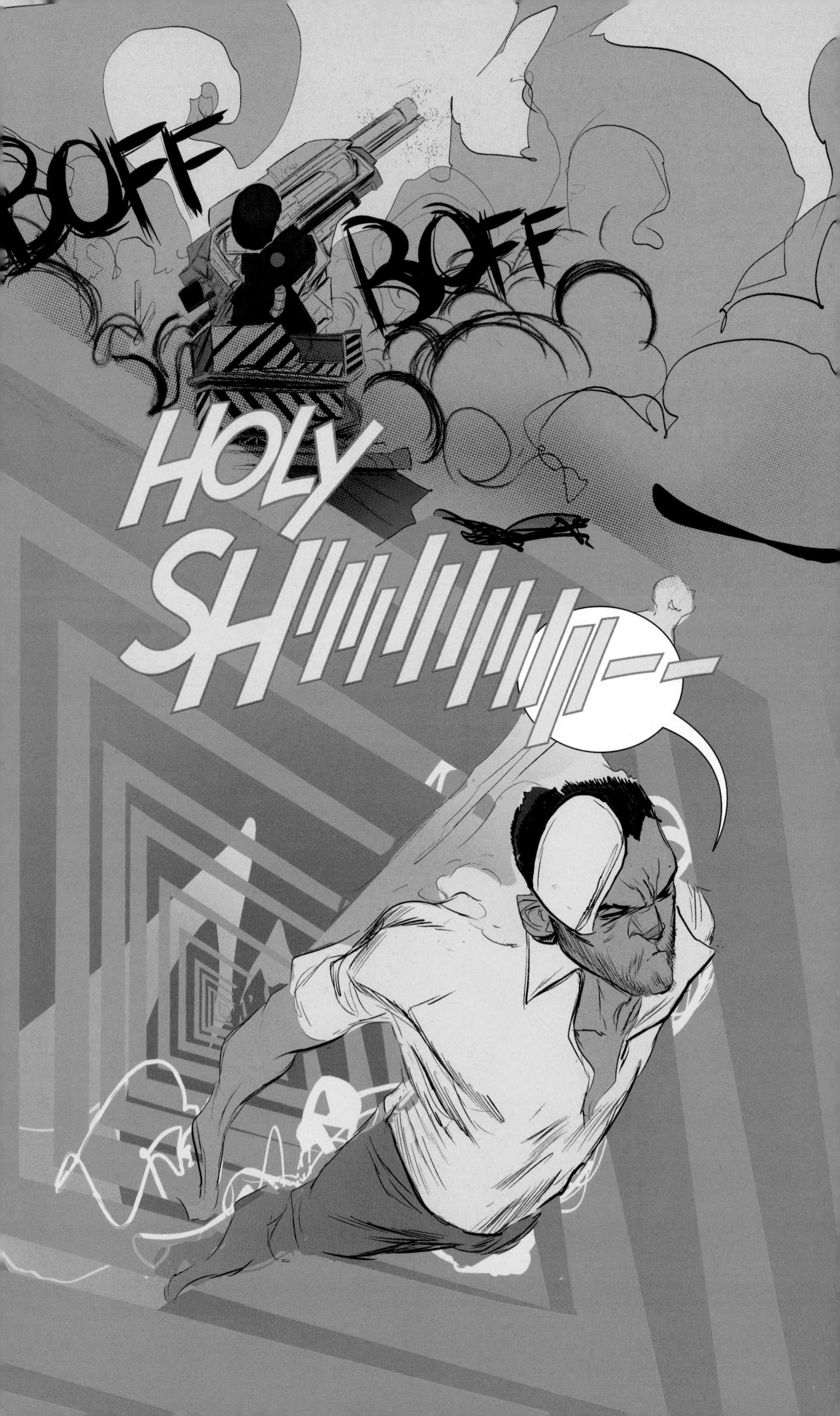
BOFF
BOFF
HOLY SHIIIIIIIIII--

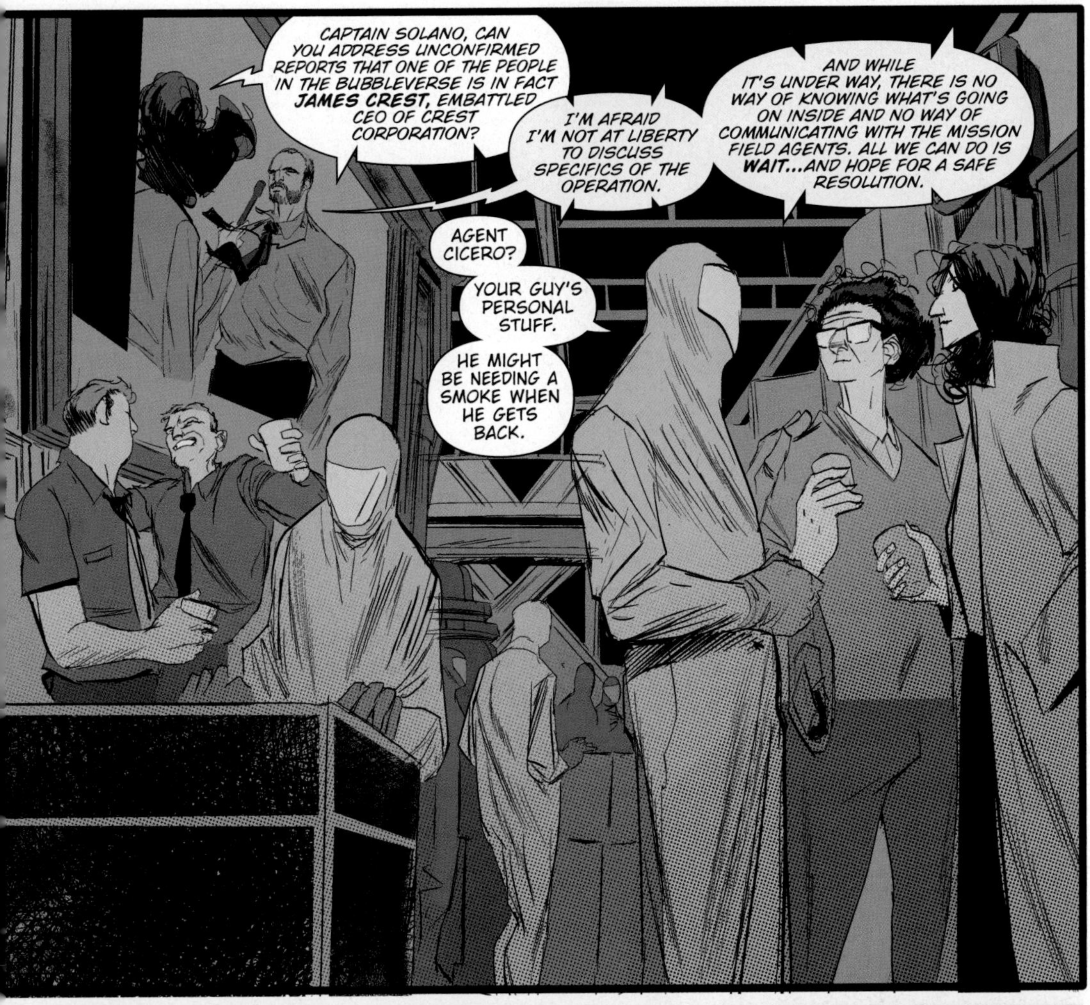
CAPTAIN SOLANO, CAN YOU ADDRESS UNCONFIRMED REPORTS THAT ONE OF THE PEOPLE IN THE BUBBLEVERSE IS IN FACT JAMES CREST, EMBATTLED CEO OF CREST CORPORATION?
I'M AFRAID I'M NOT AT LIBERTY TO DISCUSS SPECIFICS OF THE OPERATION.
AND WHILE IT'S UNDER WAY, THERE IS NO WAY OF KNOWING WHAT'S GOING ON INSIDE AND NO WAY OF COMMUNICATING WITH THE MISSION FIELD AGENTS. ALL WE CAN DO IS WAIT...AND HOPE FOR A SAFE RESOLUTION.
AGENT CICERO?
YOUR GUY'S PERSONAL STUFF.
HE MIGHT BE NEEDING A SMOKE WHEN HE GETS BACK.

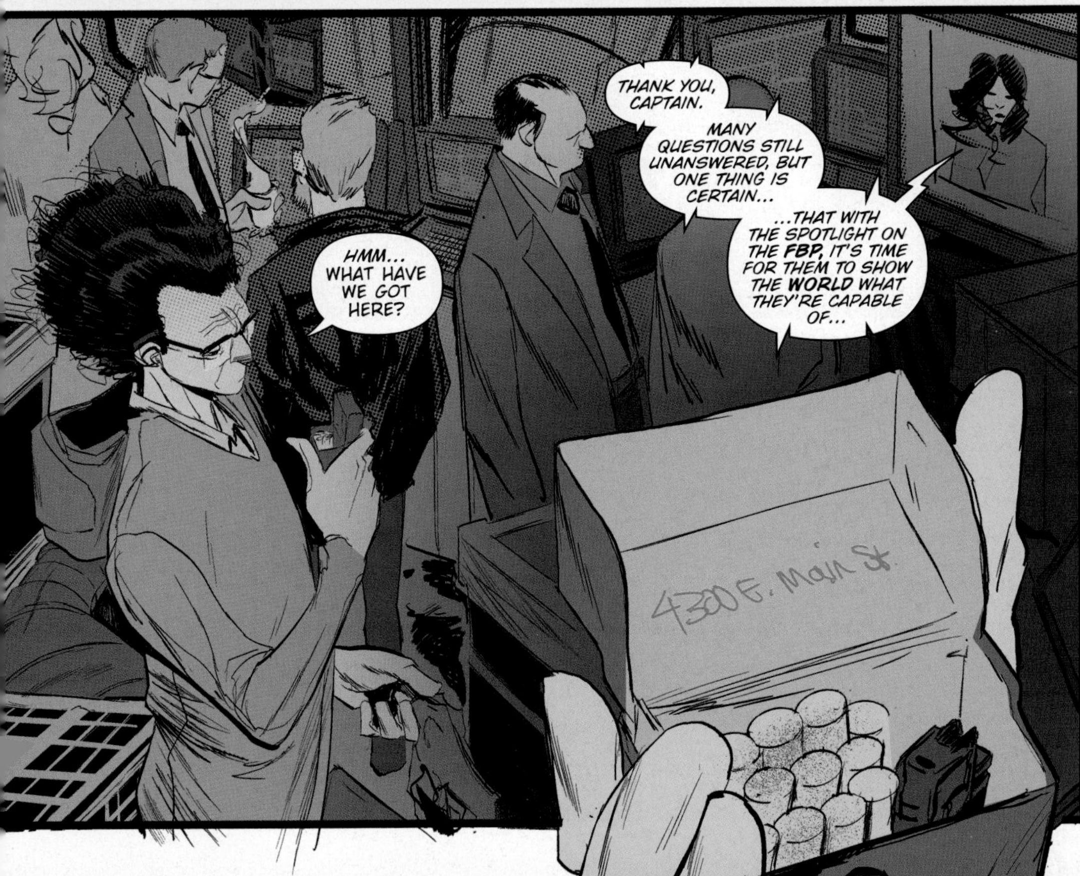
THANK YOU, CAPTAIN.
MANY QUESTIONS STILL UNANSWERED, BUT ONE THING IS CERTAIN...
...THAT WITH THE SPOTLIGHT ON THE FBP, IT'S TIME FOR THEM TO SHOW THE WORLD WHAT THEY'RE CAPABLE OF...
HMM... WHAT HAVE WE GOT HERE?
4300 E. Main St.

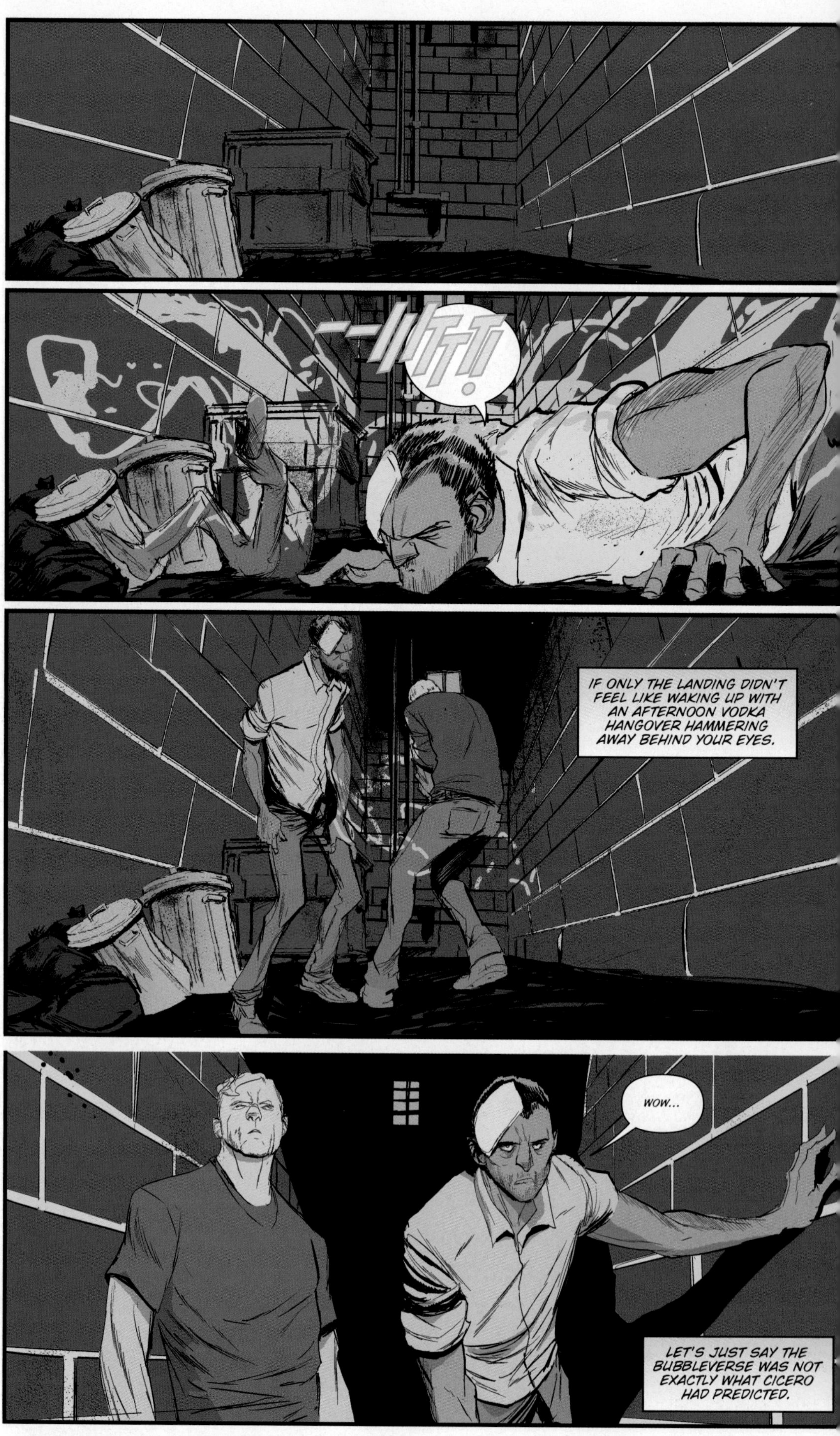

--HTTT!
IF ONLY THE LANDING DIDN'T FEEL LIKE WAKING UP WITH AN AFTERNOON VODKA HANGOVER HAMMERING AWAY BEHIND YOUR EYES.
WOW...
LET'S JUST SAY THE BUBBLEVERSE WAS NOT EXACTLY WHAT CICERO HAD PREDICTED.

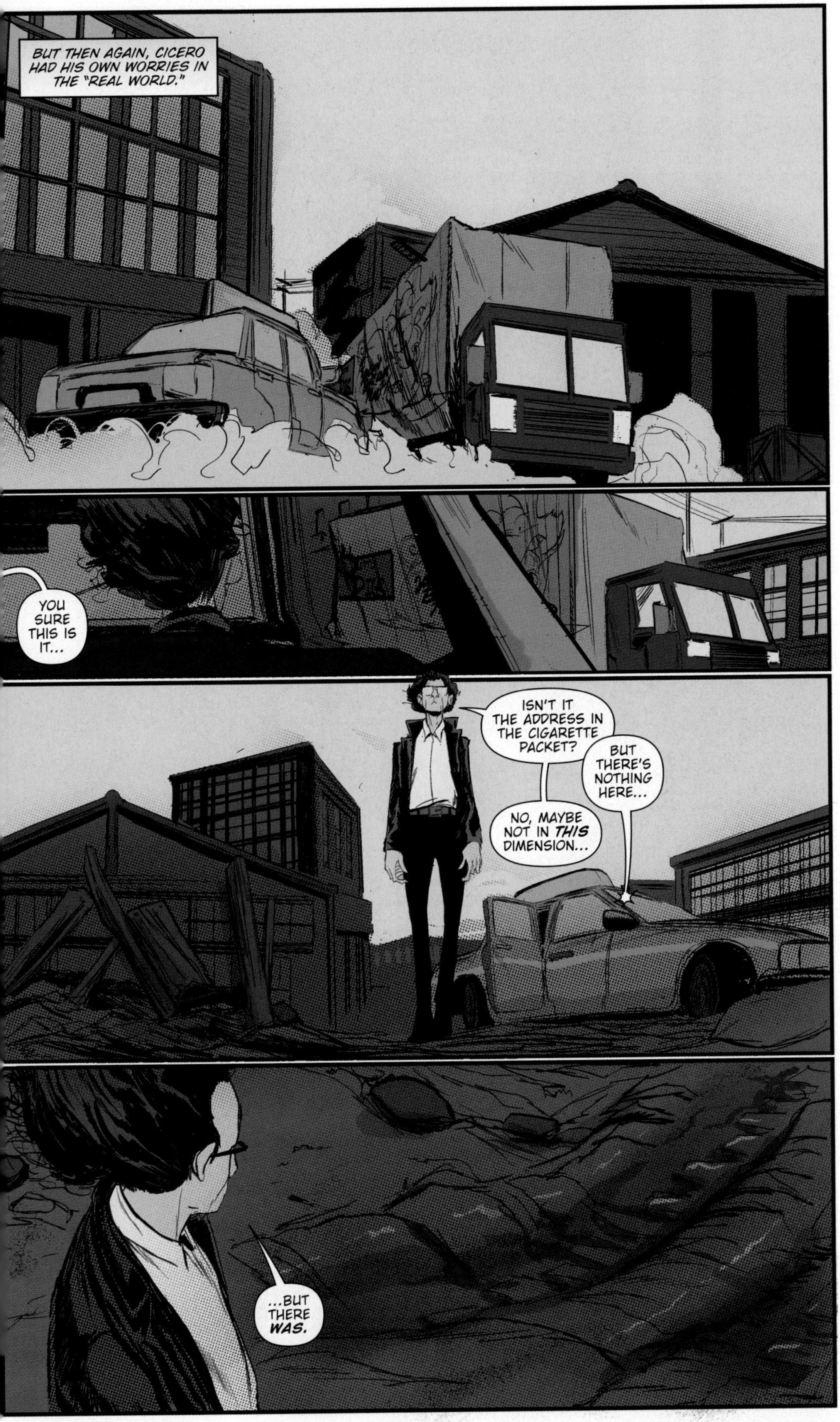
BUT THEN AGAIN, CICERO HAD HIS OWN WORRIES IN THE "REAL WORLD."
YOU SURE THIS IS IT...
ISN'T IT THE ADDRESS IN THE CIGARETTE PACKET?
NO, MAYBE NOT IN *THIS* DIMENSION...
BUT THERE'S NOTHING HERE...
...BUT THERE *WAS.*

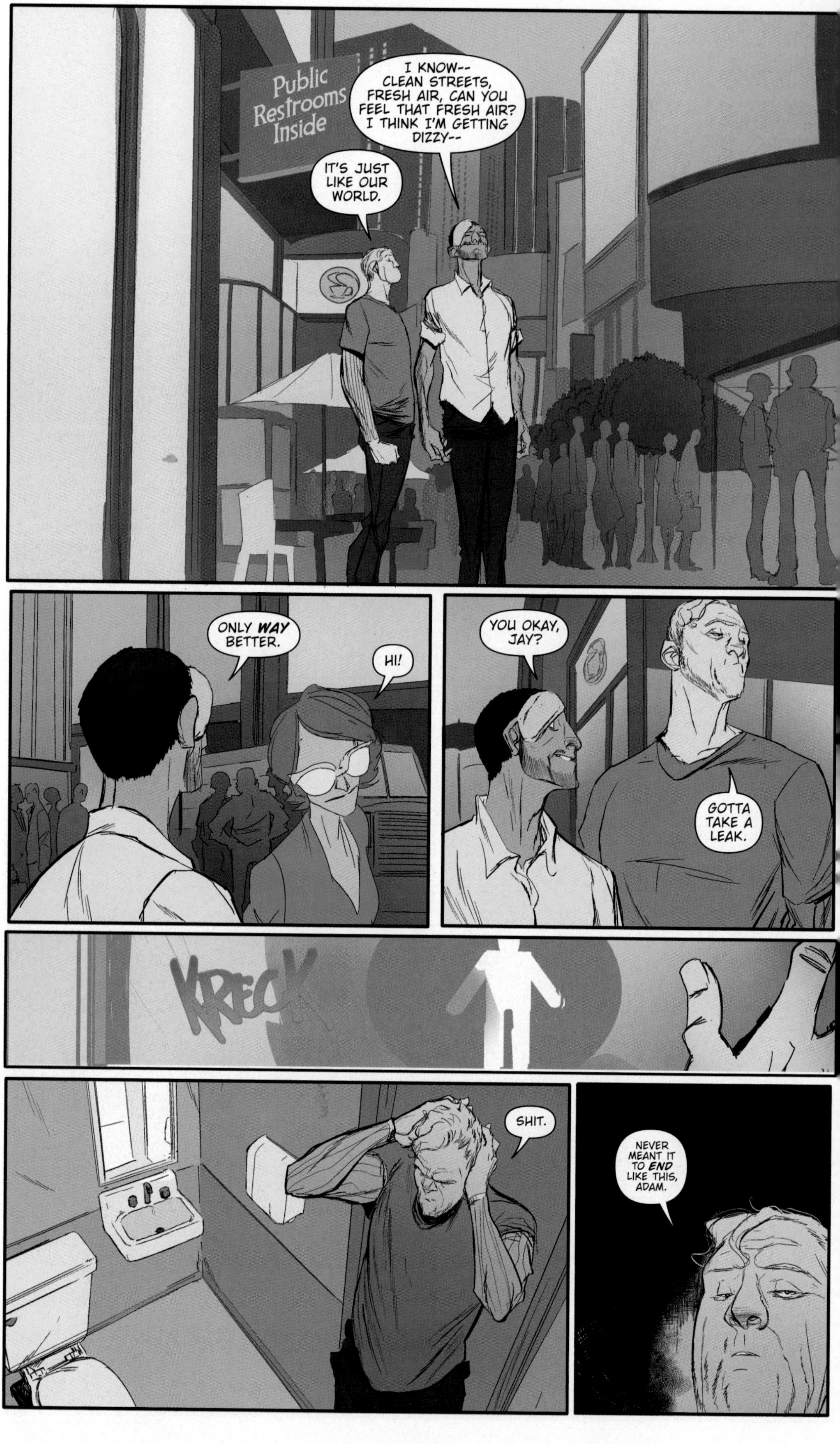
Public Restrooms Inside
I KNOW-- CLEAN STREETS, FRESH AIR, CAN YOU FEEL THAT FRESH AIR? I THINK I'M GETTING DIZZY--
IT'S JUST LIKE OUR WORLD.
ONLY WAY BETTER.
HI!
YOU OKAY, JAY?
GOTTA TAKE A LEAK.
KRECK
SHIT.
NEVER MEANT IT TO END LIKE THIS, ADAM.

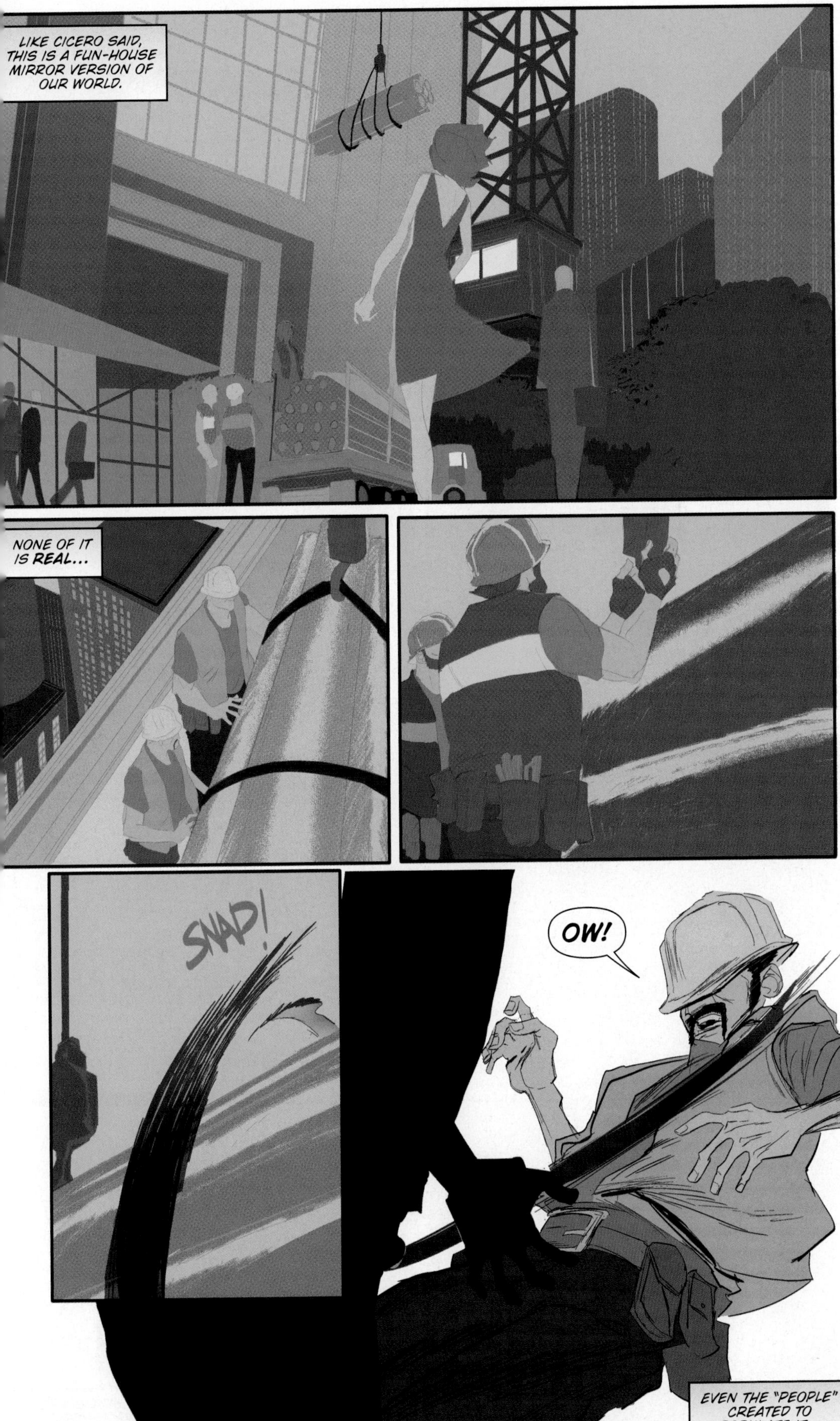
LIKE CICERO SAID, THIS IS A FUN-HOUSE MIRROR VERSION OF OUR WORLD.
NONE OF IT IS REAL...
SNAP!
OW!
EVEN THE "PEOPLE" CREATED TO POPULATE IT...

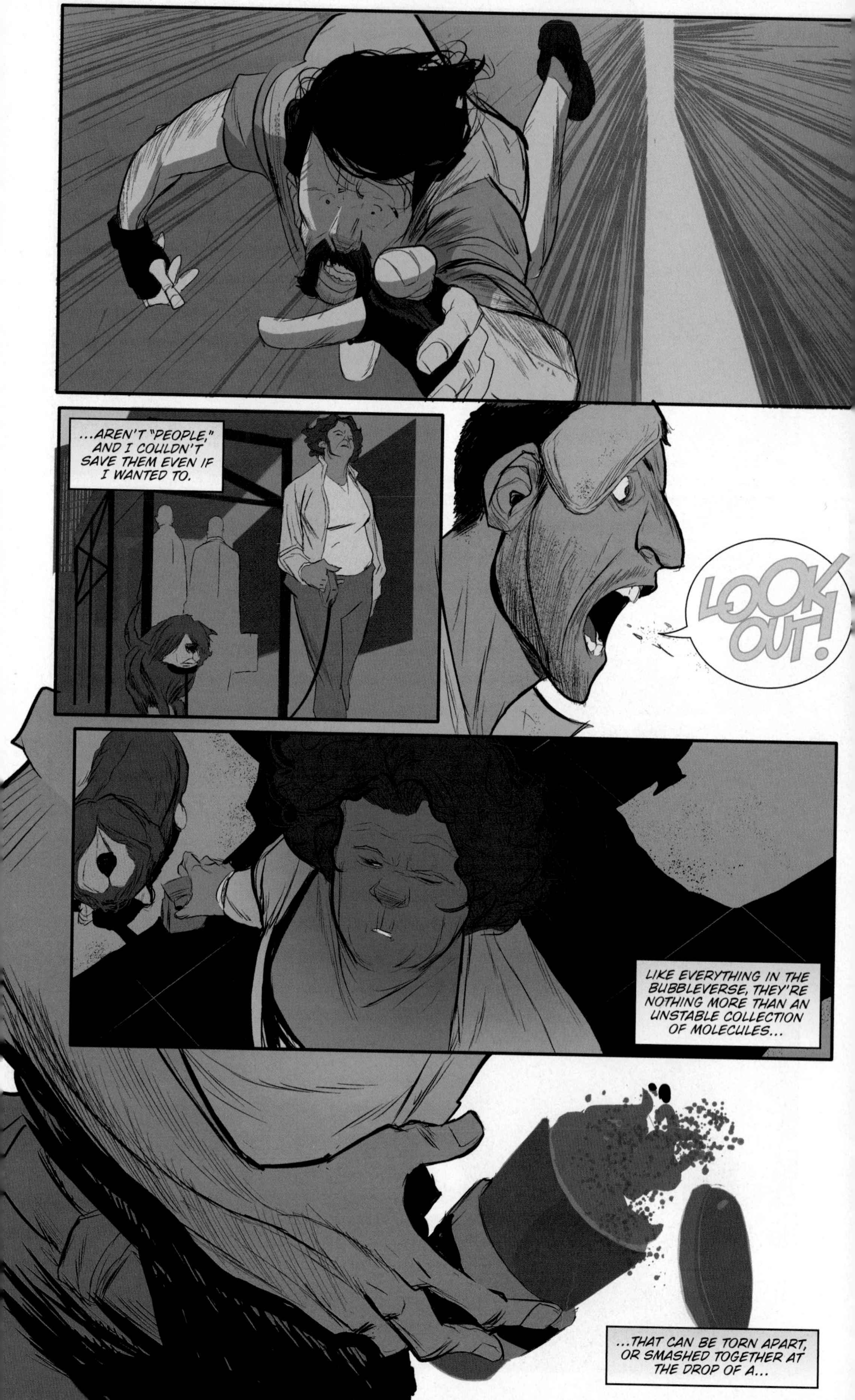
...AREN'T "PEOPLE," AND I COULDN'T SAVE THEM EVEN IF I WANTED TO.
LOOK OUT!
LIKE EVERYTHING IN THE BUBBLEVERSE, THEY'RE NOTHING MORE THAN AN UNSTABLE COLLECTION OF MOLECULES...
...THAT CAN BE TORN APART, OR SMASHED TOGETHER AT THE DROP OF A...

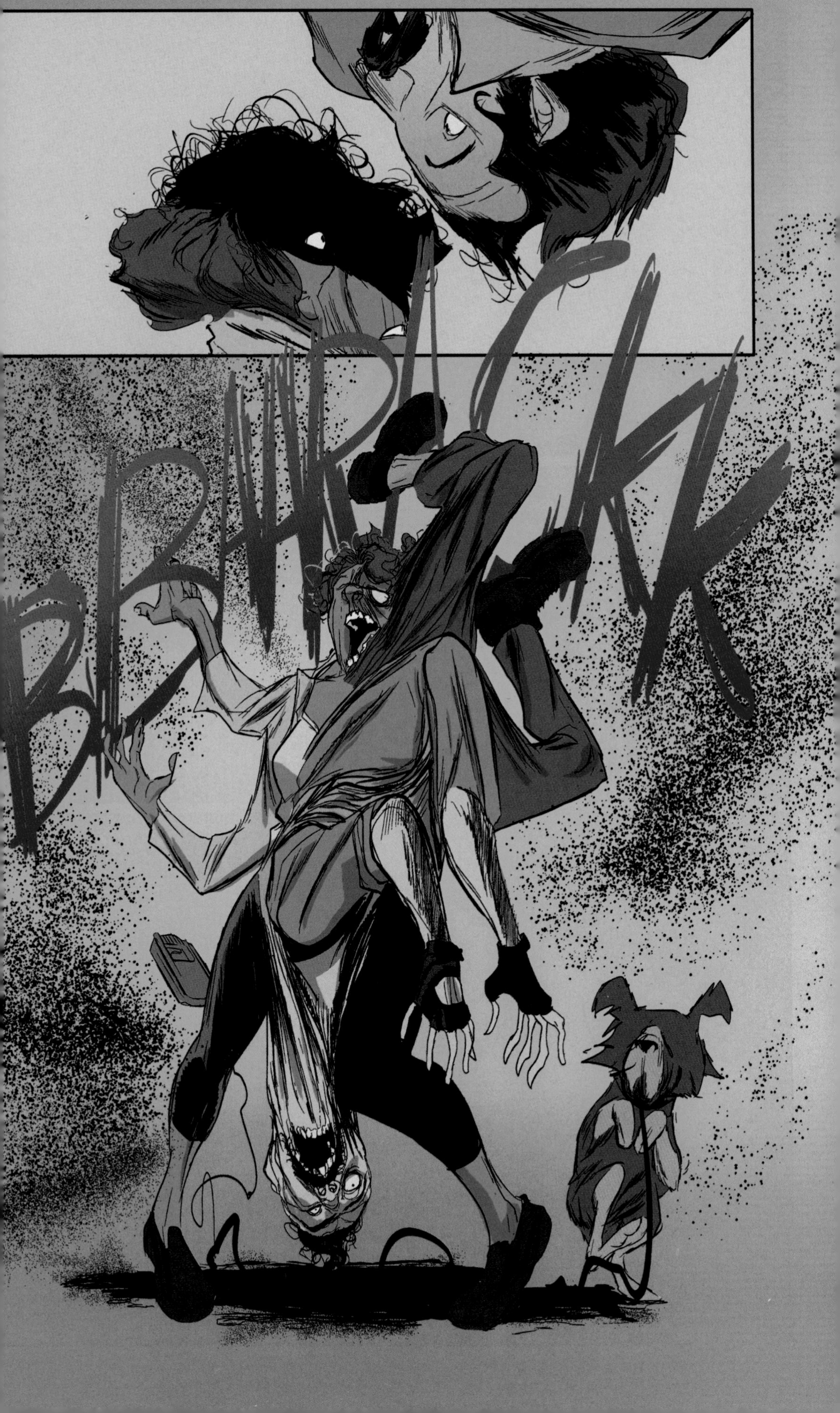

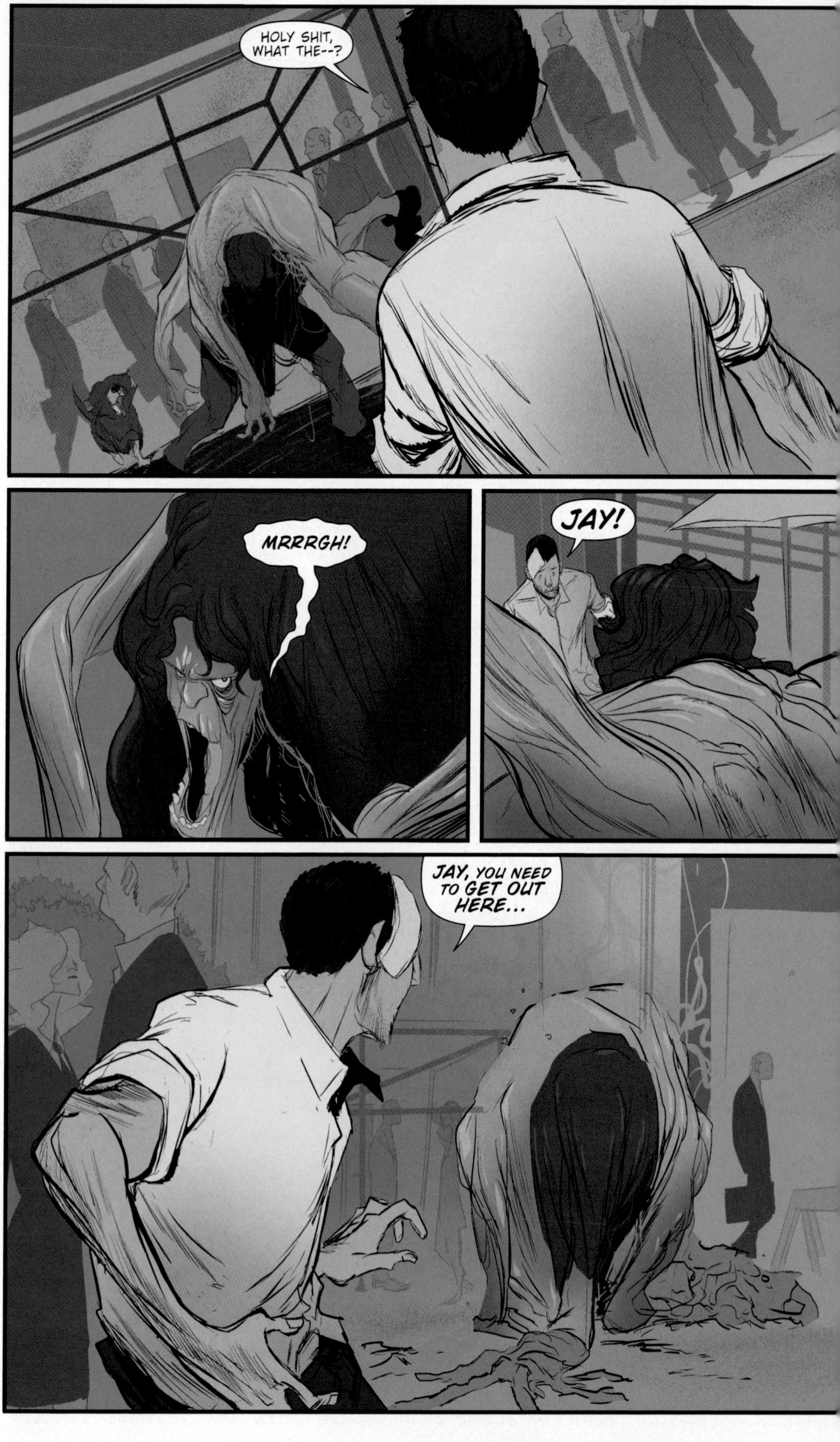
HOLY SHIT, WHAT THE--?
MRRRGH!
JAY!
JAY, YOU NEED TO GET OUT HERE...

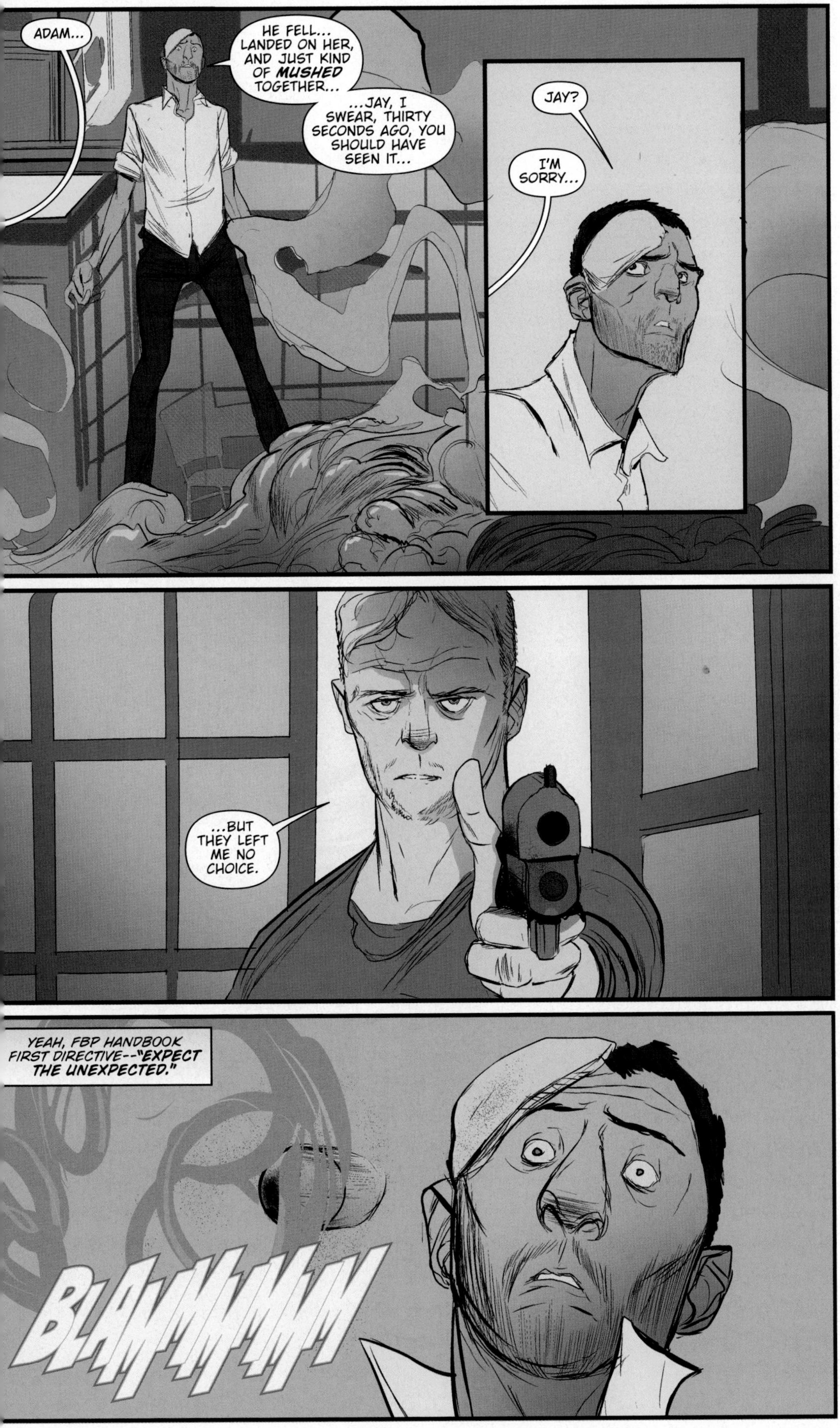
ADAM...
HE FELL... LANDED ON HER, AND JUST KIND OF **MUSHED** TOGETHER...
...JAY, I SWEAR, THIRTY SECONDS AGO, YOU SHOULD HAVE SEEN IT...
JAY?
I'M SORRY...
...BUT THEY LEFT ME NO CHOICE.
*YEAH, FBP HANDBOOK FIRST DIRECTIVE--"**EXPECT THE UNEXPECTED.**"*
BLAMMMMMM

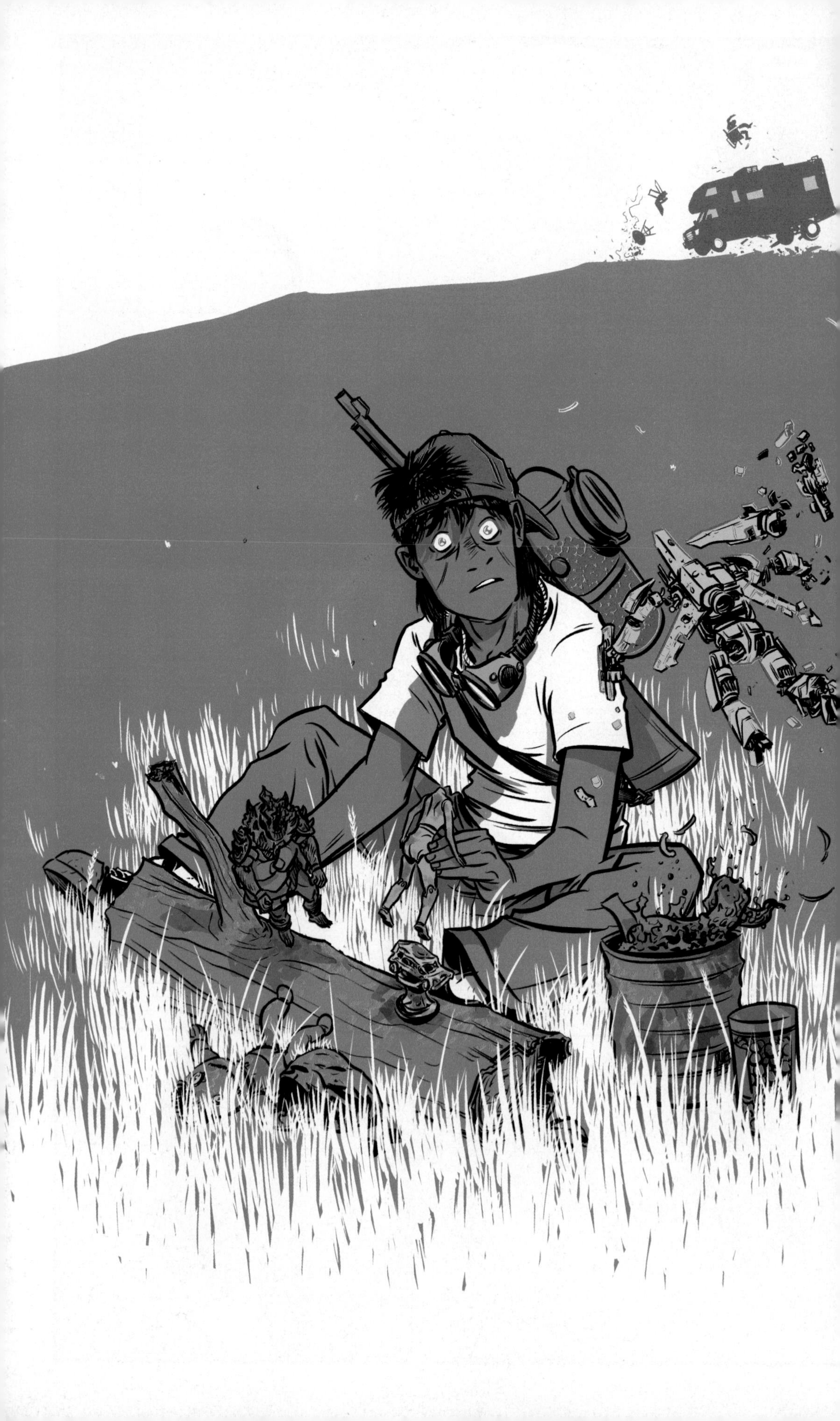

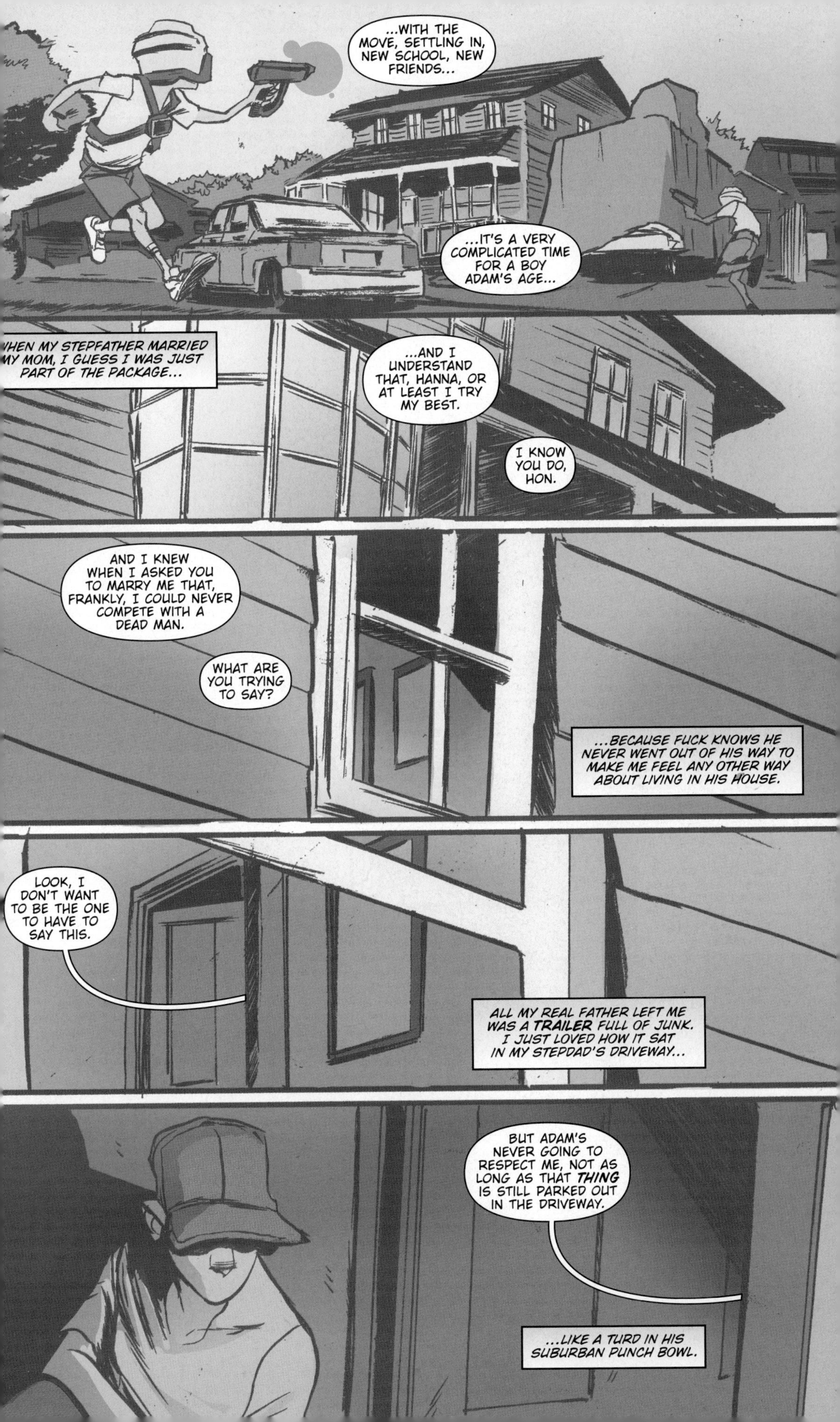
...WITH THE MOVE, SETTLING IN, NEW SCHOOL, NEW FRIENDS...
...IT'S A VERY COMPLICATED TIME FOR A BOY ADAM'S AGE...
WHEN MY STEPFATHER MARRIED MY MOM, I GUESS I WAS JUST PART OF THE PACKAGE...
...AND I UNDERSTAND THAT, HANNA, OR AT LEAST I TRY MY BEST.
I KNOW YOU DO, HON.
AND I KNEW WHEN I ASKED YOU TO MARRY ME THAT, FRANKLY, I COULD NEVER COMPETE WITH A DEAD MAN.
WHAT ARE YOU TRYING TO SAY?
...BECAUSE FUCK KNOWS HE NEVER WENT OUT OF HIS WAY TO MAKE ME FEEL ANY OTHER WAY ABOUT LIVING IN HIS HOUSE.
LOOK, I DON'T WANT TO BE THE ONE TO HAVE TO SAY THIS.
ALL MY REAL FATHER LEFT ME WAS A TRAILER FULL OF JUNK. I JUST LOVED HOW IT SAT IN MY STEPDAD'S DRIVEWAY...
BUT ADAM'S NEVER GOING TO RESPECT ME, NOT AS LONG AS THAT THING IS STILL PARKED OUT IN THE DRIVEWAY.
...LIKE A TURD IN HIS SUBURBAN PUNCH BOWL.

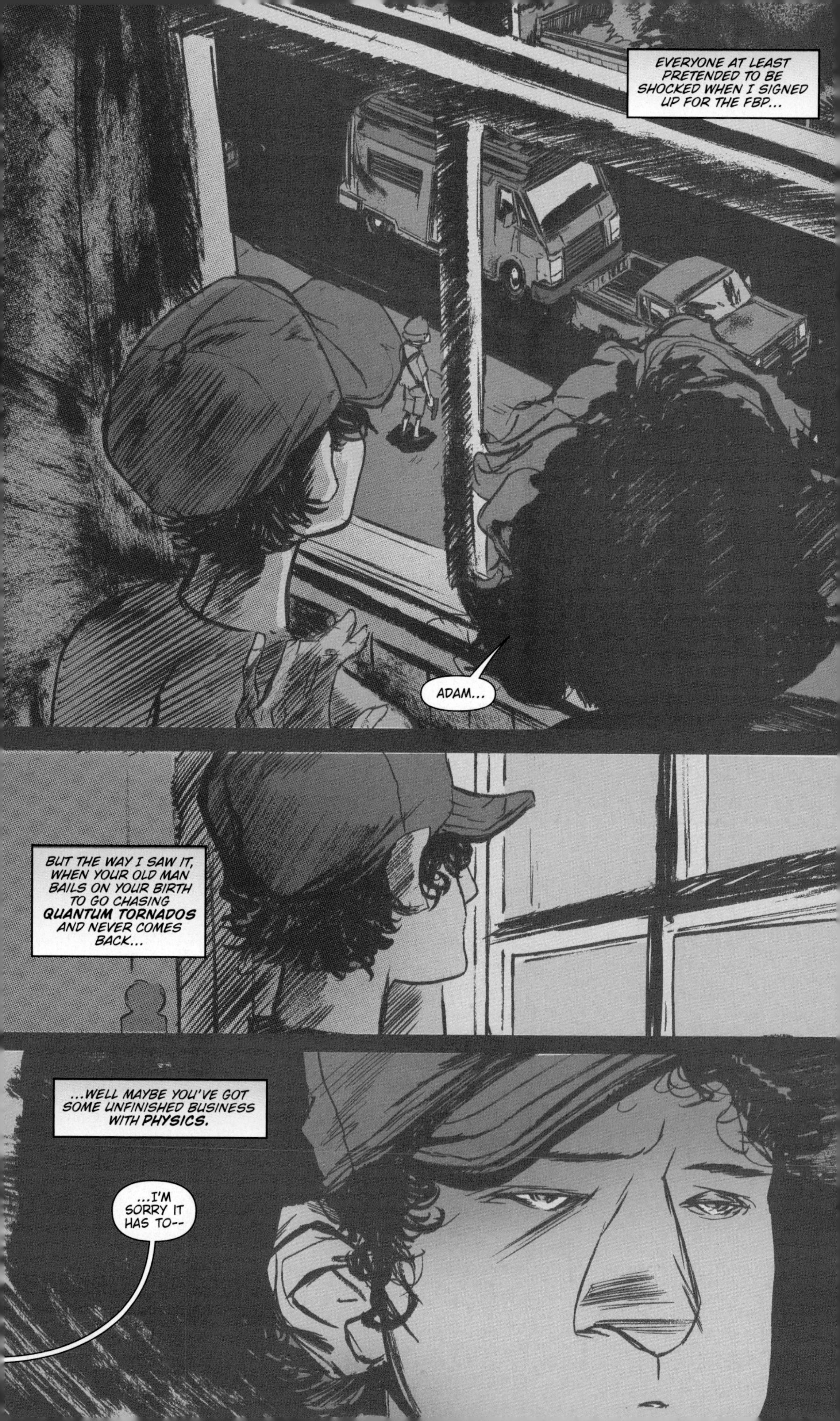
EVERYONE AT LEAST PRETENDED TO BE SHOCKED WHEN I SIGNED UP FOR THE FBP...
ADAM...
BUT THE WAY I SAW IT, WHEN YOUR OLD MAN BAILS ON YOUR BIRTH TO GO CHASING **QUANTUM TORNADOS** AND NEVER COMES BACK...
...WELL MAYBE YOU'VE GOT SOME UNFINISHED BUSINESS WITH **PHYSICS.**
...I'M SORRY IT HAS TO--

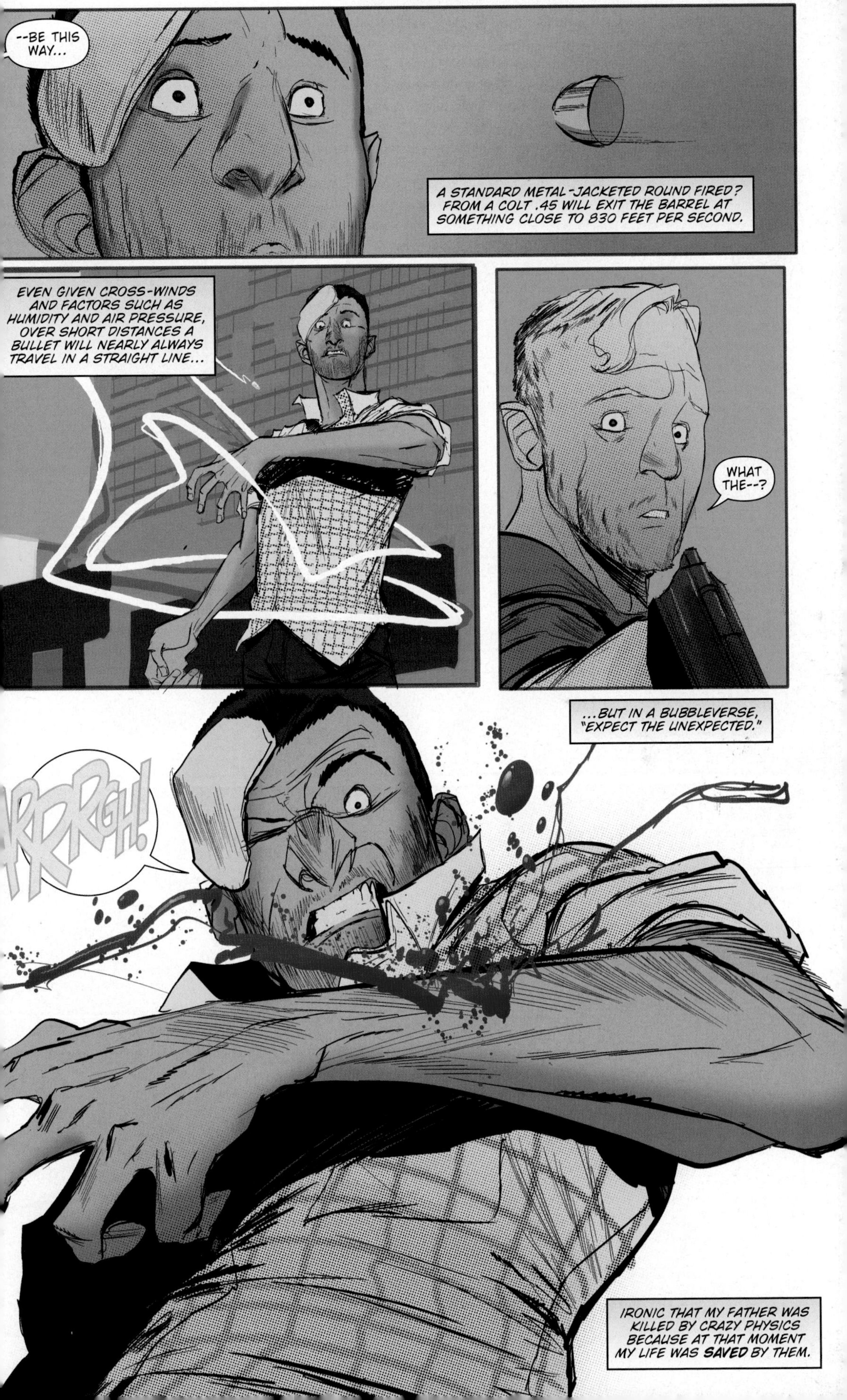
--BE THIS WAY...
A STANDARD METAL-JACKETED ROUND FIRED FROM A COLT .45 WILL EXIT THE BARREL AT SOMETHING CLOSE TO 830 FEET PER SECOND.
EVEN GIVEN CROSS-WINDS AND FACTORS SUCH AS HUMIDITY AND AIR PRESSURE, OVER SHORT DISTANCES A BULLET WILL NEARLY ALWAYS TRAVEL IN A STRAIGHT LINE...
WHAT THE--?
ARRRGH!
...BUT IN A BUBBLEVERSE, "EXPECT THE UNEXPECTED."
IRONIC THAT MY FATHER WAS KILLED BY CRAZY PHYSICS BECAUSE AT THAT MOMENT MY LIFE WAS SAVED BY THEM.

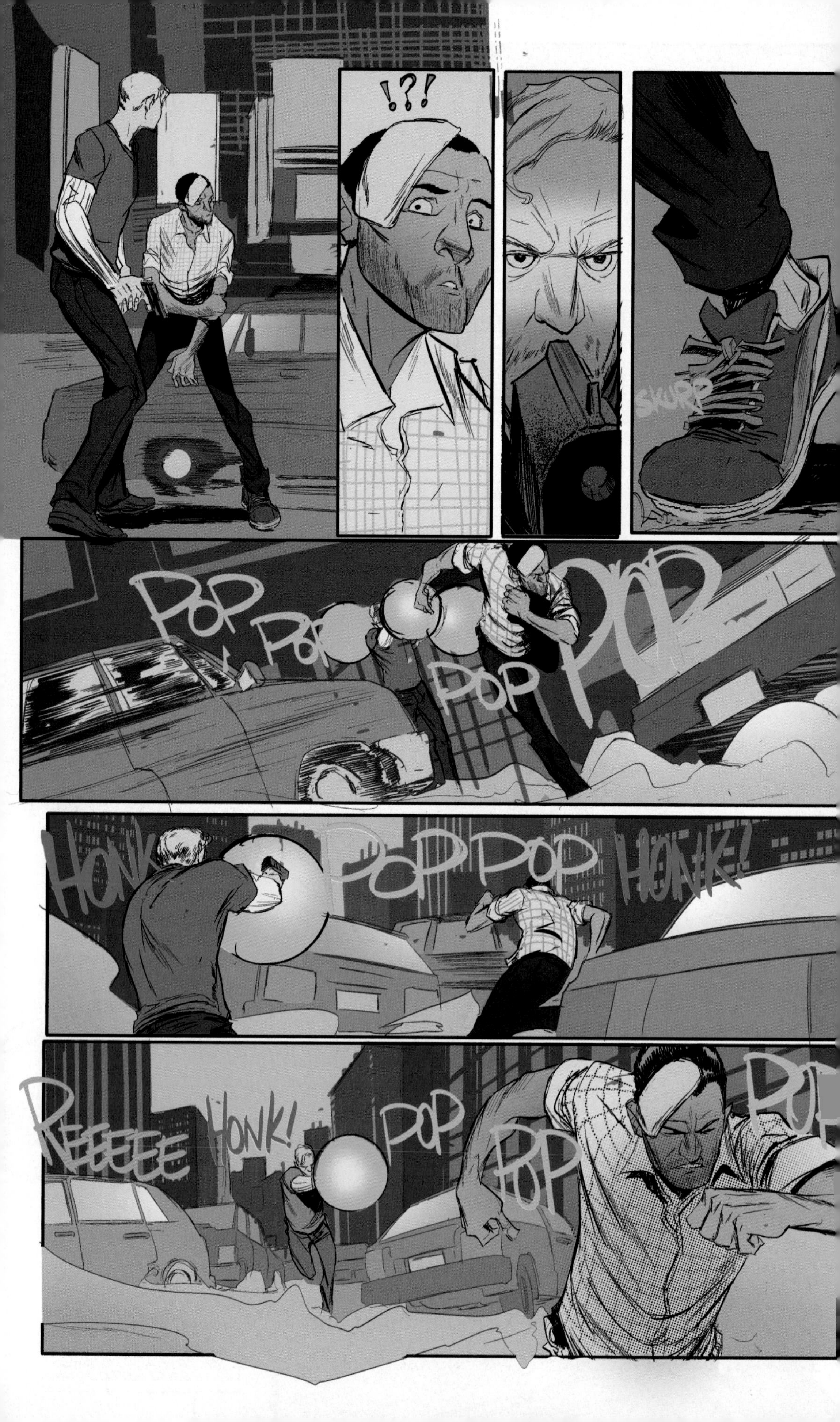
!?!
SKURP
POP
POP
POP
POP
HONK
POP POP POP
HONK!
REEEEEE
HONK!
POP
POP
POP

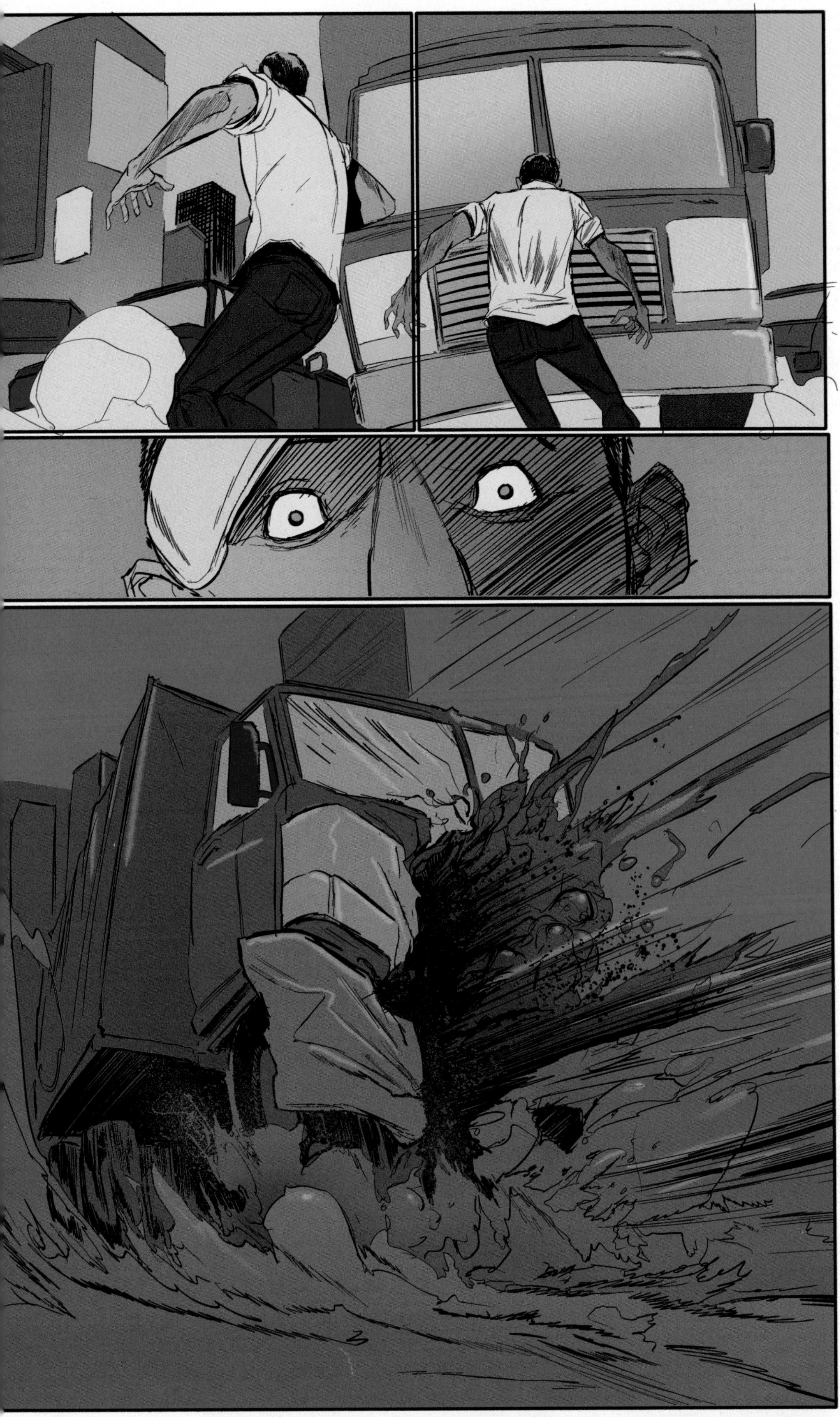

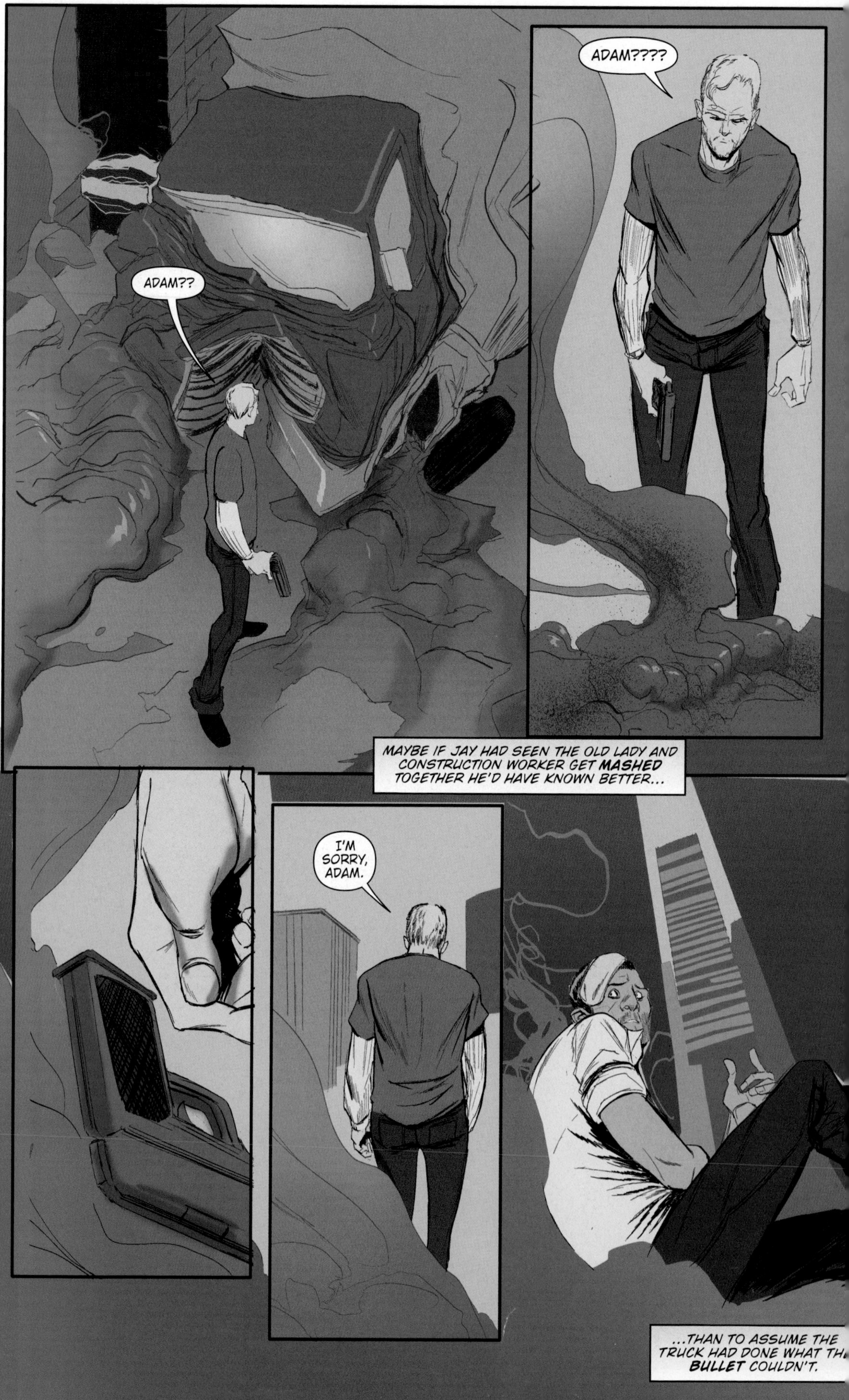
ADAM??
ADAM????
MAYBE IF JAY HAD SEEN THE OLD LADY AND CONSTRUCTION WORKER GET MASHED TOGETHER HE'D HAVE KNOWN BETTER...
I'M SORRY, ADAM.
...THAN TO ASSUME THE TRUCK HAD DONE WHAT TH BULLET COULDN'T.

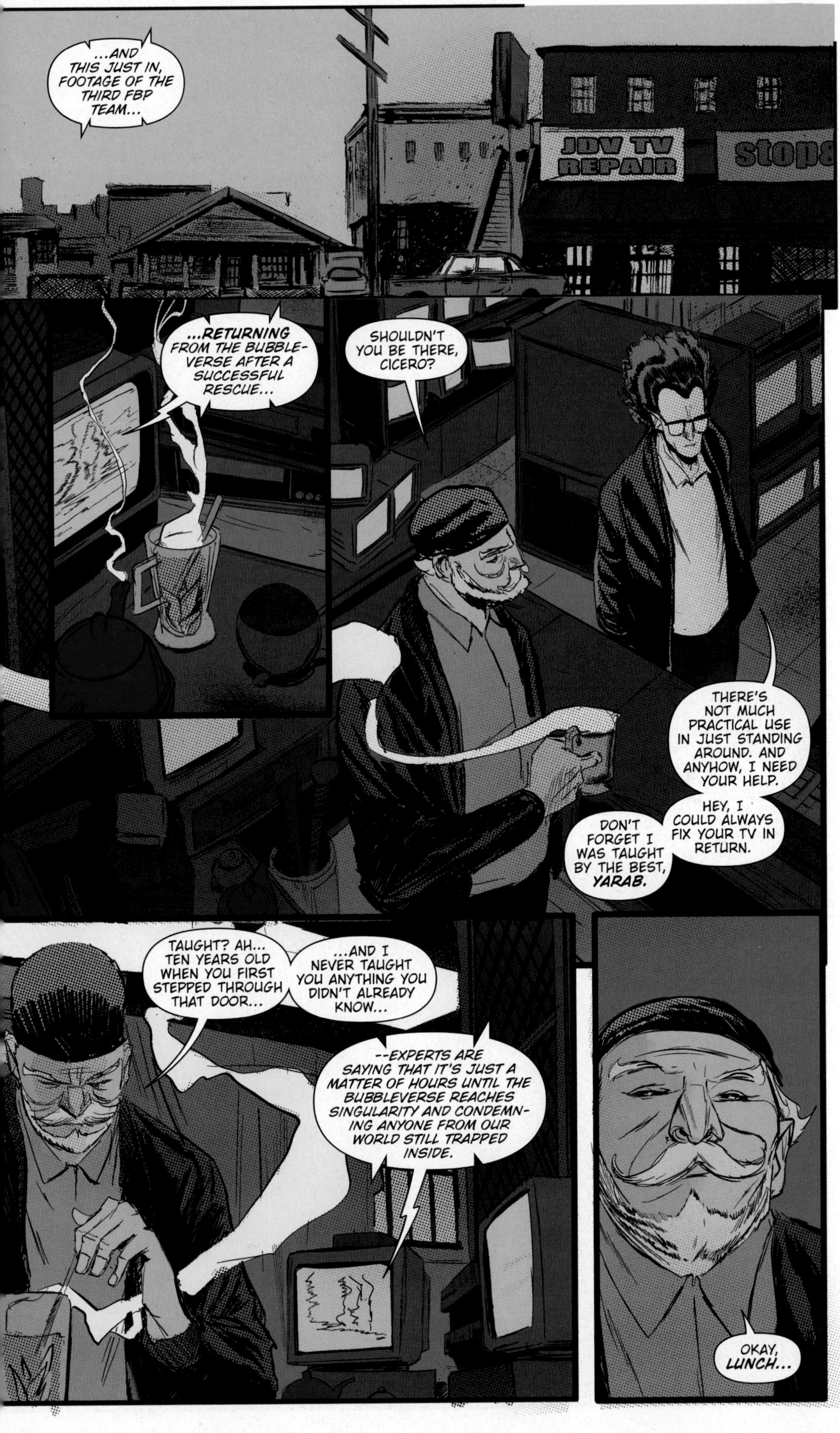
...AND THIS JUST IN, FOOTAGE OF THE THIRD FBP TEAM...
JDV TV REPAIR
stop
...RETURNING FROM THE BUBBLE-VERSE AFTER A SUCCESSFUL RESCUE...
SHOULDN'T YOU BE THERE, CICERO?
THERE'S NOT MUCH PRACTICAL USE IN JUST STANDING AROUND. AND ANYHOW, I NEED YOUR HELP.
HEY, I COULD ALWAYS FIX YOUR TV IN RETURN.
DON'T FORGET I WAS TAUGHT BY THE BEST, YARAB.
TAUGHT? AH... TEN YEARS OLD WHEN YOU FIRST STEPPED THROUGH THAT DOOR...
...AND I NEVER TAUGHT YOU ANYTHING YOU DIDN'T ALREADY KNOW...
--EXPERTS ARE SAYING THAT IT'S JUST A MATTER OF HOURS UNTIL THE BUBBLEVERSE REACHES SINGULARITY AND CONDEMN-ING ANYONE FROM OUR WORLD STILL TRAPPED INSIDE.
OKAY, LUNCH...

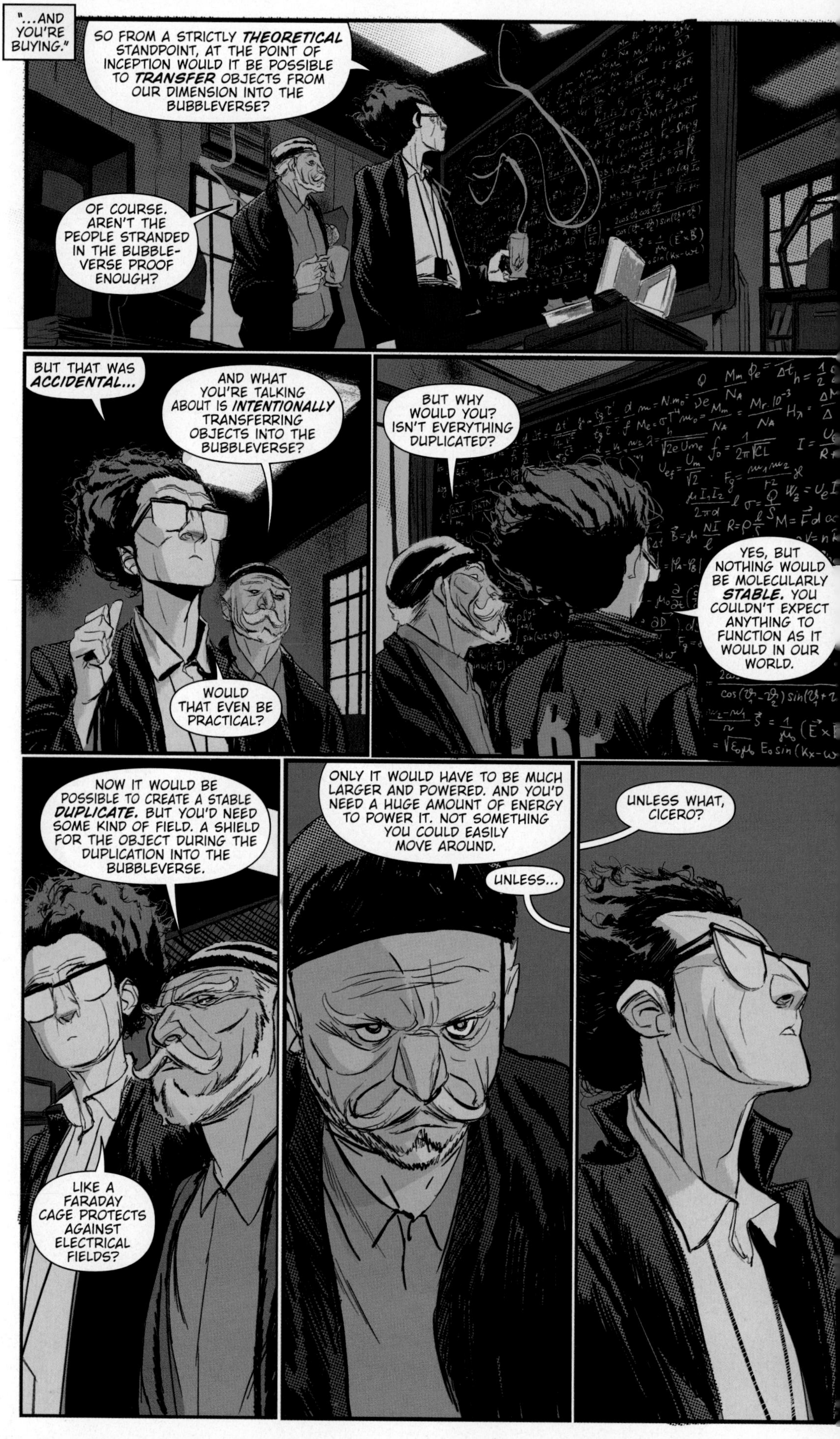
"...AND YOU'RE BUYING."
SO FROM A STRICTLY THEORETICAL STANDPOINT, AT THE POINT OF INCEPTION WOULD IT BE POSSIBLE TO TRANSFER OBJECTS FROM OUR DIMENSION INTO THE BUBBLEVERSE?
OF COURSE. AREN'T THE PEOPLE STRANDED IN THE BUBBLE-VERSE PROOF ENOUGH?
BUT THAT WAS ACCIDENTAL...
AND WHAT YOU'RE TALKING ABOUT IS INTENTIONALLY TRANSFERRING OBJECTS INTO THE BUBBLEVERSE?
WOULD THAT EVEN BE PRACTICAL?
BUT WHY WOULD YOU? ISN'T EVERYTHING DUPLICATED?
YES, BUT NOTHING WOULD BE MOLECULARLY STABLE. YOU COULDN'T EXPECT ANYTHING TO FUNCTION AS IT WOULD IN OUR WORLD.
NOW IT WOULD BE POSSIBLE TO CREATE A STABLE DUPLICATE. BUT YOU'D NEED SOME KIND OF FIELD. A SHIELD FOR THE OBJECT DURING THE DUPLICATION INTO THE BUBBLEVERSE.
LIKE A FARADAY CAGE PROTECTS AGAINST ELECTRICAL FIELDS?
ONLY IT WOULD HAVE TO BE MUCH LARGER AND POWERED. AND YOU'D NEED A HUGE AMOUNT OF ENERGY TO POWER IT. NOT SOMETHING YOU COULD EASILY MOVE AROUND.
UNLESS...
UNLESS WHAT, CICERO?

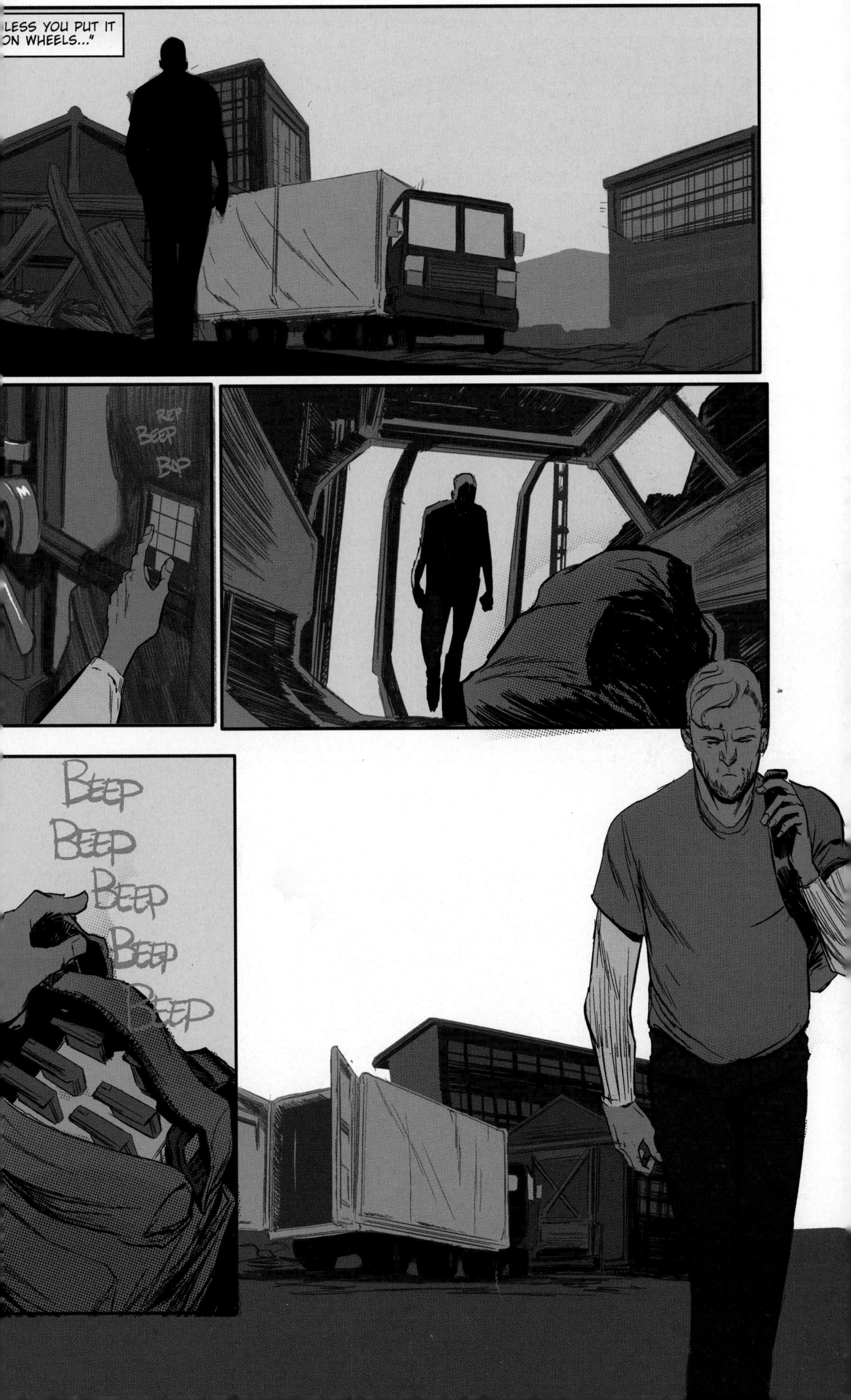
LESS YOU PUT IT
ON WHEELS..."
REP
BEEP
BOP
BEEP
BEEP
BEEP
BEEP
BEEP

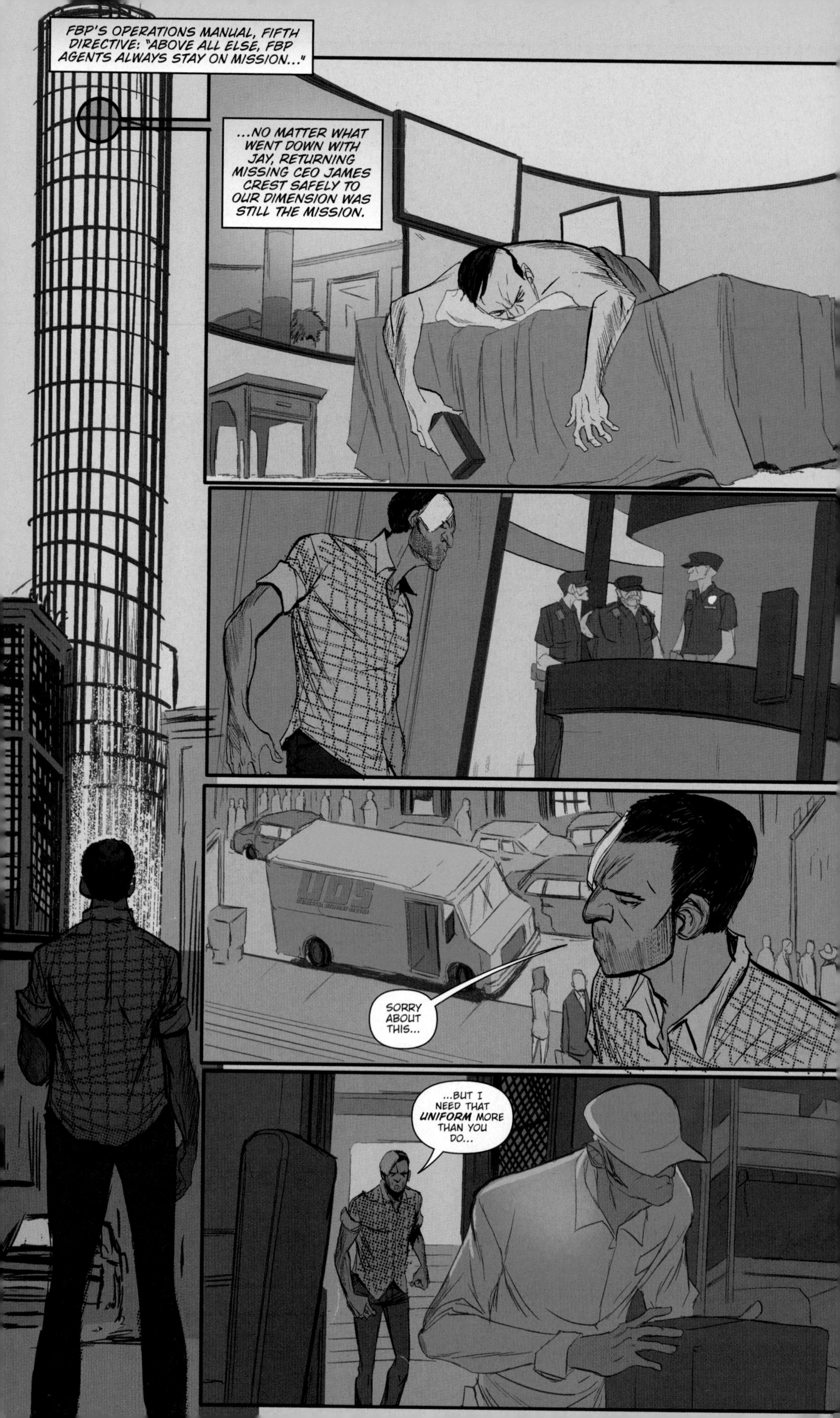

FBP'S OPERATIONS MANUAL, FIFTH DIRECTIVE: "ABOVE ALL ELSE, FBP AGENTS ALWAYS STAY ON MISSION..."
...NO MATTER WHAT WENT DOWN WITH JAY, RETURNING MISSING CEO JAMES CREST SAFELY TO OUR DIMENSION WAS STILL THE MISSION.
SORRY ABOUT THIS...
...BUT I NEED THAT UNIFORM MORE THAN YOU DO...

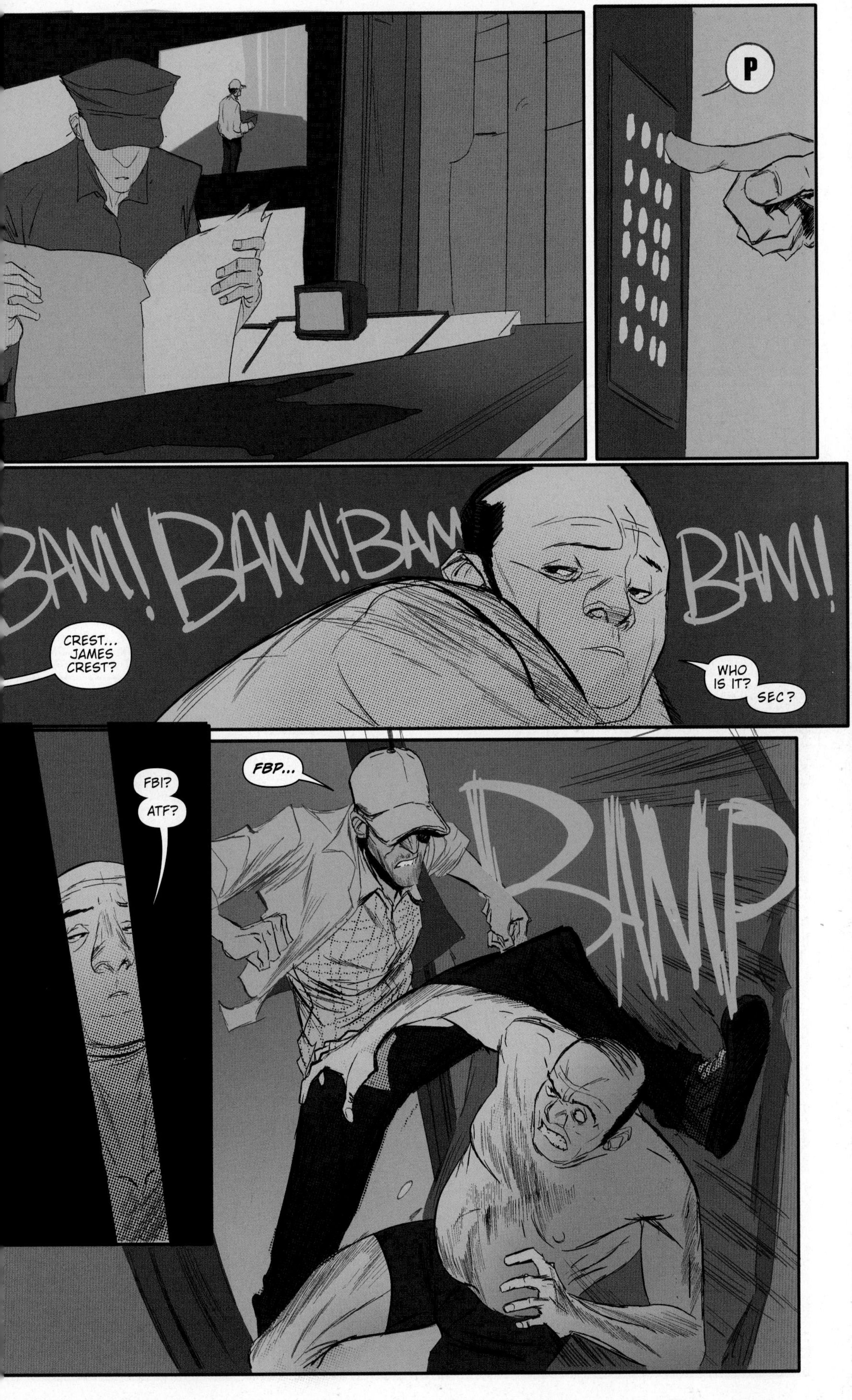
P
BAM! BAM! BAM
BAM!
CREST... JAMES CREST?
WHO IS IT?
SEC?
FBI?
ATF?
FBP...
BAMP

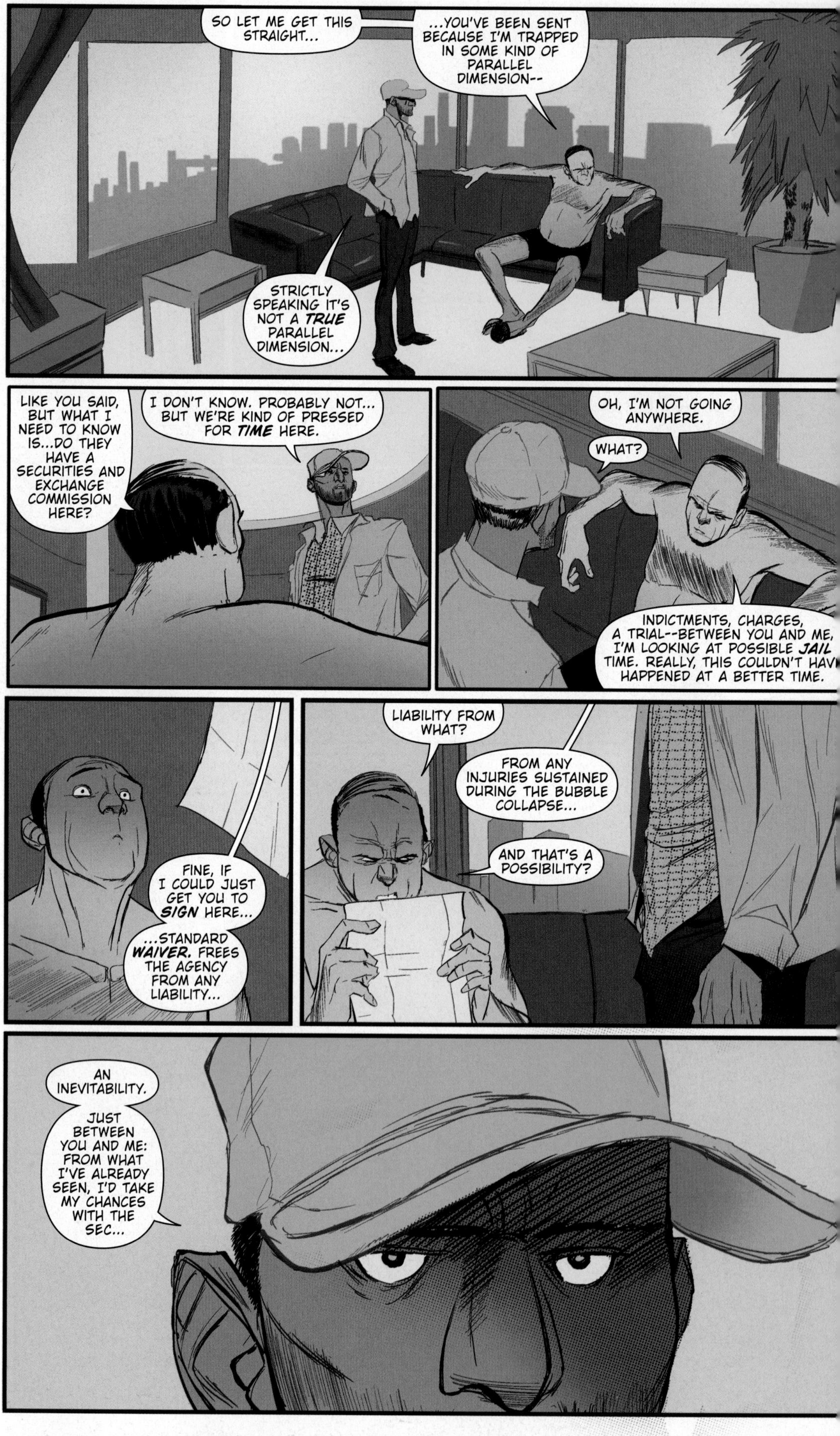
SO LET ME GET THIS STRAIGHT...
...YOU'VE BEEN SENT BECAUSE I'M TRAPPED IN SOME KIND OF PARALLEL DIMENSION--
STRICTLY SPEAKING IT'S NOT A TRUE PARALLEL DIMENSION...
LIKE YOU SAID, BUT WHAT I NEED TO KNOW IS...DO THEY HAVE A SECURITIES AND EXCHANGE COMMISSION HERE?
I DON'T KNOW. PROBABLY NOT... BUT WE'RE KIND OF PRESSED FOR TIME HERE.
OH, I'M NOT GOING ANYWHERE.
WHAT?
INDICTMENTS, CHARGES, A TRIAL--BETWEEN YOU AND ME, I'M LOOKING AT POSSIBLE JAIL TIME. REALLY, THIS COULDN'T HAV HAPPENED AT A BETTER TIME.
FINE, IF I COULD JUST GET YOU TO SIGN HERE...
...STANDARD WAIVER. FREES THE AGENCY FROM ANY LIABILITY...
LIABILITY FROM WHAT?
FROM ANY INJURIES SUSTAINED DURING THE BUBBLE COLLAPSE...
AND THAT'S A POSSIBILITY?
AN INEVITABILITY.
JUST BETWEEN YOU AND ME: FROM WHAT I'VE ALREADY SEEN, I'D TAKE MY CHANCES WITH THE SEC...

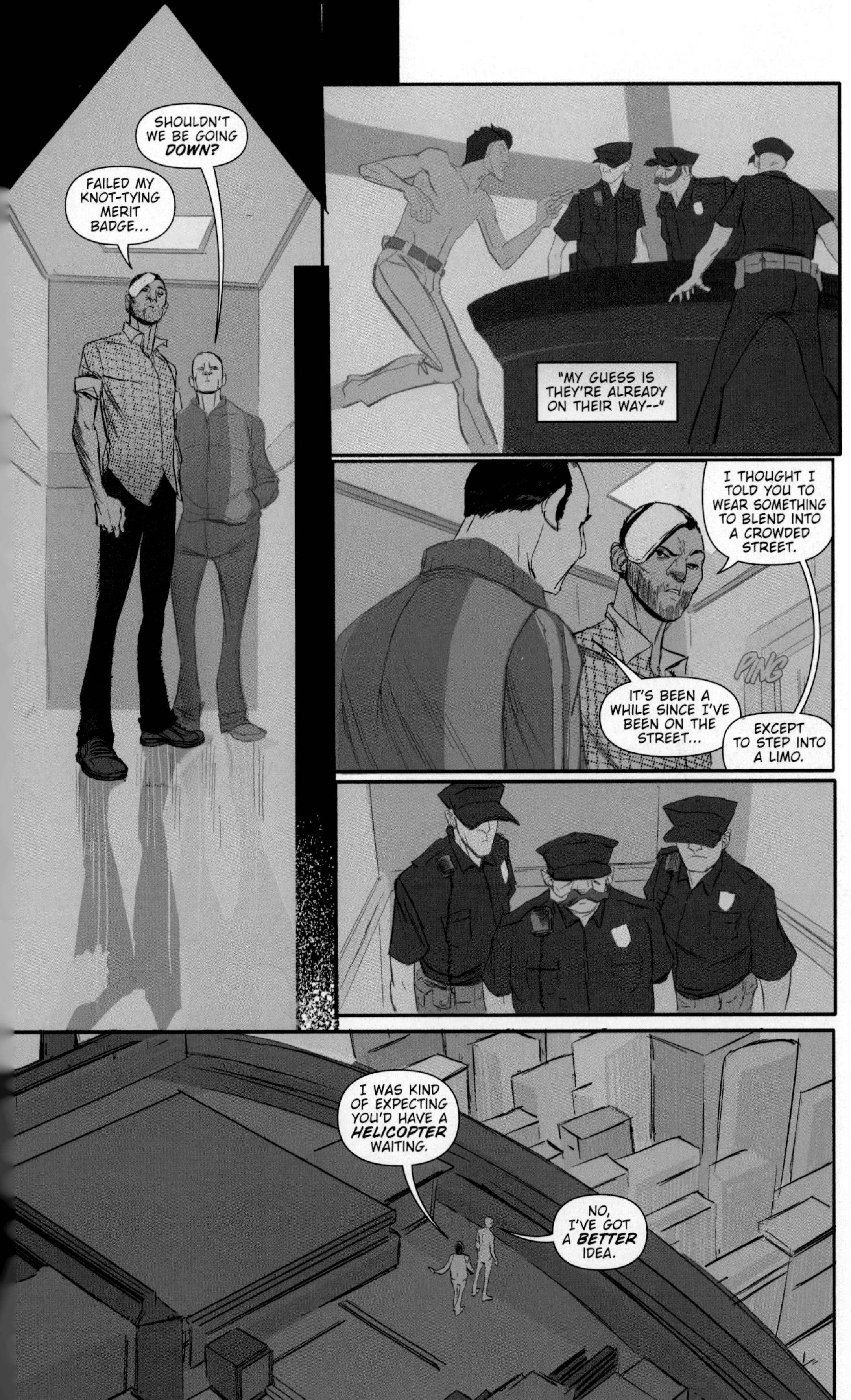
FAILED MY KNOT-TYING MERIT BADGE...
SHOULDN'T WE BE GOING DOWN?
"MY GUESS IS THEY'RE ALREADY ON THEIR WAY--"
I THOUGHT I TOLD YOU TO WEAR SOMETHING TO BLEND INTO A CROWDED STREET.
IT'S BEEN A WHILE SINCE I'VE BEEN ON THE STREET...
EXCEPT TO STEP INTO A LIMO.
PING
I WAS KIND OF EXPECTING YOU'D HAVE A HELICOPTER WAITING.
NO, I'VE GOT A BETTER IDEA.

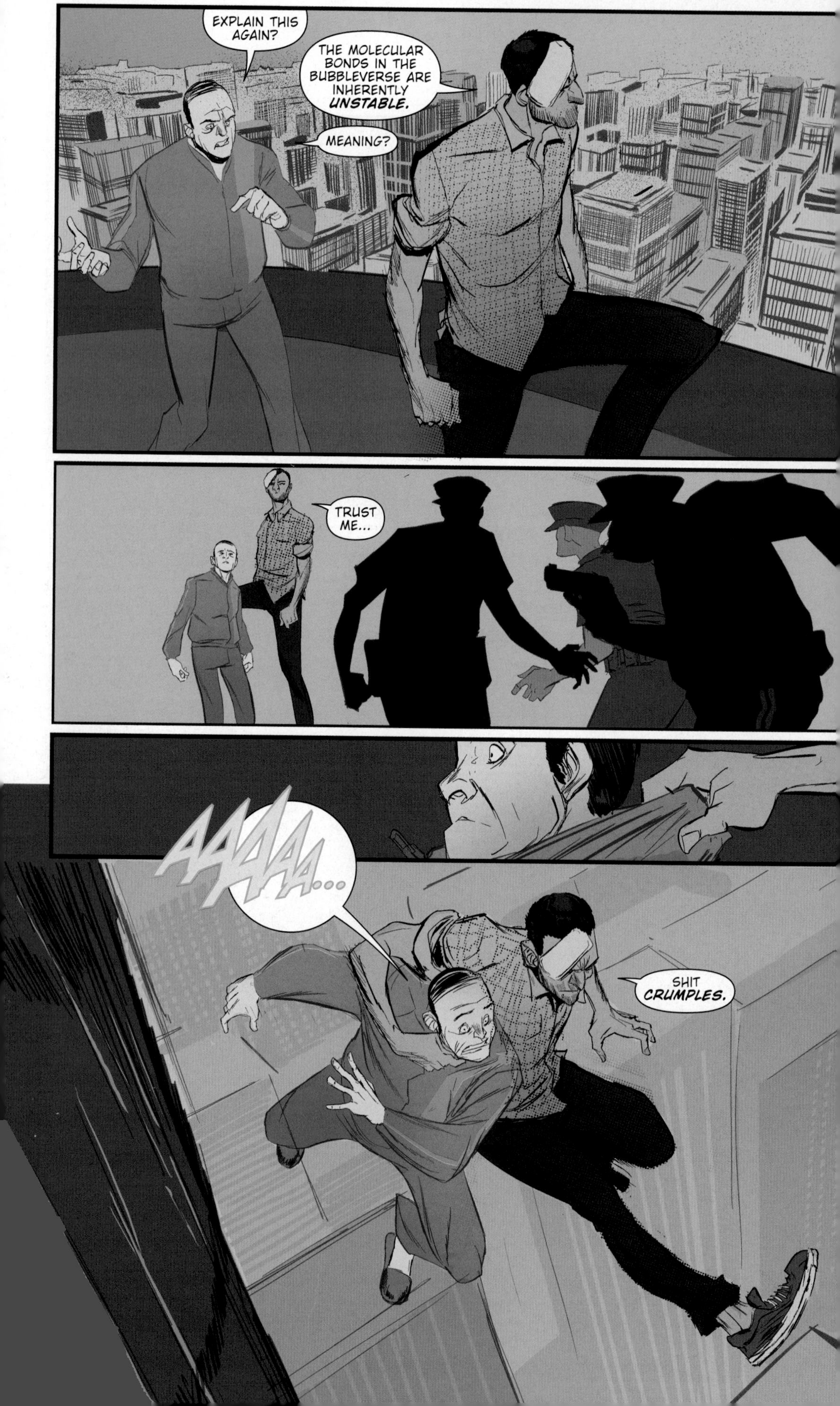
EXPLAIN THIS AGAIN?
THE MOLECULAR BONDS IN THE BUBBLEVERSE ARE INHERENTLY UNSTABLE.
MEANING?
TRUST ME...
AAAAA...
SHIT CRUMPLES.

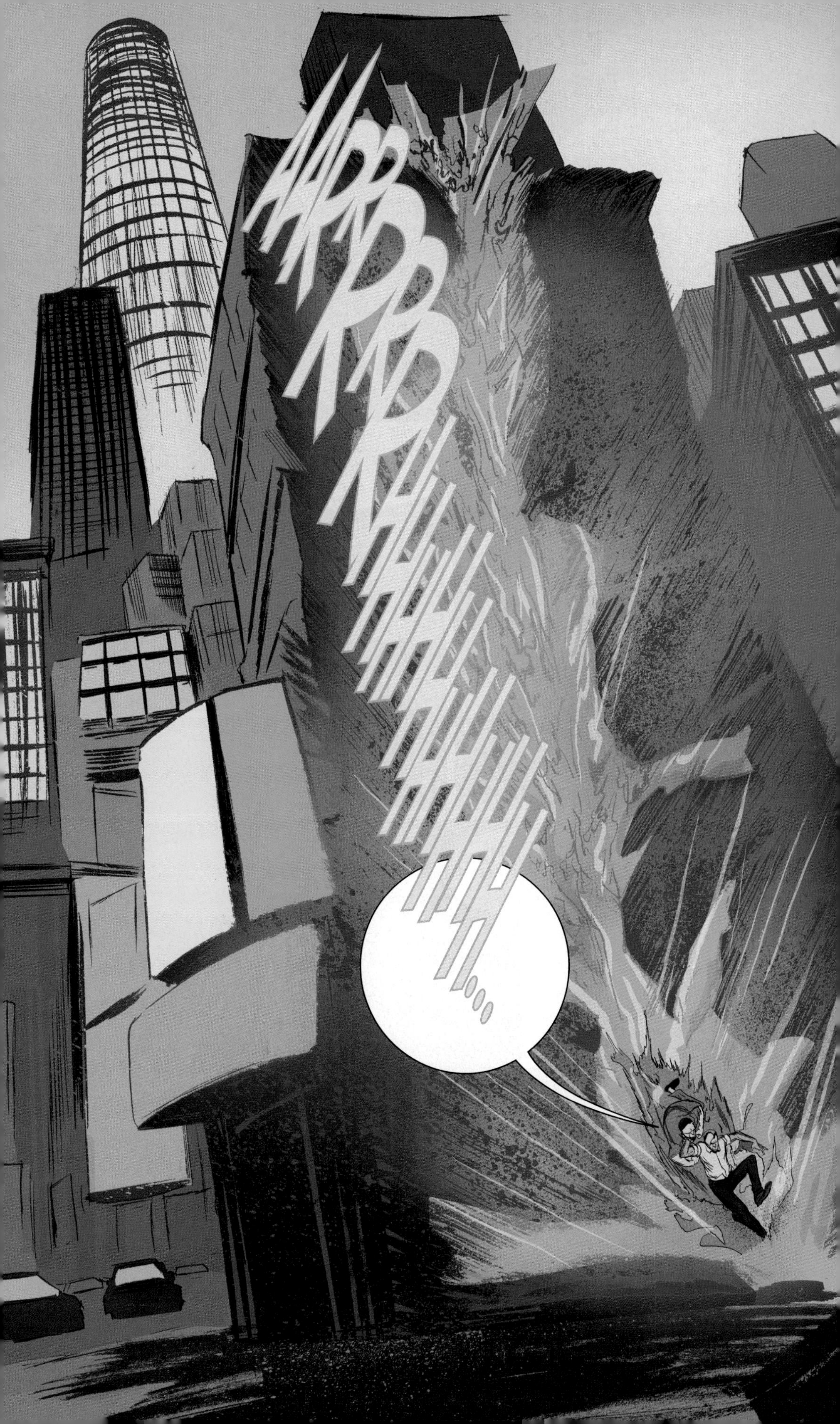
AARRRRRHHHHHHHHHHHH...

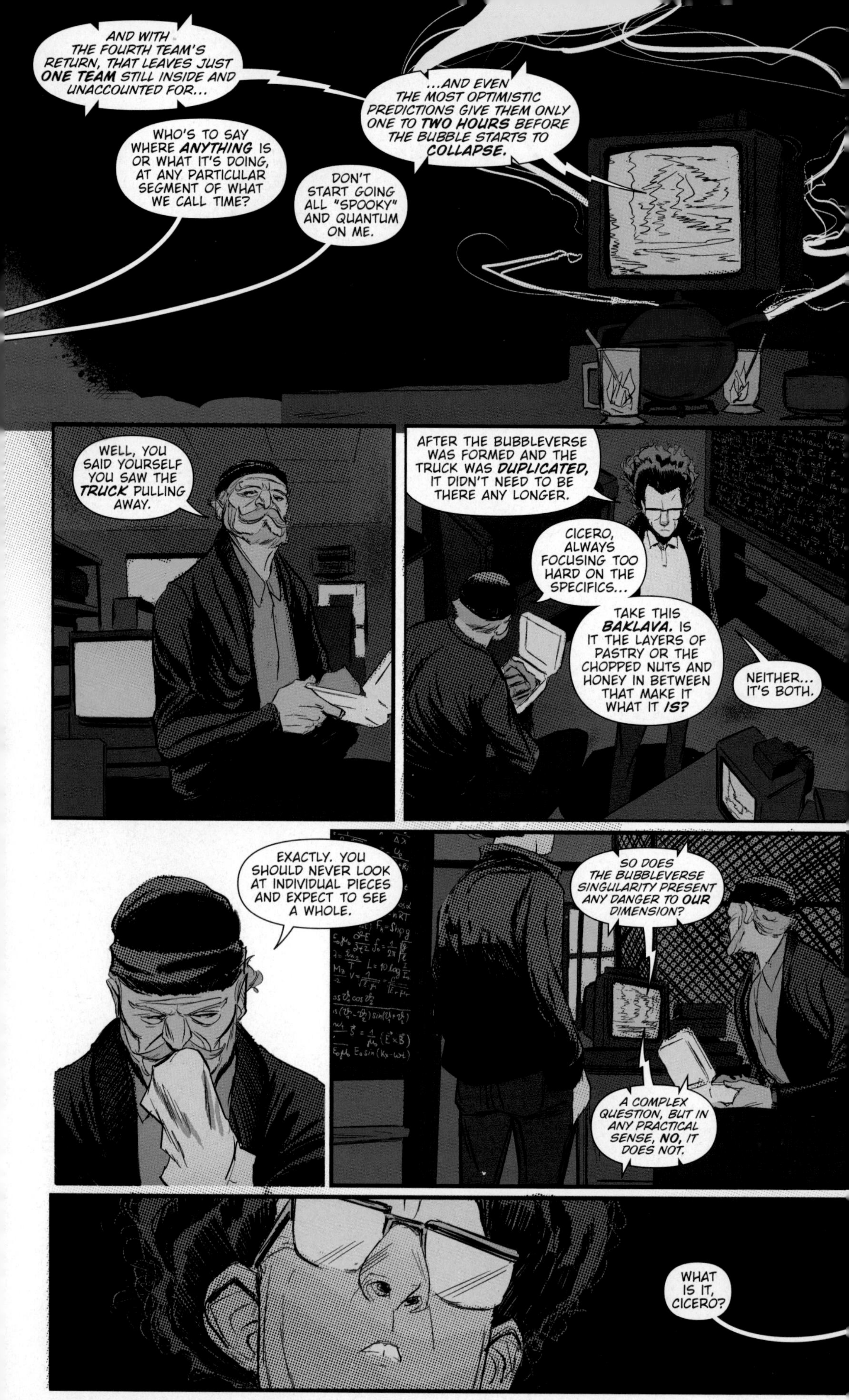
AND WITH THE FOURTH TEAM'S RETURN, THAT LEAVES JUST ONE TEAM STILL INSIDE AND UNACCOUNTED FOR...
...AND EVEN THE MOST OPTIMISTIC PREDICTIONS GIVE THEM ONLY ONE TO TWO HOURS BEFORE THE BUBBLE STARTS TO COLLAPSE.
WHO'S TO SAY WHERE ANYTHING IS OR WHAT IT'S DOING, AT ANY PARTICULAR SEGMENT OF WHAT WE CALL TIME?
DON'T START GOING ALL "SPOOKY" AND QUANTUM ON ME.
WELL, YOU SAID YOURSELF YOU SAW THE TRUCK PULLING AWAY.
AFTER THE BUBBLEVERSE WAS FORMED AND THE TRUCK WAS DUPLICATED, IT DIDN'T NEED TO BE THERE ANY LONGER.
CICERO, ALWAYS FOCUSING TOO HARD ON THE SPECIFICS...
TAKE THIS BAKLAVA. IS IT THE LAYERS OF PASTRY OR THE CHOPPED NUTS AND HONEY IN BETWEEN THAT MAKE IT WHAT IT IS?
NEITHER... IT'S BOTH.
EXACTLY. YOU SHOULD NEVER LOOK AT INDIVIDUAL PIECES AND EXPECT TO SEE A WHOLE.
SO DOES THE BUBBLEVERSE SINGULARITY PRESENT ANY DANGER TO OUR DIMENSION?
A COMPLEX QUESTION, BUT IN ANY PRACTICAL SENSE, NO, IT DOES NOT.
WHAT IS IT, CICERO?

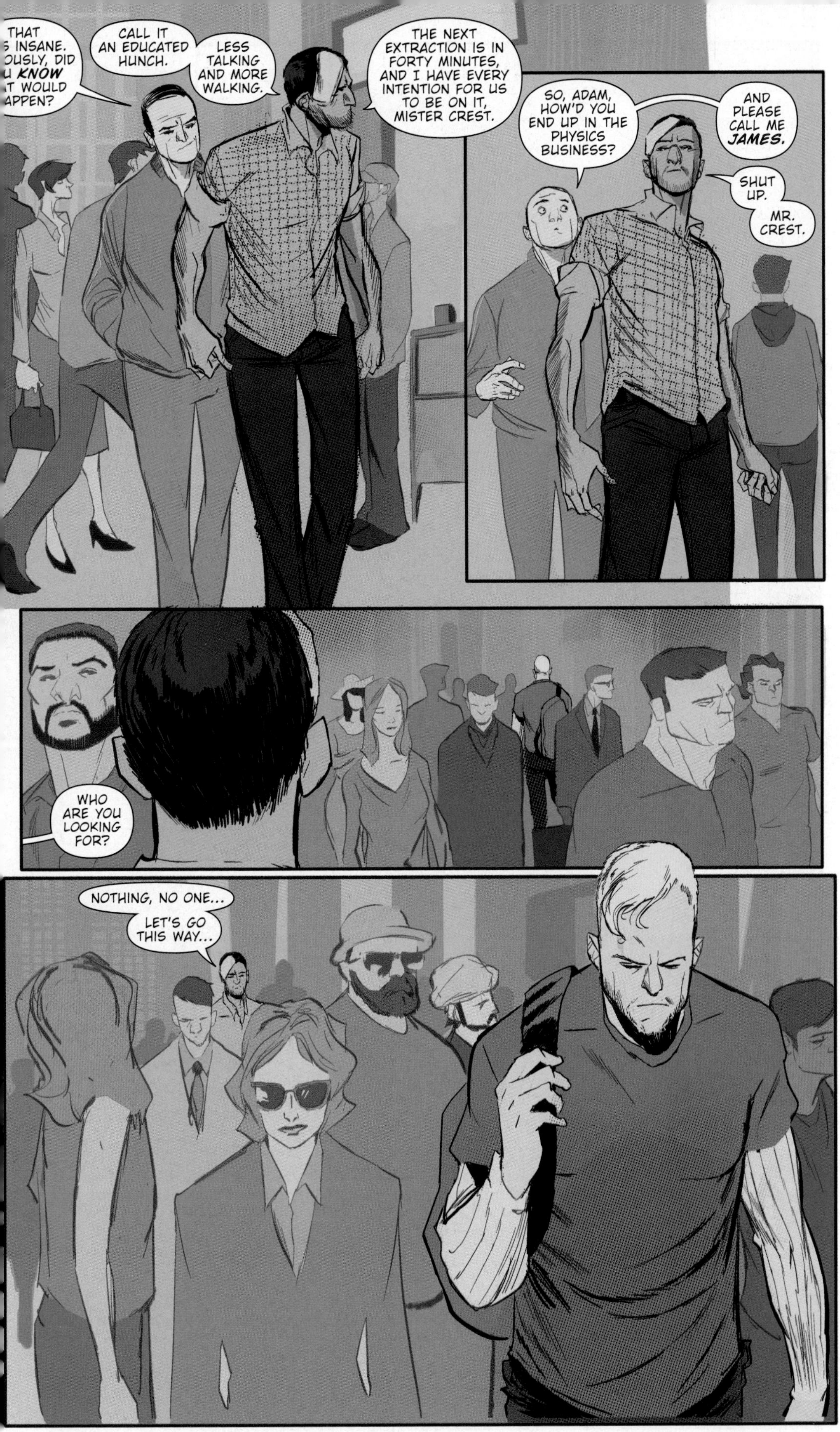

THAT
S INSANE.
OUSLY, DID
U KNOW
T WOULD
APPEN?
CALL IT AN EDUCATED HUNCH.
LESS TALKING AND MORE WALKING.
THE NEXT EXTRACTION IS IN FORTY MINUTES, AND I HAVE EVERY INTENTION FOR US TO BE ON IT, MISTER CREST.
SO, ADAM, HOW'D YOU END UP IN THE PHYSICS BUSINESS?
AND PLEASE CALL ME JAMES.
SHUT UP.
MR. CREST.
WHO ARE YOU LOOKING FOR?
NOTHING, NO ONE...
LET'S GO THIS WAY...

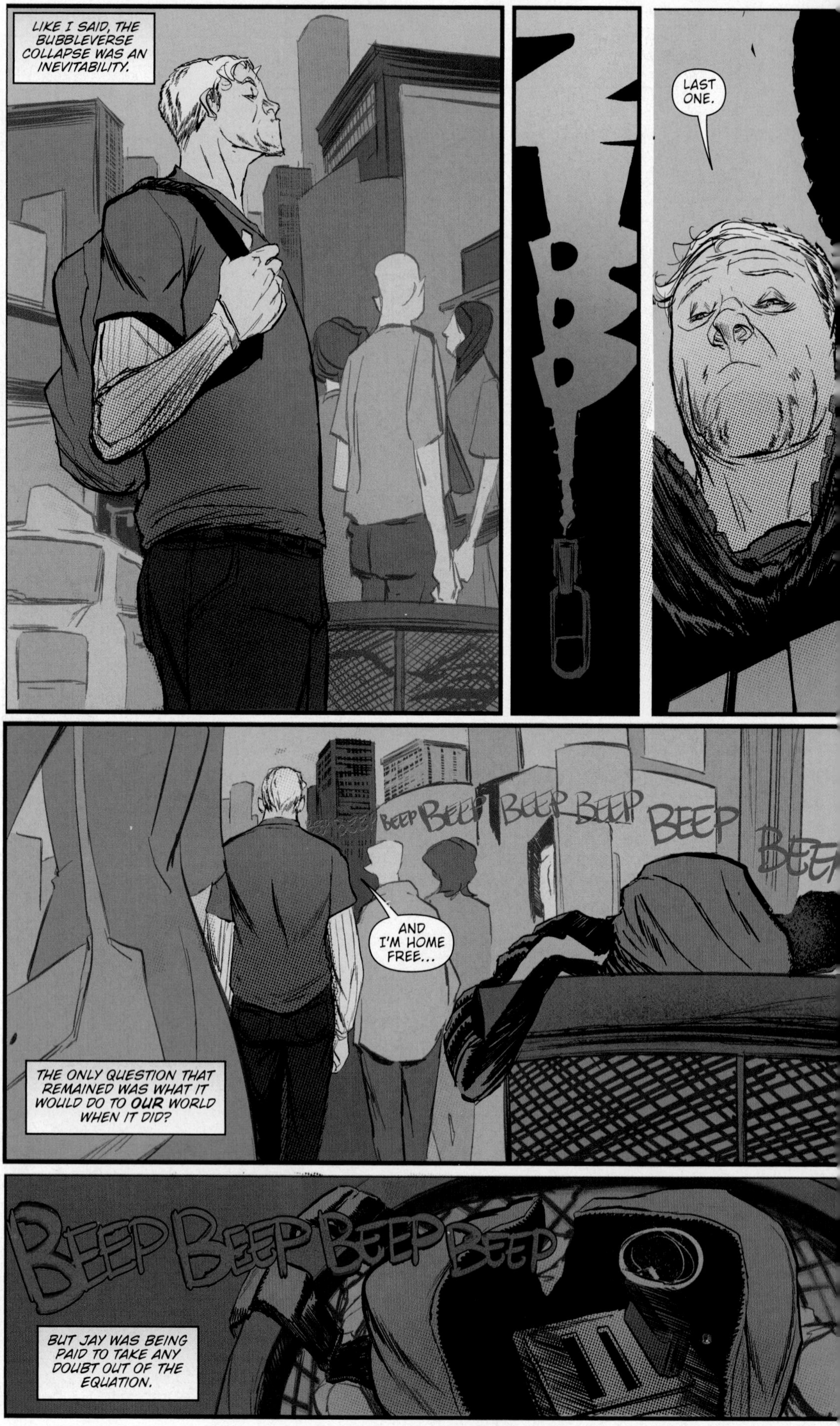
LIKE I SAID, THE BUBBLEVERSE COLLAPSE WAS AN INEVITABILITY.
LAST ONE.
BEEP BEEP BEEP BEEP BEEP BEEP
AND I'M HOME FREE...
THE ONLY QUESTION THAT REMAINED WAS WHAT IT WOULD DO TO OUR WORLD WHEN IT DID?
BEEP BEEP BEEP BEEP
BUT JAY WAS BEING PAID TO TAKE ANY DOUBT OUT OF THE EQUATION.

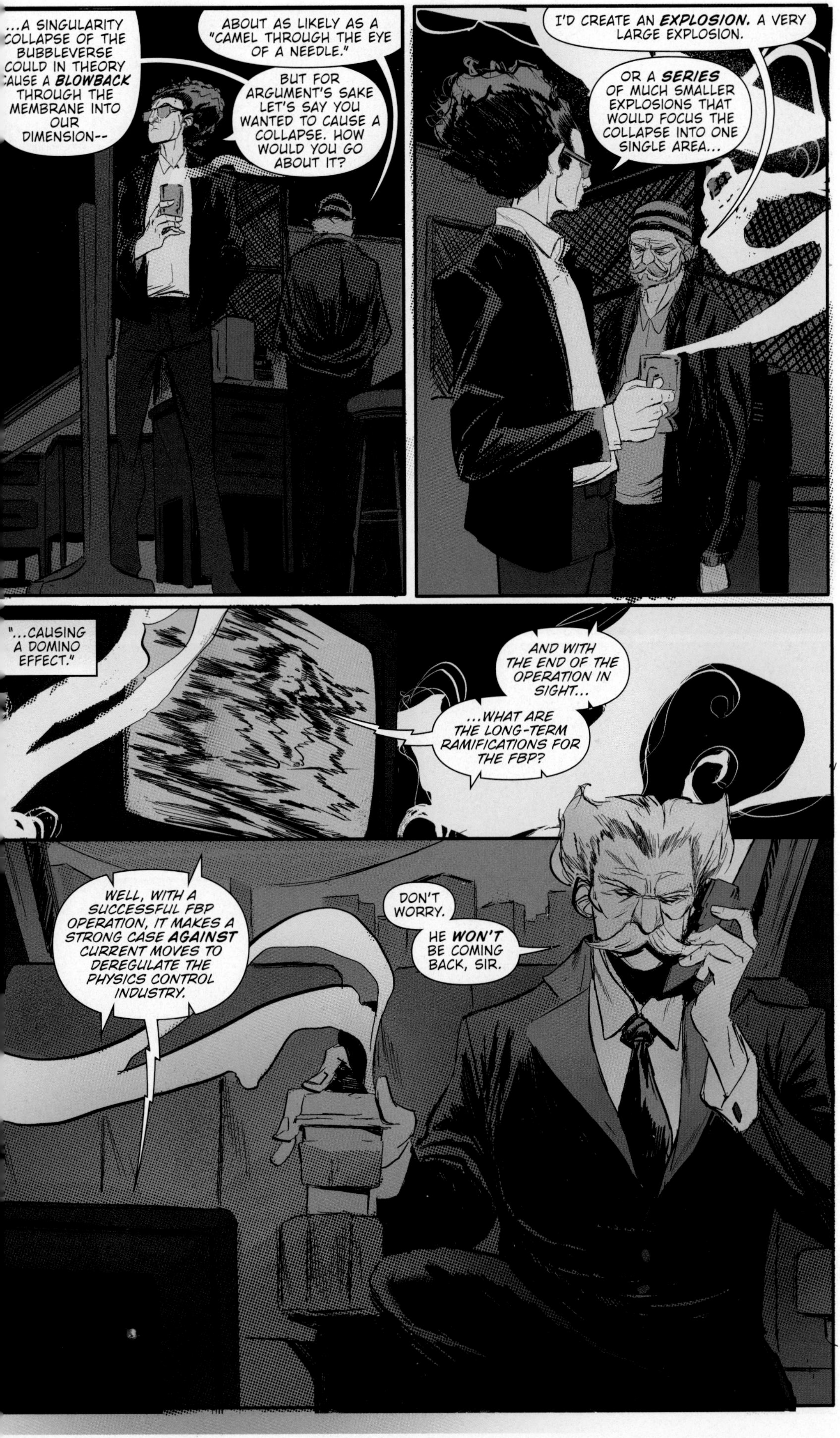

...A SINGULARITY COLLAPSE OF THE BUBBLEVERSE COULD IN THEORY CAUSE A BLOWBACK THROUGH THE MEMBRANE INTO OUR DIMENSION--
ABOUT AS LIKELY AS A "CAMEL THROUGH THE EYE OF A NEEDLE."
BUT FOR ARGUMENT'S SAKE LET'S SAY YOU WANTED TO CAUSE A COLLAPSE. HOW WOULD YOU GO ABOUT IT?
I'D CREATE AN EXPLOSION. A VERY LARGE EXPLOSION.
OR A SERIES OF MUCH SMALLER EXPLOSIONS THAT WOULD FOCUS THE COLLAPSE INTO ONE SINGLE AREA...
"...CAUSING A DOMINO EFFECT."
AND WITH THE END OF THE OPERATION IN SIGHT...
...WHAT ARE THE LONG-TERM RAMIFICATIONS FOR THE FBP?
WELL, WITH A SUCCESSFUL FBP OPERATION, IT MAKES A STRONG CASE AGAINST CURRENT MOVES TO DEREGULATE THE PHYSICS CONTROL INDUSTRY.
DON'T WORRY.
HE WON'T BE COMING BACK, SIR.

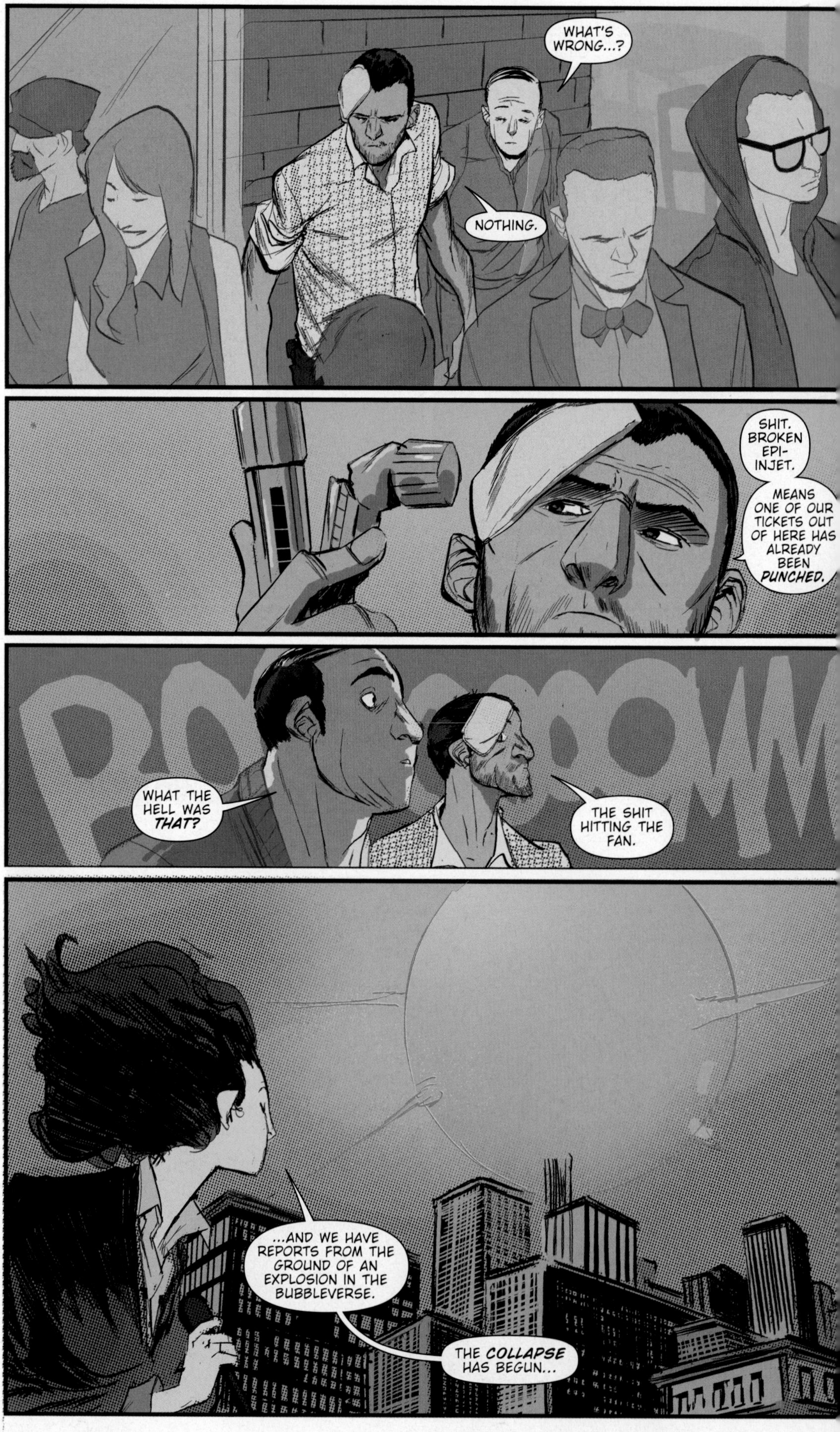
WHAT'S WRONG...?
NOTHING.
SHIT. BROKEN EPI-INJET.
MEANS ONE OF OUR TICKETS OUT OF HERE HAS ALREADY BEEN *PUNCHED.*
WHAT THE HELL WAS *THAT?*
THE SHIT HITTING THE FAN.
...AND WE HAVE REPORTS FROM THE GROUND OF AN EXPLOSION IN THE BUBBLEVERSE.
THE *COLLAPSE* HAS BEGUN...

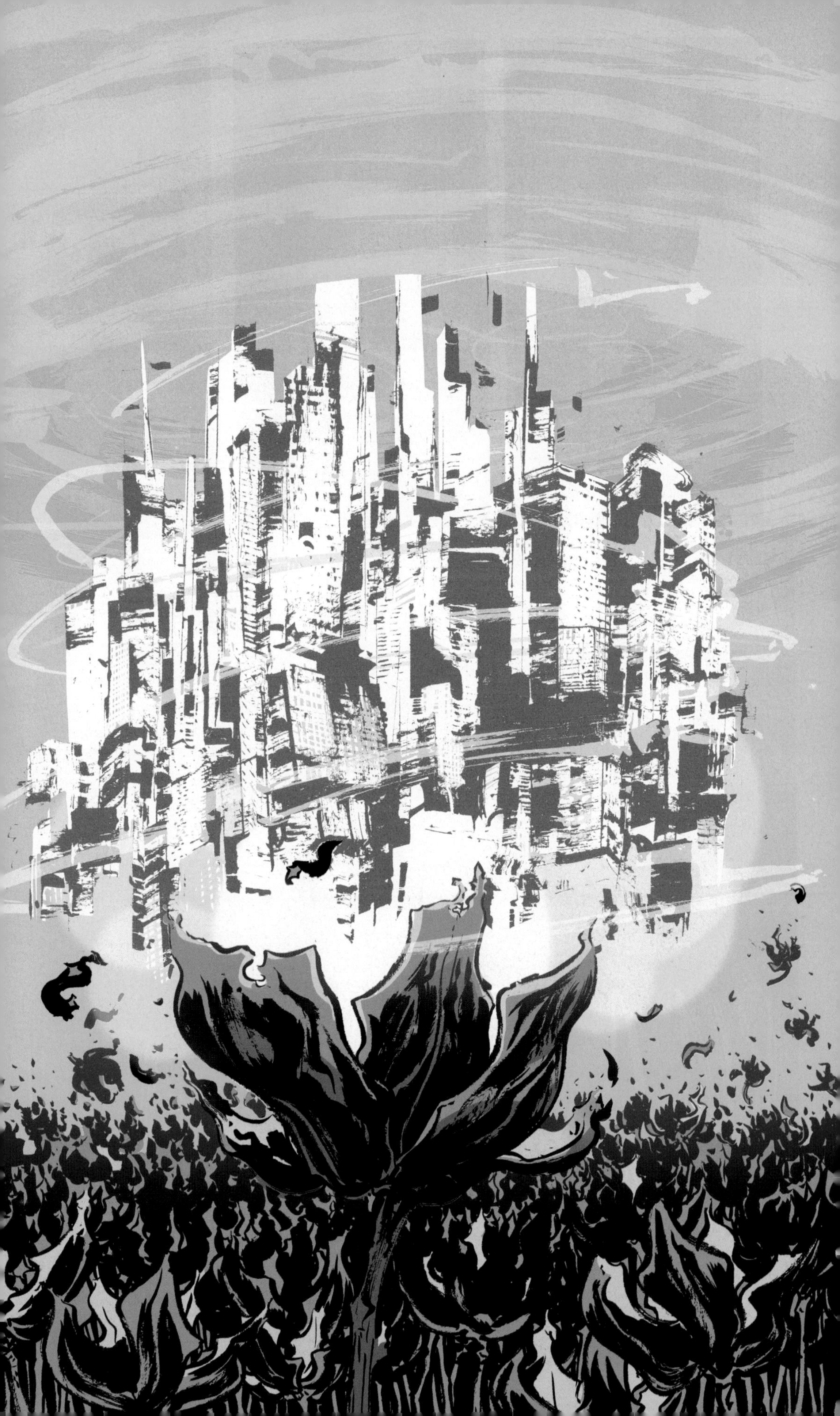

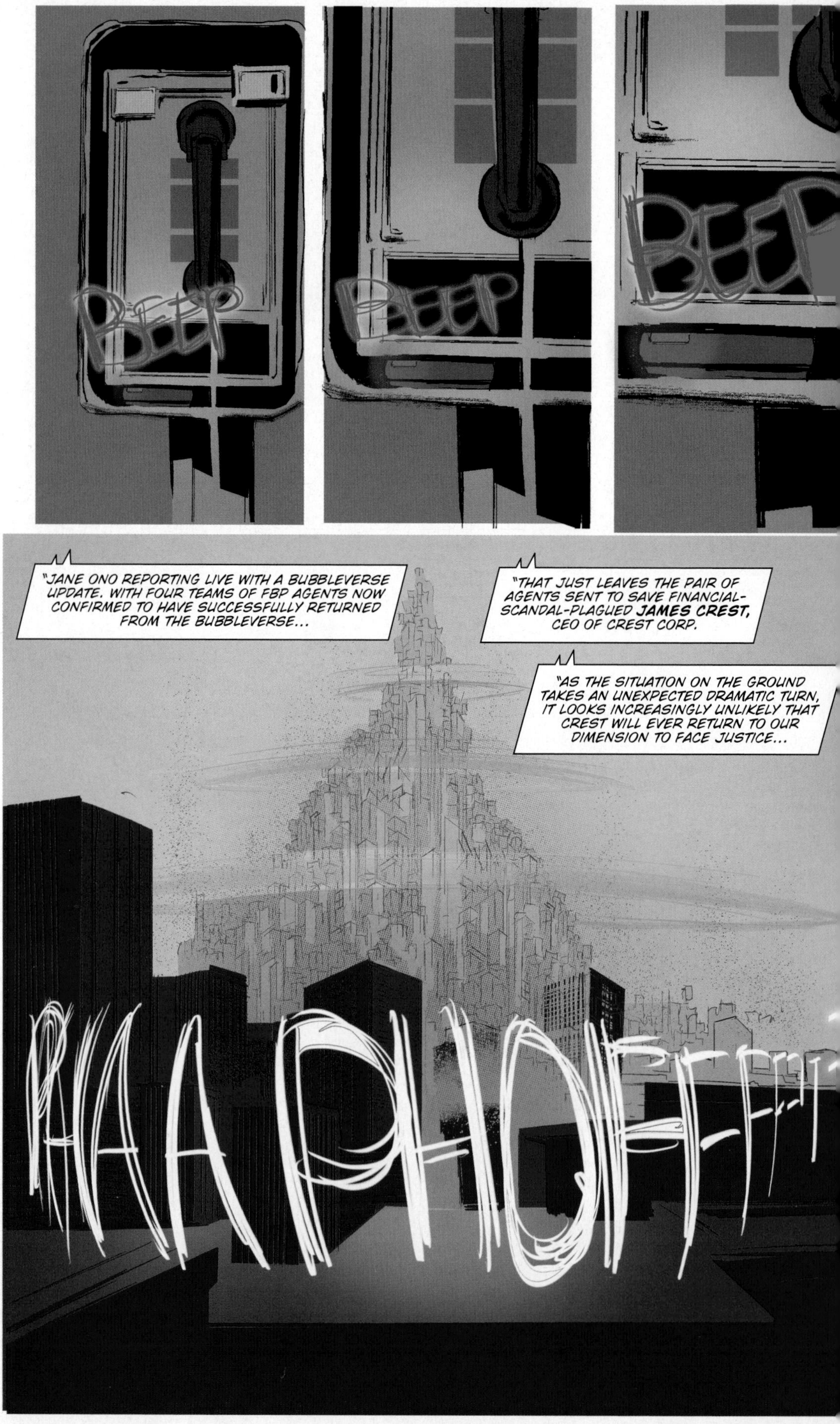
BEEP
BEEP
BEEP
"JANE ONO REPORTING LIVE WITH A BUBBLEVERSE UPDATE. WITH FOUR TEAMS OF FBP AGENTS NOW CONFIRMED TO HAVE SUCCESSFULLY RETURNED FROM THE BUBBLEVERSE...
"THAT JUST LEAVES THE PAIR OF AGENTS SENT TO SAVE FINANCIAL-SCANDAL-PLAGUED **JAMES CREST,** CEO OF CREST CORP.
"AS THE SITUATION ON THE GROUND TAKES AN UNEXPECTED DRAMATIC TURN, IT LOOKS INCREASINGLY UNLIKELY THAT CREST WILL EVER RETURN TO OUR DIMENSION TO FACE JUSTICE...

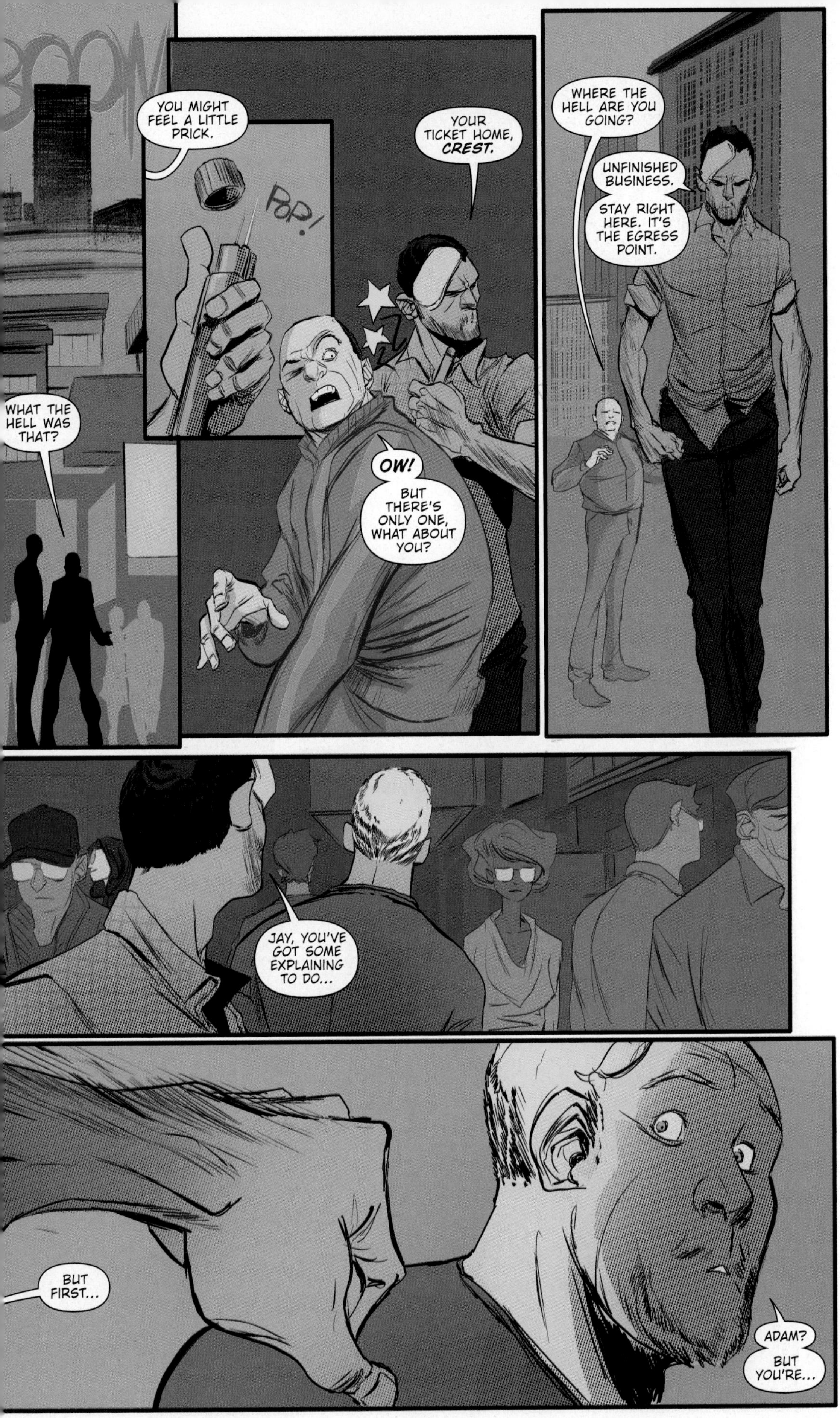
BOOM
WHAT THE HELL WAS THAT?
YOU MIGHT FEEL A LITTLE PRICK.
POP!
YOUR TICKET HOME, ***CREST.***
OW!
BUT THERE'S ONLY ONE, WHAT ABOUT YOU?
WHERE THE HELL ARE YOU GOING?
UNFINISHED BUSINESS.
STAY RIGHT HERE. IT'S THE EGRESS POINT.
JAY, YOU'VE GOT SOME EXPLAINING TO DO...
BUT FIRST...
ADAM?
BUT YOU'RE...

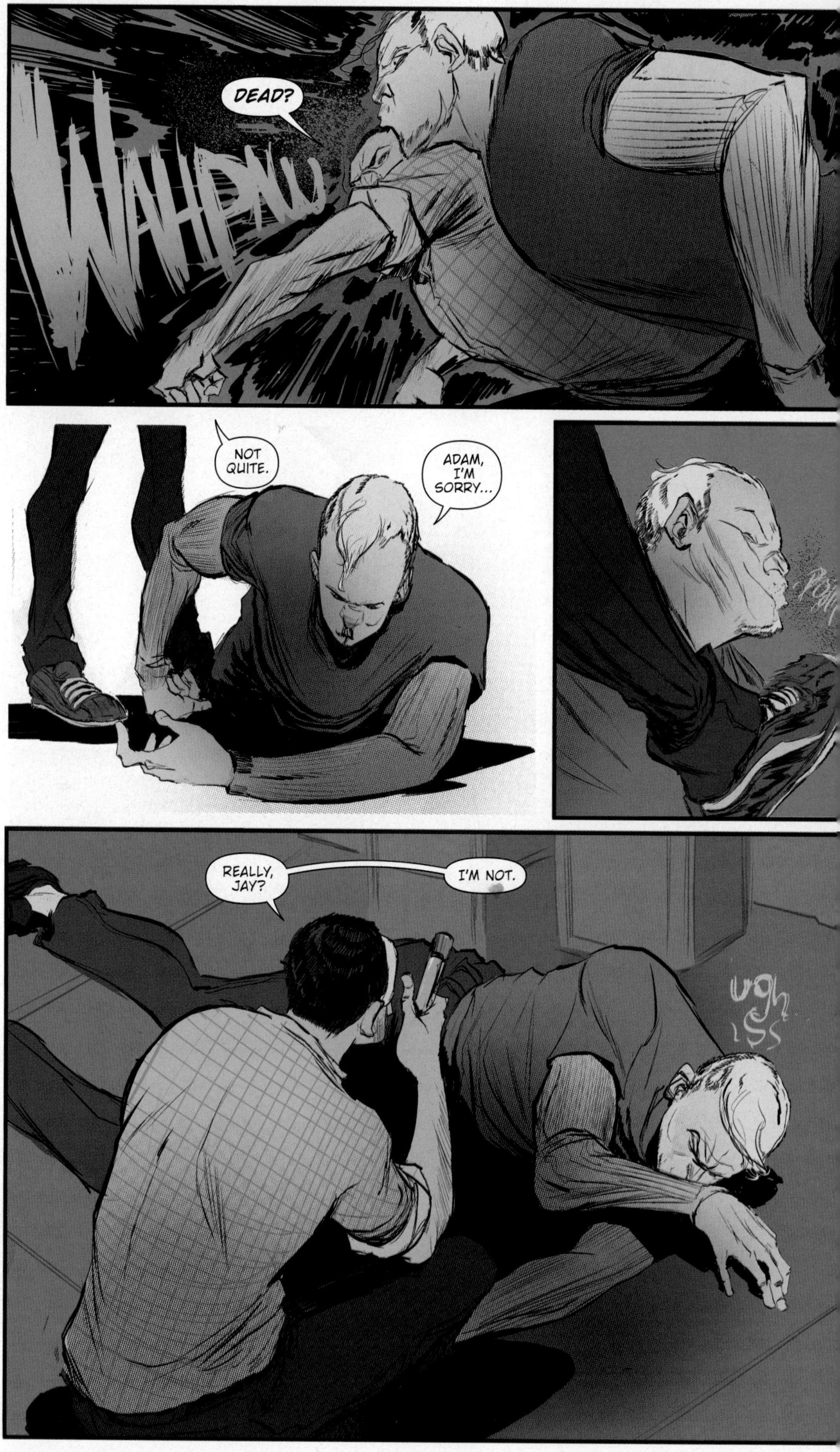
WAHPW
DEAD?
NOT QUITE.
ADAM, I'M SORRY...
REALLY, JAY?
I'M NOT.
ugh
ss

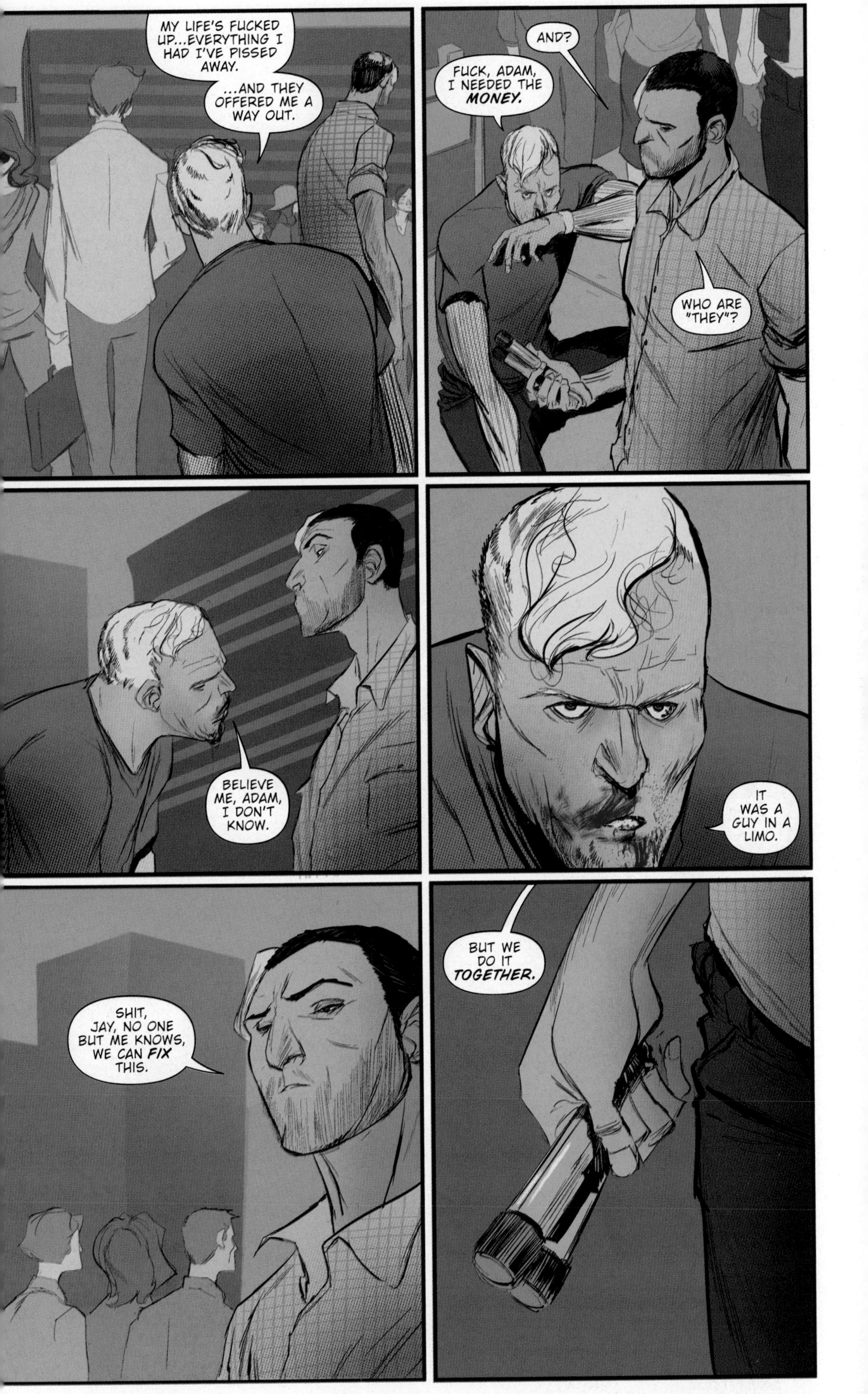
MY LIFE'S FUCKED UP...EVERYTHING I HAD I'VE PISSED AWAY.
...AND THEY OFFERED ME A WAY OUT.
AND?
FUCK, ADAM, I NEEDED THE MONEY.
WHO ARE "THEY"?
BELIEVE ME, ADAM, I DON'T KNOW.
IT WAS A GUY IN A LIMO.
SHIT, JAY, NO ONE BUT ME KNOWS, WE CAN FIX THIS.
BUT WE DO IT TOGETHER.

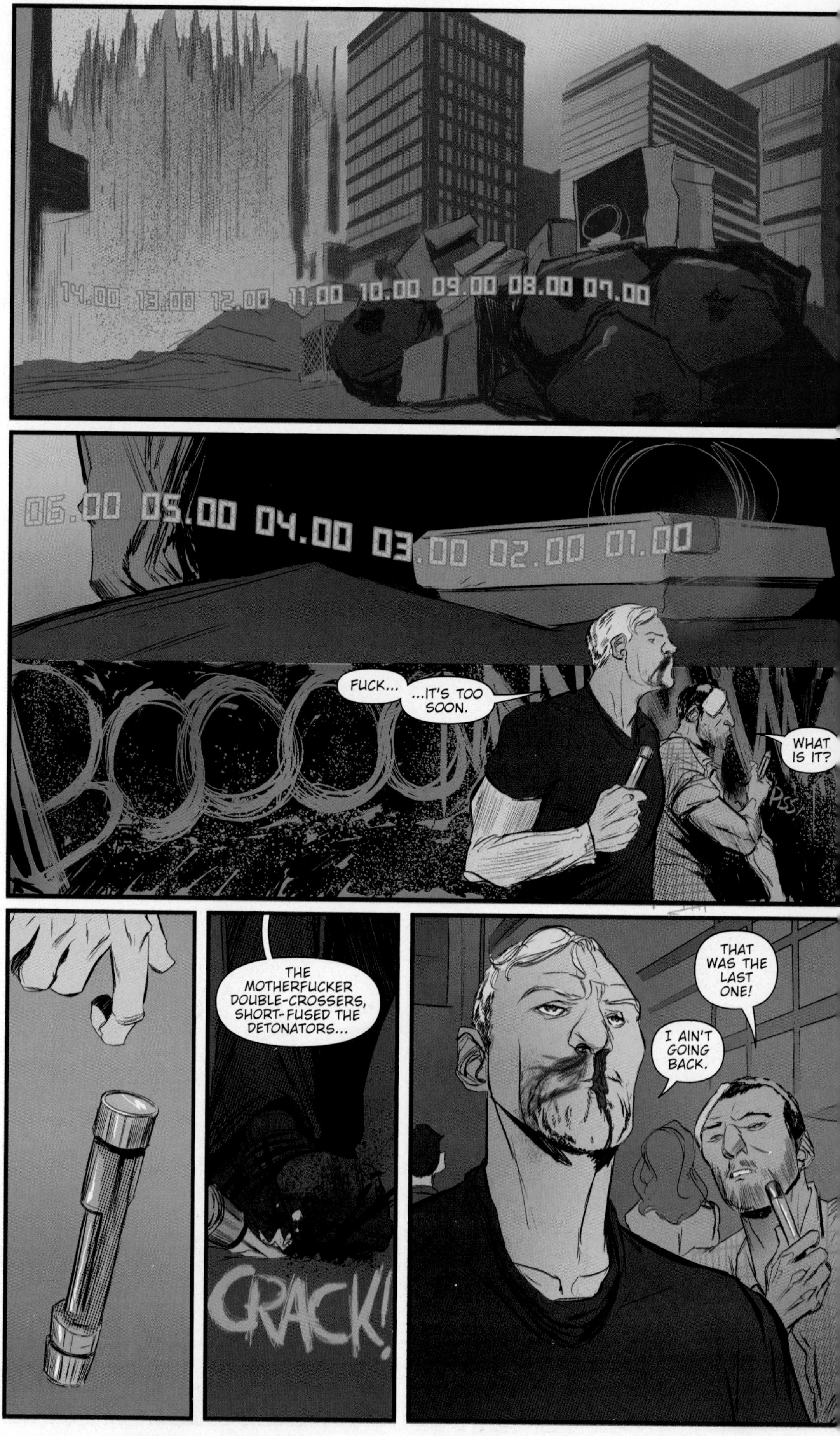
14.00 13.00 12.00 11.00 10.00 09.00 08.00 07.00
06.00 05.00 04.00 03.00 02.00 01.00
FUCK...
...IT'S TOO SOON.
WHAT IS IT?
THE MOTHERFUCKER DOUBLE-CROSSERS, SHORT-FUSED THE DETONATORS...
CRACK!
THAT WAS THE LAST ONE!
I AIN'T GOING BACK.

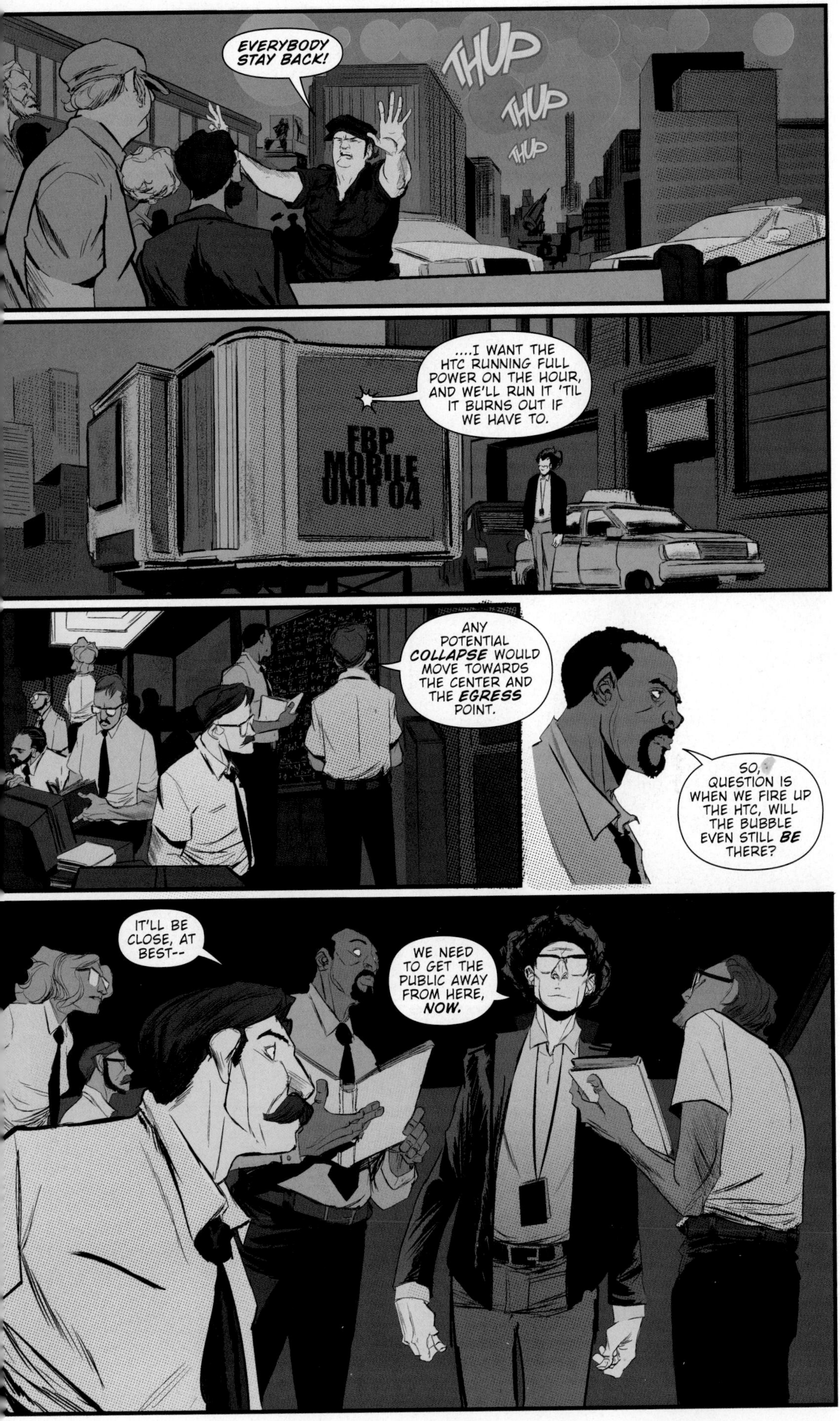
EVERYBODY STAY BACK!
THUP
THUP
THUP
....I WANT THE HTC RUNNING FULL POWER ON THE HOUR, AND WE'LL RUN IT 'TIL IT BURNS OUT IF WE HAVE TO.
FBP MOBILE UNIT 04
ANY POTENTIAL COLLAPSE WOULD MOVE TOWARDS THE CENTER AND THE EGRESS POINT.
SO, QUESTION IS WHEN WE FIRE UP THE HTC, WILL THE BUBBLE EVEN STILL BE THERE?
IT'LL BE CLOSE, AT BEST--
WE NEED TO GET THE PUBLIC AWAY FROM HERE, NOW.

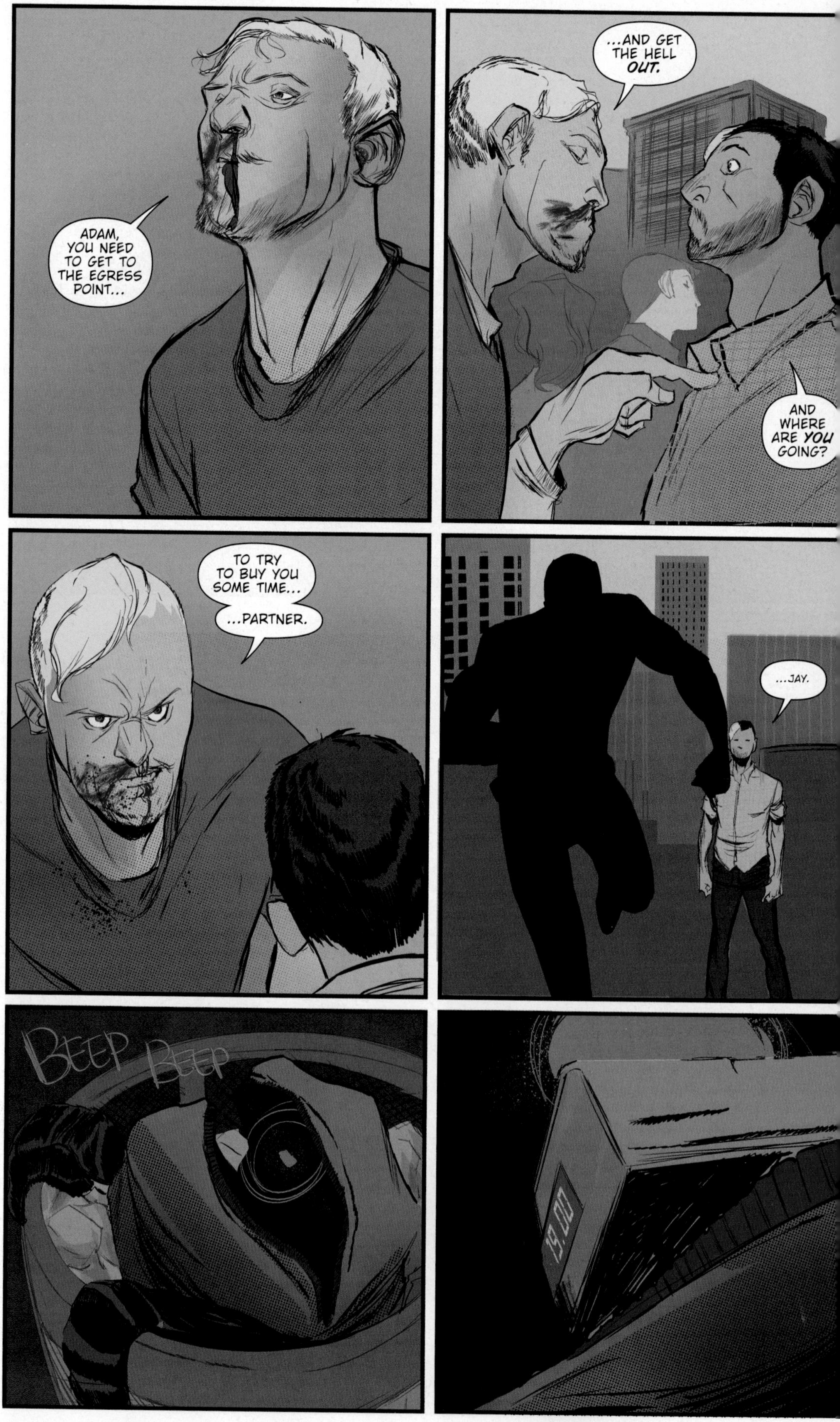
ADAM, YOU NEED TO GET TO THE EGRESS POINT...
...AND GET THE HELL OUT.
AND WHERE ARE YOU GOING?
TO TRY TO BUY YOU SOME TIME...
...PARTNER.
...JAY.
BEEP BEEP
19:00

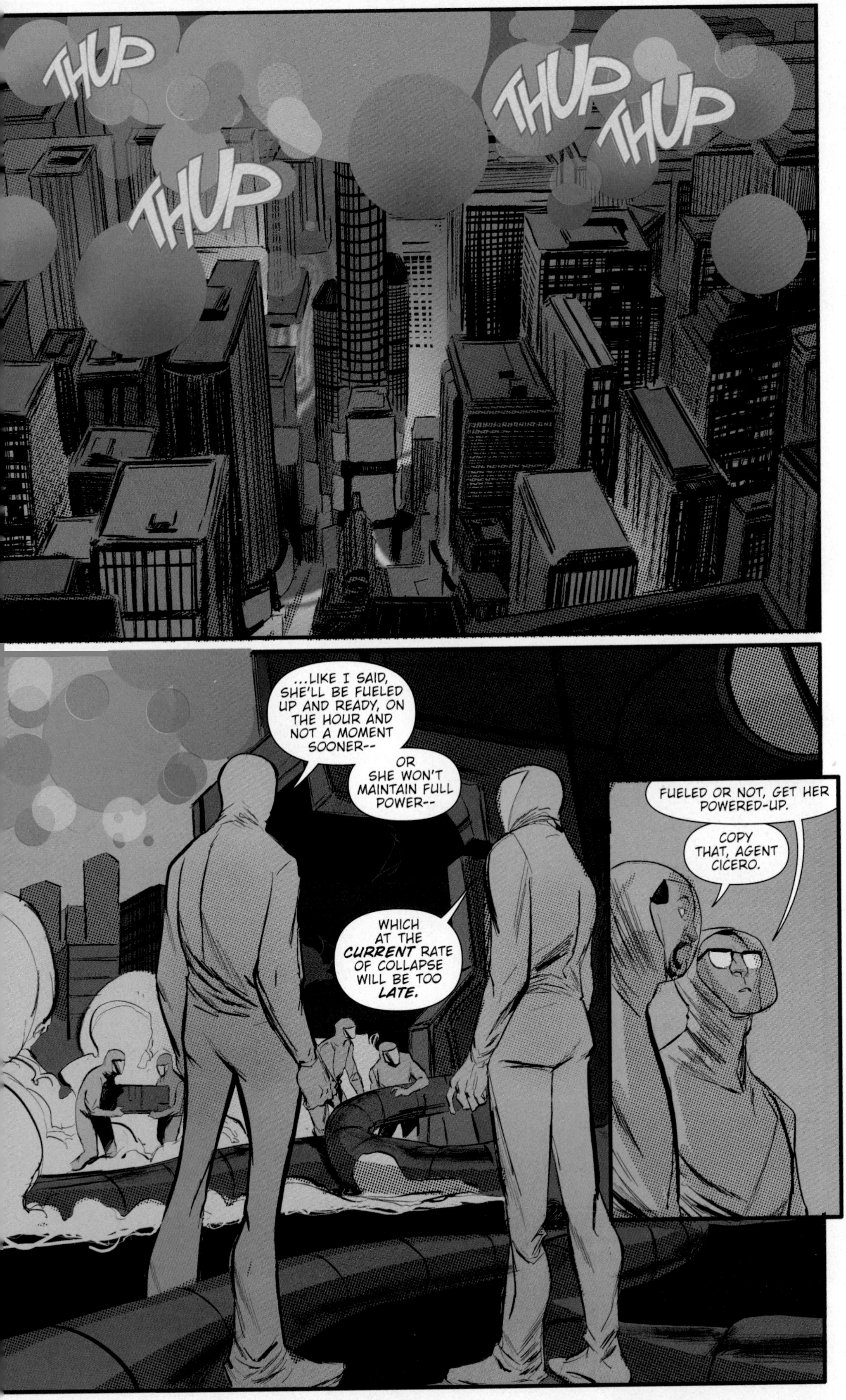
THUP
THUP
THUP THUP
...LIKE I SAID, SHE'LL BE FUELED UP AND READY, ON THE HOUR AND NOT A MOMENT SOONER--
OR SHE WON'T MAINTAIN FULL POWER--
WHICH AT THE CURRENT RATE OF COLLAPSE WILL BE TOO LATE.
FUELED OR NOT, GET HER POWERED-UP.
COPY THAT, AGENT CICERO.

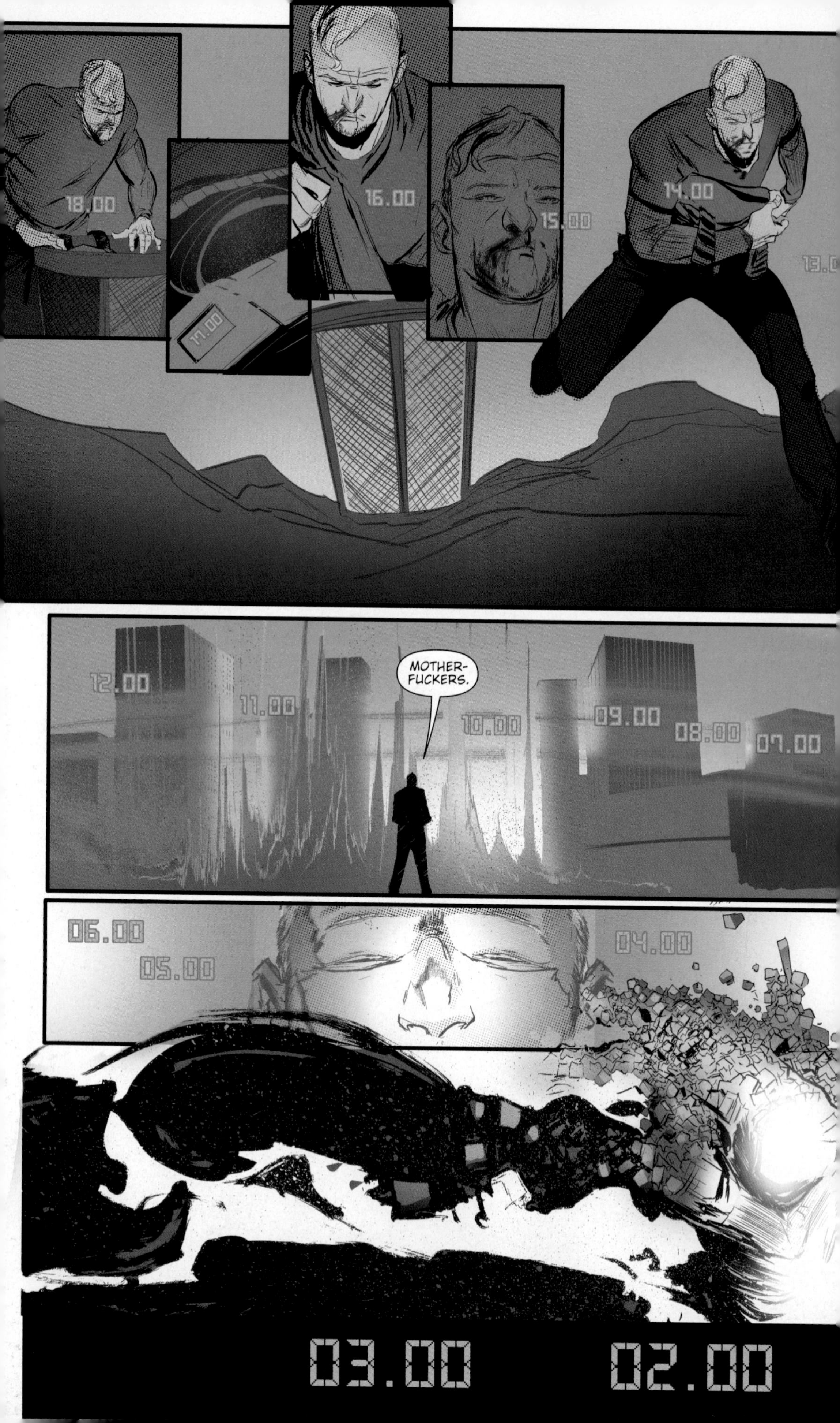
18.00
17.00
16.00
15.00
14.00
13.0
12.00
11.00
MOTHER-FUCKERS.
10.00
09.00
08.00
07.00
06.00
05.00
04.00
03.00
02.00

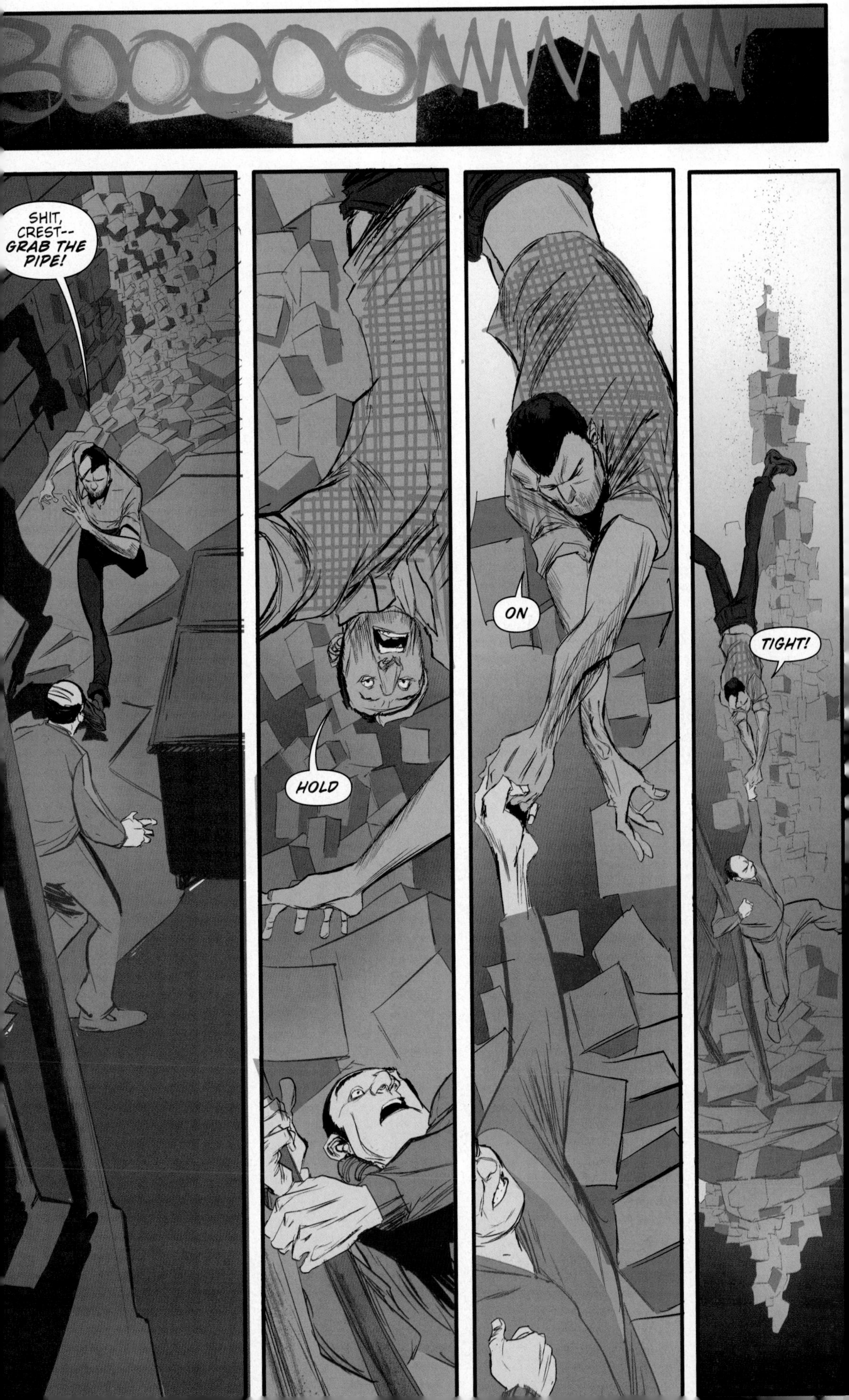
BOOOOOOMMMMMM
SHIT, CREST-- GRAB THE PIPE!
HOLD
ON
TIGHT!

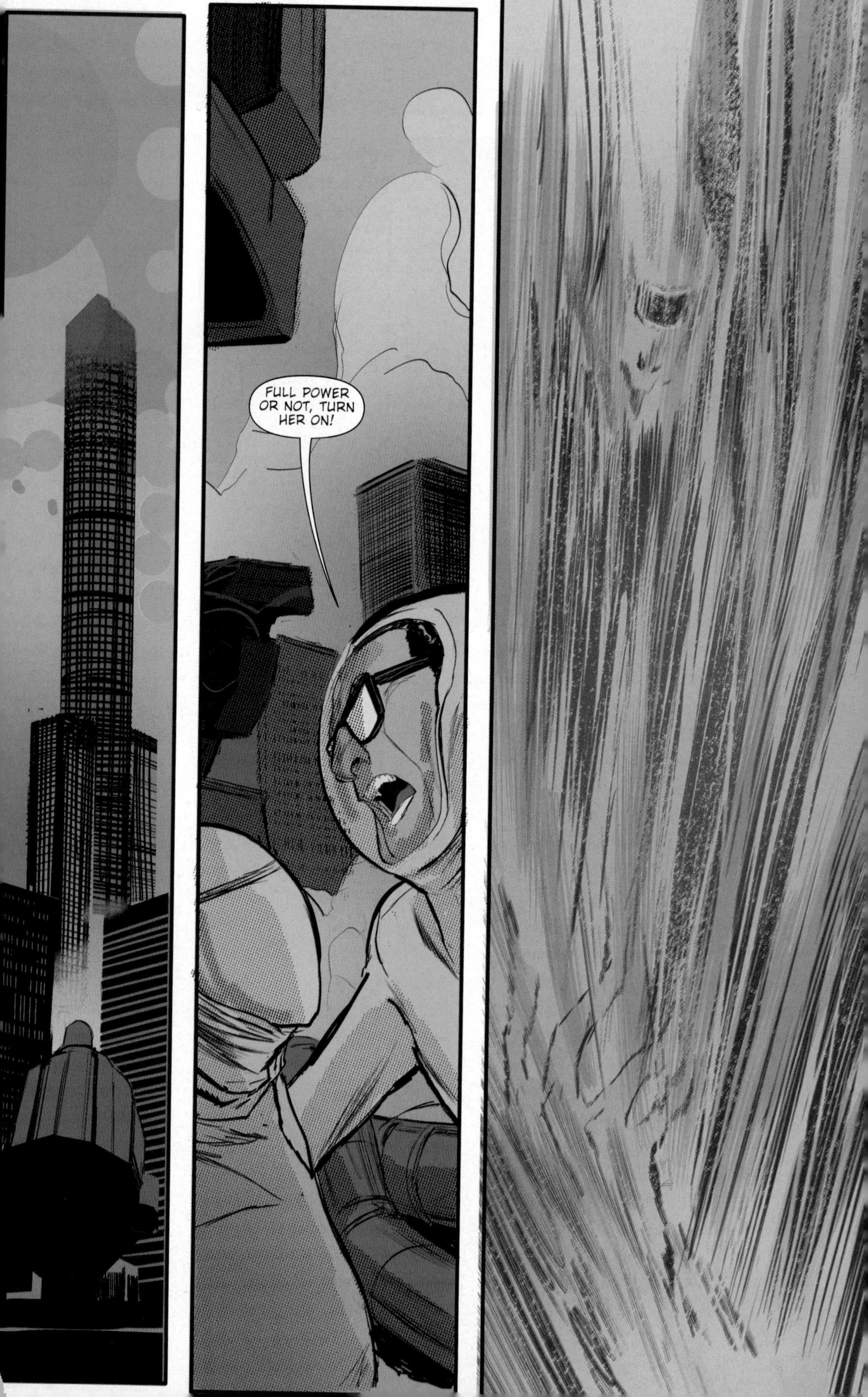
FULL POWER OR NOT, TURN HER ON!

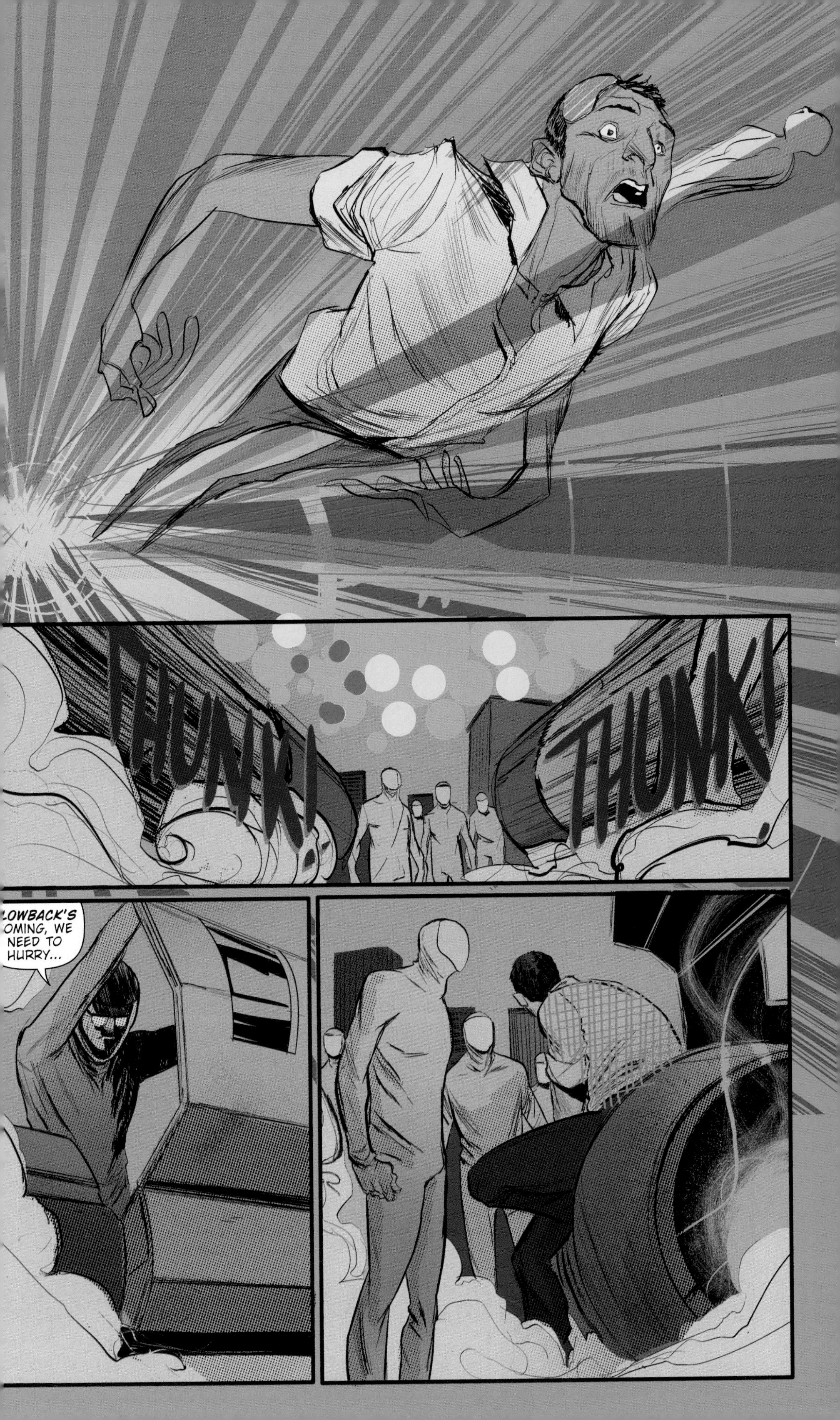
THUNK!
THUNK!
LOWBACK'S OMING, WE NEED TO HURRY...

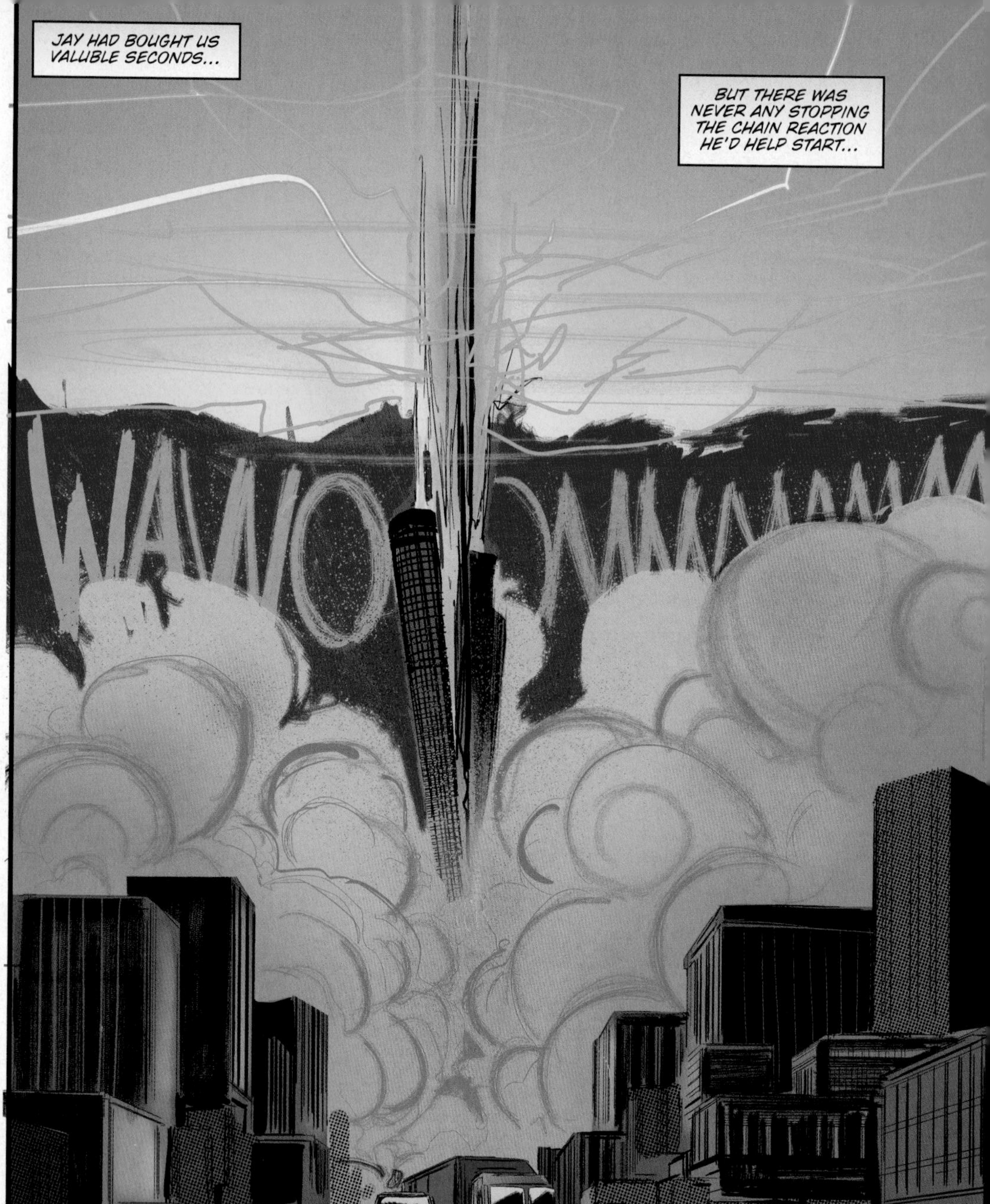
JAY HAD BOUGHT US VALUBLE SECONDS...
BUT THERE WAS NEVER ANY STOPPING THE CHAIN REACTION HE'D HELP START...
WAWOOMMMMM

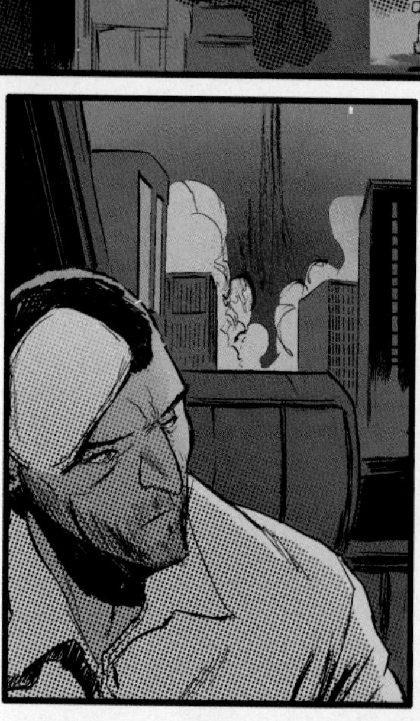

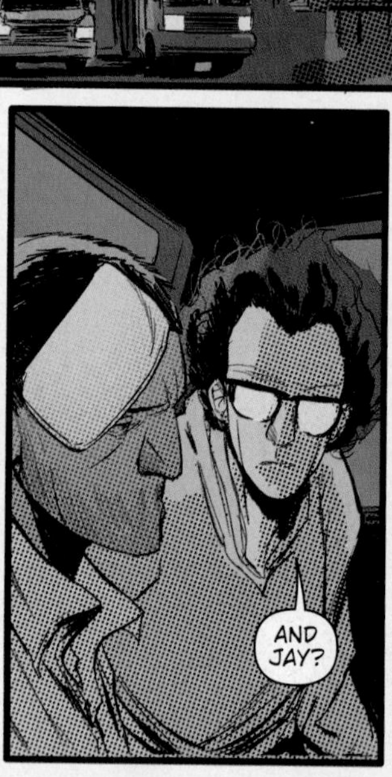
AND JAY?

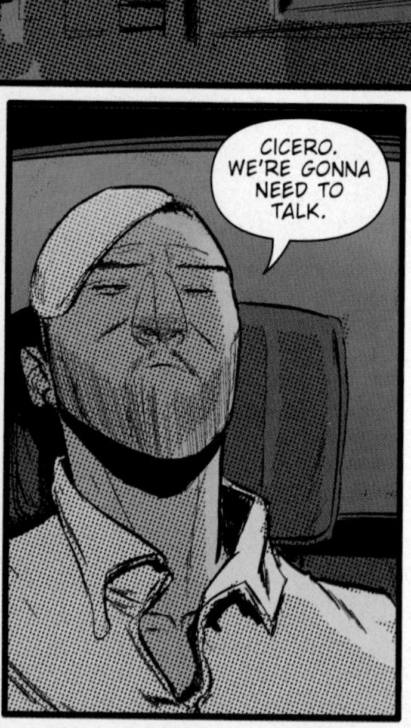
CICERO. WE'RE GONNA NEED TO TALK.

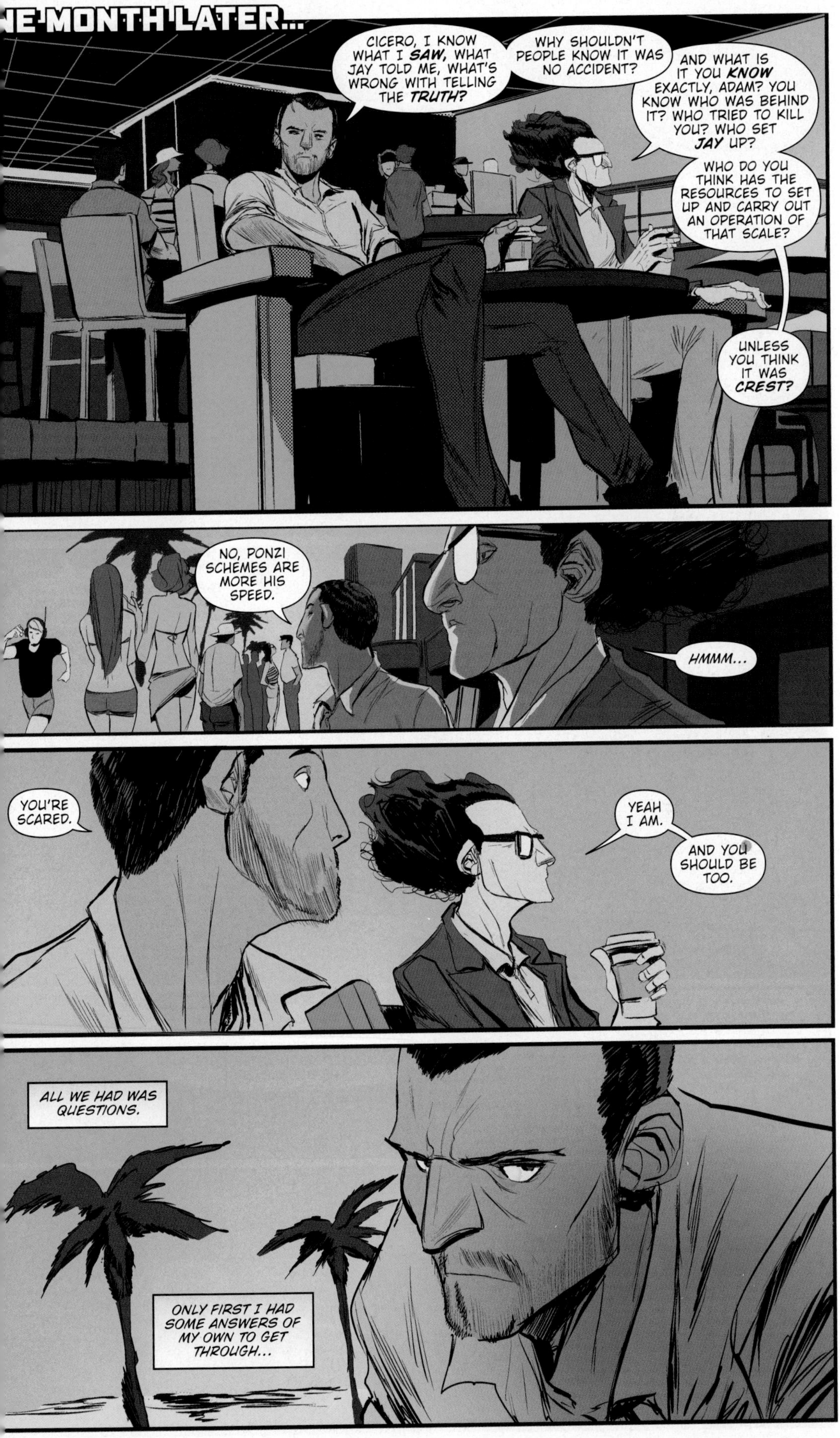

NE MONTH LATER...
CICERO, I KNOW WHAT I SAW, WHAT JAY TOLD ME, WHAT'S WRONG WITH TELLING THE TRUTH?
WHY SHOULDN'T PEOPLE KNOW IT WAS NO ACCIDENT?
AND WHAT IS IT YOU KNOW EXACTLY, ADAM? YOU KNOW WHO WAS BEHIND IT? WHO TRIED TO KILL YOU? WHO SET JAY UP?
WHO DO YOU THINK HAS THE RESOURCES TO SET UP AND CARRY OUT AN OPERATION OF THAT SCALE?
UNLESS YOU THINK IT WAS CREST?
NO, PONZI SCHEMES ARE MORE HIS SPEED.
HMMM...
YOU'RE SCARED.
YEAH I AM.
AND YOU SHOULD BE TOO.
ALL WE HAD WAS QUESTIONS.
ONLY FIRST I HAD SOME ANSWERS OF MY OWN TO GET THROUGH...

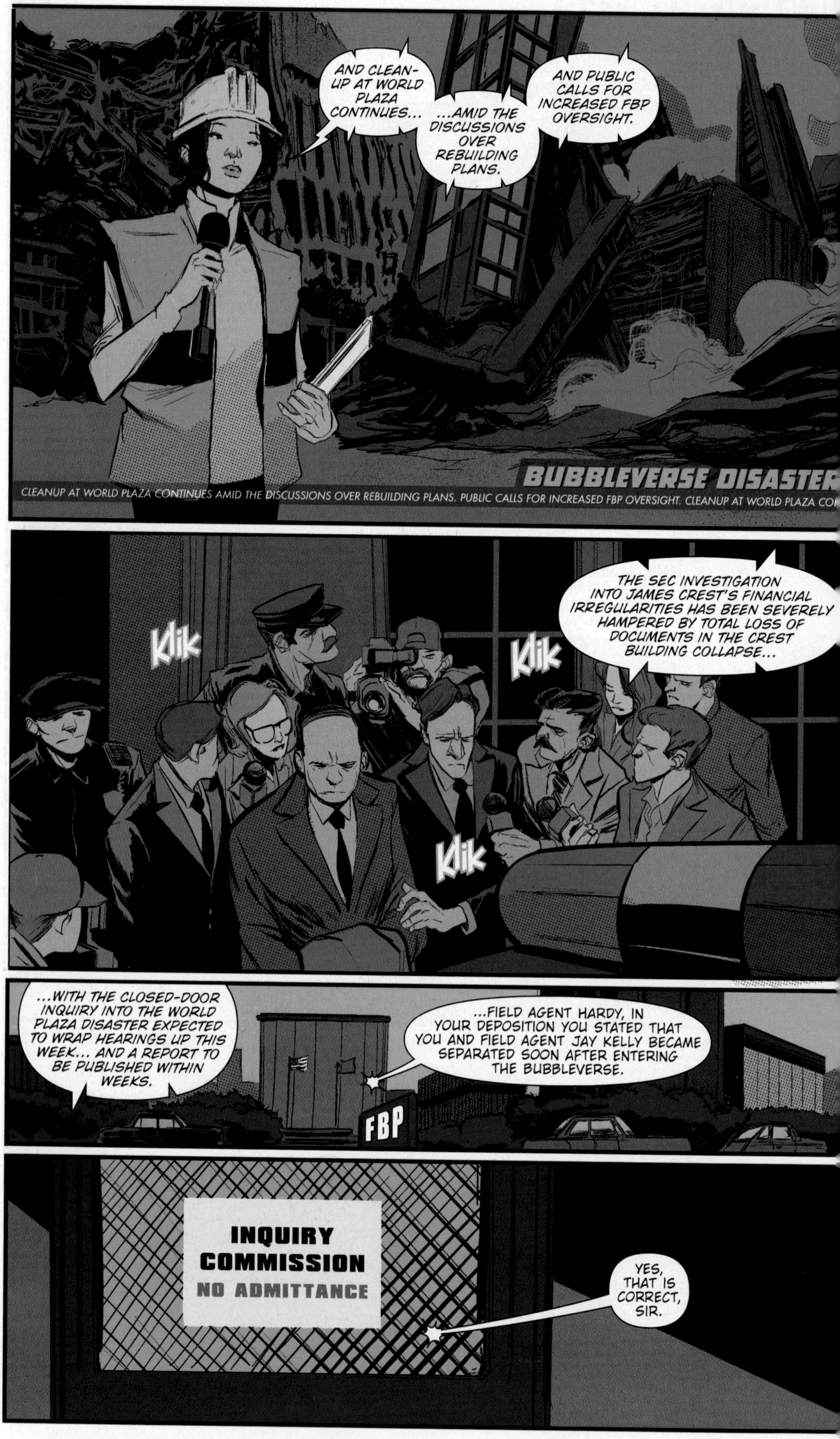
AND CLEAN-UP AT WORLD PLAZA CONTINUES...
...AMID THE DISCUSSIONS OVER REBUILDING PLANS.
AND PUBLIC CALLS FOR INCREASED FBP OVERSIGHT.
BUBBLEVERSE DISASTER
CLEANUP AT WORLD PLAZA CONTINUES AMID THE DISCUSSIONS OVER REBUILDING PLANS. PUBLIC CALLS FOR INCREASED FBP OVERSIGHT. CLEANUP AT WORLD PLAZA CO
KLIK
KLIK
THE SEC INVESTIGATION INTO JAMES CREST'S FINANCIAL IRREGULARITIES HAS BEEN SEVERELY HAMPERED BY TOTAL LOSS OF DOCUMENTS IN THE CREST BUILDING COLLAPSE...
KLIK
...WITH THE CLOSED-DOOR INQUIRY INTO THE WORLD PLAZA DISASTER EXPECTED TO WRAP HEARINGS UP THIS WEEK... AND A REPORT TO BE PUBLISHED WITHIN WEEKS.
...FIELD AGENT HARDY, IN YOUR DEPOSITION YOU STATED THAT YOU AND FIELD AGENT JAY KELLY BECAME SEPARATED SOON AFTER ENTERING THE BUBBLEVERSE.
FBP
INQUIRY COMMISSION
NO ADMITTANCE
YES, THAT IS CORRECT, SIR.

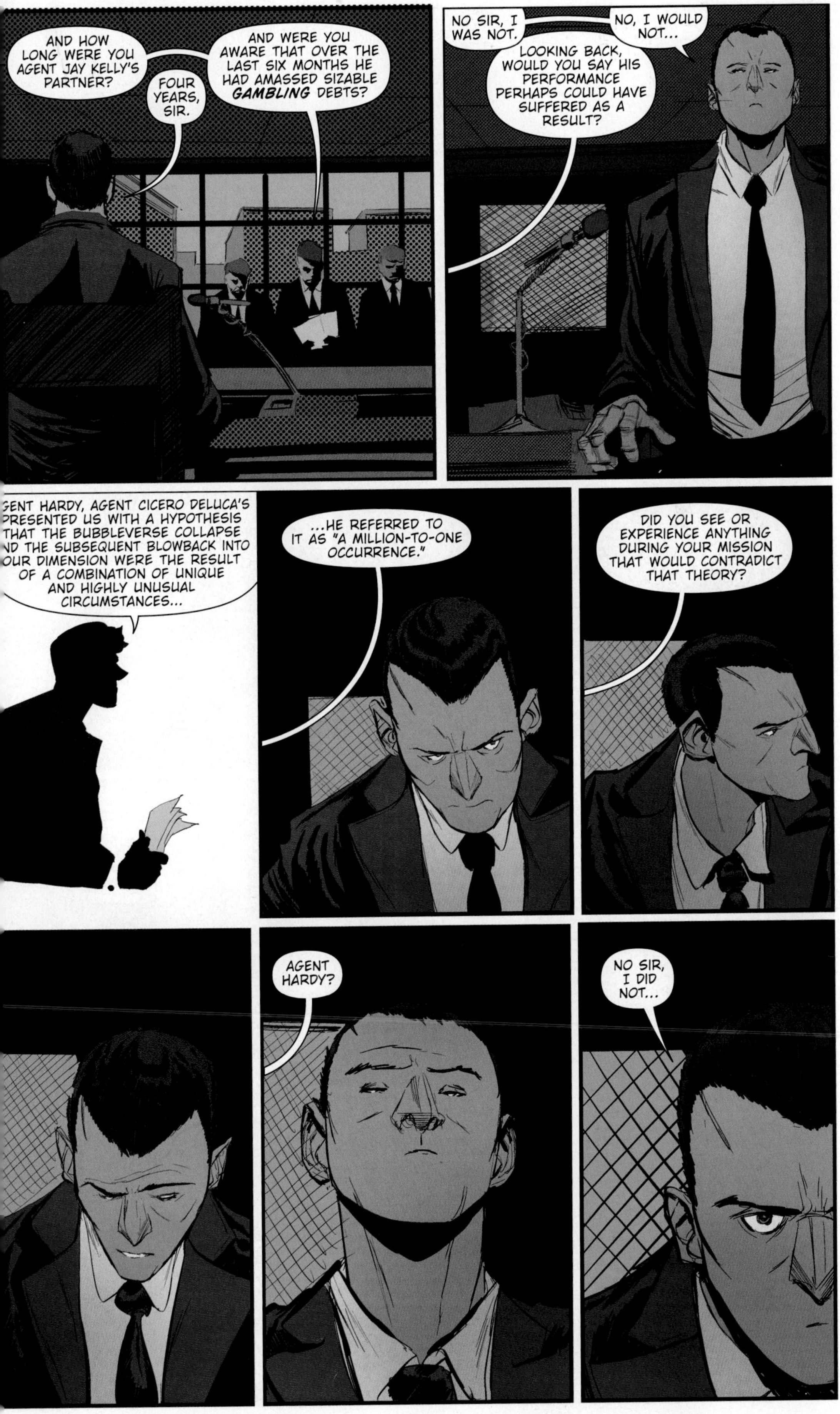
AND HOW LONG WERE YOU AGENT JAY KELLY'S PARTNER?
FOUR YEARS, SIR.
AND WERE YOU AWARE THAT OVER THE LAST SIX MONTHS HE HAD AMASSED SIZABLE GAMBLING DEBTS?
NO SIR, I WAS NOT.
LOOKING BACK, WOULD YOU SAY HIS PERFORMANCE PERHAPS COULD HAVE SUFFERED AS A RESULT?
NO, I WOULD NOT...
GENT HARDY, AGENT CICERO DELUCA'S RESENTED US WITH A HYPOTHESIS THAT THE BUBBLEVERSE COLLAPSE ND THE SUBSEQUENT BLOWBACK INTO UR DIMENSION WERE THE RESULT OF A COMBINATION OF UNIQUE AND HIGHLY UNUSUAL CIRCUMSTANCES...
...HE REFERRED TO IT AS "A MILLION-TO-ONE OCCURRENCE."
DID YOU SEE OR EXPERIENCE ANYTHING DURING YOUR MISSION THAT WOULD CONTRADICT THAT THEORY?
AGENT HARDY?
NO SIR, I DID NOT...

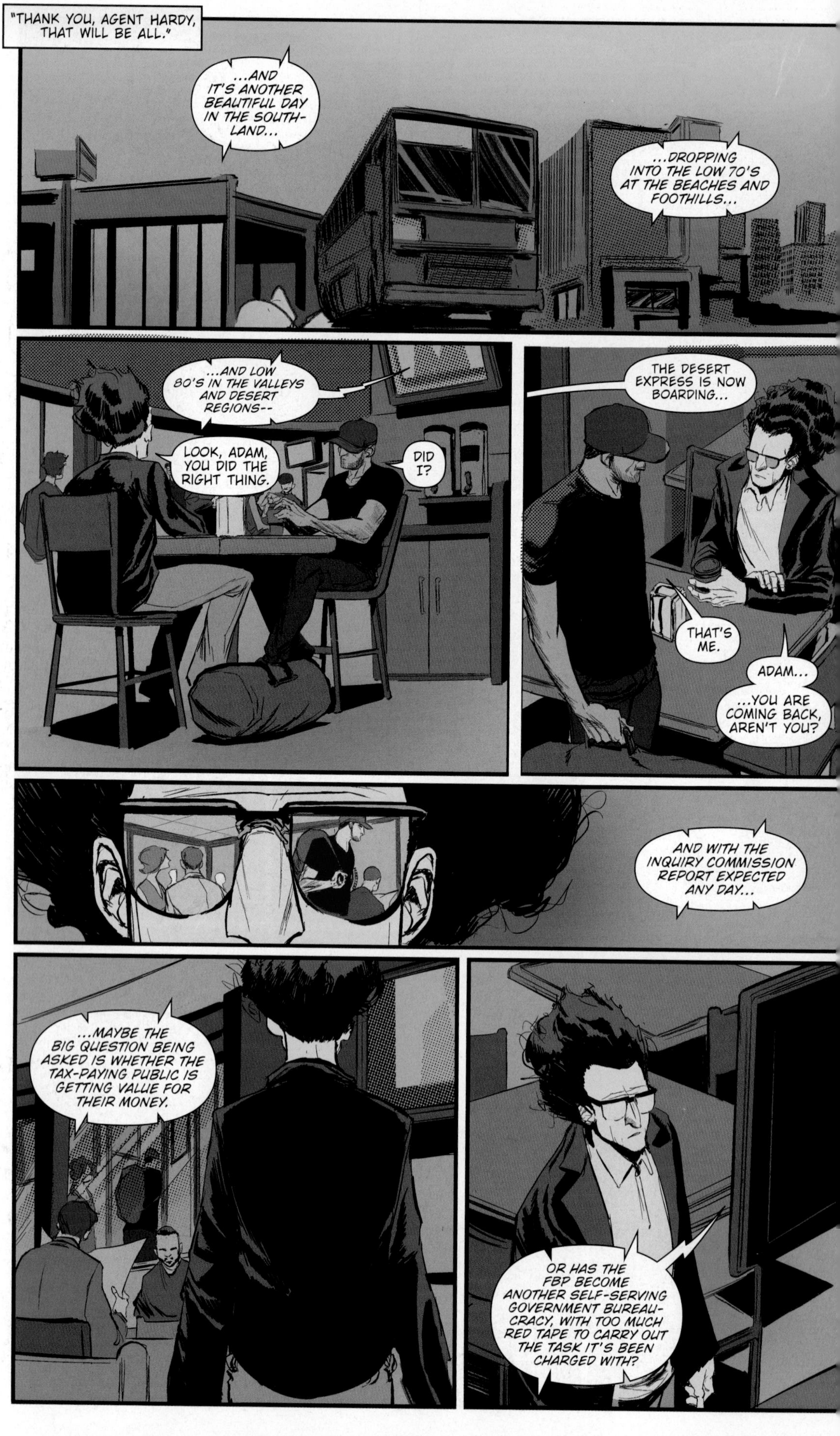
"THANK YOU, AGENT HARDY, THAT WILL BE ALL."
...AND IT'S ANOTHER BEAUTIFUL DAY IN THE SOUTH-LAND...
...DROPPING INTO THE LOW 70'S AT THE BEACHES AND FOOTHILLS...
...AND LOW 80'S IN THE VALLEYS AND DESERT REGIONS--
LOOK, ADAM, YOU DID THE RIGHT THING.
DID I?
THE DESERT EXPRESS IS NOW BOARDING...
THAT'S ME.
ADAM...
...YOU ARE COMING BACK, AREN'T YOU?
AND WITH THE INQUIRY COMMISSION REPORT EXPECTED ANY DAY...
...MAYBE THE BIG QUESTION BEING ASKED IS WHETHER THE TAX-PAYING PUBLIC IS GETTING VALUE FOR THEIR MONEY.
OR HAS THE FBP BECOME ANOTHER SELF-SERVING GOVERNMENT BUREAU-CRACY, WITH TOO MUCH RED TAPE TO CARRY OUT THE TASK IT'S BEEN CHARGED WITH?

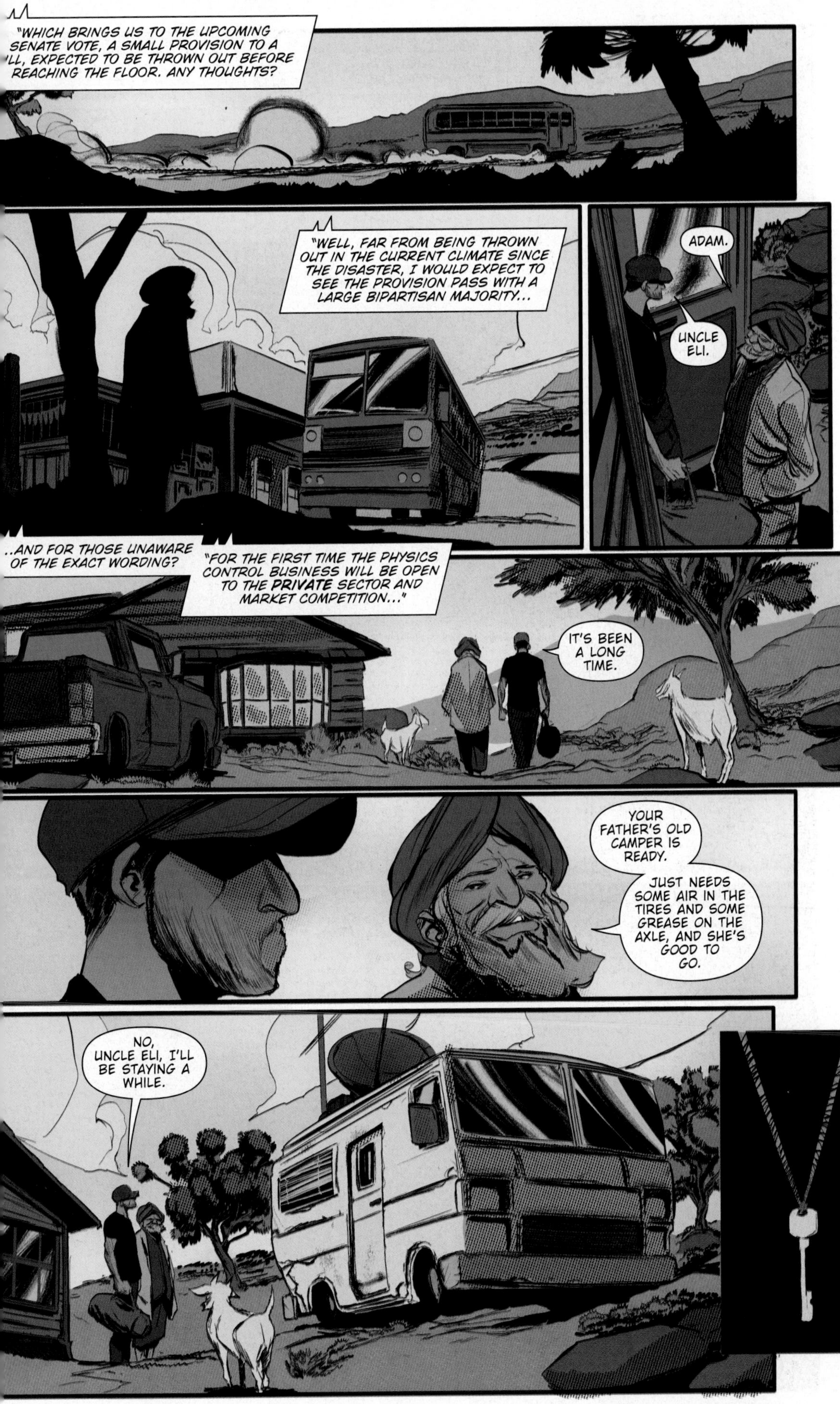
"WHICH BRINGS US TO THE UPCOMING SENATE VOTE, A SMALL PROVISION TO A 'LL, EXPECTED TO BE THROWN OUT BEFORE REACHING THE FLOOR. ANY THOUGHTS?
"WELL, FAR FROM BEING THROWN OUT IN THE CURRENT CLIMATE SINCE THE DISASTER, I WOULD EXPECT TO SEE THE PROVISION PASS WITH A LARGE BIPARTISAN MAJORITY...
ADAM.
UNCLE ELI.
..AND FOR THOSE UNAWARE OF THE EXACT WORDING?
"FOR THE FIRST TIME THE PHYSICS CONTROL BUSINESS WILL BE OPEN TO THE PRIVATE SECTOR AND MARKET COMPETITION..."
IT'S BEEN A LONG TIME.
YOUR FATHER'S OLD CAMPER IS READY.
JUST NEEDS SOME AIR IN THE TIRES AND SOME GREASE ON THE AXLE, AND SHE'S GOOD TO GO.
NO, UNCLE ELI, I'LL BE STAYING A WHILE.

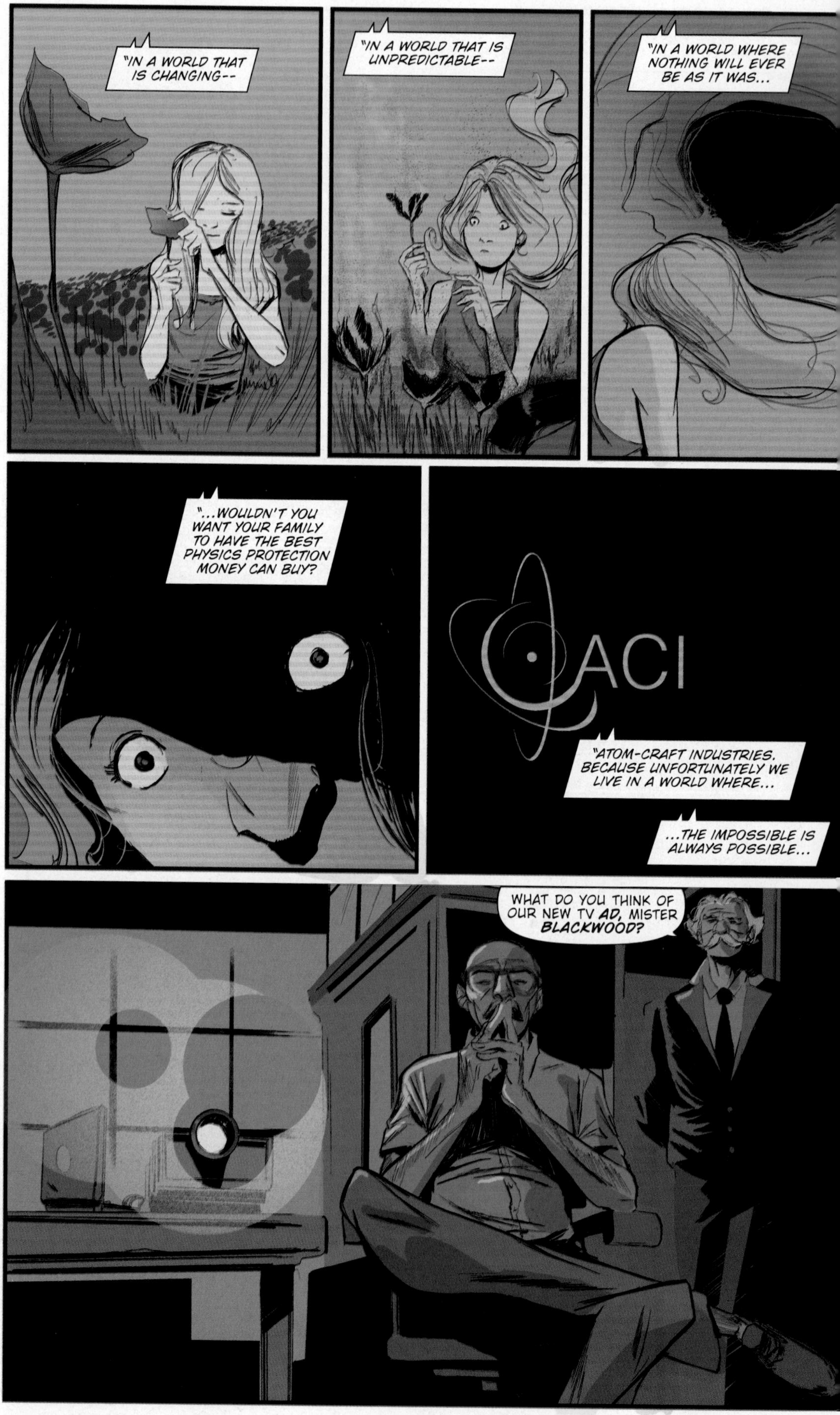
"IN A WORLD THAT IS CHANGING--
"IN A WORLD THAT IS UNPREDICTABLE--
"IN A WORLD WHERE NOTHING WILL EVER BE AS IT WAS...
"...WOULDN'T YOU WANT YOUR FAMILY TO HAVE THE BEST PHYSICS PROTECTION MONEY CAN BUY?
ACI
"ATOM-CRAFT INDUSTRIES. BECAUSE UNFORTUNATELY WE LIVE IN A WORLD WHERE...
...THE IMPOSSIBLE IS ALWAYS POSSIBLE...
WHAT DO YOU THINK OF OUR NEW TV AD, MISTER BLACKWOOD?

Things That Have Been

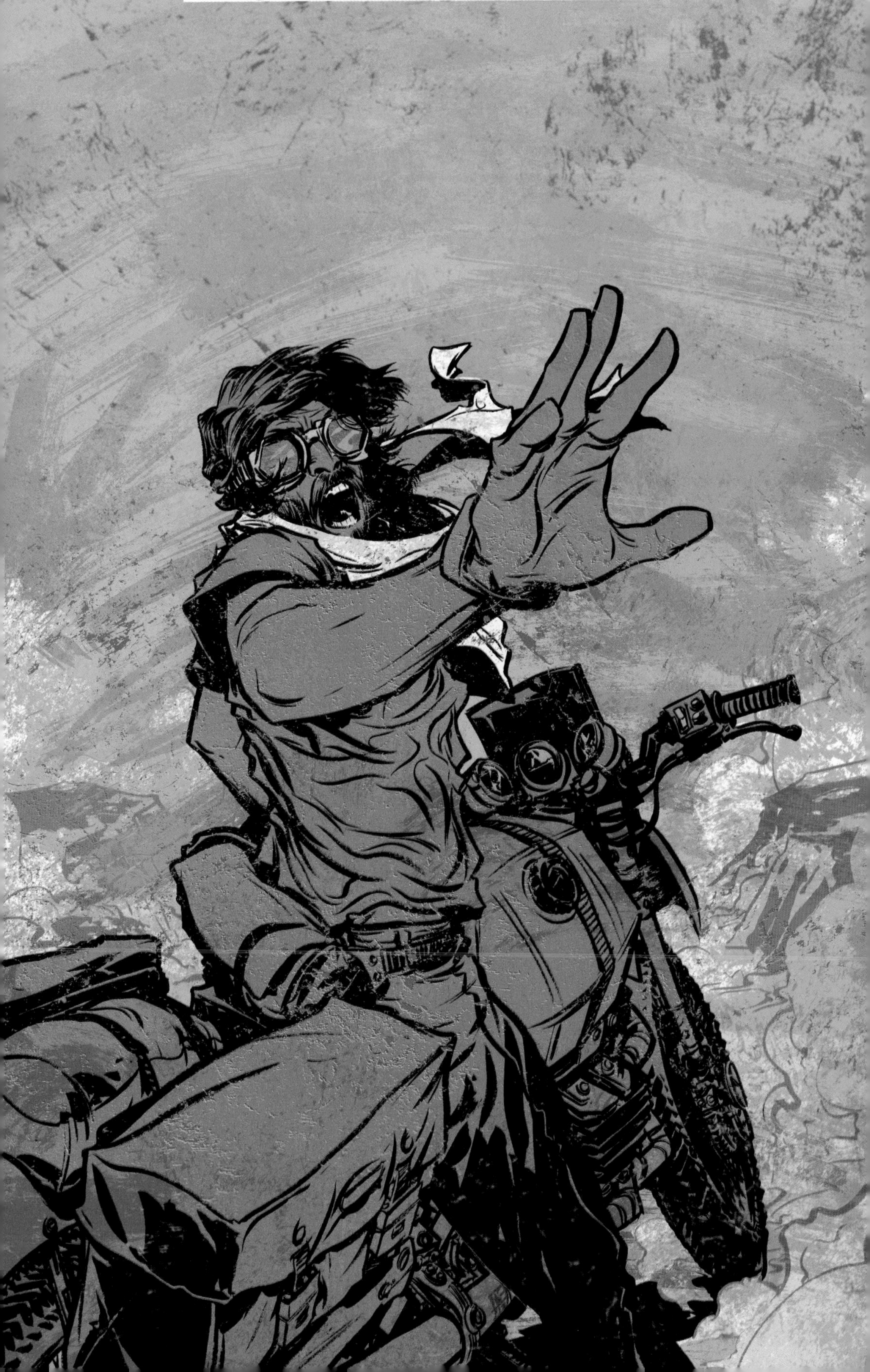

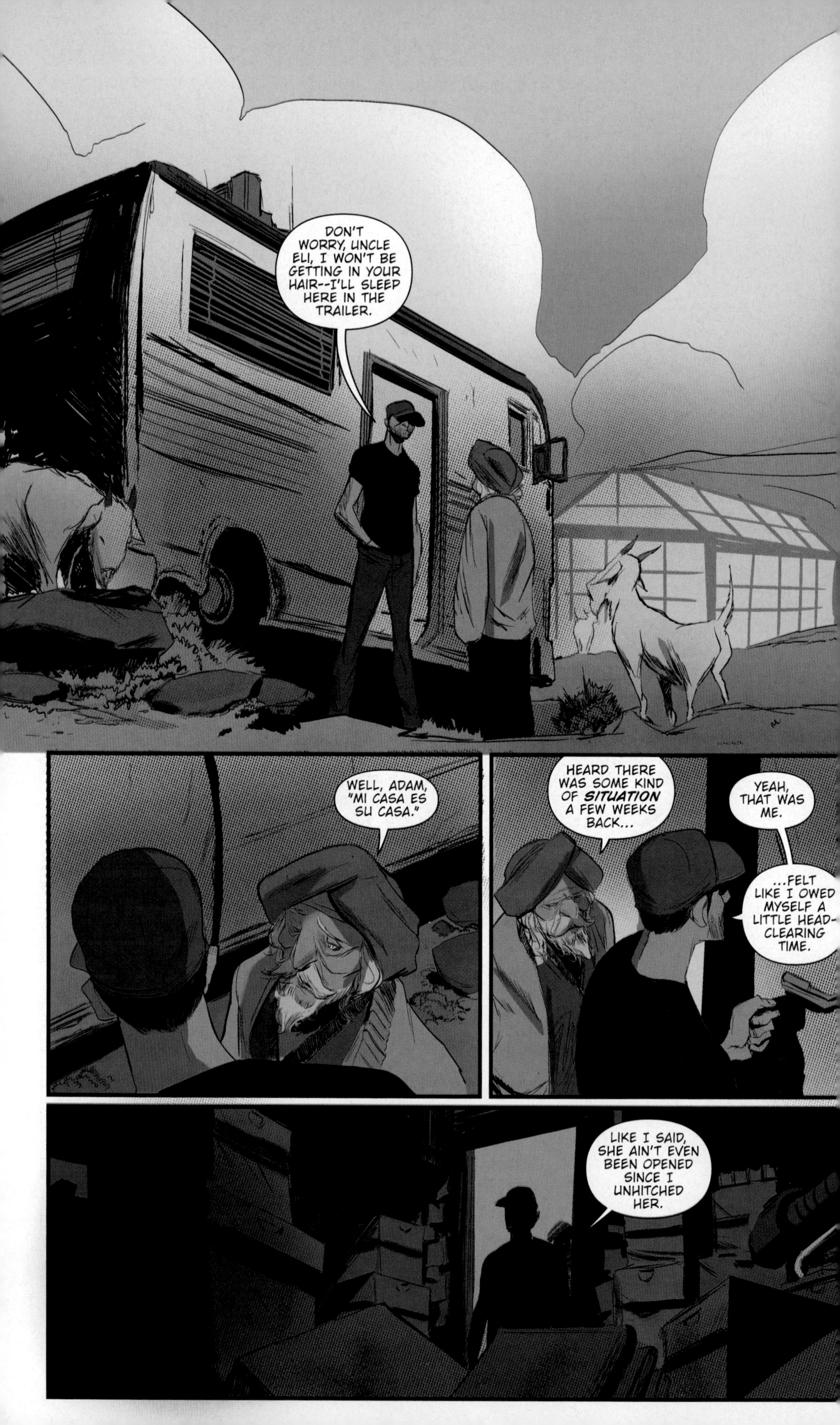
DON'T WORRY, UNCLE ELI, I WON'T BE GETTING IN YOUR HAIR--I'LL SLEEP HERE IN THE TRAILER.
WELL, ADAM, "MI CASA ES SU CASA."
HEARD THERE WAS SOME KIND OF *SITUATION* A FEW WEEKS BACK...
YEAH, THAT WAS ME.
...FELT LIKE I OWED MYSELF A LITTLE HEAD-CLEARING TIME.
LIKE I SAID, SHE AIN'T EVEN BEEN OPENED SINCE I UNHITCHED HER.

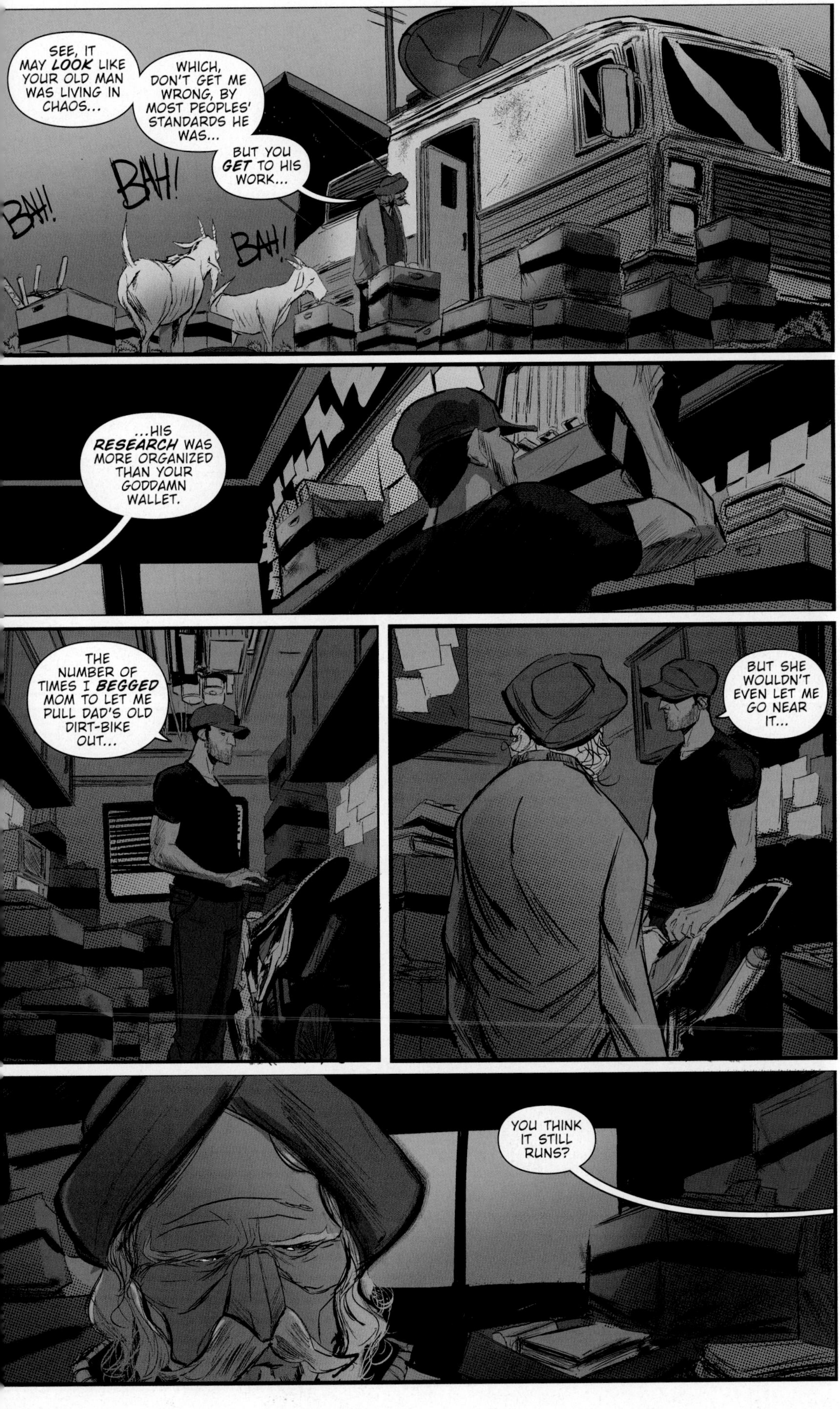
SEE, IT MAY LOOK LIKE YOUR OLD MAN WAS LIVING IN CHAOS...
WHICH, DON'T GET ME WRONG, BY MOST PEOPLES' STANDARDS HE WAS...
BUT YOU GET TO HIS WORK...
BAH!
BAH!
BAH!
...HIS RESEARCH WAS MORE ORGANIZED THAN YOUR GODDAMN WALLET.
THE NUMBER OF TIMES I BEGGED MOM TO LET ME PULL DAD'S OLD DIRT-BIKE OUT...
BUT SHE WOULDN'T EVEN LET ME GO NEAR IT...
YOU THINK IT STILL RUNS?

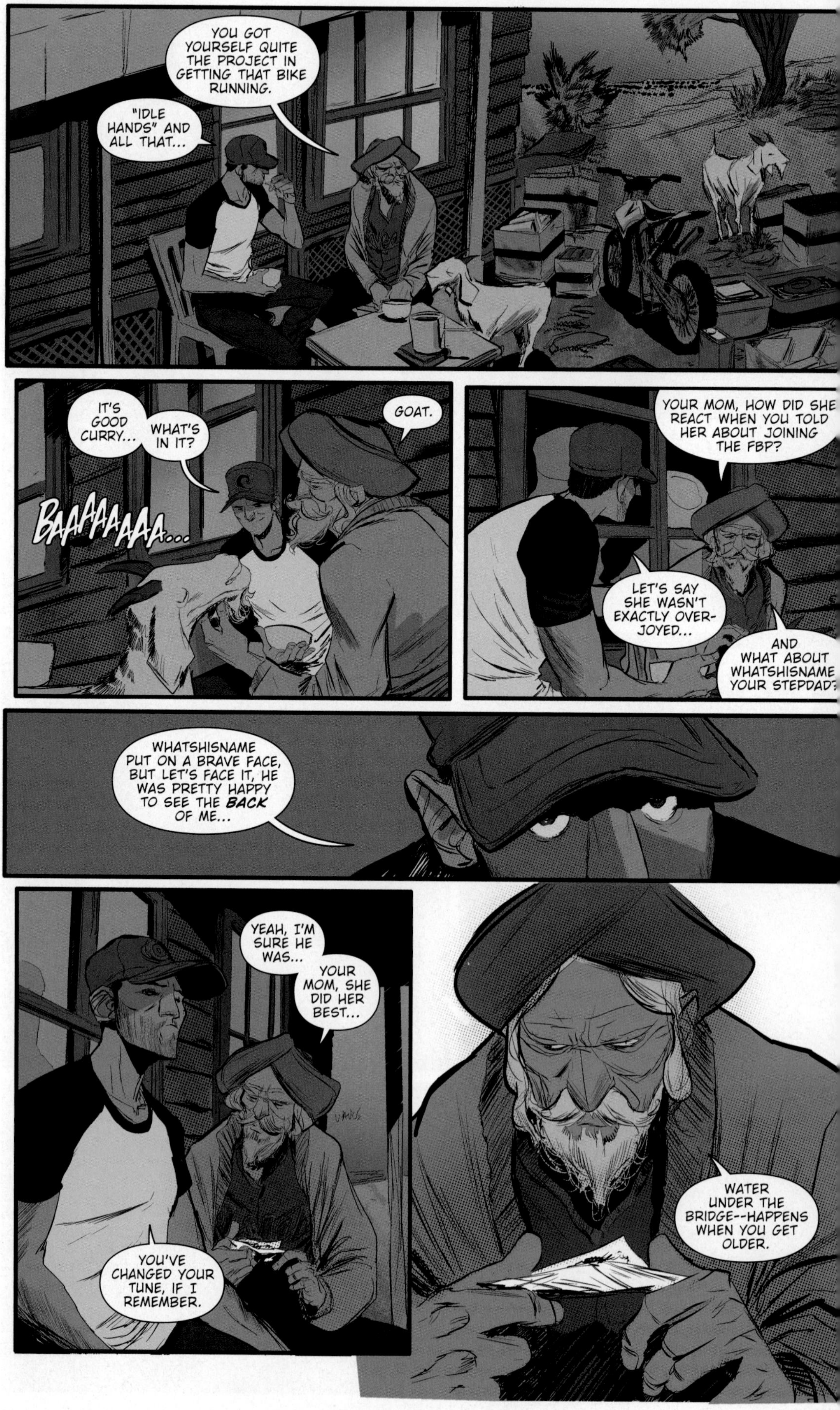
"IDLE HANDS" AND ALL THAT...
YOU GOT YOURSELF QUITE THE PROJECT IN GETTING THAT BIKE RUNNING.
IT'S GOOD CURRY...
WHAT'S IN IT?
GOAT.
BAAAAAAAA...
YOUR MOM, HOW DID SHE REACT WHEN YOU TOLD HER ABOUT JOINING THE FBP?
LET'S SAY SHE WASN'T EXACTLY OVER-JOYED...
AND WHAT ABOUT WHATSHISNAME YOUR STEPDAD?
WHATSHISNAME PUT ON A BRAVE FACE, BUT LET'S FACE IT, HE WAS PRETTY HAPPY TO SEE THE ***BACK*** OF ME...
YEAH, I'M SURE HE WAS...
YOUR MOM, SHE DID HER BEST...
YOU'VE CHANGED YOUR TUNE, IF I REMEMBER.
WATER UNDER THE BRIDGE--HAPPENS WHEN YOU GET OLDER.

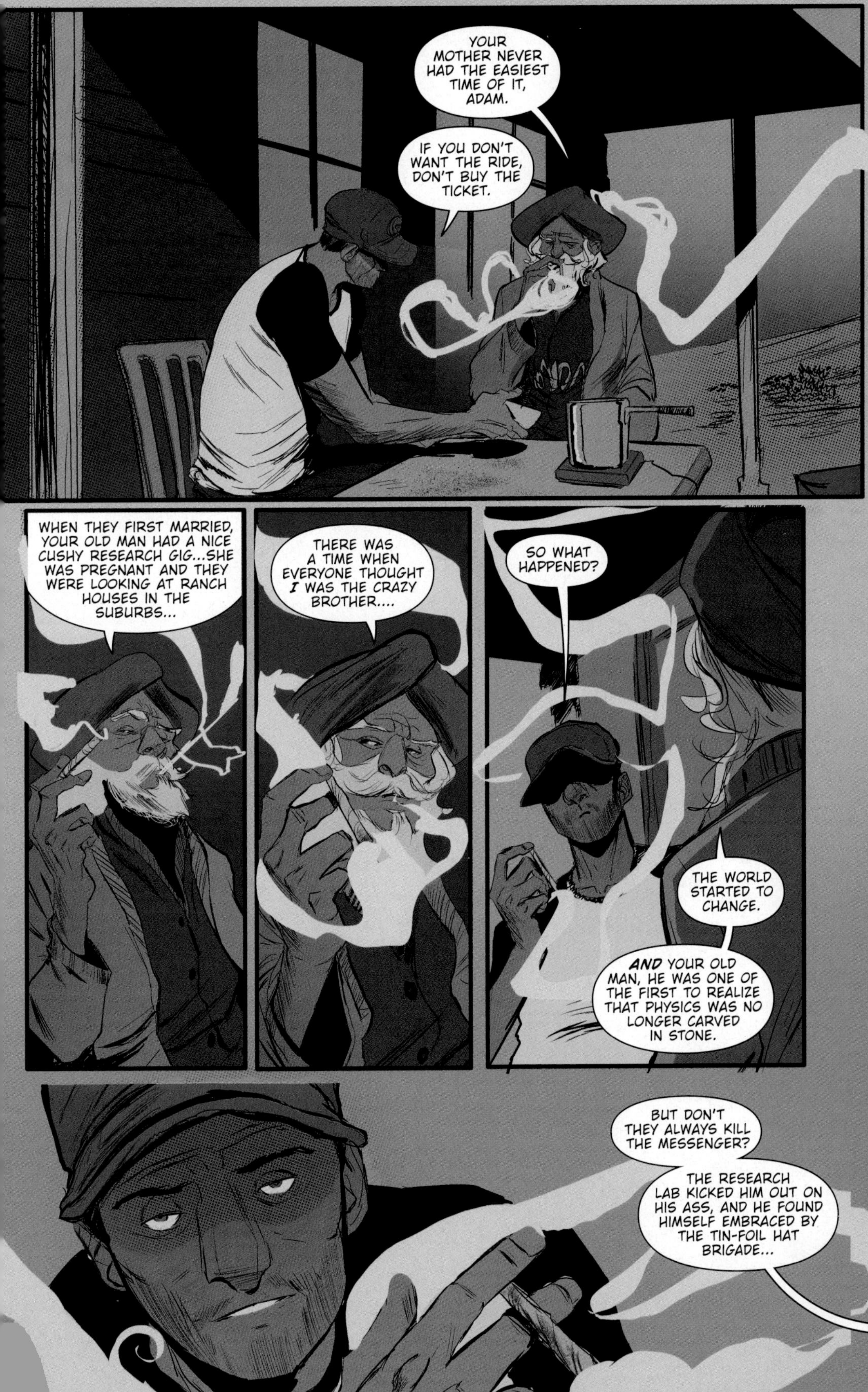
YOUR MOTHER NEVER HAD THE EASIEST TIME OF IT, ADAM.
IF YOU DON'T WANT THE RIDE, DON'T BUY THE TICKET.
WHEN THEY FIRST MARRIED, YOUR OLD MAN HAD A NICE CUSHY RESEARCH GIG...SHE WAS PREGNANT AND THEY WERE LOOKING AT RANCH HOUSES IN THE SUBURBS...
THERE WAS A TIME WHEN EVERYONE THOUGHT *I* WAS THE CRAZY BROTHER....
SO WHAT HAPPENED?
THE WORLD STARTED TO CHANGE.
AND YOUR OLD MAN, HE WAS ONE OF THE FIRST TO REALIZE THAT PHYSICS WAS NO LONGER CARVED IN STONE.
BUT DON'T THEY ALWAYS KILL THE MESSENGER?
THE RESEARCH LAB KICKED HIM OUT ON HIS ASS, AND HE FOUND HIMSELF EMBRACED BY THE TIN-FOIL HAT BRIGADE...

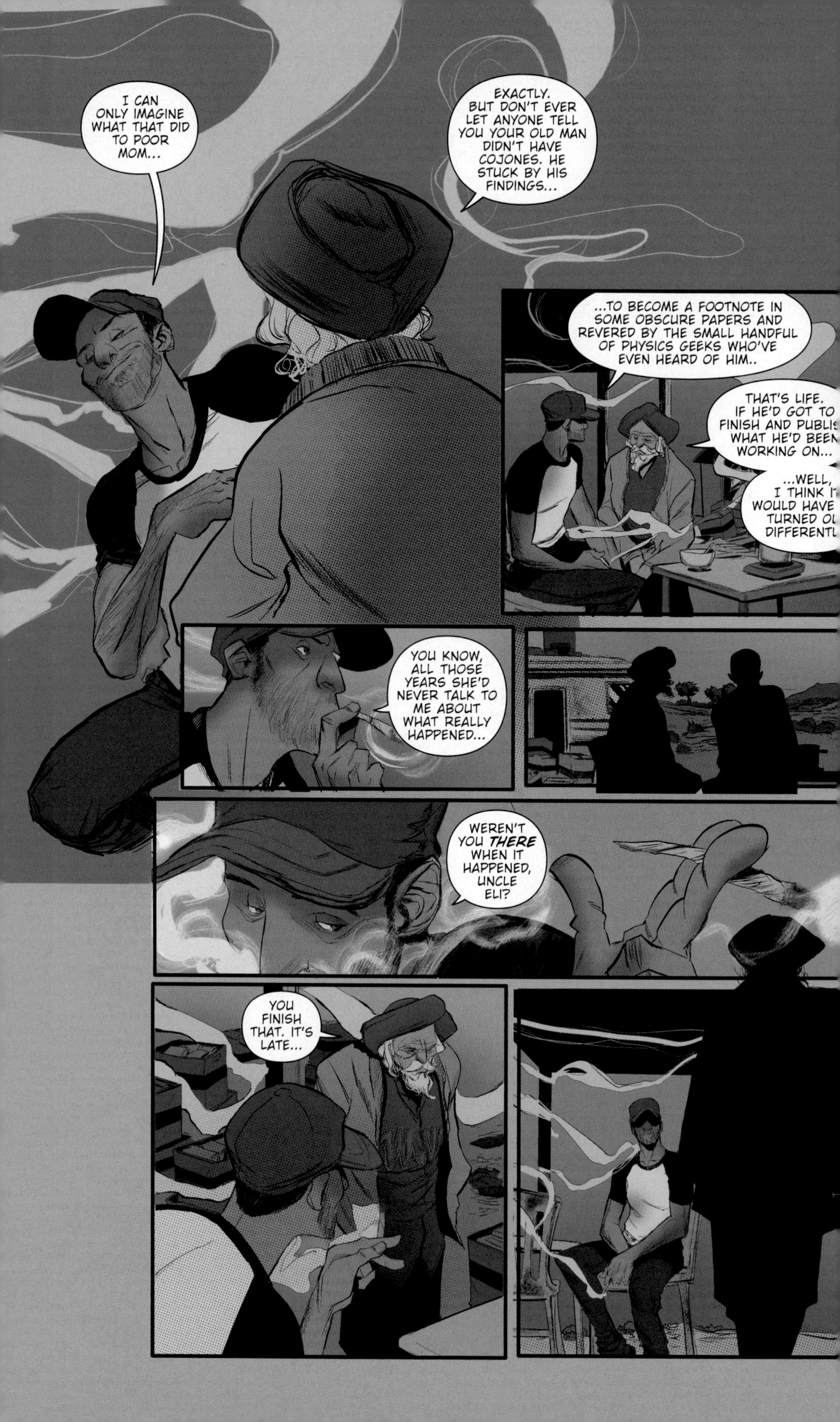
I CAN ONLY IMAGINE WHAT THAT DID TO POOR MOM...
EXACTLY. BUT DON'T EVER LET ANYONE TELL YOU YOUR OLD MAN DIDN'T HAVE COJONES. HE STUCK BY HIS FINDINGS...
...TO BECOME A FOOTNOTE IN SOME OBSCURE PAPERS AND REVERED BY THE SMALL HANDFUL OF PHYSICS GEEKS WHO'VE EVEN HEARD OF HIM..
THAT'S LIFE. IF HE'D GOT TO FINISH AND PUBLIS WHAT HE'D BEEN WORKING ON...
...WELL, I THINK I WOULD HAVE TURNED O DIFFERENTL
YOU KNOW, ALL THOSE YEARS SHE'D NEVER TALK TO ME ABOUT WHAT REALLY HAPPENED...
WEREN'T YOU *THERE* WHEN IT HAPPENED, UNCLE ELI?
YOU FINISH THAT. IT'S LATE...

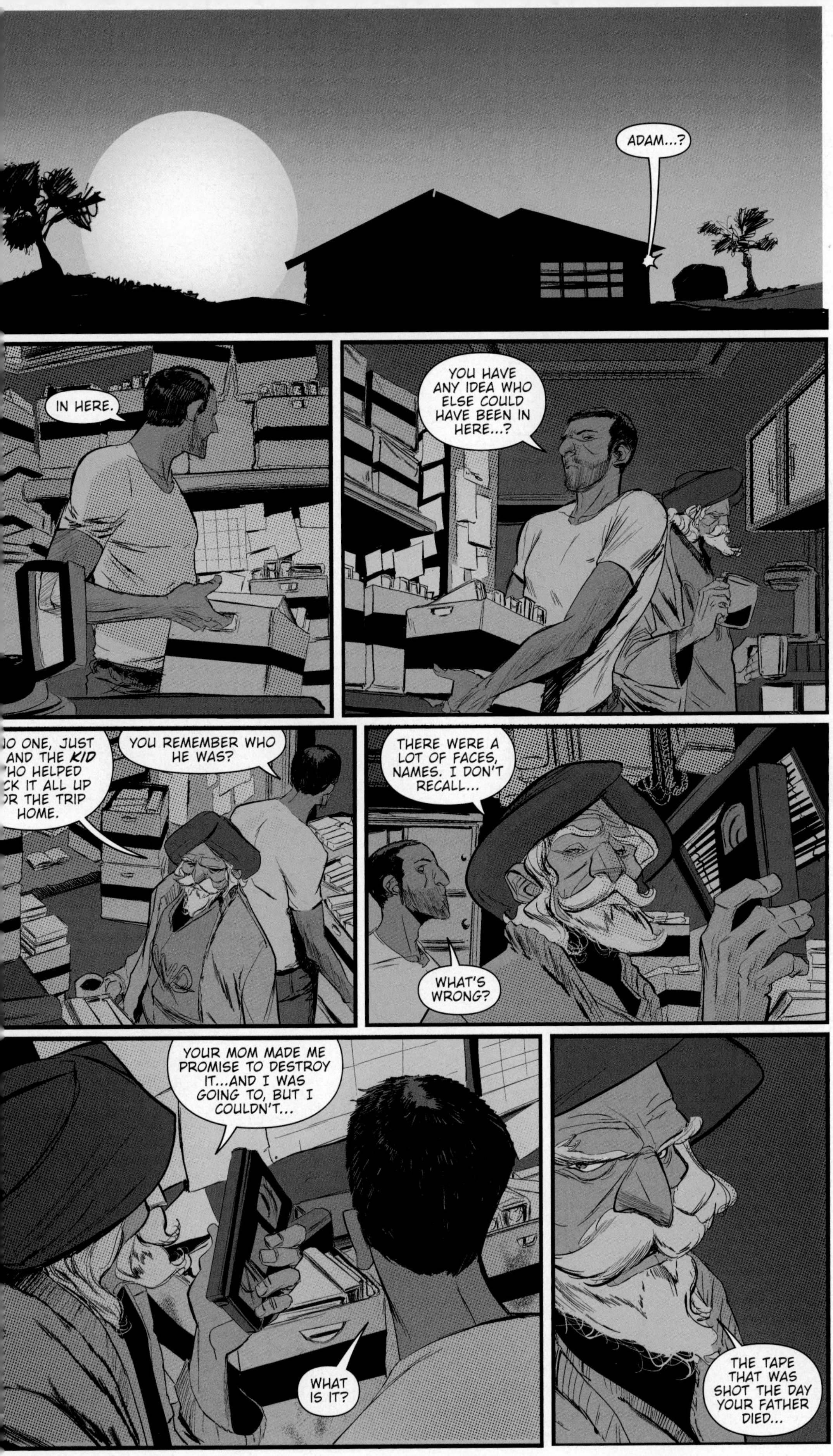
ADAM...?
IN HERE.
YOU HAVE ANY IDEA WHO ELSE COULD HAVE BEEN IN HERE...?
NO ONE, JUST AND THE KID HO HELPED CK IT ALL UP OR THE TRIP HOME.
YOU REMEMBER WHO HE WAS?
THERE WERE A LOT OF FACES, NAMES. I DON'T RECALL...
WHAT'S WRONG?
YOUR MOM MADE ME PROMISE TO DESTROY IT...AND I WAS GOING TO, BUT I COULDN'T...
WHAT IS IT?
THE TAPE THAT WAS SHOT THE DAY YOUR FATHER DIED...

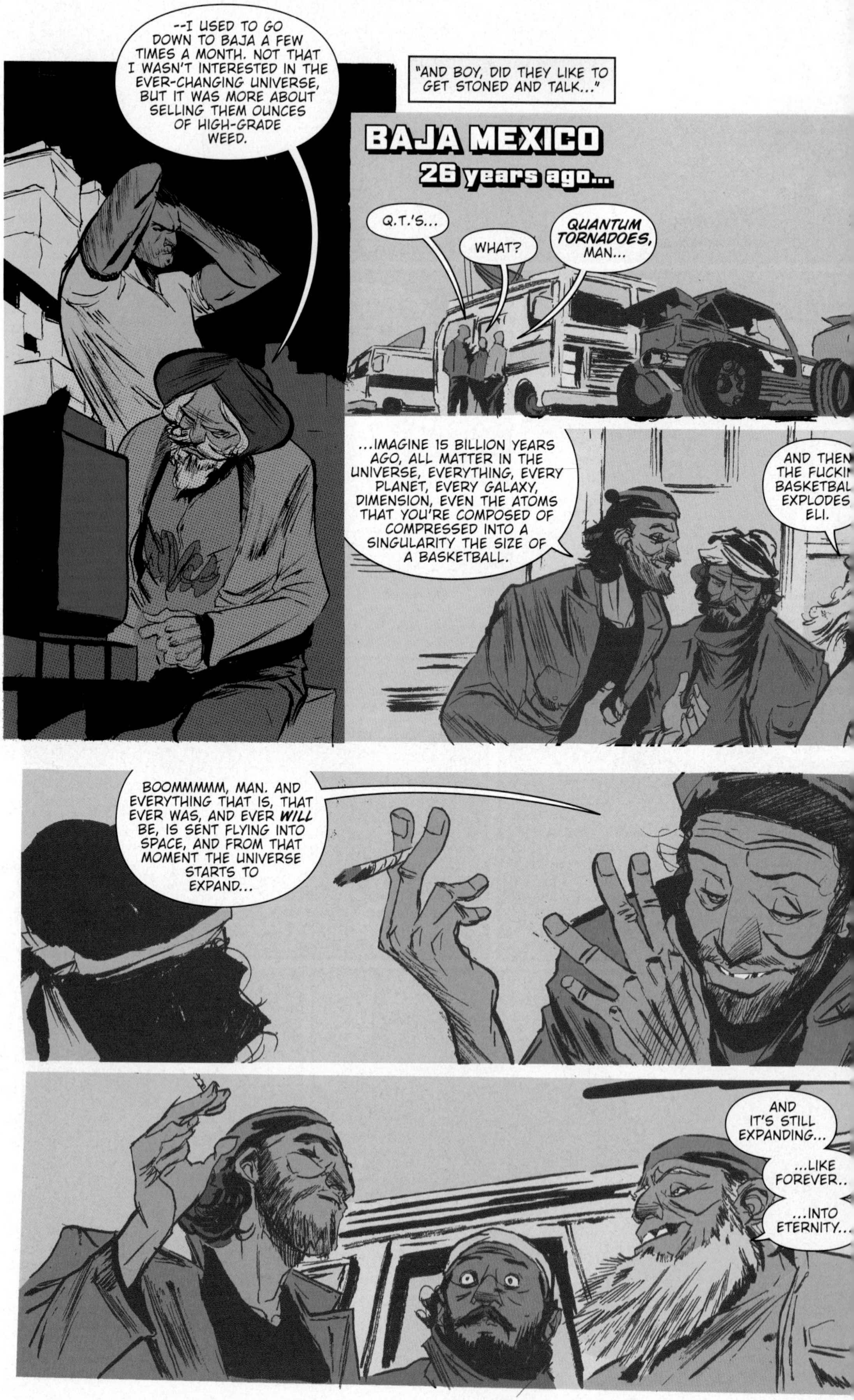
--I USED TO GO DOWN TO BAJA A FEW TIMES A MONTH. NOT THAT I WASN'T INTERESTED IN THE EVER-CHANGING UNIVERSE, BUT IT WAS MORE ABOUT SELLING THEM OUNCES OF HIGH-GRADE WEED.
"AND BOY, DID THEY LIKE TO GET STONED AND TALK..."
BAJA MEXICO
26 years ago...
Q.T.'S...
WHAT?
QUANTUM TORNADOES, MAN...
...IMAGINE 15 BILLION YEARS AGO, ALL MATTER IN THE UNIVERSE, EVERYTHING, EVERY PLANET, EVERY GALAXY, DIMENSION, EVEN THE ATOMS THAT YOU'RE COMPOSED OF COMPRESSED INTO A SINGULARITY THE SIZE OF A BASKETBALL.
AND THEN THE FUCKIN BASKETBAL EXPLODES ELI.
BOOMMMMM, MAN. AND EVERYTHING THAT IS, THAT EVER WAS, AND EVER WILL BE, IS SENT FLYING INTO SPACE, AND FROM THAT MOMENT THE UNIVERSE STARTS TO EXPAND...
AND IT'S STILL EXPANDING...
...LIKE FOREVER..
...INTO ETERNITY...

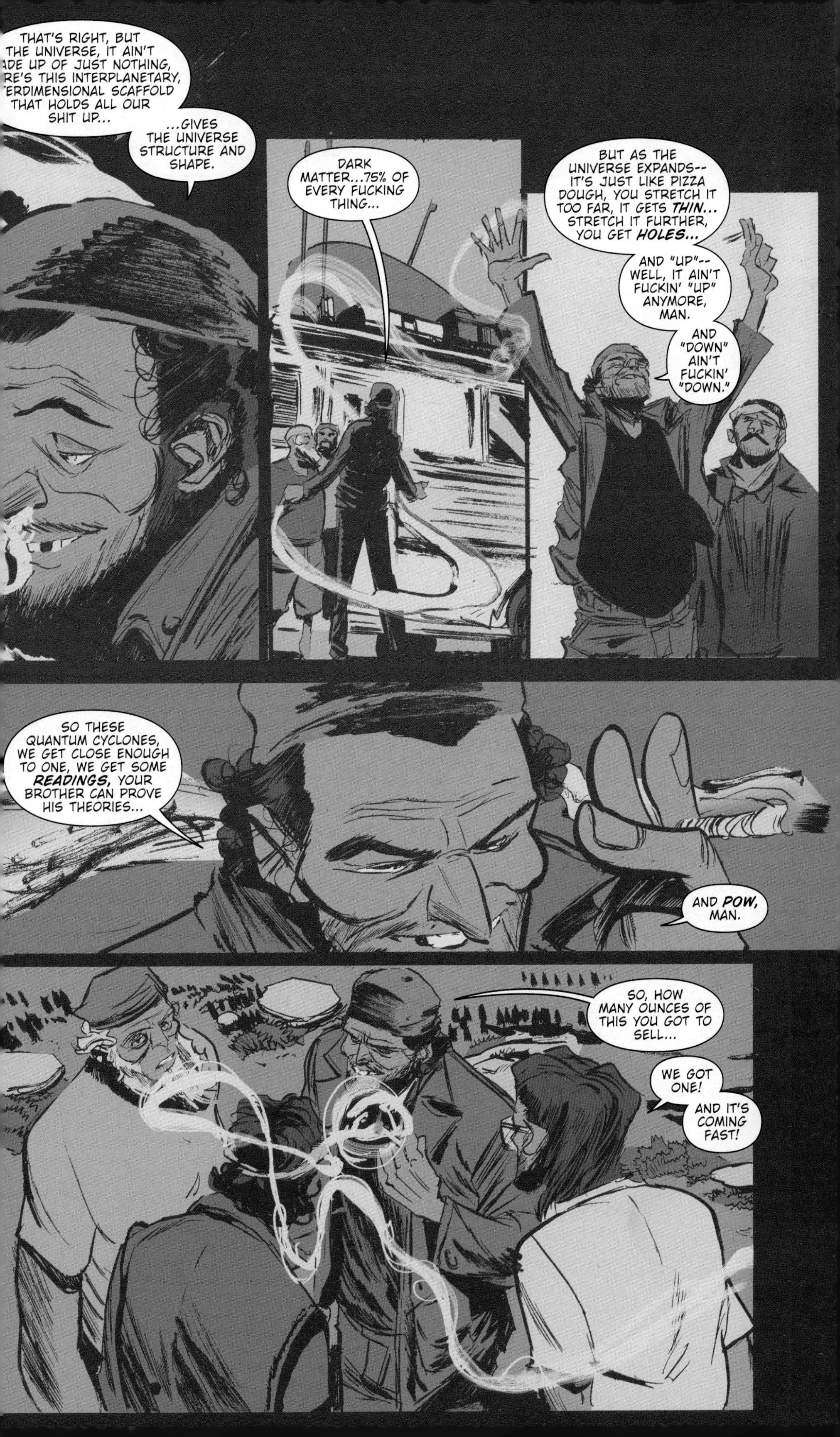
THAT'S RIGHT, BUT THE UNIVERSE, IT AIN'T ADE UP OF JUST NOTHING, RE'S THIS INTERPLANETARY, ERDIMENSIONAL SCAFFOLD THAT HOLDS ALL OUR SHIT UP...
...GIVES THE UNIVERSE STRUCTURE AND SHAPE.
DARK MATTER...75% OF EVERY FUCKING THING...
BUT AS THE UNIVERSE EXPANDS--IT'S JUST LIKE PIZZA DOUGH, YOU STRETCH IT TOO FAR, IT GETS THIN... STRETCH IT FURTHER, YOU GET HOLES...
AND "UP"--WELL, IT AIN'T FUCKIN' "UP" ANYMORE, MAN.
AND "DOWN" AIN'T FUCKIN' "DOWN."
SO THESE QUANTUM CYCLONES, WE GET CLOSE ENOUGH TO ONE, WE GET SOME READINGS, YOUR BROTHER CAN PROVE HIS THEORIES...
AND POW, MAN.
SO, HOW MANY OUNCES OF THIS YOU GOT TO SELL...
WE GOT ONE!
AND IT'S COMING FAST!

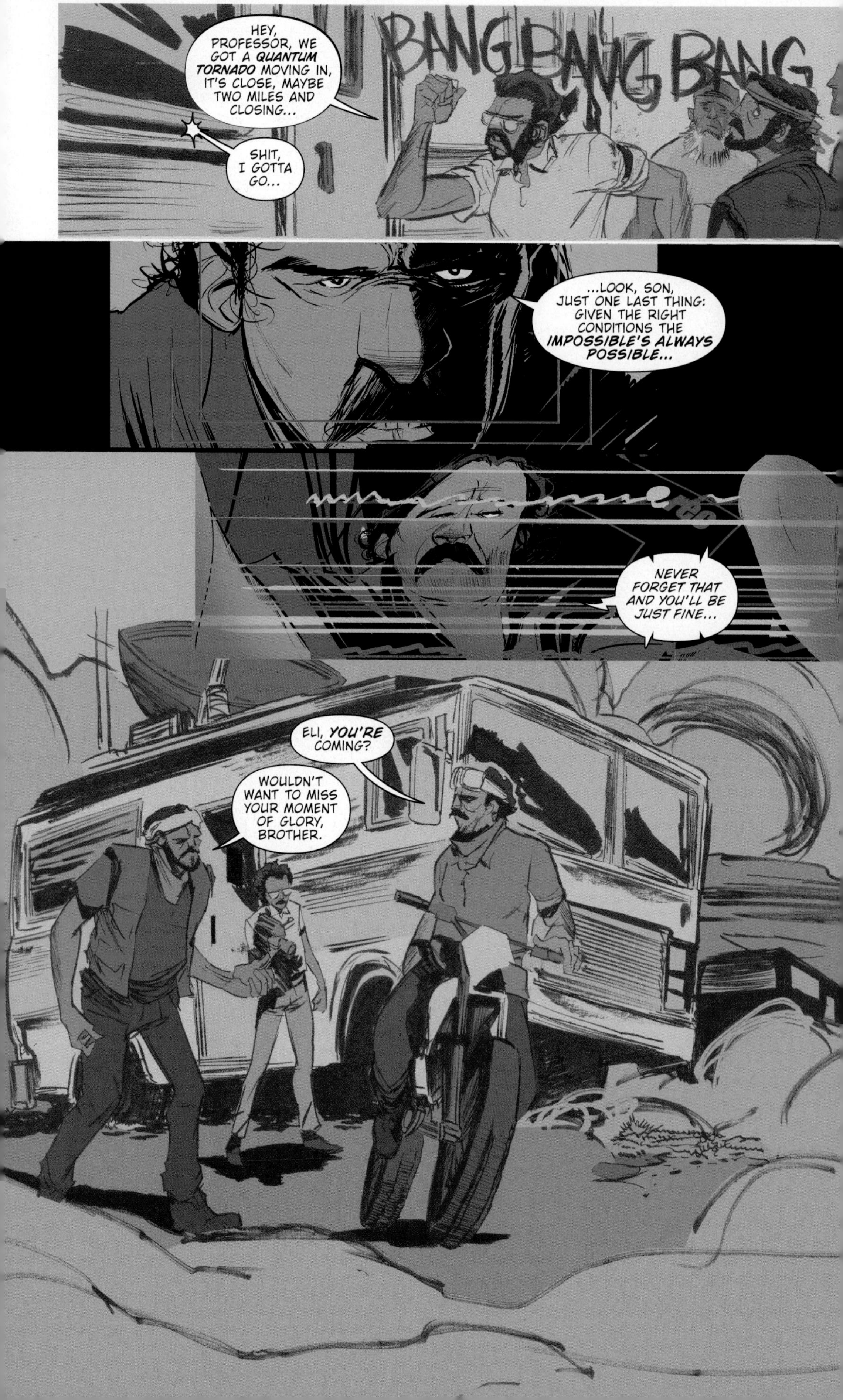
HEY, PROFESSOR, WE GOT A QUANTUM TORNADO MOVING IN, IT'S CLOSE, MAYBE TWO MILES AND CLOSING...
BANG BANG BANG
SHIT, I GOTTA GO...
...LOOK, SON, JUST ONE LAST THING: GIVEN THE RIGHT CONDITIONS THE IMPOSSIBLE'S ALWAYS POSSIBLE...
NEVER FORGET THAT AND YOU'LL BE JUST FINE...
ELI, YOU'RE COMING?
WOULDN'T WANT TO MISS YOUR MOMENT OF GLORY, BROTHER.

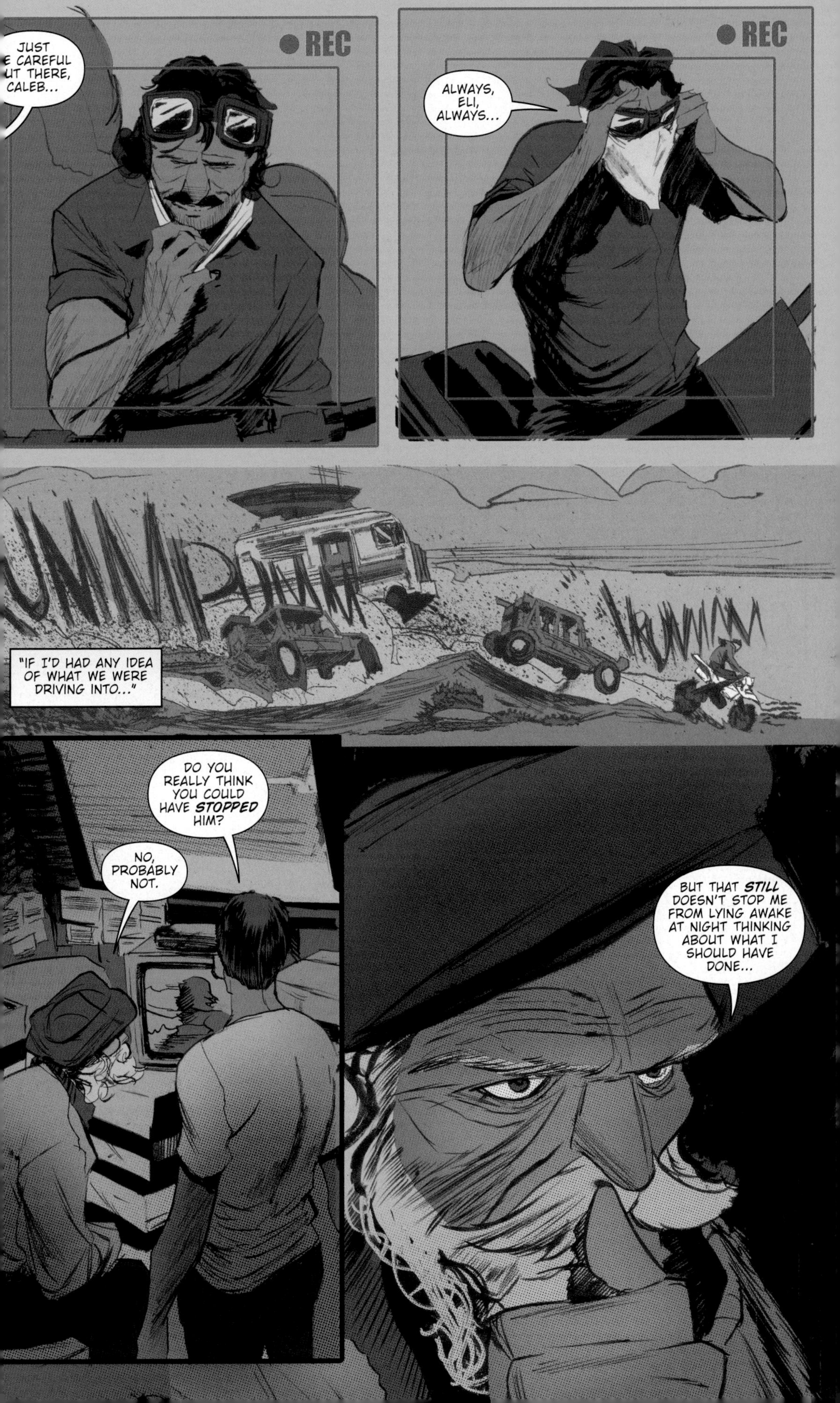

REC
JUST E CAREFUL UT THERE, CALEB...
REC
ALWAYS, ELI, ALWAYS...
"IF I'D HAD ANY IDEA OF WHAT WE WERE DRIVING INTO..."
DO YOU REALLY THINK YOU COULD HAVE STOPPED HIM?
NO, PROBABLY NOT.
BUT THAT STILL DOESN'T STOP ME FROM LYING AWAKE AT NIGHT THINKING ABOUT WHAT I SHOULD HAVE DONE...

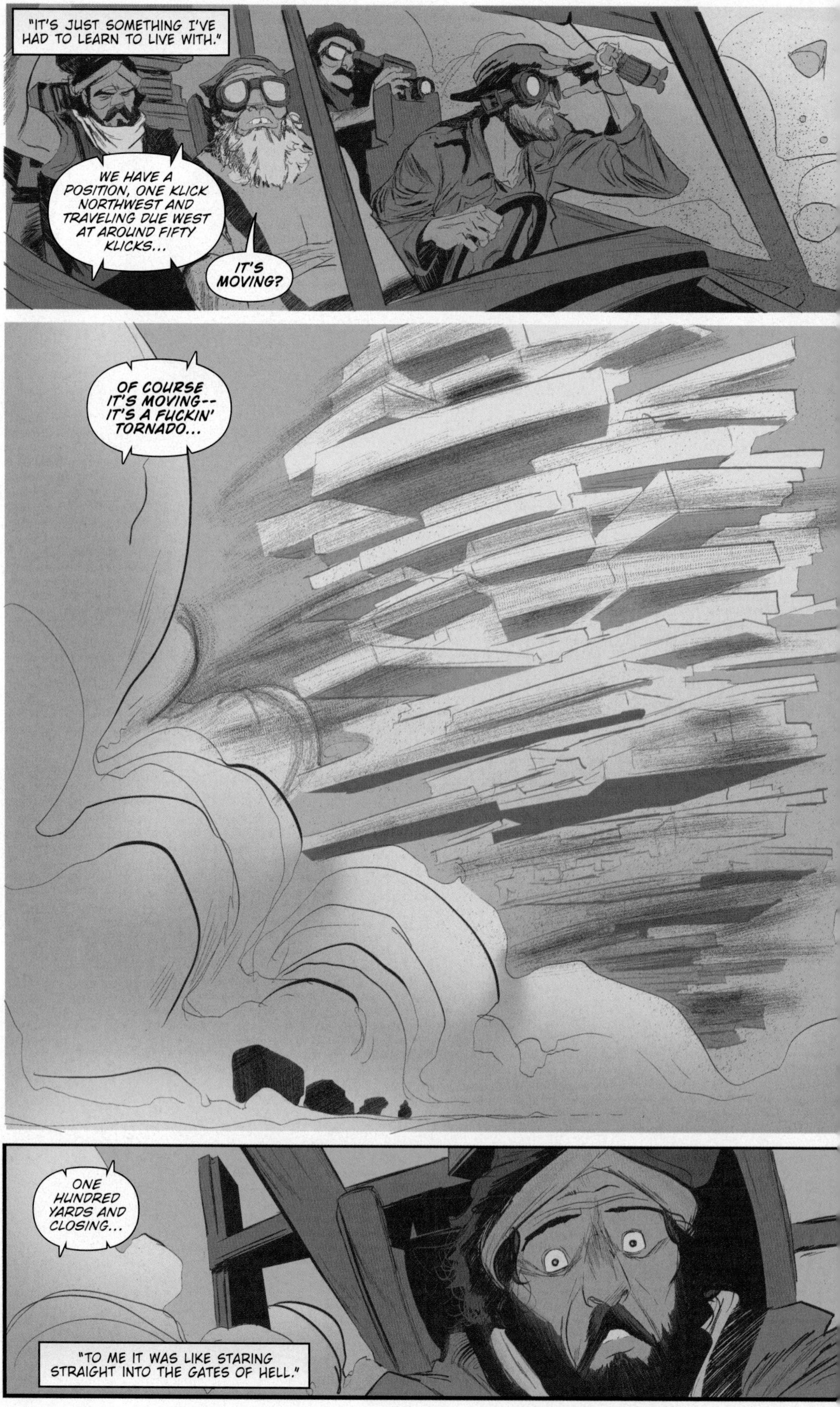
"IT'S JUST SOMETHING I'VE HAD TO LEARN TO LIVE WITH."
WE HAVE A POSITION, ONE KLICK NORTHWEST AND TRAVELING DUE WEST AT AROUND FIFTY KLICKS...
IT'S MOVING?
OF COURSE IT'S MOVING-- IT'S A FUCKIN' TORNADO...
ONE HUNDRED YARDS AND CLOSING...
"TO ME IT WAS LIKE STARING STRAIGHT INTO THE GATES OF HELL."

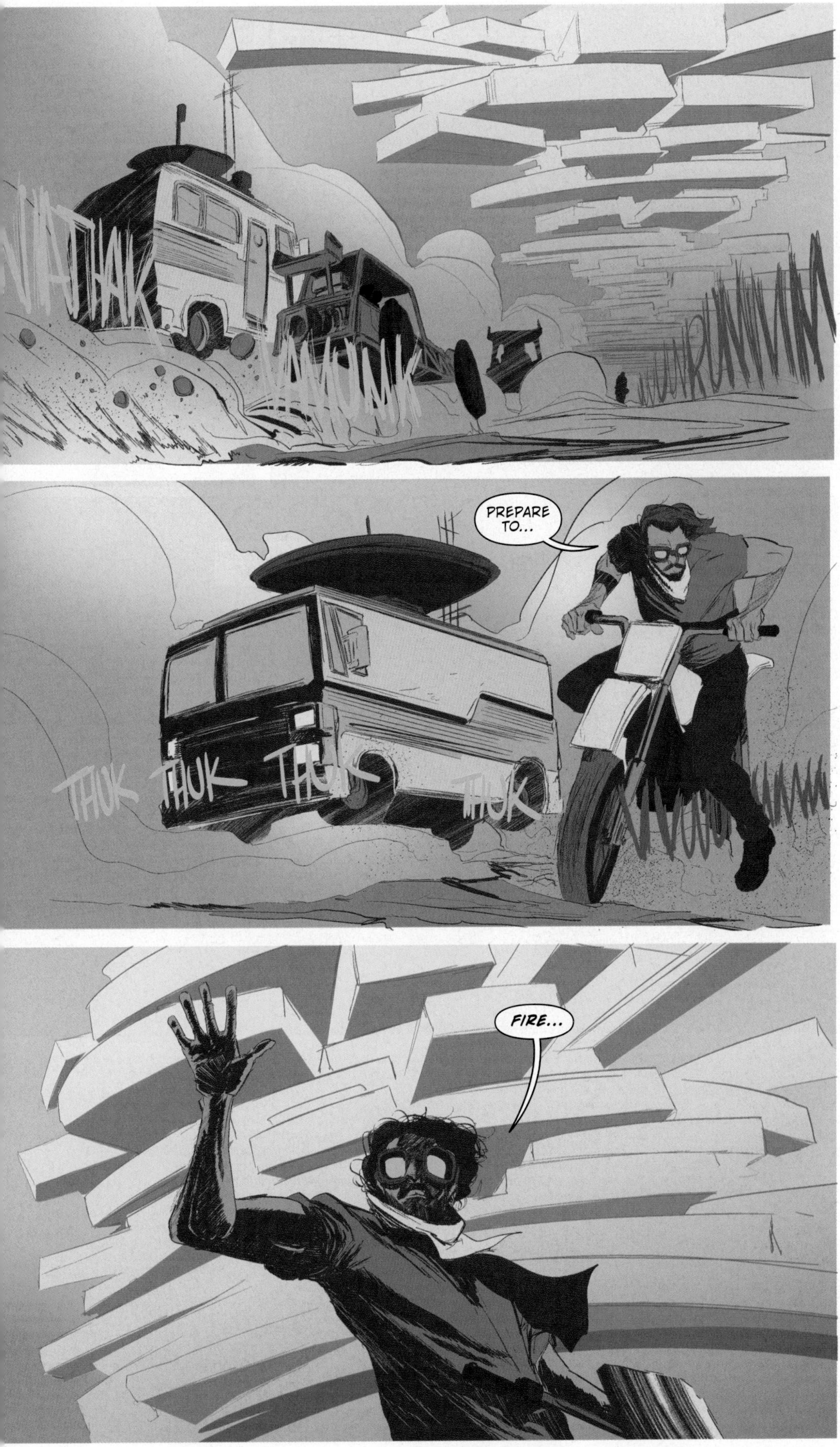
THAK
MMUNK
RUMMM
PREPARE TO...
THUK THUK THUK THUK
FIRE...

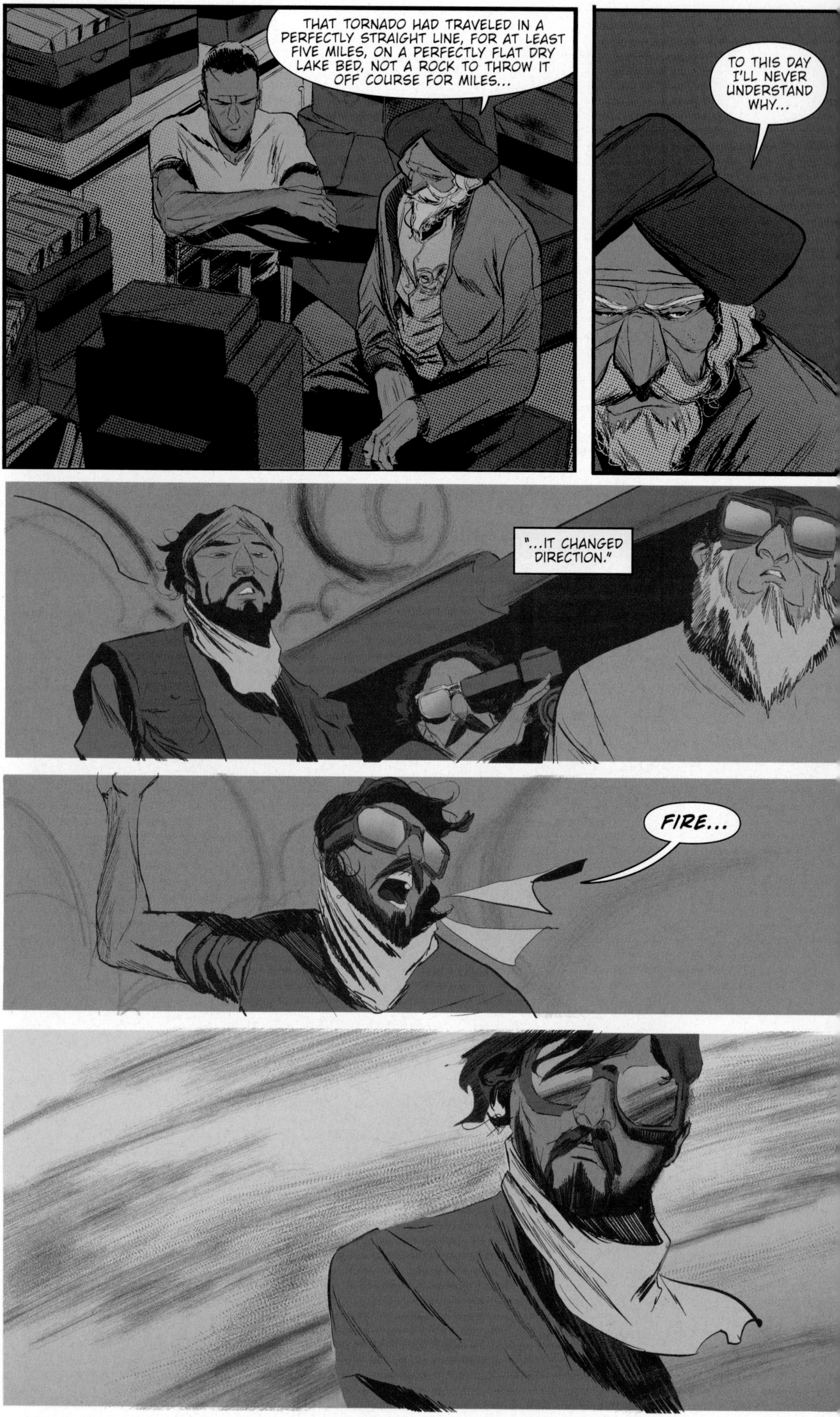
THAT TORNADO HAD TRAVELED IN A PERFECTLY STRAIGHT LINE, FOR AT LEAST FIVE MILES, ON A PERFECTLY FLAT DRY LAKE BED, NOT A ROCK TO THROW IT OFF COURSE FOR MILES...
TO THIS DAY I'LL NEVER UNDERSTAND WHY...
"...IT CHANGED DIRECTION."
FIRE...

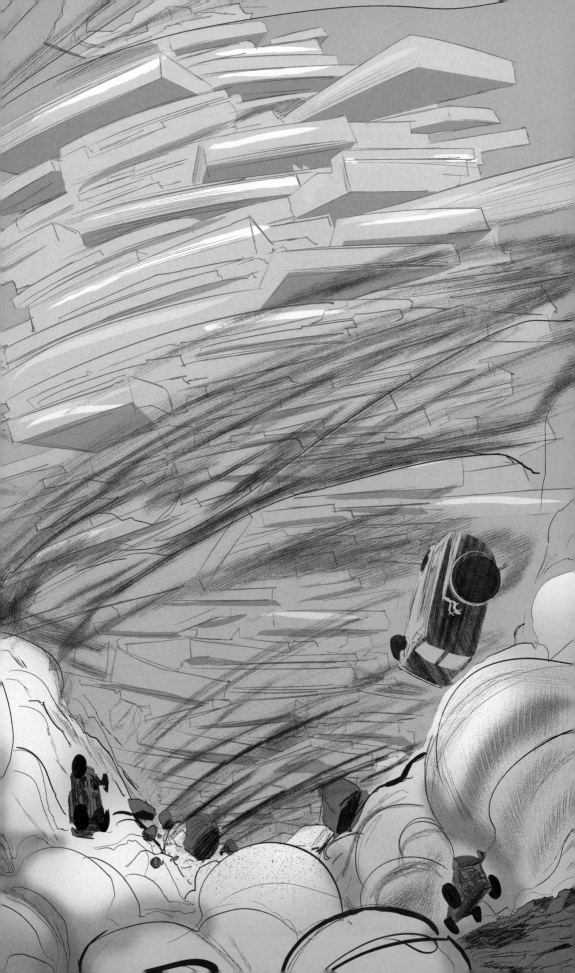

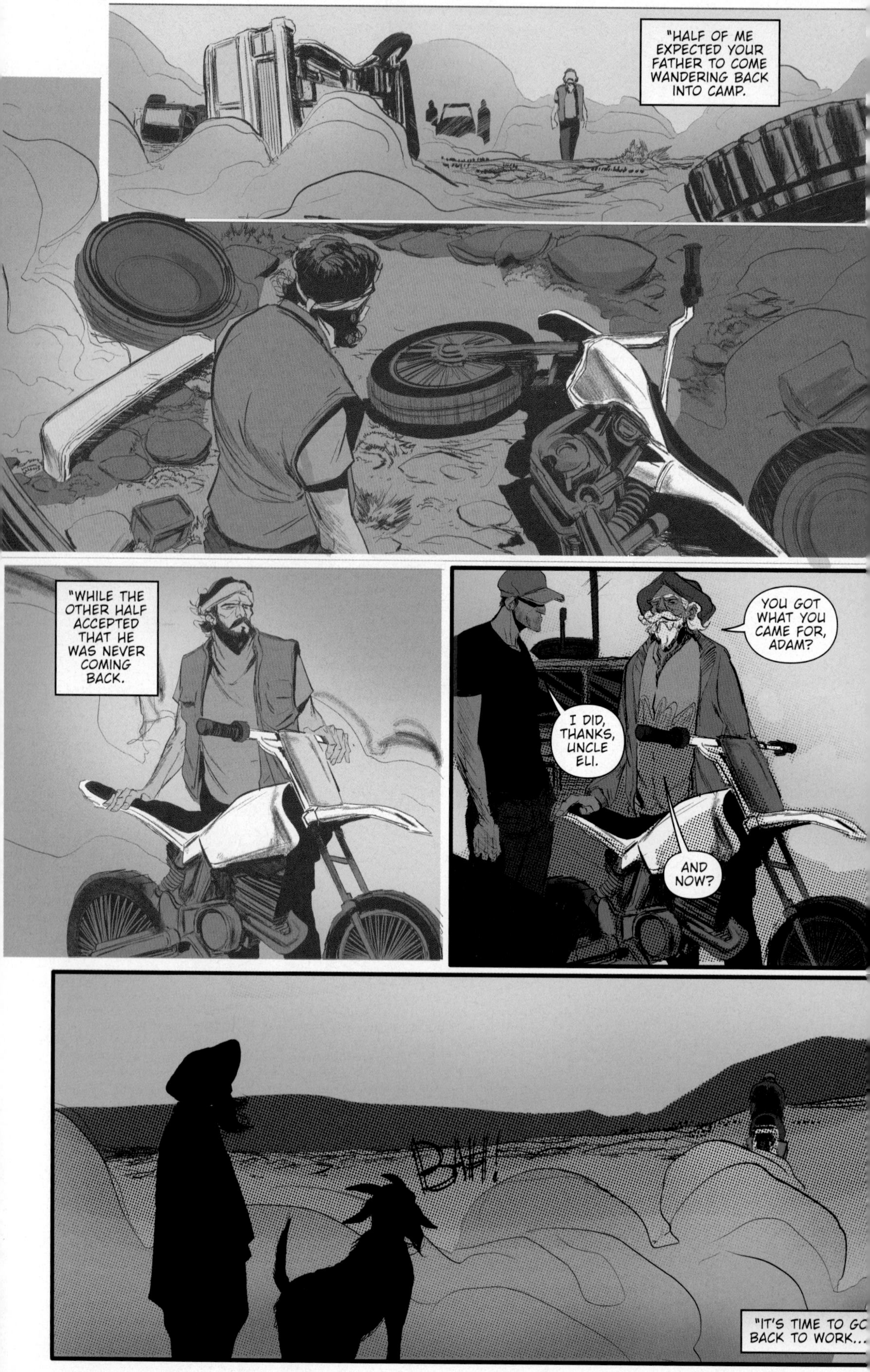
"HALF OF ME EXPECTED YOUR FATHER TO COME WANDERING BACK INTO CAMP.
"WHILE THE OTHER HALF ACCEPTED THAT HE WAS NEVER COMING BACK.
YOU GOT WHAT YOU CAME FOR, ADAM?
I DID, THANKS, UNCLE ELI.
AND NOW?
BAH!
"IT'S TIME TO GO BACK TO WORK...

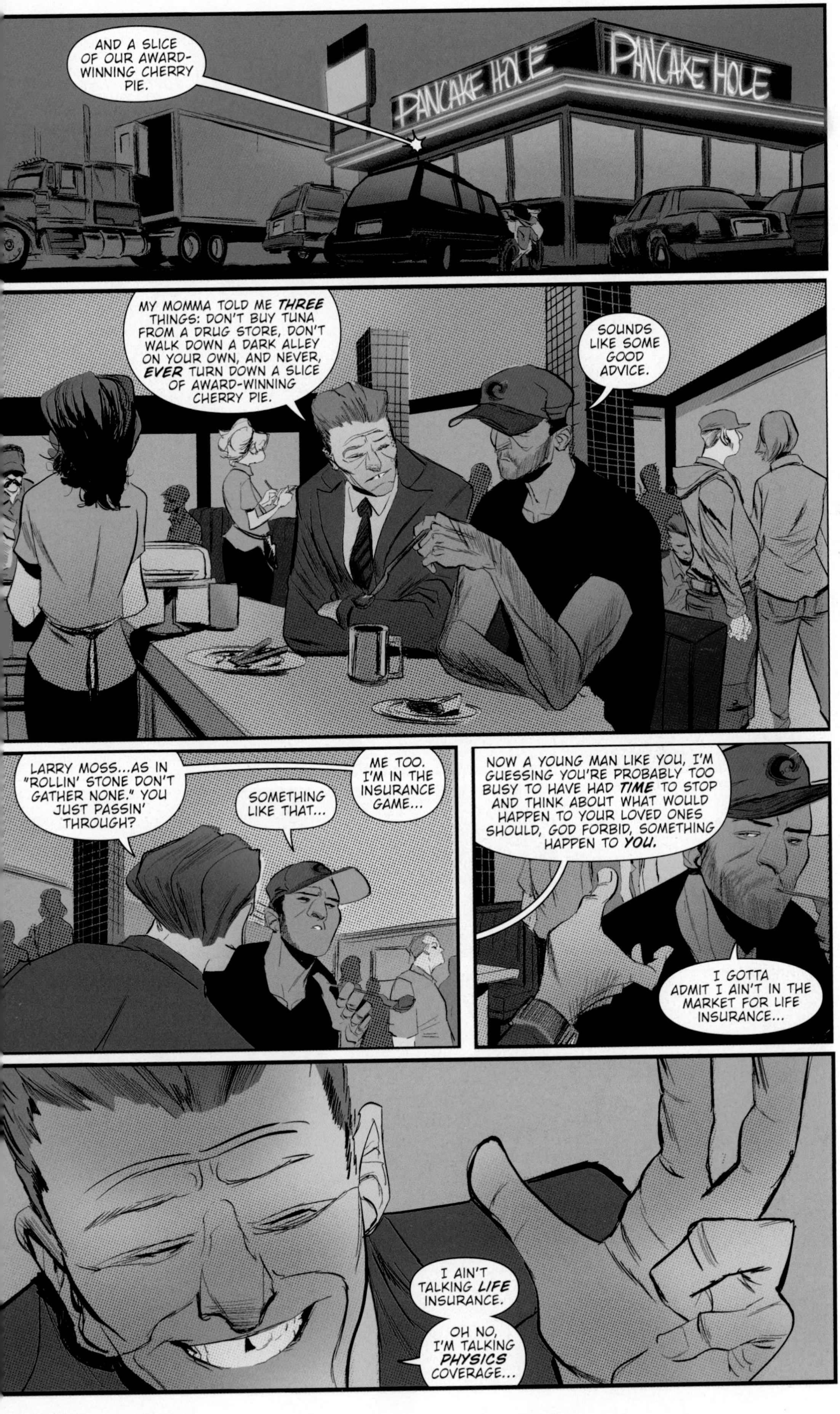
AND A SLICE OF OUR AWARD-WINNING CHERRY PIE.
PANCAKE HOLE
PANCAKE HOLE
MY MOMMA TOLD ME THREE THINGS: DON'T BUY TUNA FROM A DRUG STORE, DON'T WALK DOWN A DARK ALLEY ON YOUR OWN, AND NEVER, EVER TURN DOWN A SLICE OF AWARD-WINNING CHERRY PIE.
SOUNDS LIKE SOME GOOD ADVICE.
LARRY MOSS...AS IN "ROLLIN' STONE DON'T GATHER NONE." YOU JUST PASSIN' THROUGH?
SOMETHING LIKE THAT...
ME TOO. I'M IN THE INSURANCE GAME...
NOW A YOUNG MAN LIKE YOU, I'M GUESSING YOU'RE PROBABLY TOO BUSY TO HAVE HAD TIME TO STOP AND THINK ABOUT WHAT WOULD HAPPEN TO YOUR LOVED ONES SHOULD, GOD FORBID, SOMETHING HAPPEN TO YOU.
I GOTTA ADMIT I AIN'T IN THE MARKET FOR LIFE INSURANCE...
I AIN'T TALKING LIFE INSURANCE.
OH NO, I'M TALKING PHYSICS COVERAGE...

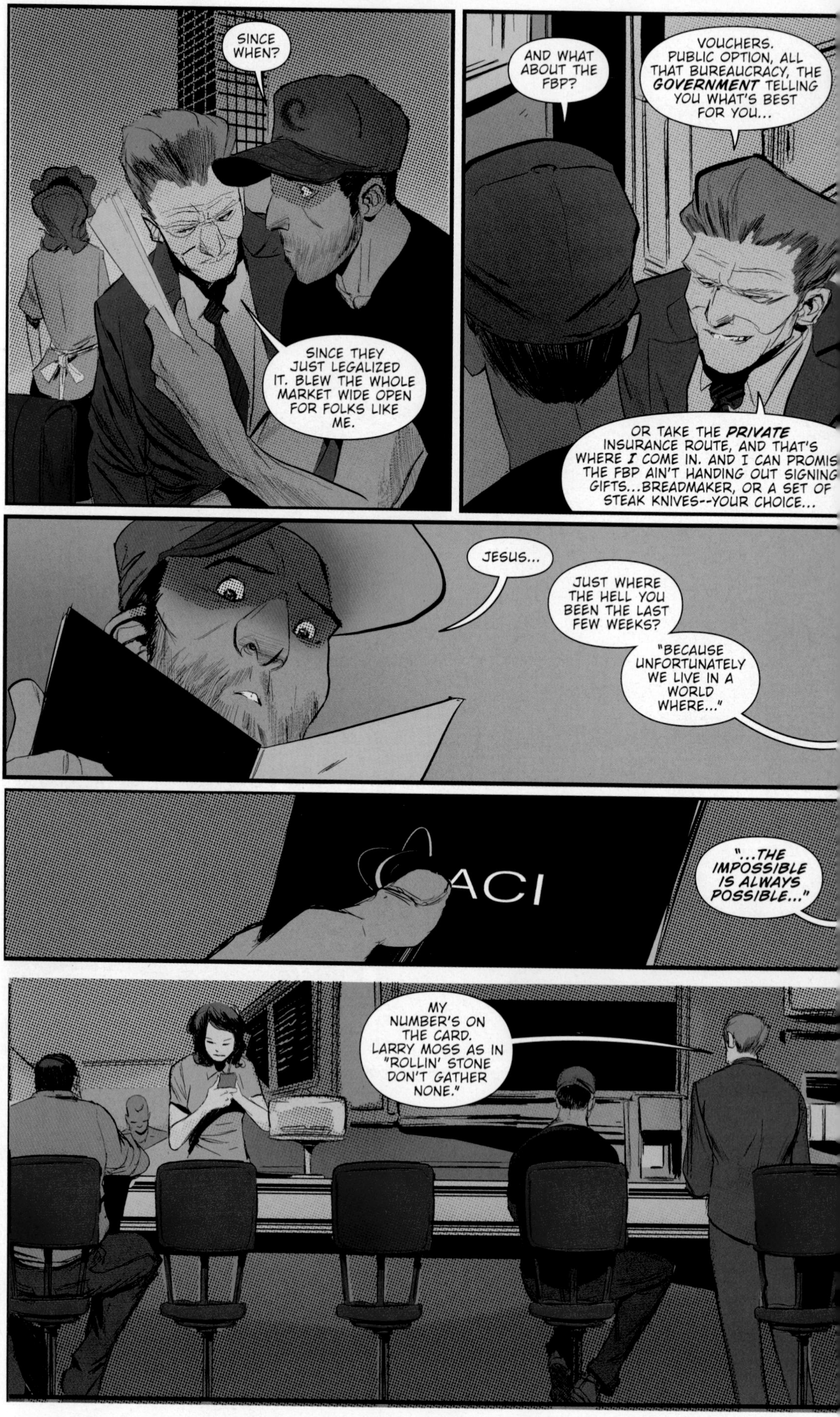
SINCE WHEN?
SINCE THEY JUST LEGALIZED IT. BLEW THE WHOLE MARKET WIDE OPEN FOR FOLKS LIKE ME.
AND WHAT ABOUT THE FBP?
VOUCHERS. PUBLIC OPTION, ALL THAT BUREAUCRACY, THE **GOVERNMENT** TELLING YOU WHAT'S BEST FOR YOU...
OR TAKE THE **PRIVATE** INSURANCE ROUTE, AND THAT'S WHERE **I** COME IN. AND I CAN PROMIS THE FBP AIN'T HANDING OUT SIGNING GIFTS...BREADMAKER, OR A SET OF STEAK KNIVES--YOUR CHOICE...
JESUS...
JUST WHERE THE HELL YOU BEEN THE LAST FEW WEEKS?
"BECAUSE UNFORTUNATELY WE LIVE IN A WORLD WHERE..."
ACI
"...THE IMPOSSIBLE IS ALWAYS POSSIBLE..."
MY NUMBER'S ON THE CARD. LARRY MOSS AS IN "ROLLIN' STONE DON'T GATHER NONE."

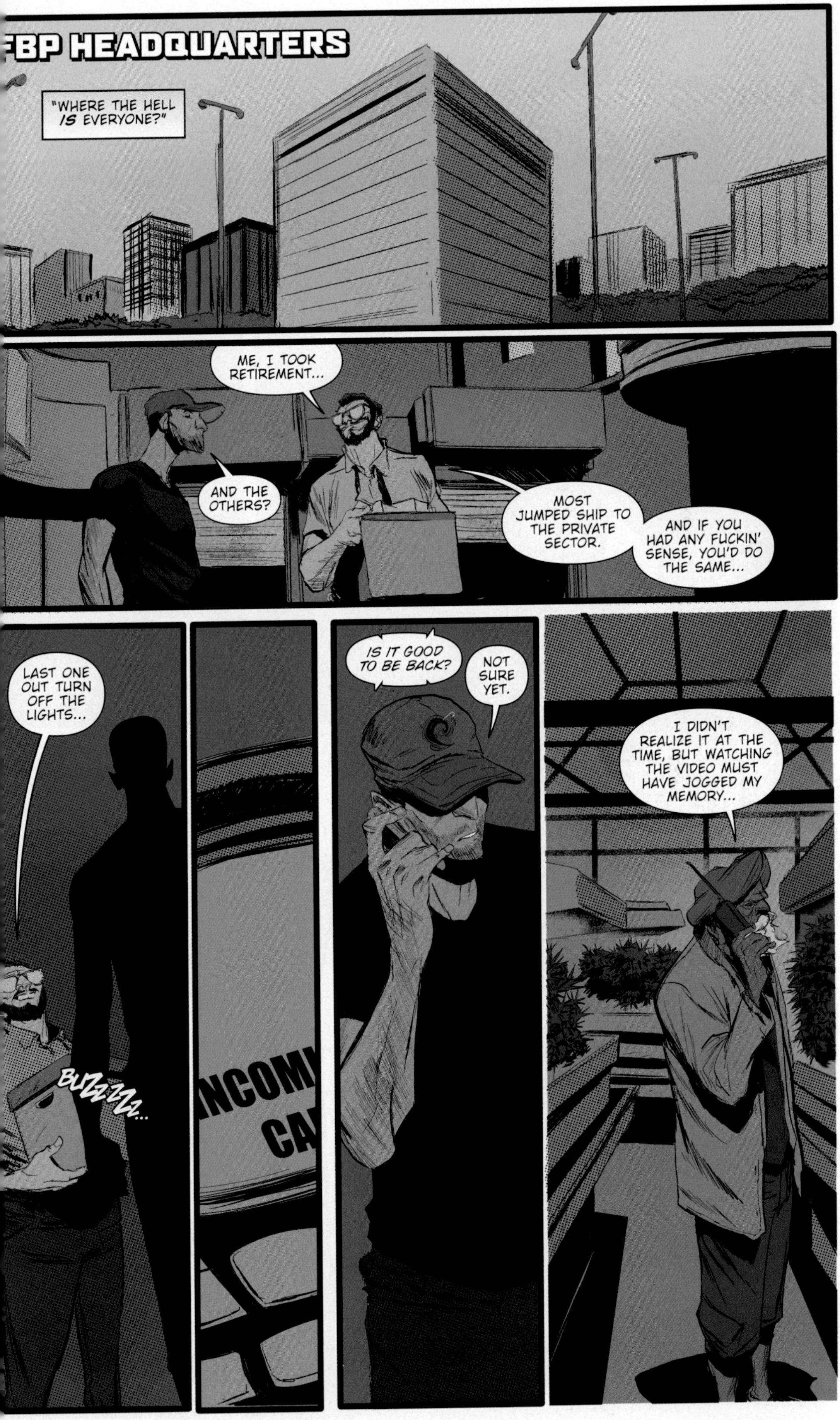

FBP HEADQUARTERS
"WHERE THE HELL *IS* EVERYONE?"
ME, I TOOK RETIREMENT...
AND THE OTHERS?
MOST JUMPED SHIP TO THE PRIVATE SECTOR.
AND IF YOU HAD ANY FUCKIN' SENSE, YOU'D DO THE SAME...
LAST ONE OUT TURN OFF THE LIGHTS...
BUZZZZZ...
INCOMI
CA
IS IT GOOD TO BE BACK?
NOT SURE YET.
I DIDN'T REALIZE IT AT THE TIME, BUT WATCHING THE VIDEO MUST HAVE JOGGED MY MEMORY...

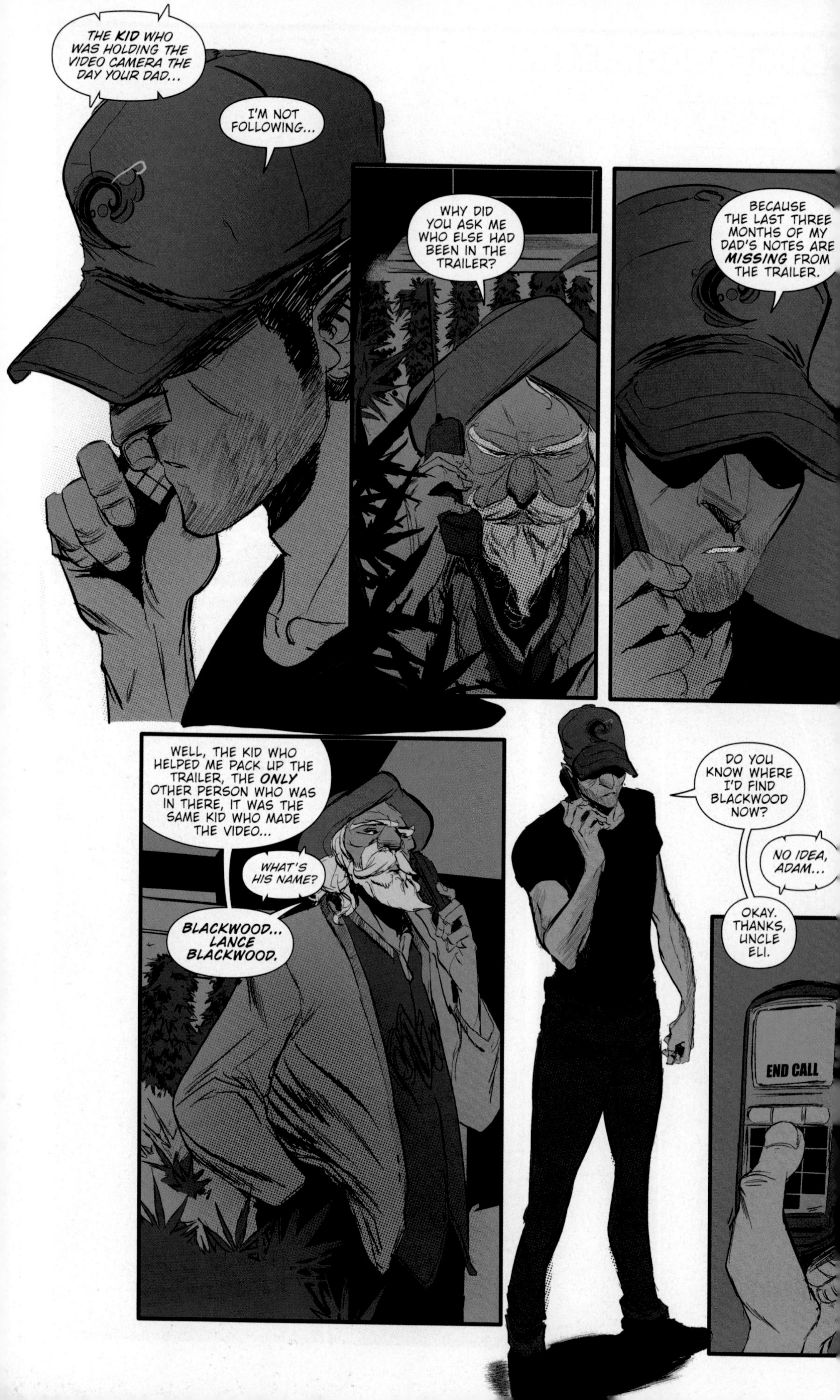
THE KID WHO WAS HOLDING THE VIDEO CAMERA THE DAY YOUR DAD...
I'M NOT FOLLOWING...
WHY DID YOU ASK ME WHO ELSE HAD BEEN IN THE TRAILER?
BECAUSE THE LAST THREE MONTHS OF MY DAD'S NOTES ARE MISSING FROM THE TRAILER.
WELL, THE KID WHO HELPED ME PACK UP THE TRAILER, THE ONLY OTHER PERSON WHO WAS IN THERE, IT WAS THE SAME KID WHO MADE THE VIDEO...
WHAT'S HIS NAME?
BLACKWOOD... LANCE BLACKWOOD.
DO YOU KNOW WHERE I'D FIND BLACKWOOD NOW?
NO IDEA, ADAM...
OKAY. THANKS, UNCLE ELI.
END CALL

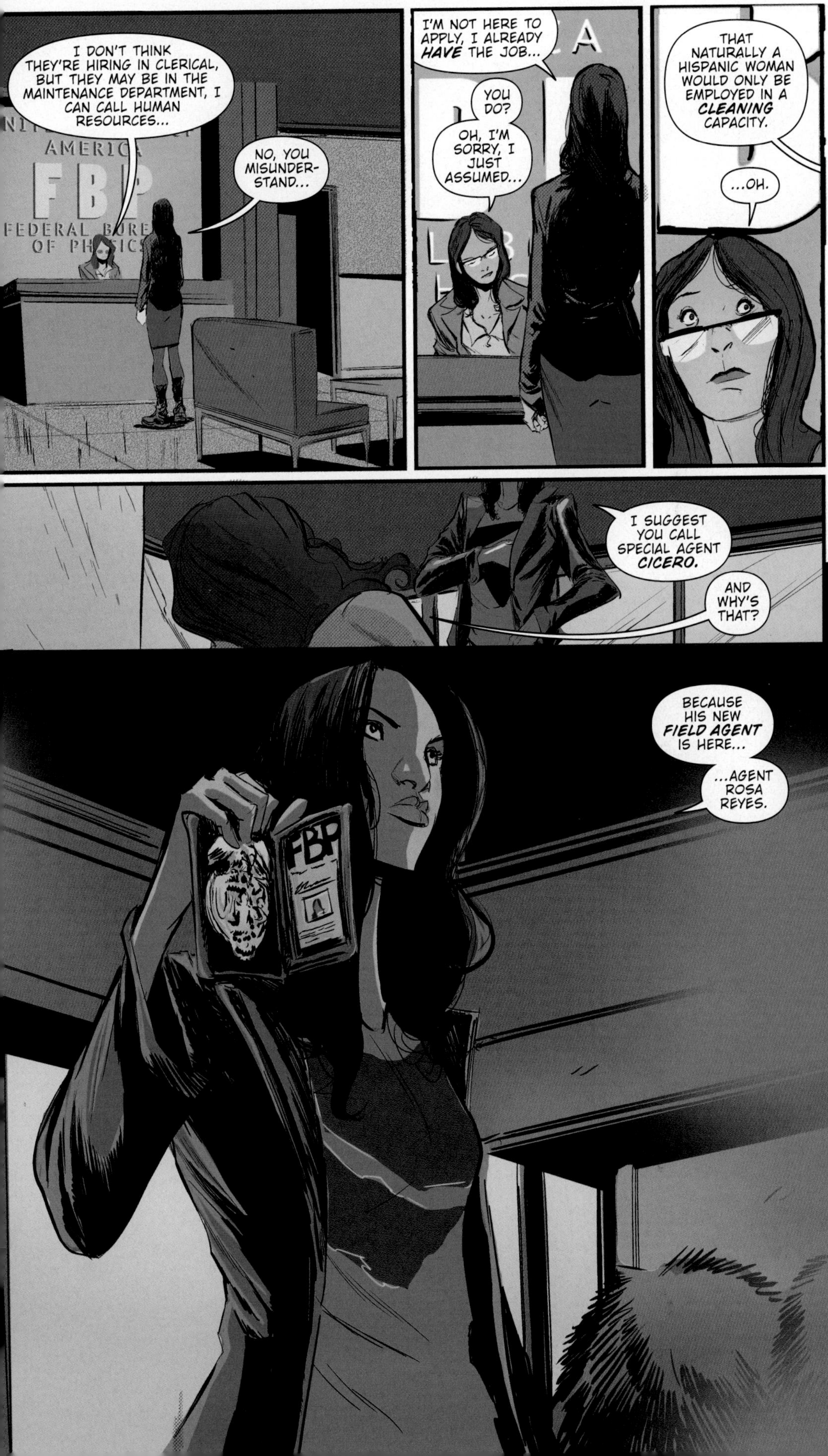
I DON'T THINK THEY'RE HIRING IN CLERICAL, BUT THEY MAY BE IN THE MAINTENANCE DEPARTMENT, I CAN CALL HUMAN RESOURCES...
AMERICA
FBP
FEDERAL BURE
OF PH
NO, YOU MISUNDER-STAND...
I'M NOT HERE TO APPLY, I ALREADY HAVE THE JOB...
YOU DO?
OH, I'M SORRY, I JUST ASSUMED...
THAT NATURALLY A HISPANIC WOMAN WOULD ONLY BE EMPLOYED IN A CLEANING CAPACITY.
...OH.
I SUGGEST YOU CALL SPECIAL AGENT CICERO.
AND WHY'S THAT?
BECAUSE HIS NEW FIELD AGENT IS HERE...
...AGENT ROSA REYES.
FBP

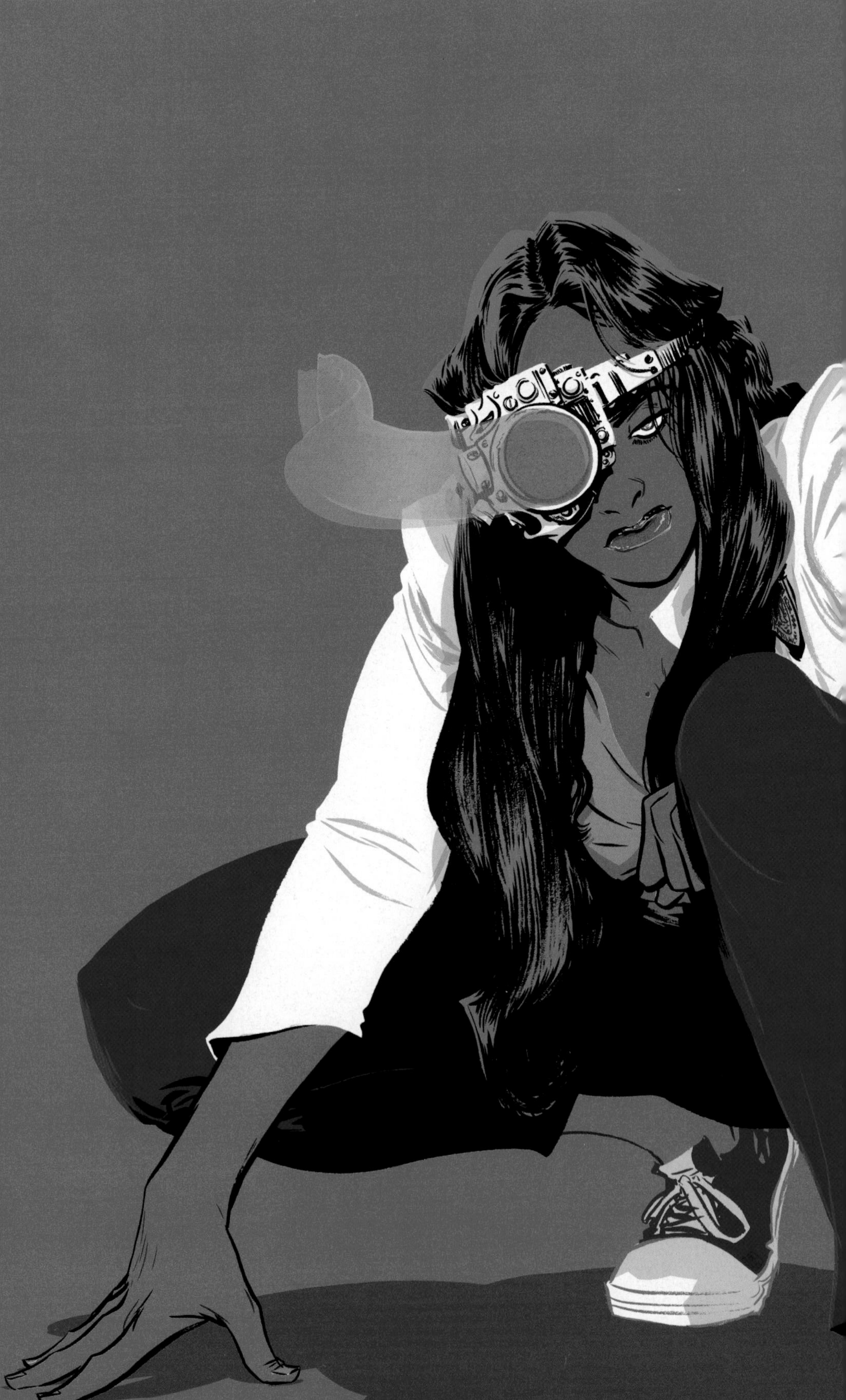

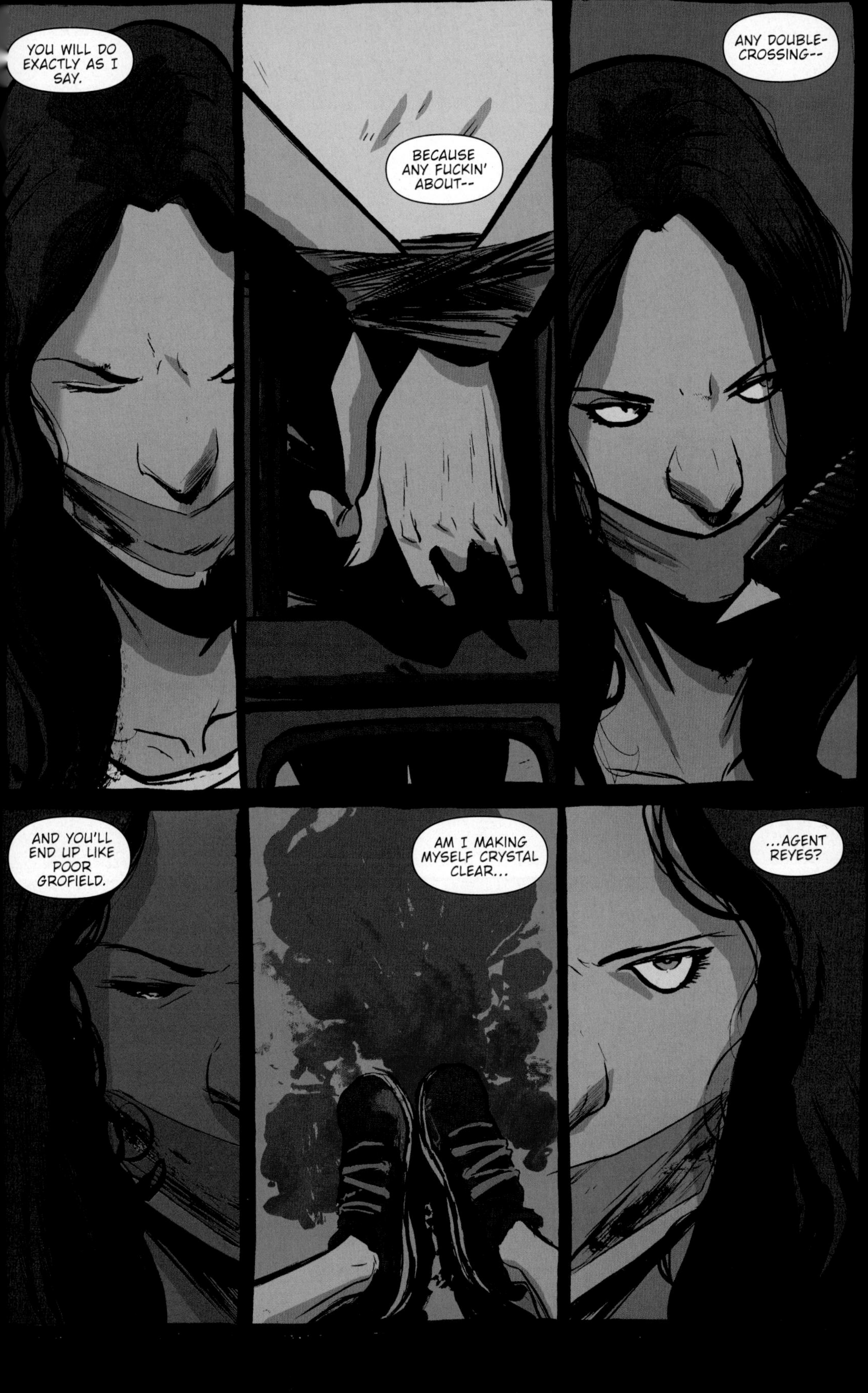
YOU WILL DO EXACTLY AS I SAY.
BECAUSE ANY FUCKIN' ABOUT--
ANY DOUBLE-CROSSING--
AND YOU'LL END UP LIKE POOR GROFIELD.
AM I MAKING MYSELF CRYSTAL CLEAR...
...AGENT REYES?

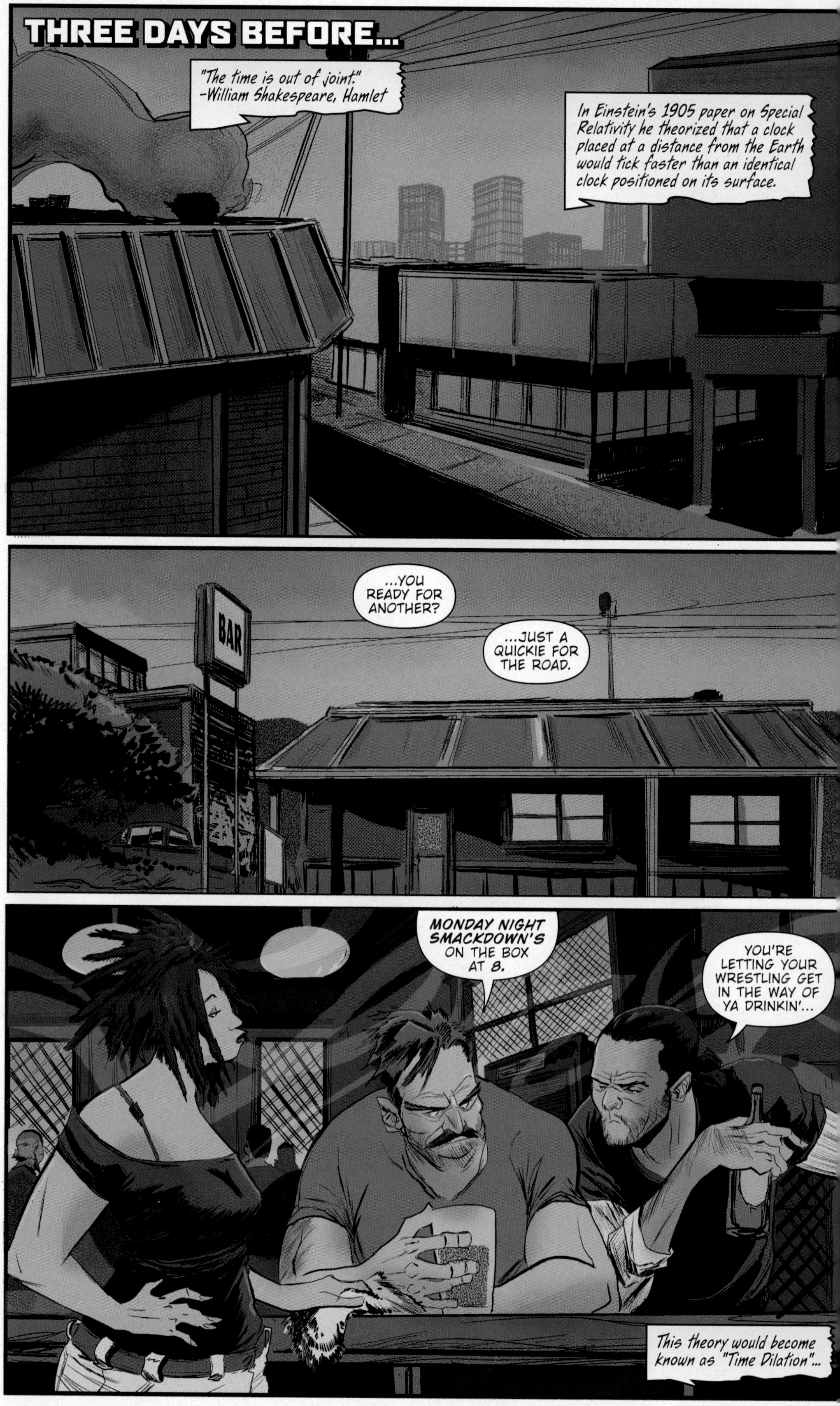
THREE DAYS BEFORE...
"The time is out of joint."
-William Shakespeare, Hamlet
In Einstein's 1905 paper on Special Relativity he theorized that a clock placed at a distance from the Earth would tick faster than an identical clock positioned on its surface.
BAR
...YOU READY FOR ANOTHER?
...JUST A QUICKIE FOR THE ROAD.
MONDAY NIGHT SMACKDOWN'S ON THE BOX AT 8.
YOU'RE LETTING YOUR WRESTLING GET IN THE WAY OF YA DRINKIN'...
This theory would become known as "Time Dilation"...

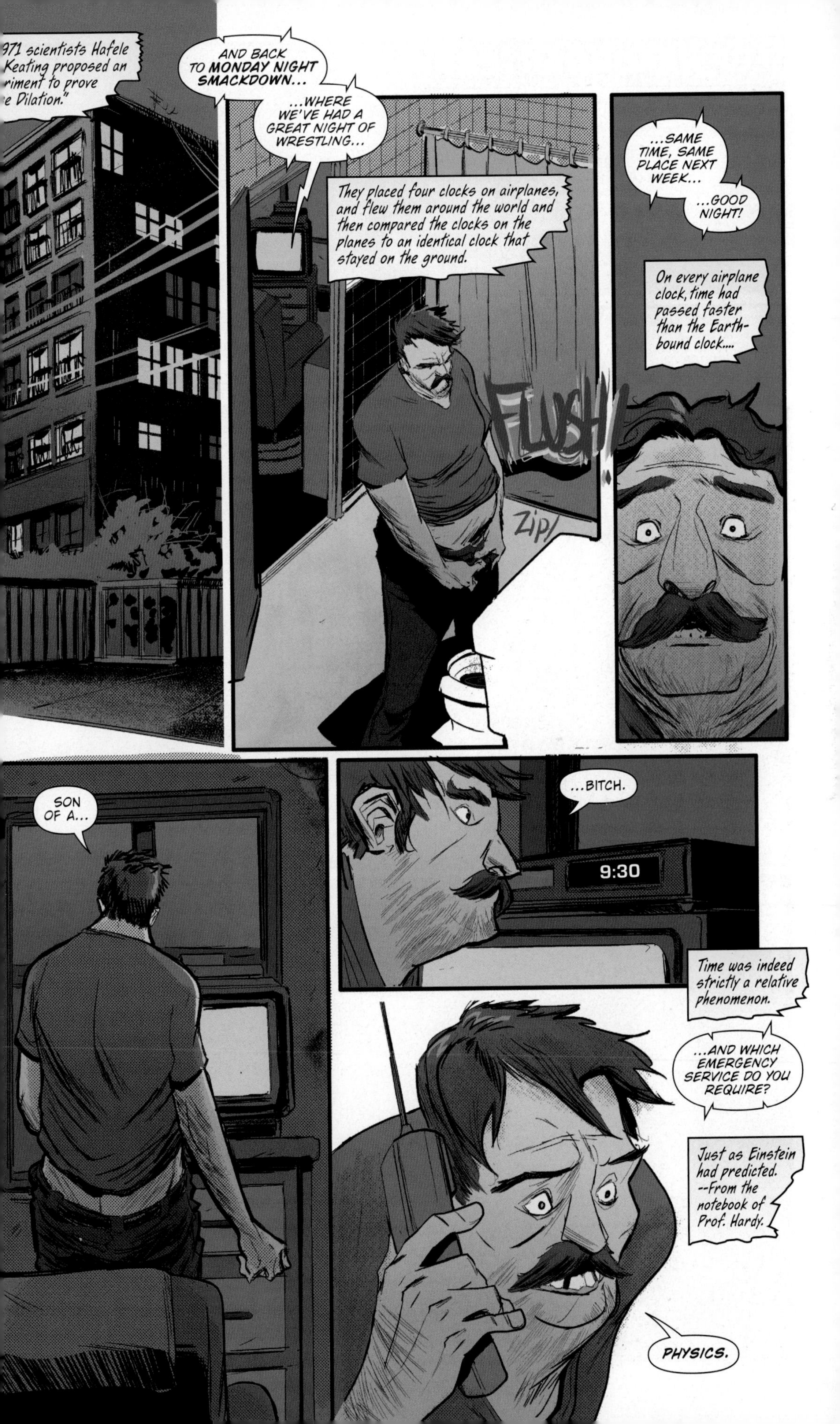
971 scientists Hafele
Keating proposed an
riment to prove
e Dilation."
AND BACK TO MONDAY NIGHT SMACKDOWN...
...WHERE WE'VE HAD A GREAT NIGHT OF WRESTLING...
They placed four clocks on airplanes, and flew them around the world and then compared the clocks on the planes to an identical clock that stayed on the ground.
...SAME TIME, SAME PLACE NEXT WEEK...
...GOOD NIGHT!
On every airplane clock, time had passed faster than the Earth-bound clock....
FLUSH!
ZIP!
SON OF A...
...BITCH.
9:30
Time was indeed strictly a relative phenomenon.
...AND WHICH EMERGENCY SERVICE DO YOU REQUIRE?
Just as Einstein had predicted. --From the notebook of Prof. Hardy.
PHYSICS.

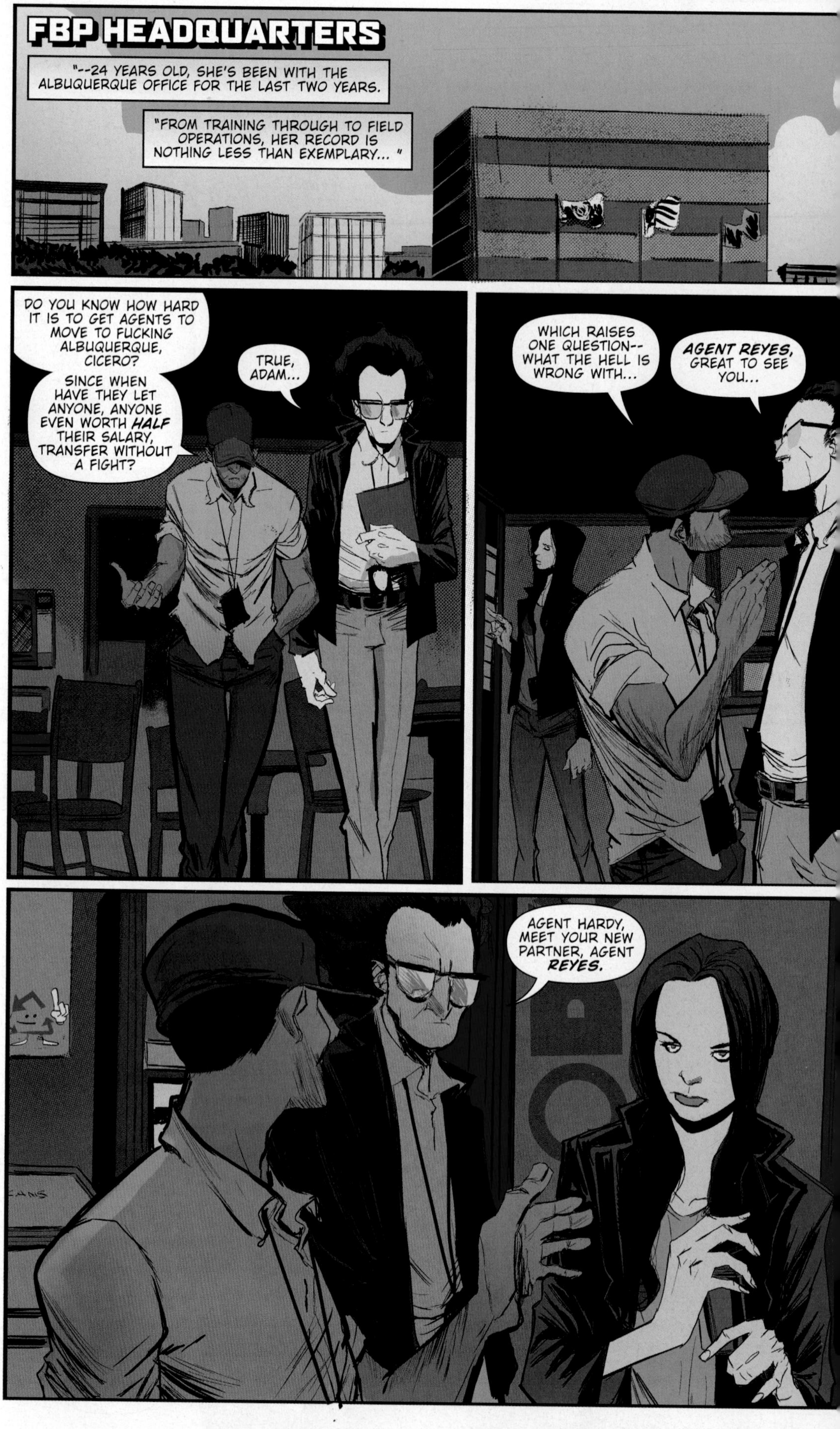
FBP HEADQUARTERS
"--24 YEARS OLD, SHE'S BEEN WITH THE ALBUQUERQUE OFFICE FOR THE LAST TWO YEARS.
"FROM TRAINING THROUGH TO FIELD OPERATIONS, HER RECORD IS NOTHING LESS THAN EXEMPLARY... "
DO YOU KNOW HOW HARD IT IS TO GET AGENTS TO MOVE TO FUCKING ALBUQUERQUE, CICERO?
SINCE WHEN HAVE THEY LET ANYONE, ANYONE EVEN WORTH HALF THEIR SALARY, TRANSFER WITHOUT A FIGHT?
TRUE, ADAM...
WHICH RAISES ONE QUESTION-- WHAT THE HELL IS WRONG WITH...
AGENT REYES, GREAT TO SEE YOU...
AGENT HARDY, MEET YOUR NEW PARTNER, AGENT REYES.

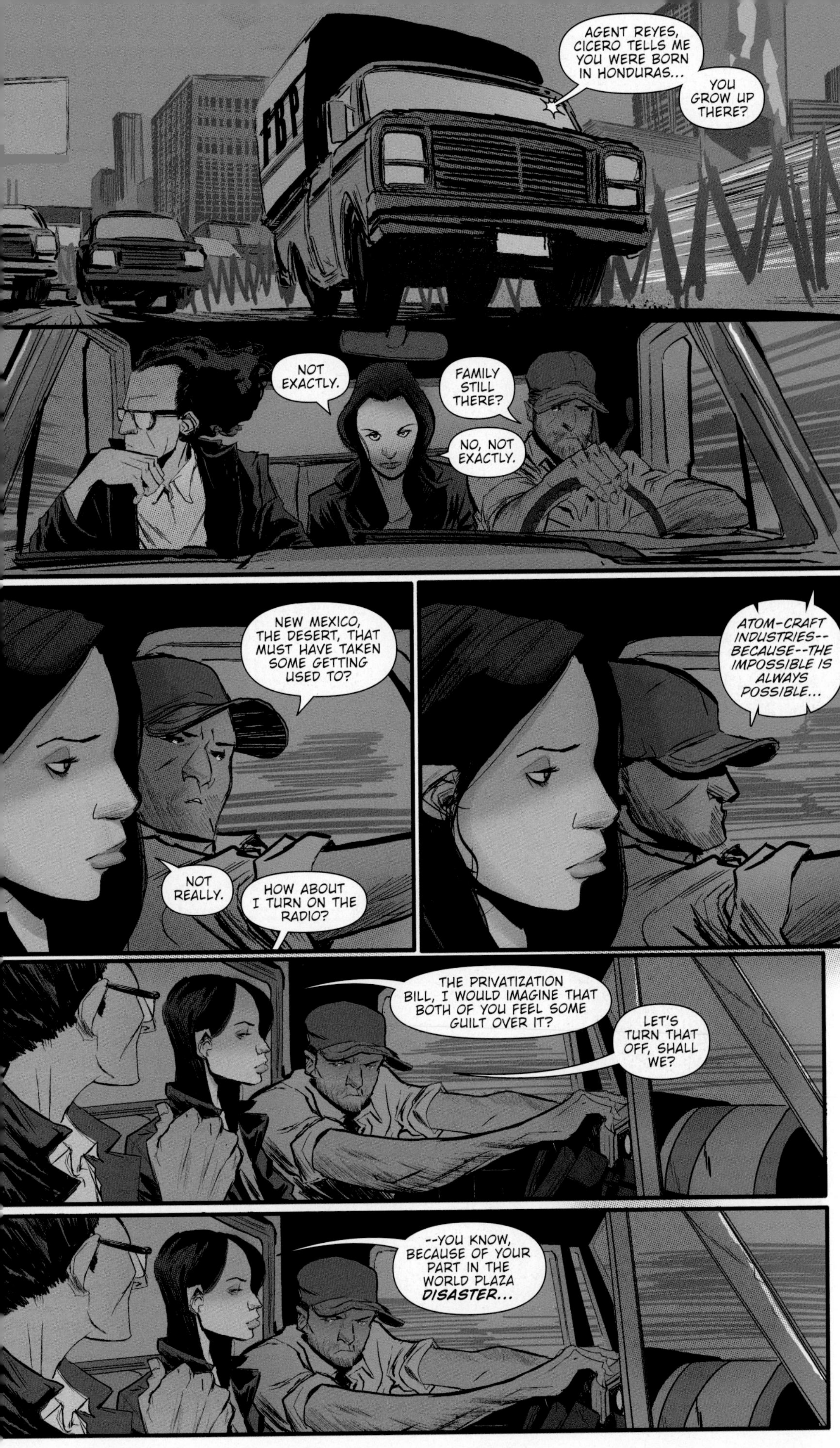
AGENT REYES, CICERO TELLS ME YOU WERE BORN IN HONDURAS...
YOU GROW UP THERE?
NOT EXACTLY.
FAMILY STILL THERE?
NO, NOT EXACTLY.
NEW MEXICO, THE DESERT, THAT MUST HAVE TAKEN SOME GETTING USED TO?
NOT REALLY.
HOW ABOUT I TURN ON THE RADIO?
ATOM-CRAFT INDUSTRIES--BECAUSE--THE IMPOSSIBLE IS ALWAYS POSSIBLE...
THE PRIVATIZATION BILL, I WOULD IMAGINE THAT BOTH OF YOU FEEL SOME GUILT OVER IT?
LET'S TURN THAT OFF, SHALL WE?
--YOU KNOW, BECAUSE OF YOUR PART IN THE WORLD PLAZA DISASTER...

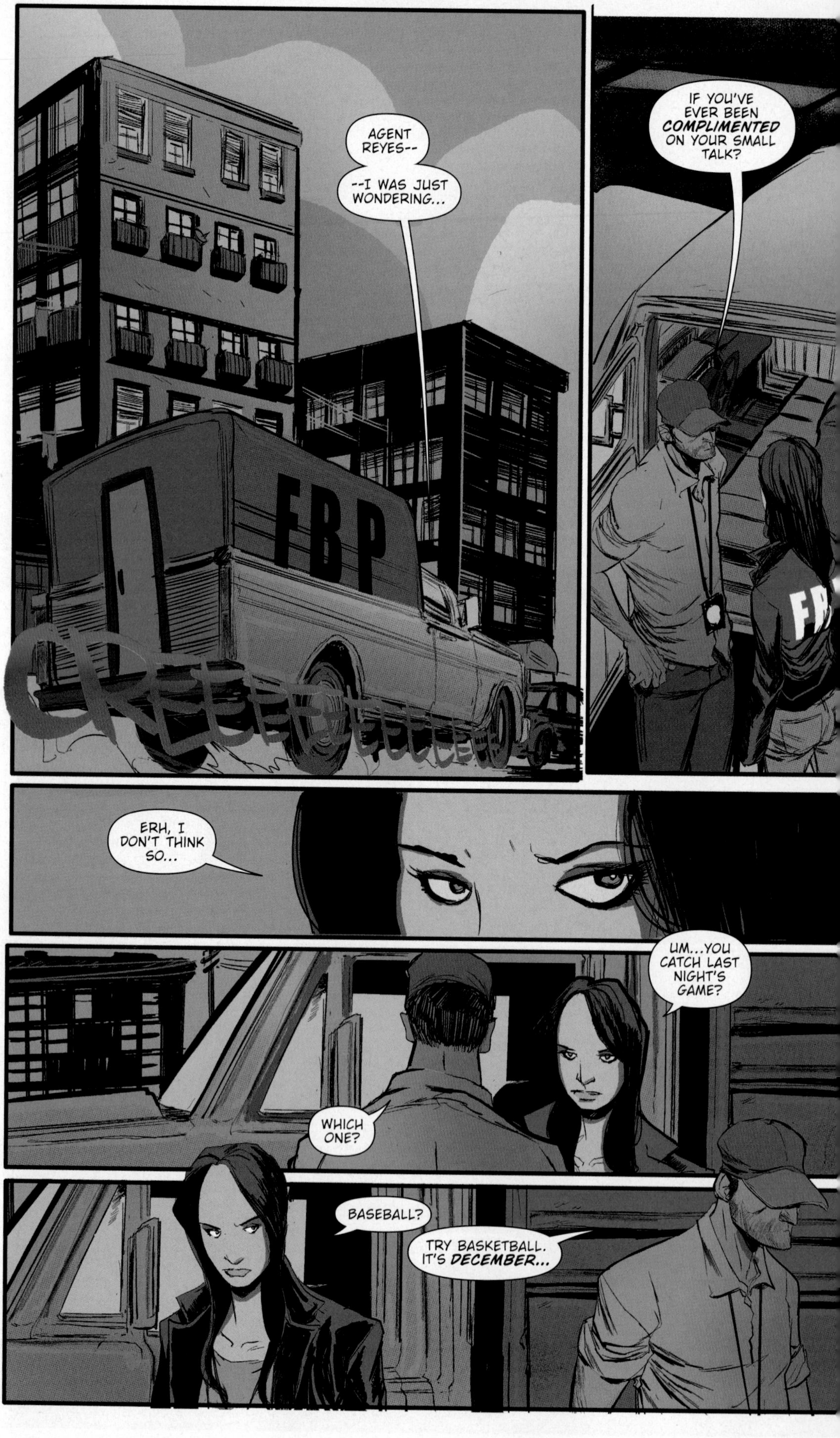
AGENT REYES--
--I WAS JUST WONDERING...
IF YOU'VE EVER BEEN COMPLIMENTED ON YOUR SMALL TALK?
ERH, I DON'T THINK SO...
UM...YOU CATCH LAST NIGHT'S GAME?
WHICH ONE?
BASEBALL?
TRY BASKETBALL. IT'S DECEMBER...

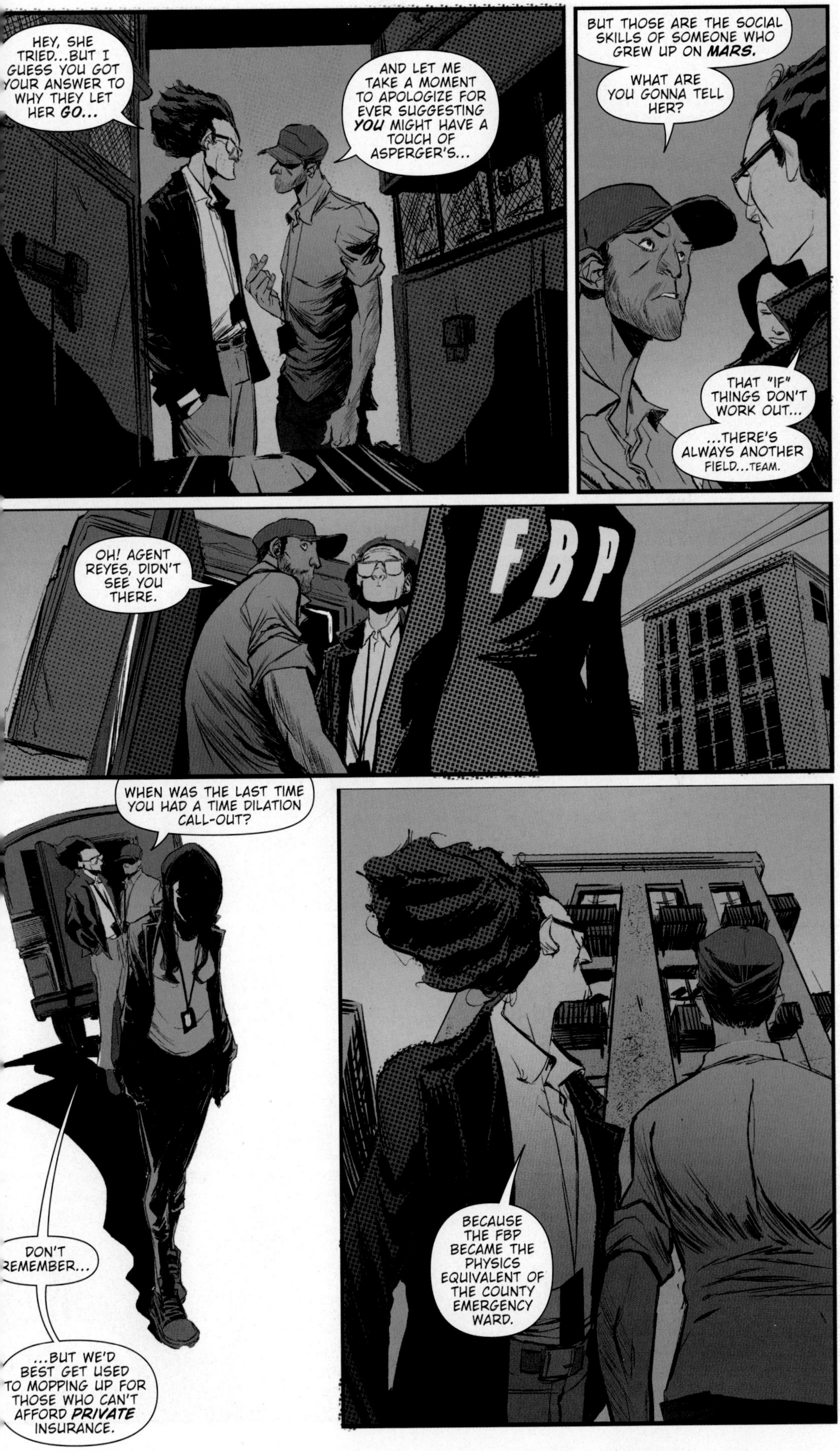
HEY, SHE TRIED...BUT I GUESS YOU GOT YOUR ANSWER TO WHY THEY LET HER GO...
AND LET ME TAKE A MOMENT TO APOLOGIZE FOR EVER SUGGESTING YOU MIGHT HAVE A TOUCH OF ASPERGER'S...
BUT THOSE ARE THE SOCIAL SKILLS OF SOMEONE WHO GREW UP ON MARS.
WHAT ARE YOU GONNA TELL HER?
THAT "IF" THINGS DON'T WORK OUT...
...THERE'S ALWAYS ANOTHER FIELD...TEAM.
OH! AGENT REYES, DIDN'T SEE YOU THERE.
FBP
WHEN WAS THE LAST TIME YOU HAD A TIME DILATION CALL-OUT?
DON'T REMEMBER...
...BUT WE'D BEST GET USED TO MOPPING UP FOR THOSE WHO CAN'T AFFORD PRIVATE INSURANCE.
BECAUSE THE FBP BECAME THE PHYSICS EQUIVALENT OF THE COUNTY EMERGENCY WARD.

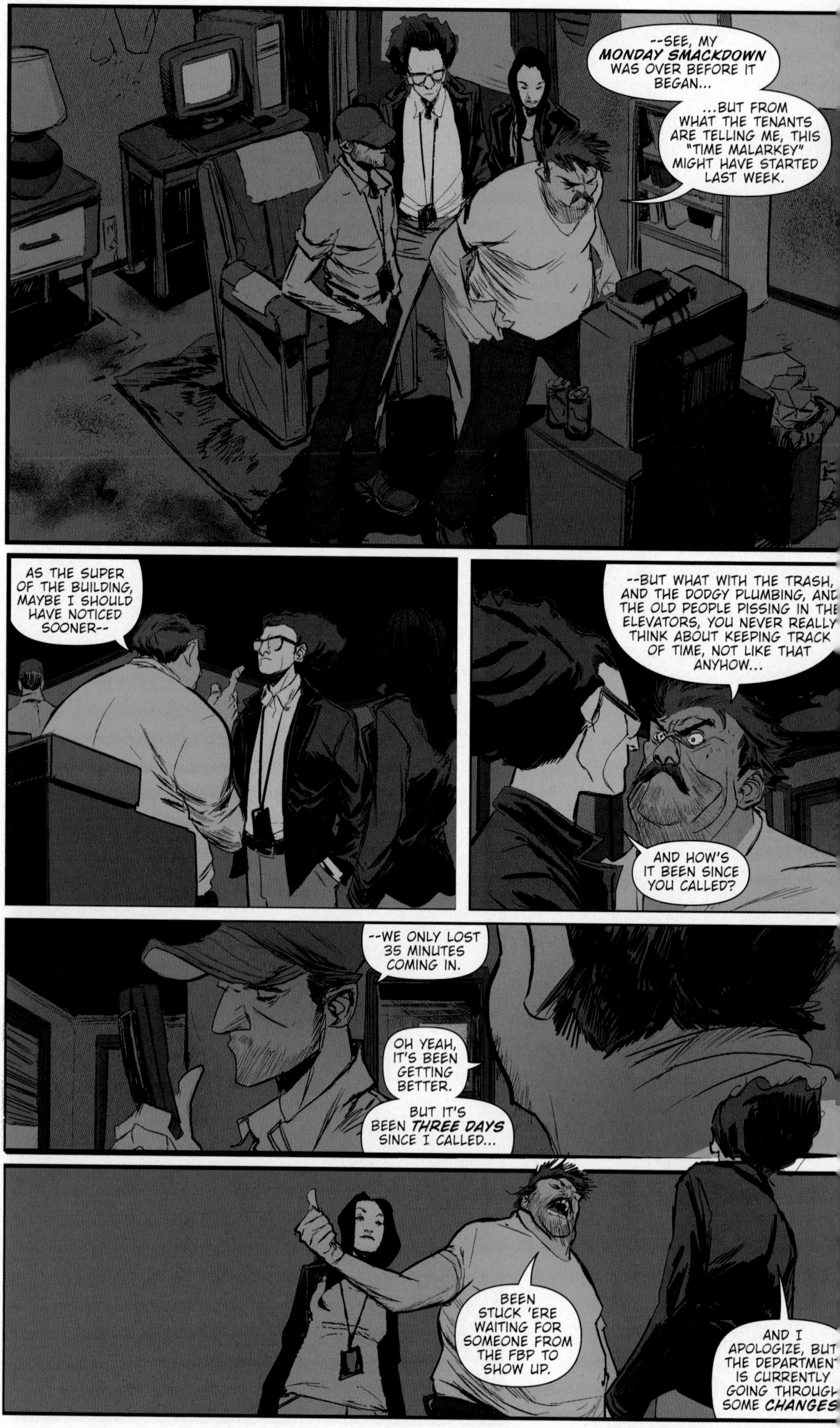
--SEE, MY MONDAY SMACKDOWN WAS OVER BEFORE IT BEGAN...
...BUT FROM WHAT THE TENANTS ARE TELLING ME, THIS "TIME MALARKEY" MIGHT HAVE STARTED LAST WEEK.
AS THE SUPER OF THE BUILDING, MAYBE I SHOULD HAVE NOTICED SOONER--
--BUT WHAT WITH THE TRASH, AND THE DODGY PLUMBING, AND THE OLD PEOPLE PISSING IN THE ELEVATORS, YOU NEVER REALLY THINK ABOUT KEEPING TRACK OF TIME, NOT LIKE THAT ANYHOW...
AND HOW'S IT BEEN SINCE YOU CALLED?
--WE ONLY LOST 35 MINUTES COMING IN.
OH YEAH, IT'S BEEN GETTING BETTER.
BUT IT'S BEEN THREE DAYS SINCE I CALLED...
BEEN STUCK 'ERE WAITING FOR SOMEONE FROM THE FBP TO SHOW UP.
AND I APOLOGIZE, BUT THE DEPARTMENT IS CURRENTLY GOING THROUGH SOME CHANGES

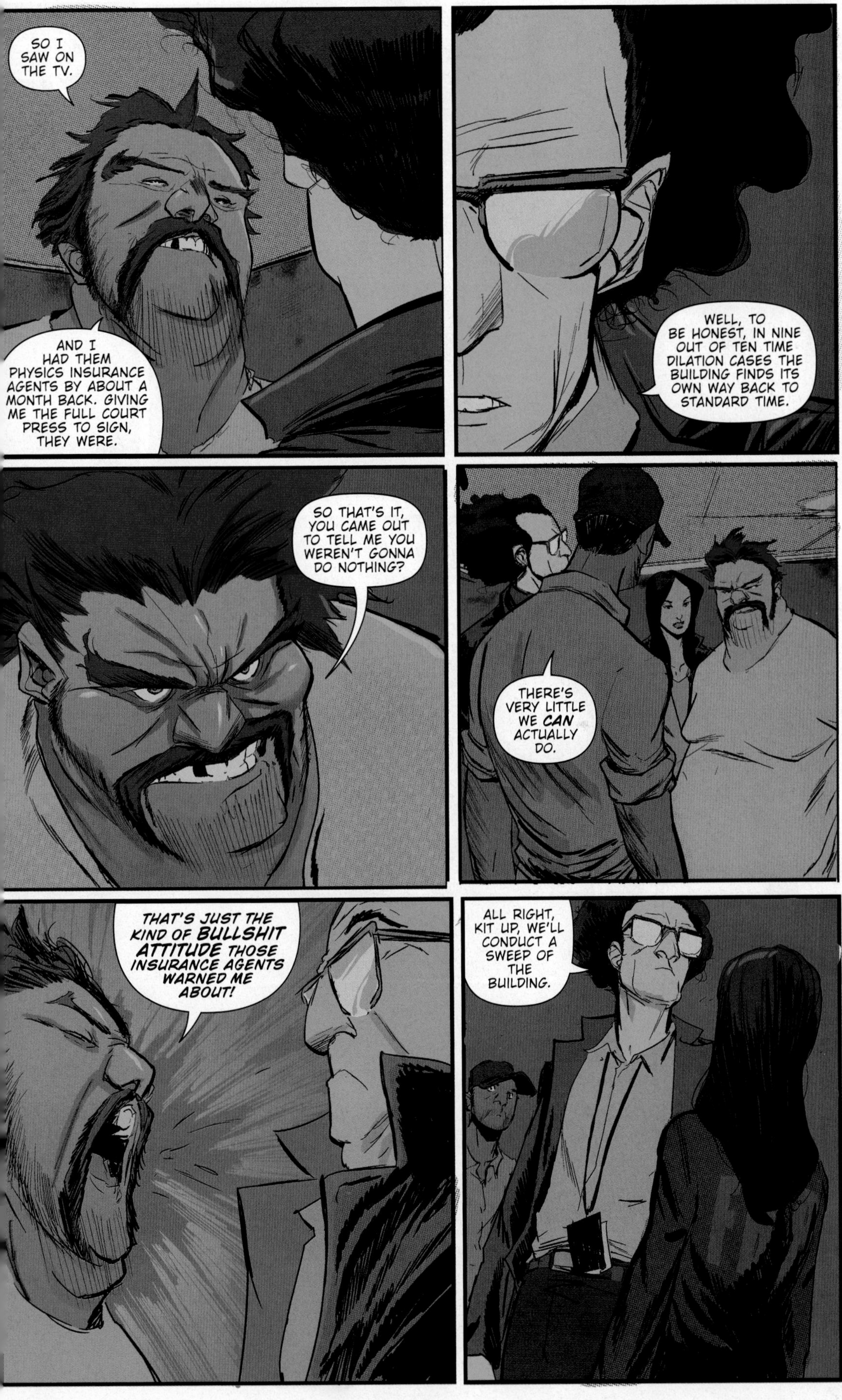
SO I SAW ON THE TV.
AND I HAD THEM PHYSICS INSURANCE AGENTS BY ABOUT A MONTH BACK. GIVING ME THE FULL COURT PRESS TO SIGN, THEY WERE.
WELL, TO BE HONEST, IN NINE OUT OF TEN TIME DILATION CASES THE BUILDING FINDS ITS OWN WAY BACK TO STANDARD TIME.
SO THAT'S IT, YOU CAME OUT TO TELL ME YOU WEREN'T GONNA DO NOTHING?
THERE'S VERY LITTLE WE CAN ACTUALLY DO.
THAT'S JUST THE KIND OF BULLSHIT ATTITUDE THOSE INSURANCE AGENTS WARNED ME ABOUT!
ALL RIGHT, KIT UP, WE'LL CONDUCT A SWEEP OF THE BUILDING.

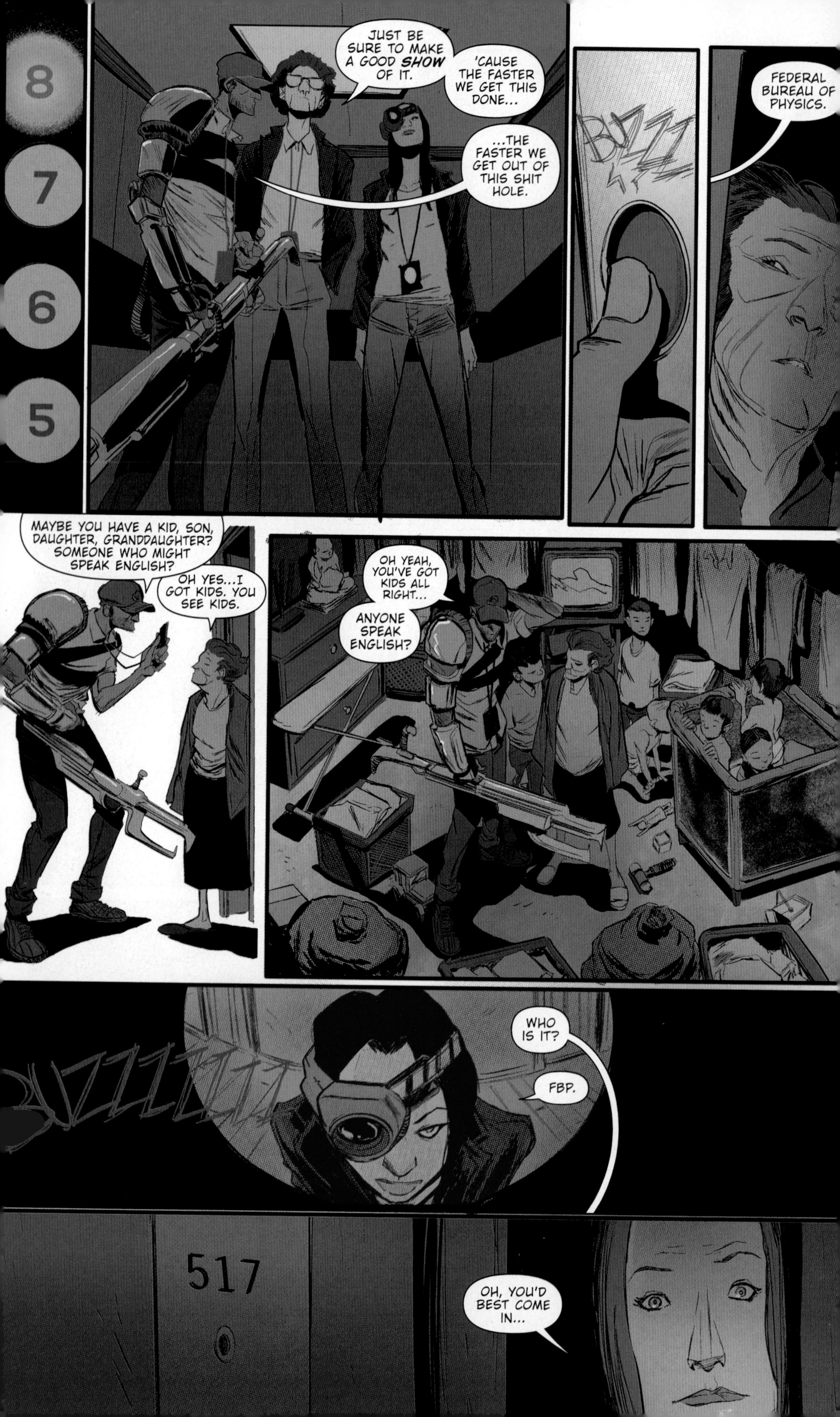
8
7
6
5
JUST BE SURE TO MAKE A GOOD SHOW OF IT.
'CAUSE THE FASTER WE GET THIS DONE...
...THE FASTER WE GET OUT OF THIS SHIT HOLE.
BZZZ
FEDERAL BUREAU OF PHYSICS.
MAYBE YOU HAVE A KID, SON, DAUGHTER, GRANDDAUGHTER? SOMEONE WHO MIGHT SPEAK ENGLISH?
OH YES...I GOT KIDS. YOU SEE KIDS.
OH YEAH, YOU'VE GOT KIDS ALL RIGHT...
ANYONE SPEAK ENGLISH?
BZZZZZZZZ
WHO IS IT?
FBP.
517
OH, YOU'D BEST COME IN...

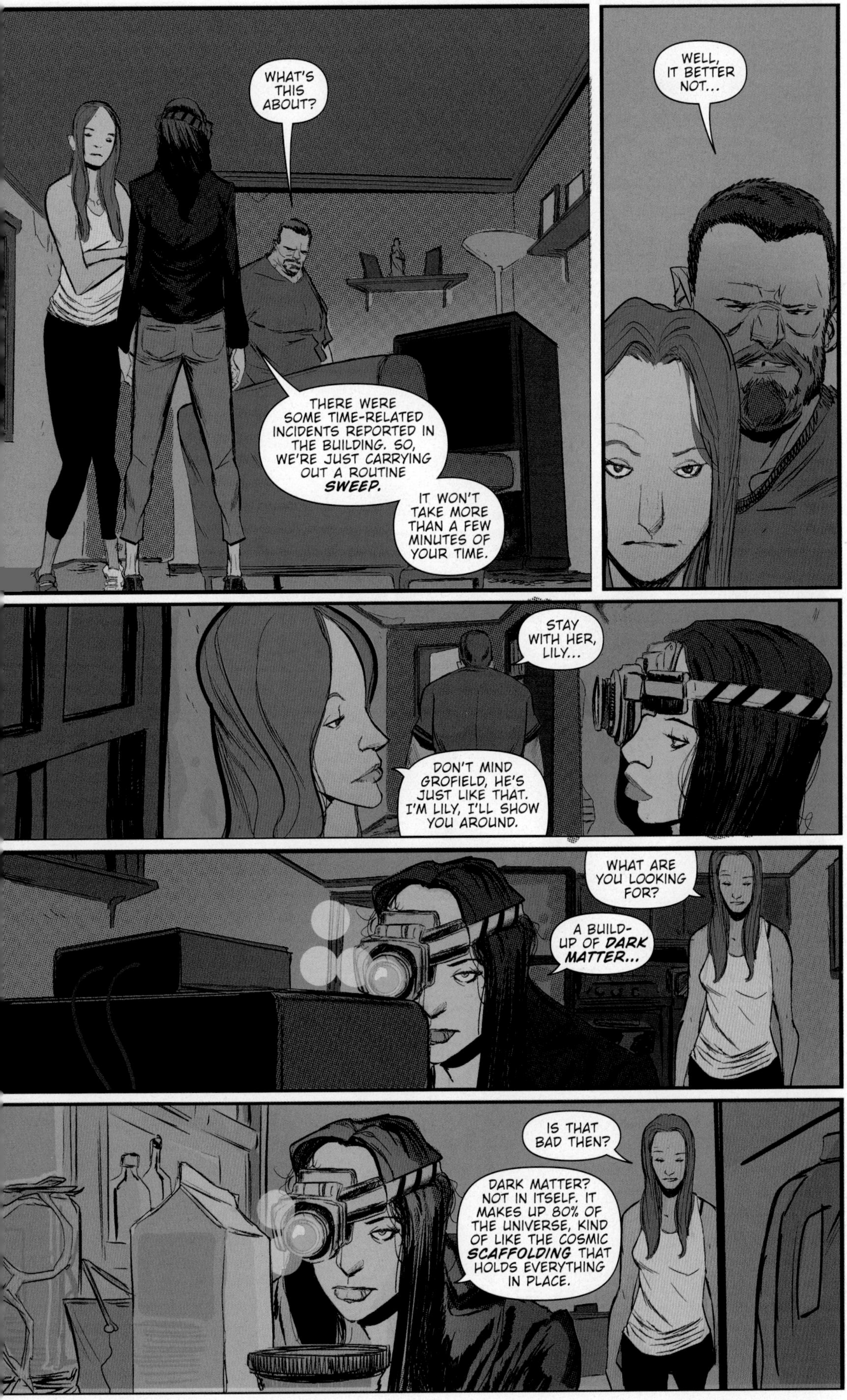
WHAT'S THIS ABOUT?
THERE WERE SOME TIME-RELATED INCIDENTS REPORTED IN THE BUILDING. SO, WE'RE JUST CARRYING OUT A ROUTINE SWEEP.
IT WON'T TAKE MORE THAN A FEW MINUTES OF YOUR TIME.
WELL, IT BETTER NOT...
STAY WITH HER, LILY...
DON'T MIND GROFIELD, HE'S JUST LIKE THAT. I'M LILY, I'LL SHOW YOU AROUND.
WHAT ARE YOU LOOKING FOR?
A BUILD-UP OF DARK MATTER...
IS THAT BAD THEN?
DARK MATTER? NOT IN ITSELF. IT MAKES UP 80% OF THE UNIVERSE, KIND OF LIKE THE COSMIC SCAFFOLDING THAT HOLDS EVERYTHING IN PLACE.

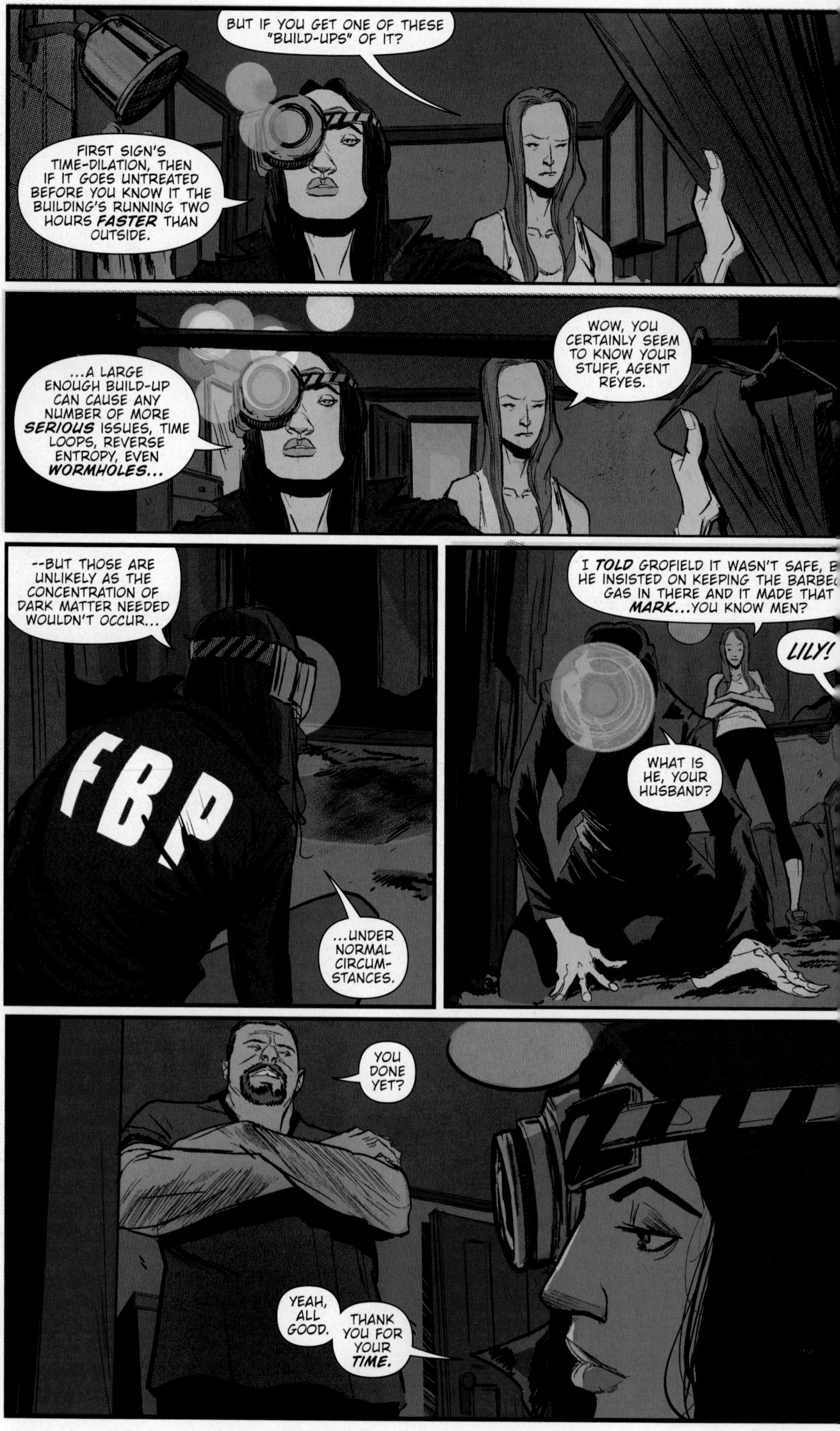
BUT IF YOU GET ONE OF THESE "BUILD-UPS" OF IT?
FIRST SIGN'S TIME-DILATION, THEN IF IT GOES UNTREATED BEFORE YOU KNOW IT THE BUILDING'S RUNNING TWO HOURS FASTER THAN OUTSIDE.
...A LARGE ENOUGH BUILD-UP CAN CAUSE ANY NUMBER OF MORE SERIOUS ISSUES, TIME LOOPS, REVERSE ENTROPY, EVEN WORMHOLES...
WOW, YOU CERTAINLY SEEM TO KNOW YOUR STUFF, AGENT REYES.
--BUT THOSE ARE UNLIKELY AS THE CONCENTRATION OF DARK MATTER NEEDED WOULDN'T OCCUR...
FBI
...UNDER NORMAL CIRCUM-STANCES.
I TOLD GROFIELD IT WASN'T SAFE, B HE INSISTED ON KEEPING THE BARBE GAS IN THERE AND IT MADE THAT MARK...YOU KNOW MEN?
LILY!
WHAT IS HE, YOUR HUSBAND?
YOU DONE YET?
YEAH, ALL GOOD.
THANK YOU FOR YOUR TIME.

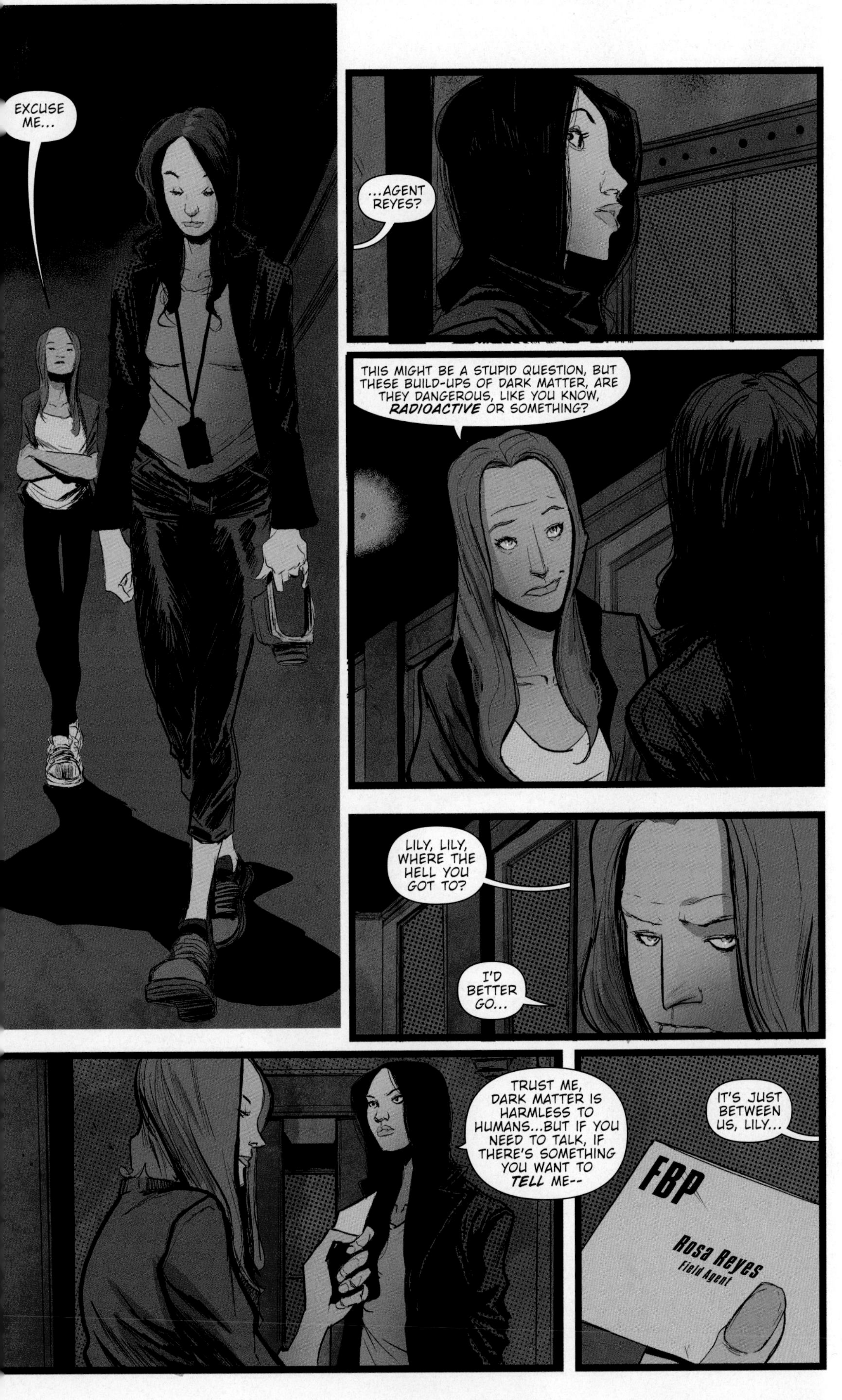
EXCUSE ME...
...AGENT REYES?
THIS MIGHT BE A STUPID QUESTION, BUT THESE BUILD-UPS OF DARK MATTER, ARE THEY DANGEROUS, LIKE YOU KNOW, RADIOACTIVE OR SOMETHING?
LILY, LILY, WHERE THE HELL YOU GOT TO?
I'D BETTER GO...
TRUST ME, DARK MATTER IS HARMLESS TO HUMANS...BUT IF YOU NEED TO TALK, IF THERE'S SOMETHING YOU WANT TO TELL ME--
IT'S JUST BETWEEN US, LILY...
FBP
Rosa Reyes
Field Agent

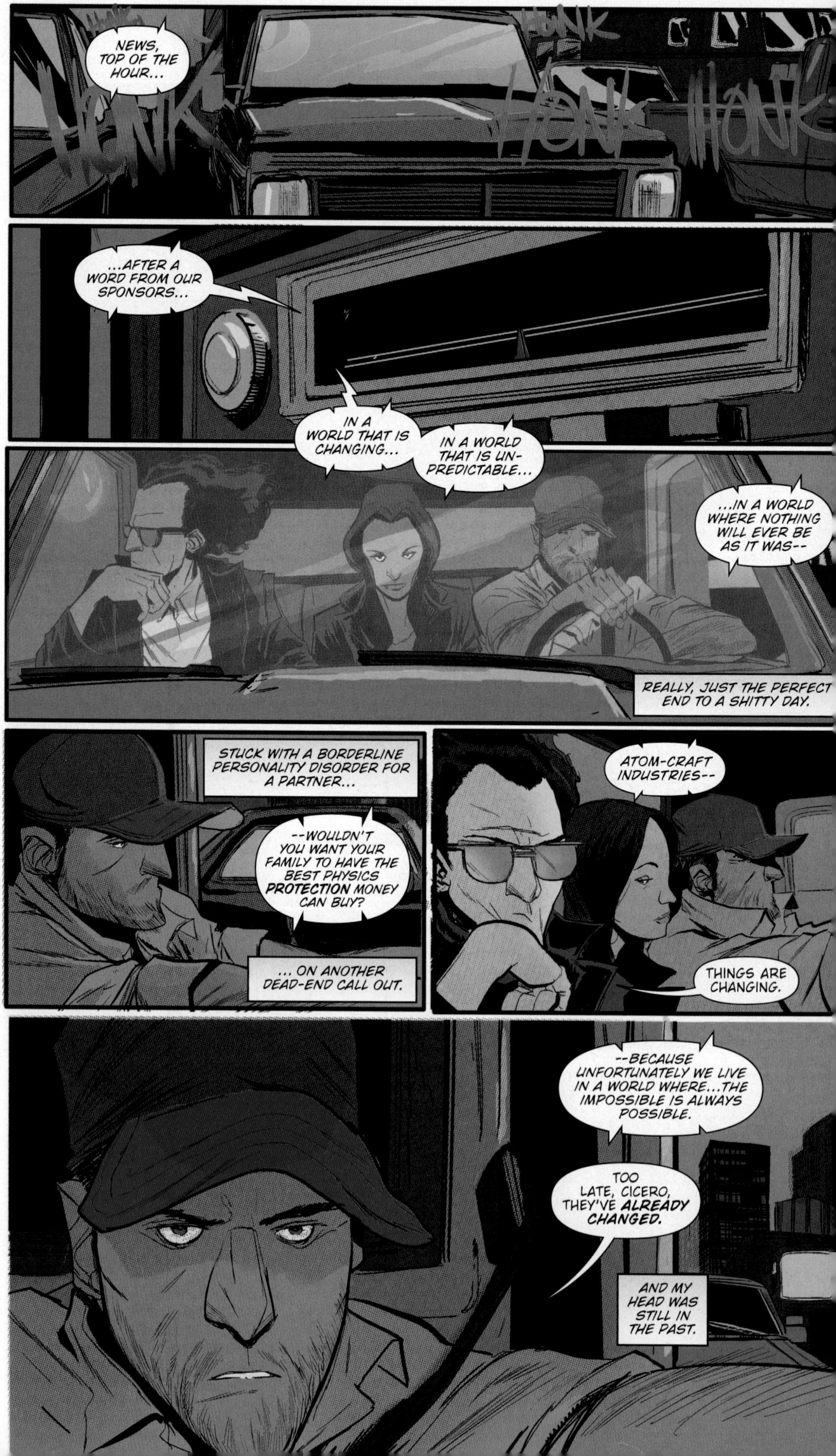

NEWS, TOP OF THE HOUR...
HONK HONK HONK HONK HONK
...AFTER A WORD FROM OUR SPONSORS...
IN A WORLD THAT IS CHANGING...
IN A WORLD THAT IS UN-PREDICTABLE...
...IN A WORLD WHERE NOTHING WILL EVER BE AS IT WAS--
REALLY, JUST THE PERFECT END TO A SHITTY DAY.
STUCK WITH A BORDERLINE PERSONALITY DISORDER FOR A PARTNER...
--WOULDN'T YOU WANT YOUR FAMILY TO HAVE THE BEST PHYSICS **PROTECTION** MONEY CAN BUY?
... ON ANOTHER DEAD-END CALL OUT.
ATOM-CRAFT INDUSTRIES--
THINGS ARE CHANGING.
--BECAUSE UNFORTUNATELY WE LIVE IN A WORLD WHERE...THE IMPOSSIBLE IS ALWAYS POSSIBLE.
TOO LATE, CICERO, THEY'VE **ALREADY CHANGED.**
AND MY HEAD WAS STILL IN THE PAST.

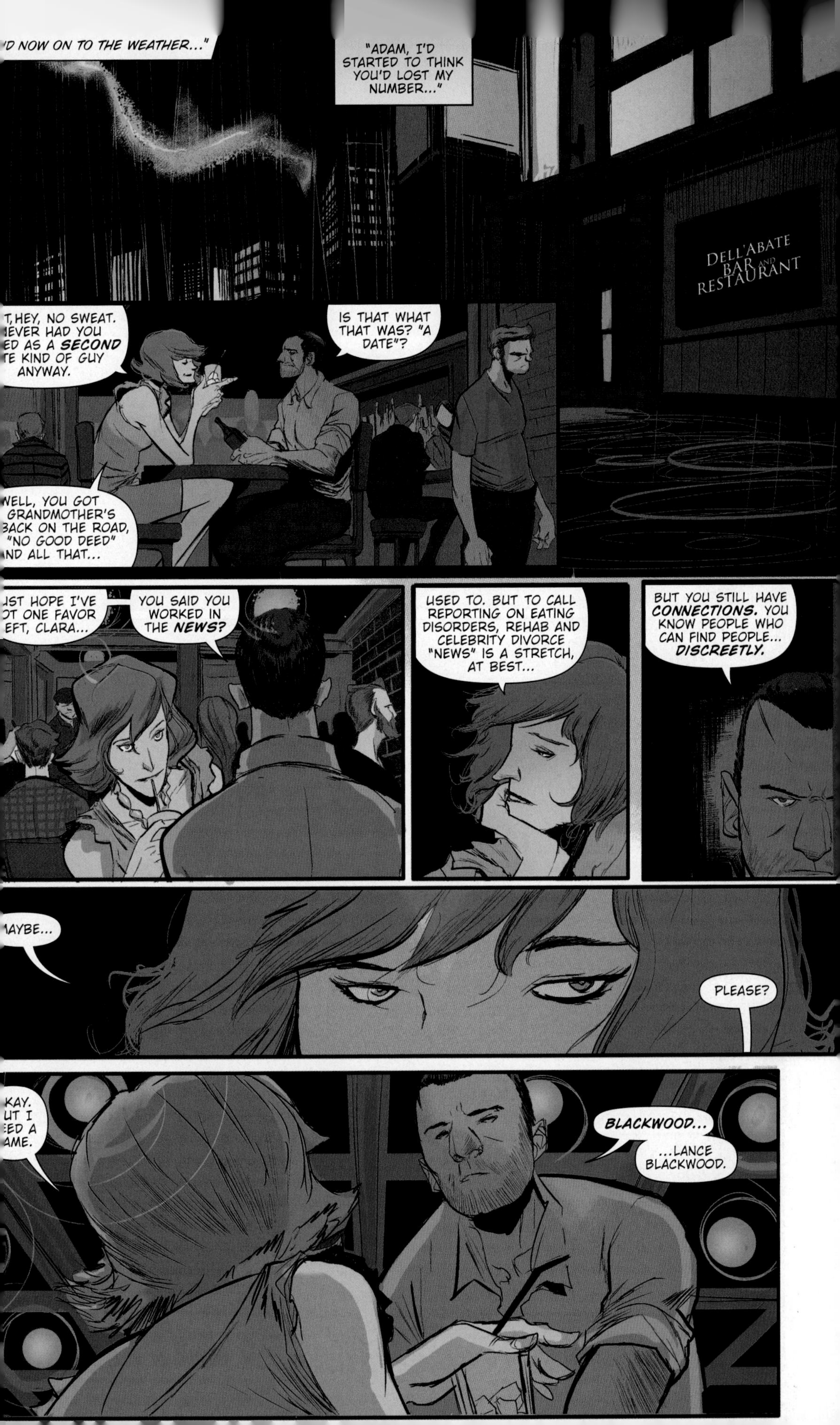
'D NOW ON TO THE WEATHER..."
"ADAM, I'D STARTED TO THINK YOU'D LOST MY NUMBER..."
DELL'ABATE BAR AND RESTAURANT
T, HEY, NO SWEAT. NEVER HAD YOU ED AS A SECOND TE KIND OF GUY ANYWAY.
IS THAT WHAT THAT WAS? "A DATE"?
WELL, YOU GOT GRANDMOTHER'S BACK ON THE ROAD, "NO GOOD DEED" AND ALL THAT...
UST HOPE I'VE OT ONE FAVOR EFT, CLARA...
YOU SAID YOU WORKED IN THE NEWS?
USED TO. BUT TO CALL REPORTING ON EATING DISORDERS, REHAB AND CELEBRITY DIVORCE "NEWS" IS A STRETCH, AT BEST...
BUT YOU STILL HAVE CONNECTIONS. YOU KNOW PEOPLE WHO CAN FIND PEOPLE... DISCREETLY.
AYBE...
PLEASE?
KAY. UT I EED A AME.
BLACKWOOD...
...LANCE BLACKWOOD.

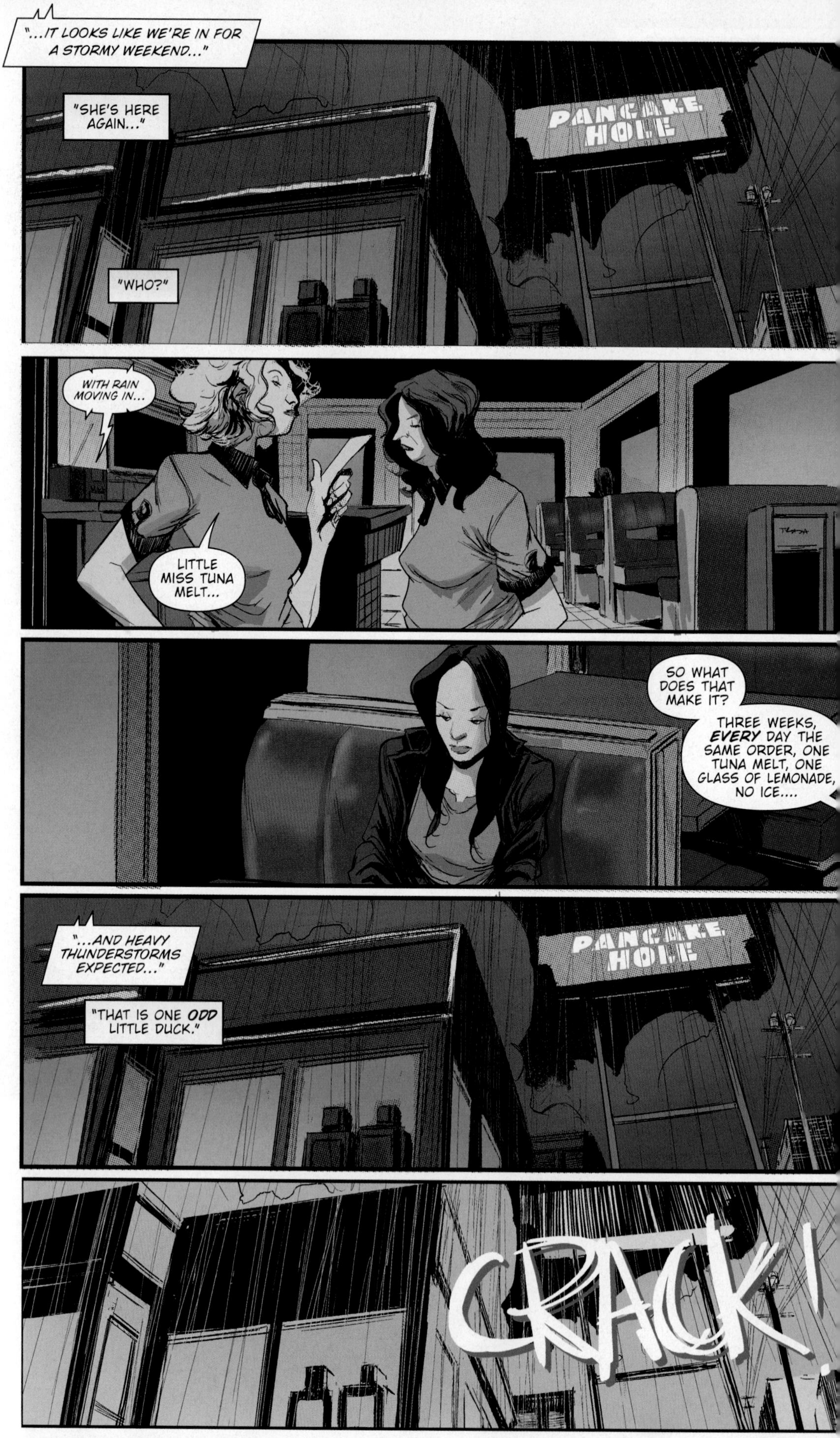
"...IT LOOKS LIKE WE'RE IN FOR A STORMY WEEKEND..."
"SHE'S HERE AGAIN..."
PANCAKE HOLE
"WHO?"
WITH RAIN MOVING IN...
LITTLE MISS TUNA MELT...
SO WHAT DOES THAT MAKE IT?
THREE WEEKS, EVERY DAY THE SAME ORDER, ONE TUNA MELT, ONE GLASS OF LEMONADE, NO ICE....
"...AND HEAVY THUNDERSTORMS EXPECTED..."
PANCAKE HOLE
"THAT IS ONE ODD LITTLE DUCK."
CRACK!

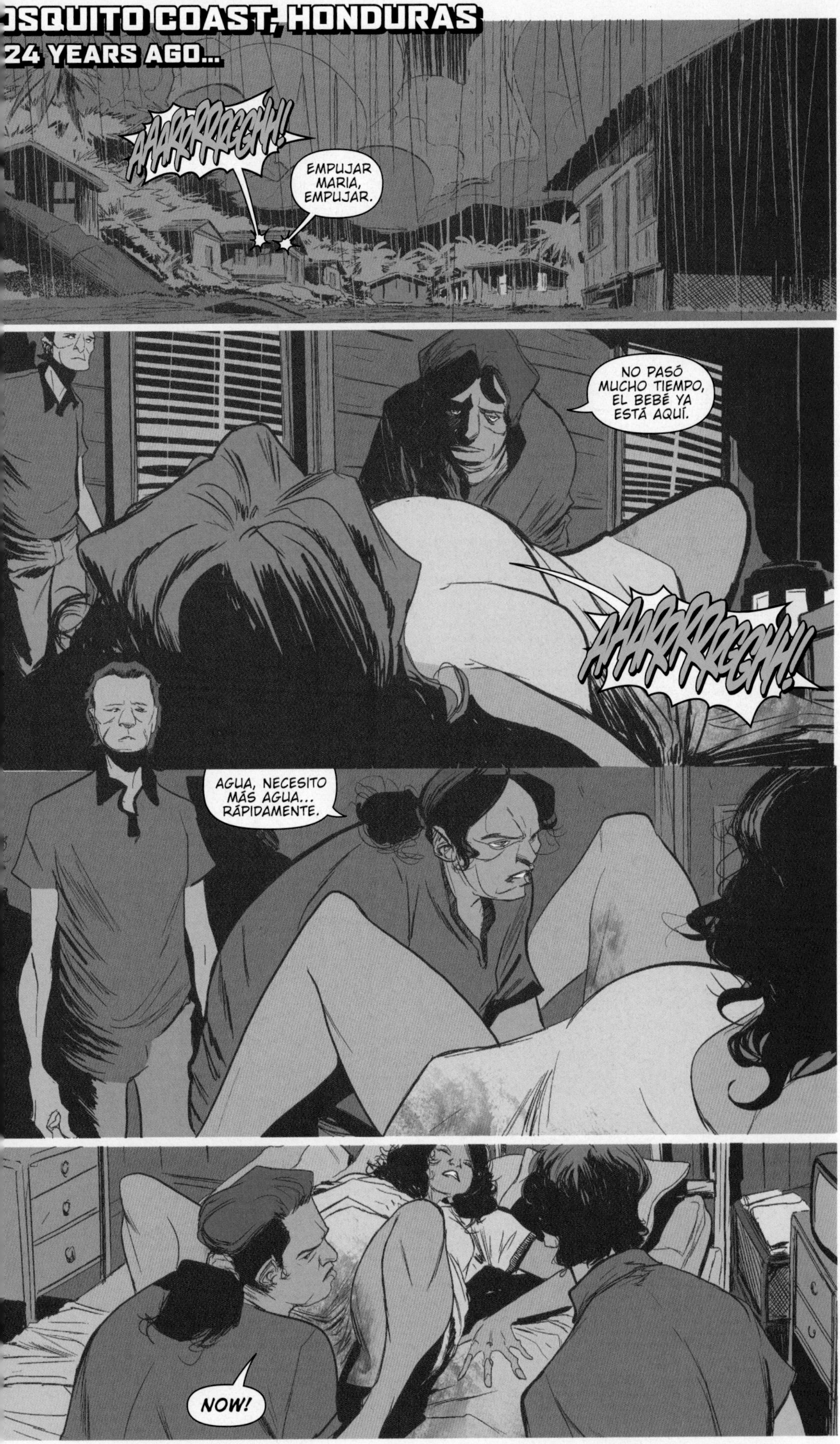

OSQUITO COAST, HONDURAS
24 YEARS AGO...
AAARRRRGGHH!
EMPUJAR MARIA, EMPUJAR.
NO PASÓ MUCHO TIEMPO, EL BEBÉ YA ESTÁ AQUÍ.
AAARRRRGGHH!
AGUA, NECESITO MÁS AGUA... RÁPIDAMENTE.
NOW!

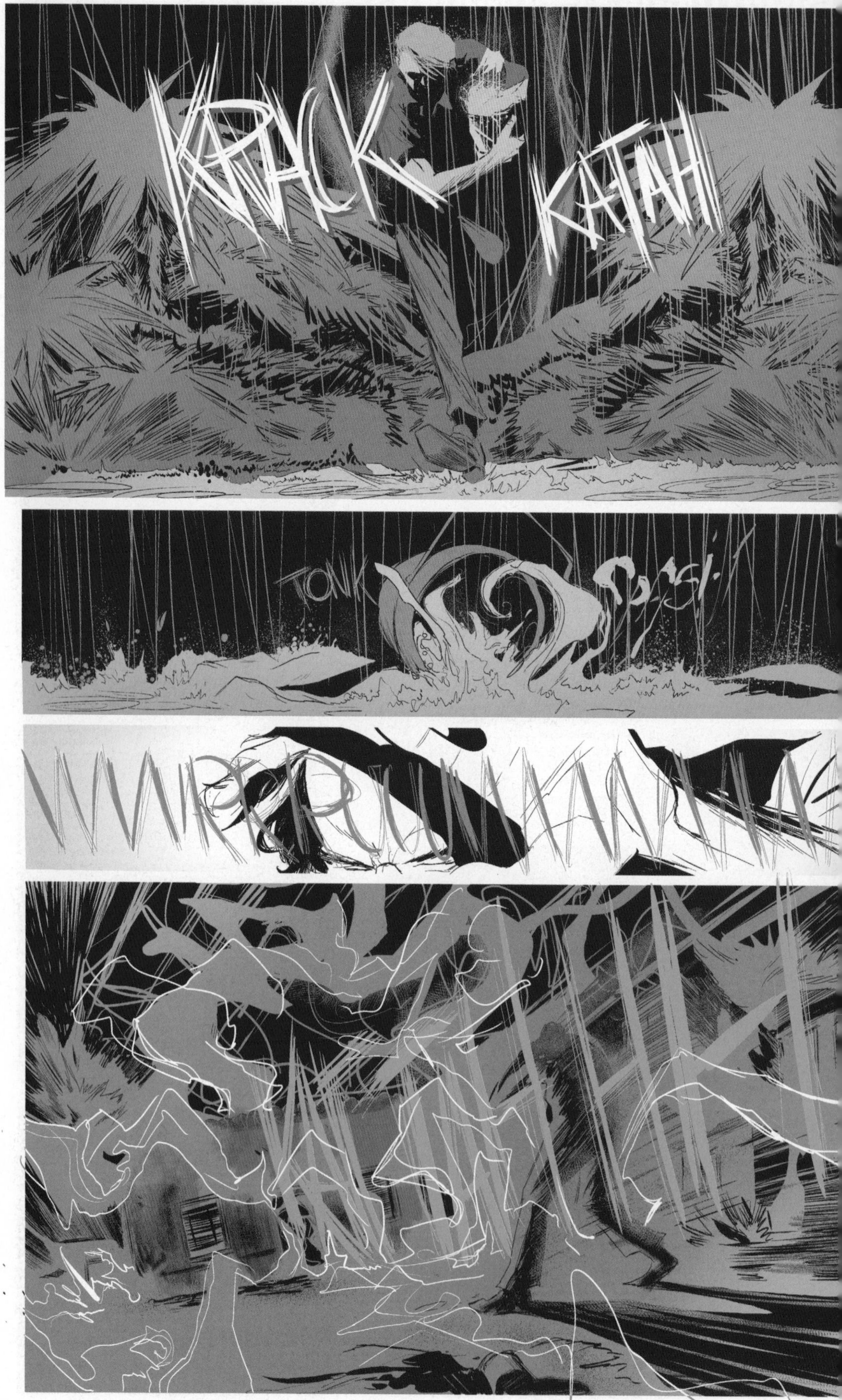
KRACK
KATAH
TONK

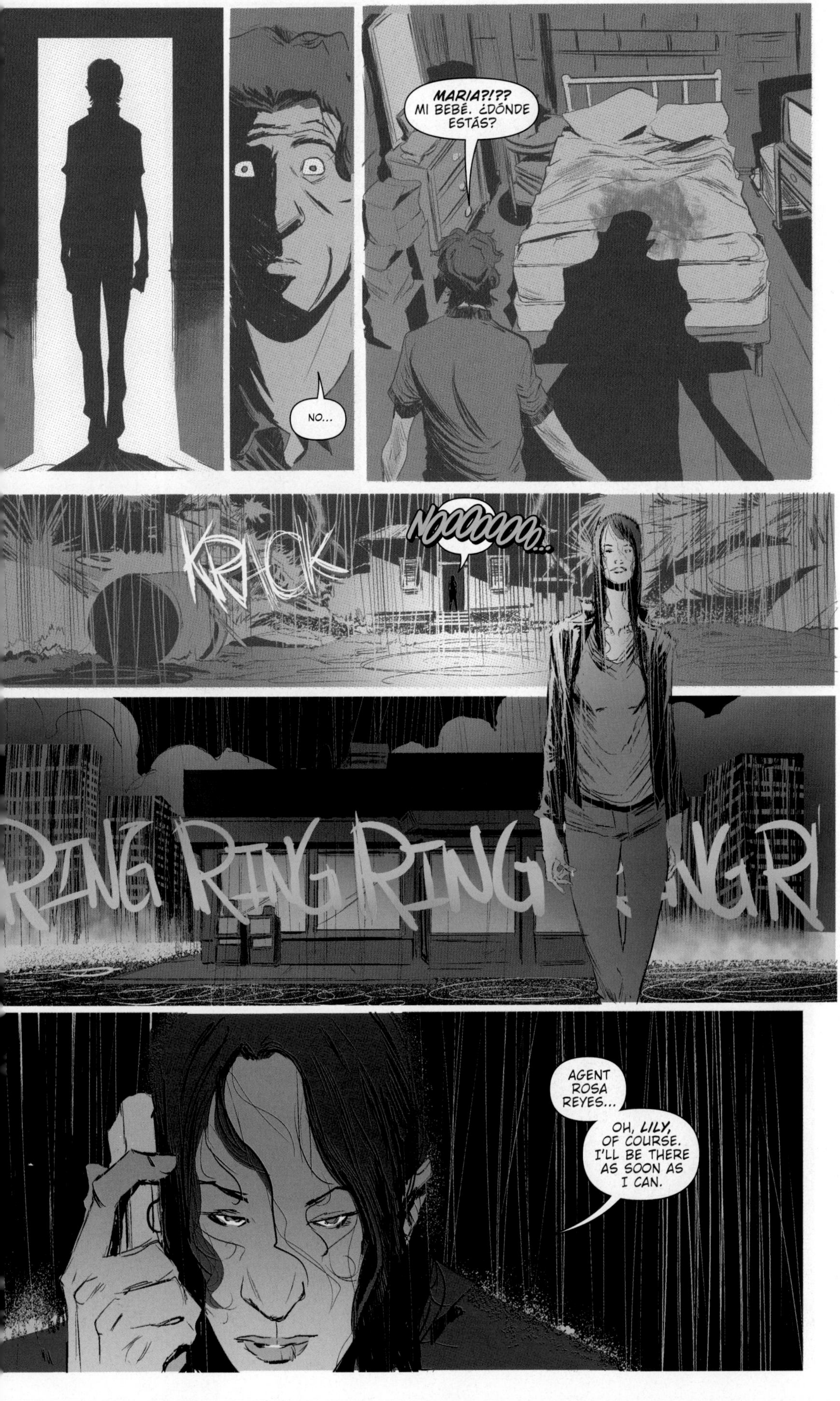

NO...
MARIA?!??
MI BEBÉ. ¿DÓNDE ESTÁS?
KRACK
NOOOOOOO...
RING RING RING
AGENT ROSA REYES...
OH, LILY, OF COURSE. I'LL BE THERE AS SOON AS I CAN.

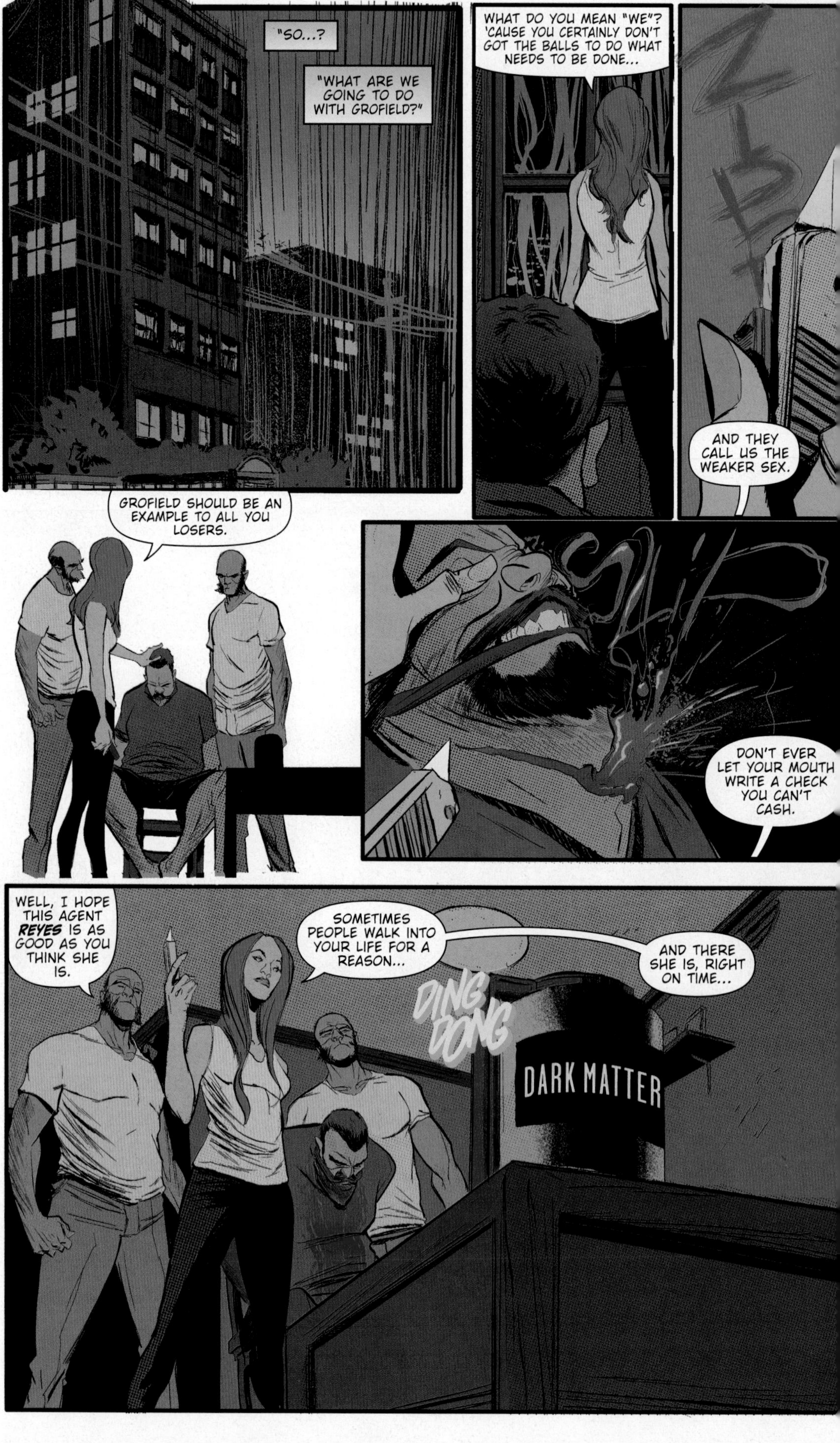
"SO...?
"WHAT ARE WE GOING TO DO WITH GROFIELD?"
WHAT DO YOU MEAN "WE"? 'CAUSE YOU CERTAINLY DON'T GOT THE BALLS TO DO WHAT NEEDS TO BE DONE...
AND THEY CALL US THE WEAKER SEX.
GROFIELD SHOULD BE AN EXAMPLE TO ALL YOU LOSERS.
DON'T EVER LET YOUR MOUTH WRITE A CHECK YOU CAN'T CASH.
WELL, I HOPE THIS AGENT **REYES** IS AS GOOD AS YOU THINK SHE IS.
SOMETIMES PEOPLE WALK INTO YOUR LIFE FOR A REASON...
AND THERE SHE IS, RIGHT ON TIME...
DING DONG
DARK MATTER

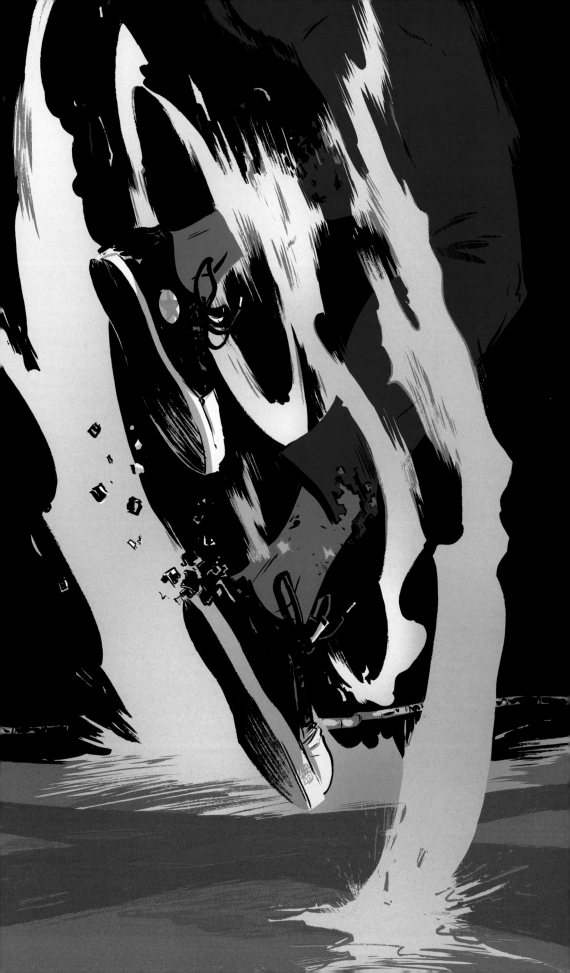

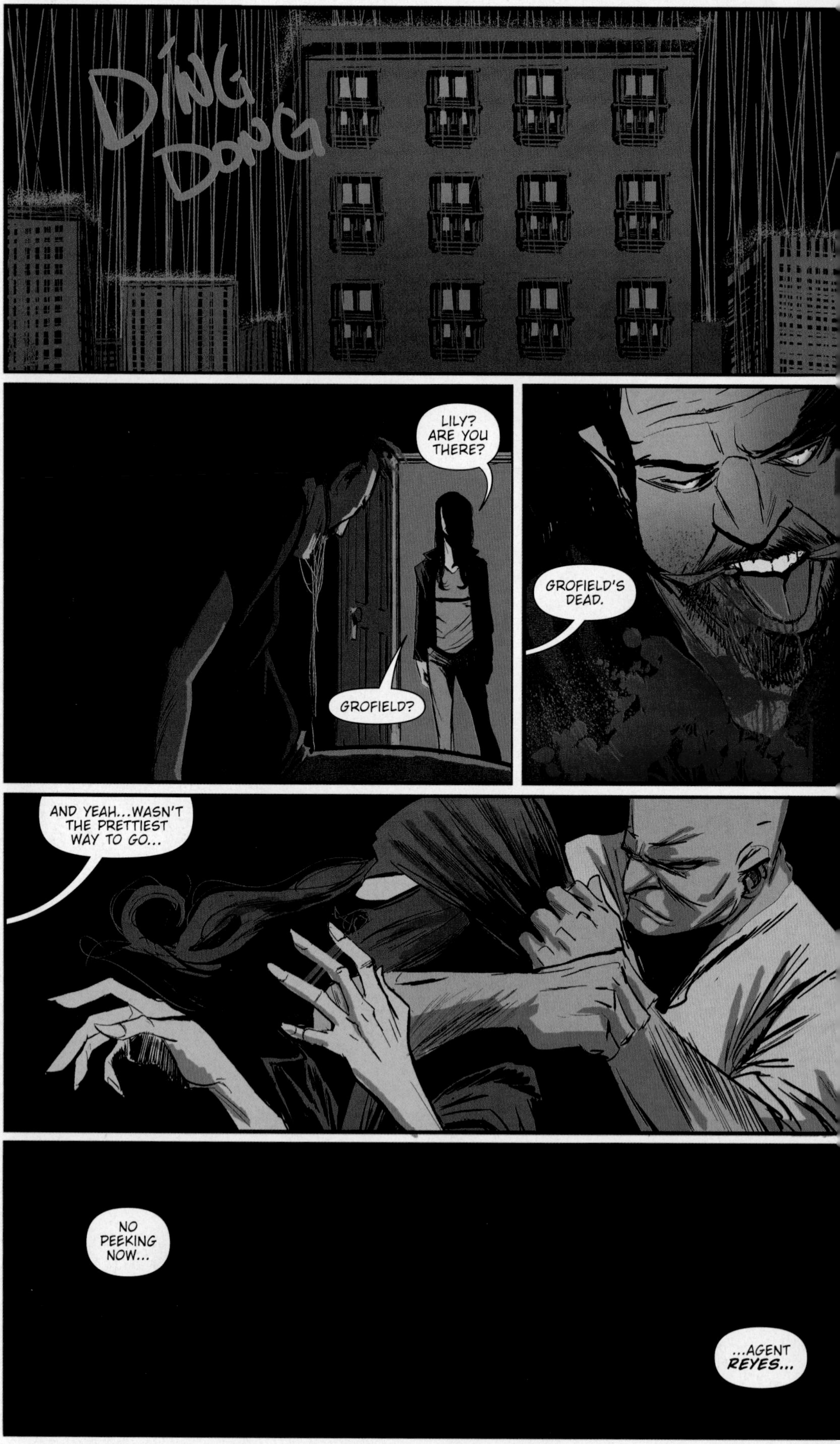
DING DONG
LILY? ARE YOU THERE?
GROFIELD?
GROFIELD'S DEAD.
AND YEAH...WASN'T THE PRETTIEST WAY TO GO...
NO PEEKING NOW...
...AGENT REYES...

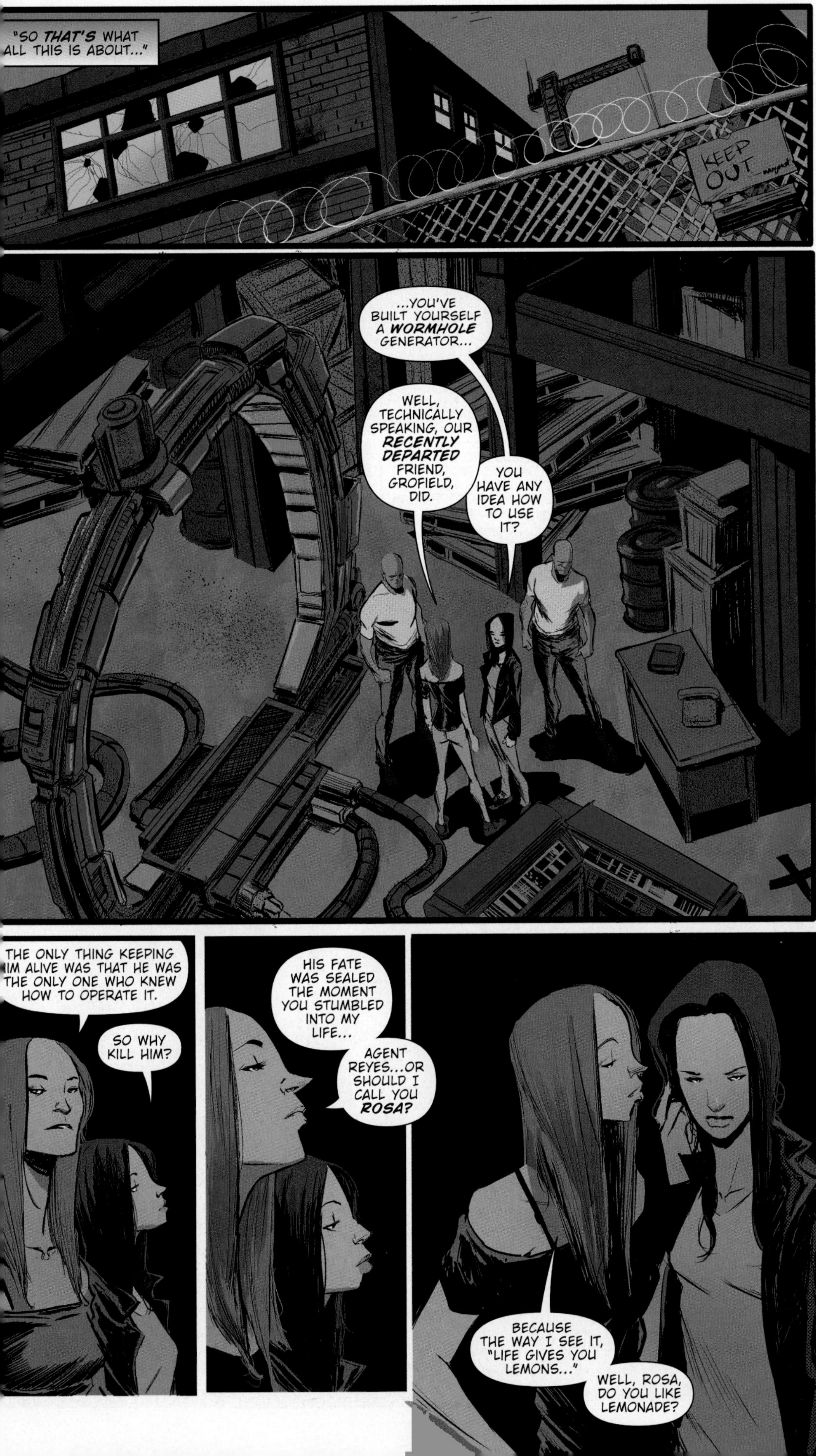
"SO THAT'S WHAT ALL THIS IS ABOUT..."
KEEP OUT
...YOU'VE BUILT YOURSELF A WORMHOLE GENERATOR...
WELL, TECHNICALLY SPEAKING, OUR RECENTLY DEPARTED FRIEND, GROFIELD, DID.
YOU HAVE ANY IDEA HOW TO USE IT?
THE ONLY THING KEEPING IM ALIVE WAS THAT HE WAS THE ONLY ONE WHO KNEW HOW TO OPERATE IT.
SO WHY KILL HIM?
HIS FATE WAS SEALED THE MOMENT YOU STUMBLED INTO MY LIFE...
AGENT REYES...OR SHOULD I CALL YOU ROSA?
BECAUSE THE WAY I SEE IT, "LIFE GIVES YOU LEMONS..."
WELL, ROSA, DO YOU LIKE LEMONADE?

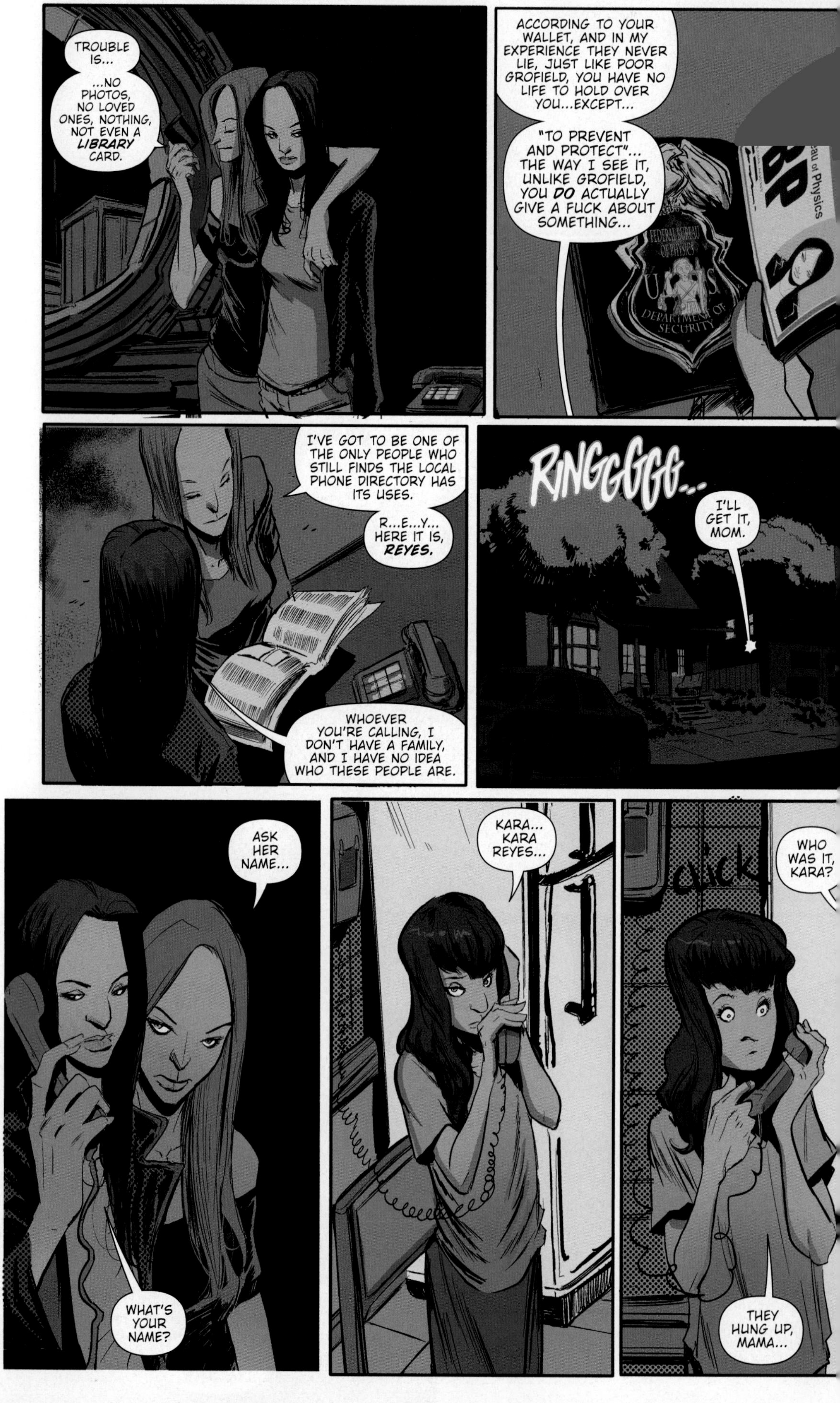
TROUBLE IS...
...NO PHOTOS, NO LOVED ONES, NOTHING, NOT EVEN A *LIBRARY* CARD.
ACCORDING TO YOUR WALLET, AND IN MY EXPERIENCE THEY NEVER LIE, JUST LIKE POOR GROFIELD, YOU HAVE NO LIFE TO HOLD OVER YOU...EXCEPT...
"TO PREVENT AND PROTECT"... THE WAY I SEE IT, UNLIKE GROFIELD, YOU *DO* ACTUALLY GIVE A FUCK ABOUT SOMETHING...
FEDERAL BUREAU OF PHYSICS
U.S. DEPARTMENT OF SECURITY
I'VE GOT TO BE ONE OF THE ONLY PEOPLE WHO STILL FINDS THE LOCAL PHONE DIRECTORY HAS ITS USES.
R...E...Y... HERE IT IS, *REYES.*
WHOEVER YOU'RE CALLING, I DON'T HAVE A FAMILY, AND I HAVE NO IDEA WHO THESE PEOPLE ARE.
RINGGGGG...
I'LL GET IT, MOM.
ASK HER NAME...
WHAT'S YOUR NAME?
KARA... KARA REYES...
CLICK
WHO WAS IT, KARA?
THEY HUNG UP, MAMA...

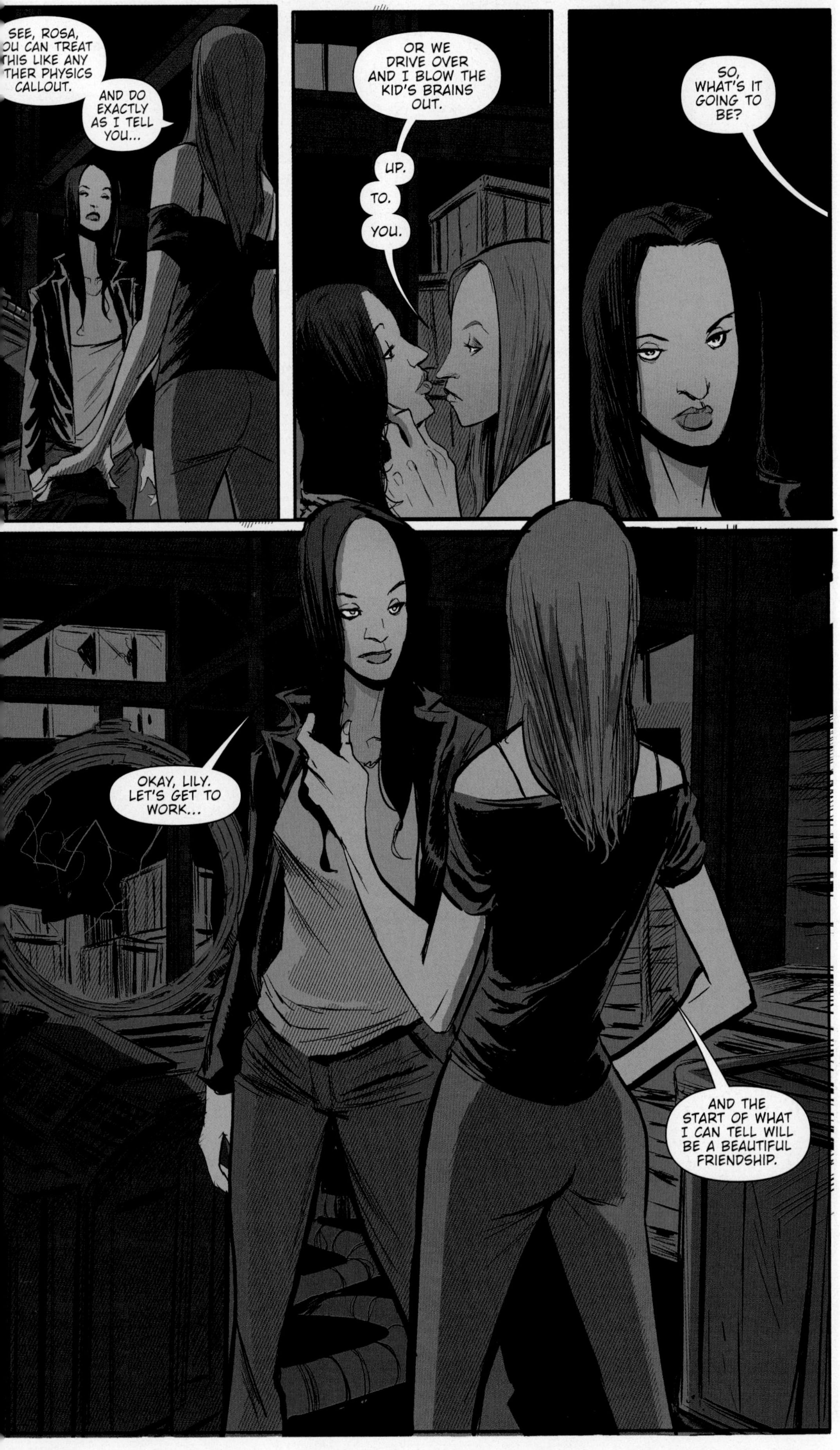
SEE, ROSA, OU CAN TREAT THIS LIKE ANY THER PHYSICS CALLOUT.
AND DO EXACTLY AS I TELL YOU...
OR WE DRIVE OVER AND I BLOW THE KID'S BRAINS OUT.
UP.
TO.
YOU.
SO, WHAT'S IT GOING TO BE?
OKAY, LILY. LET'S GET TO WORK...
AND THE START OF WHAT I CAN TELL WILL BE A BEAUTIFUL FRIENDSHIP.

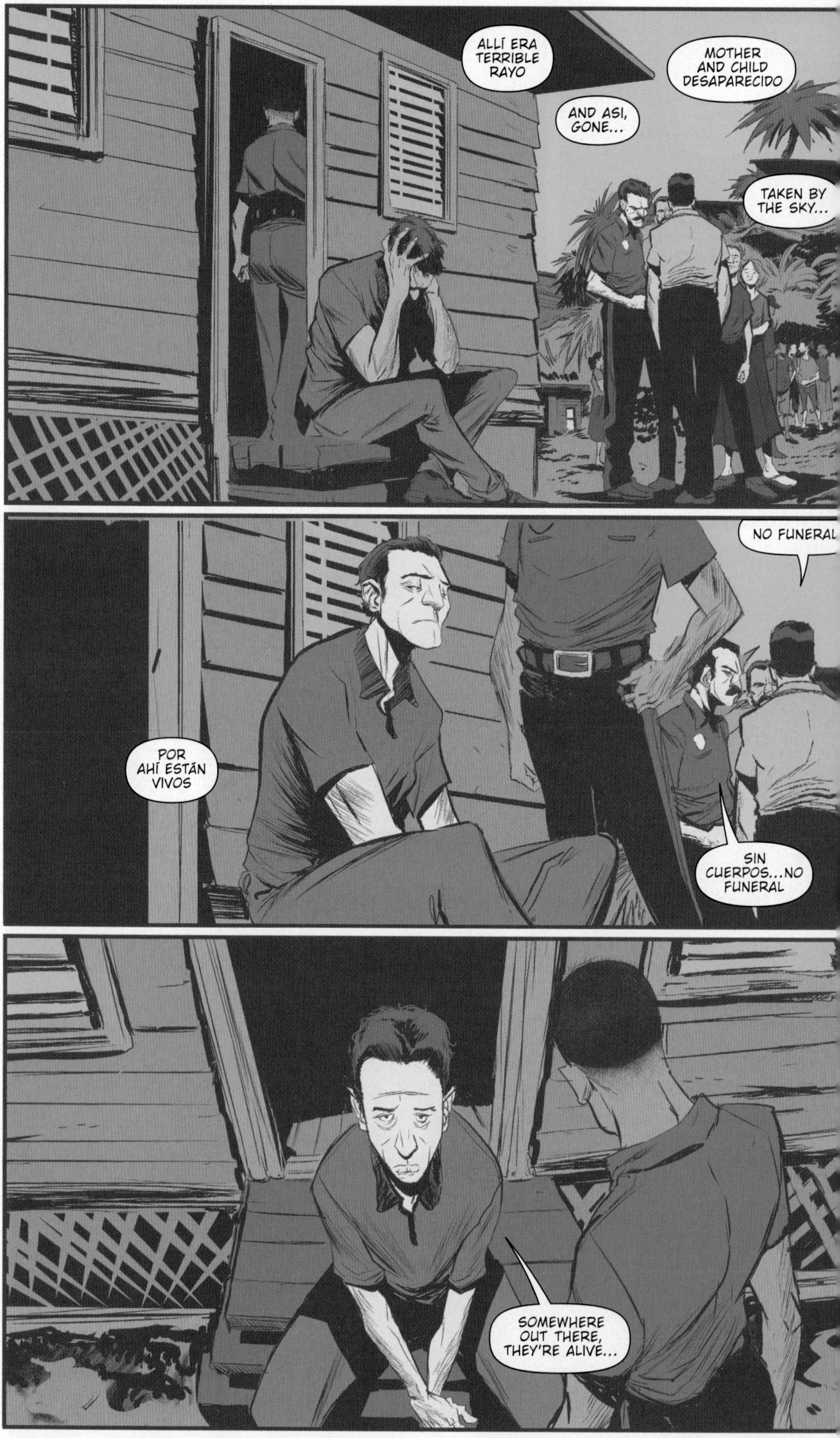
ALLÍ ERA TERRIBLE RAYO
AND ASI, GONE...
MOTHER AND CHILD DESAPARECIDO
TAKEN BY THE SKY...
NO FUNERAL
POR AHÍ ESTÁN VIVOS
SIN CUERPOS...NO FUNERAL
SOMEWHERE OUT THERE, THEY'RE ALIVE...

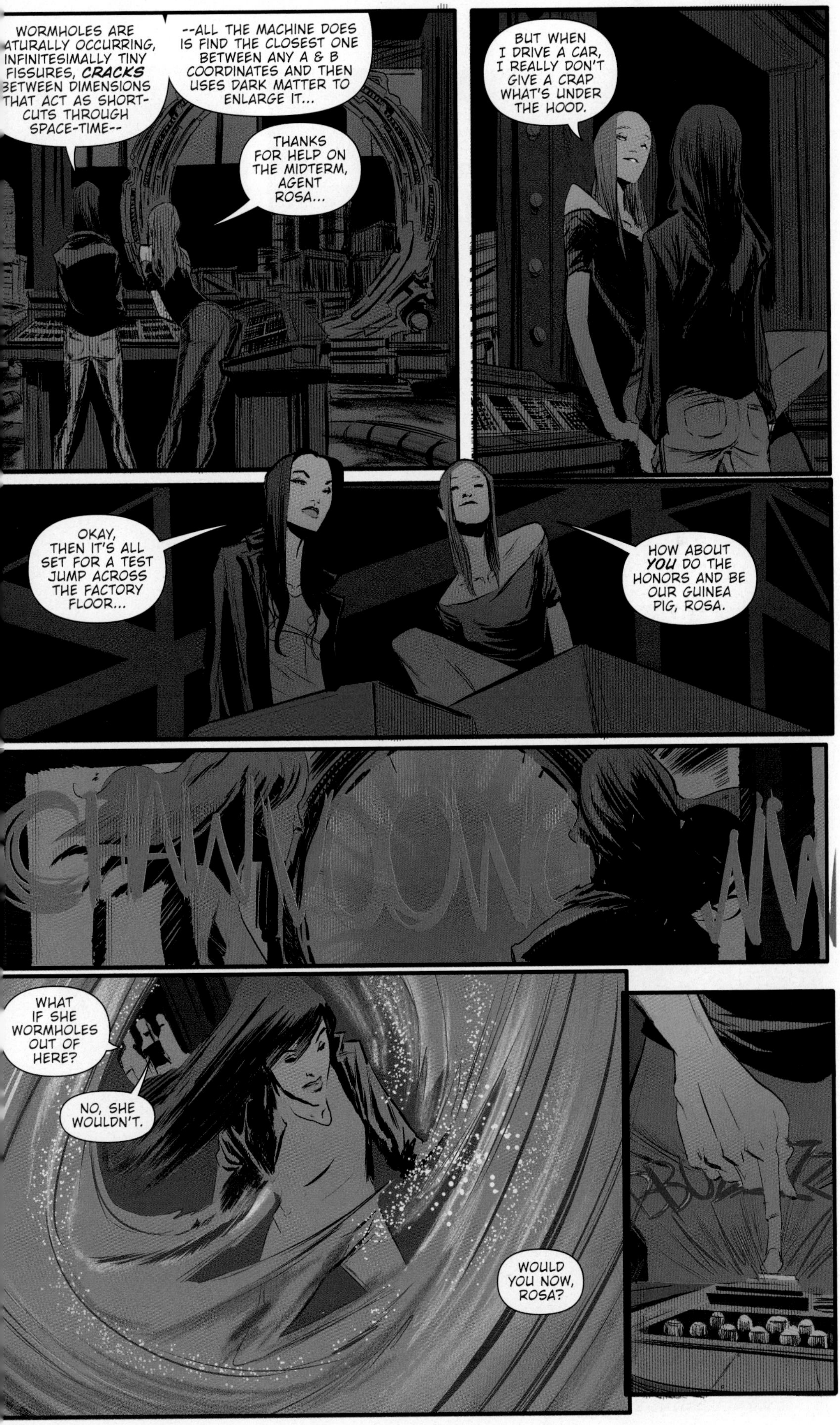
WORMHOLES ARE ATURALLY OCCURRING, INFINITESIMALLY TINY FISSURES, CRACKS BETWEEN DIMENSIONS THAT ACT AS SHORT-CUTS THROUGH SPACE-TIME--
--ALL THE MACHINE DOES IS FIND THE CLOSEST ONE BETWEEN ANY A & B COORDINATES AND THEN USES DARK MATTER TO ENLARGE IT...
THANKS FOR HELP ON THE MIDTERM, AGENT ROSA...
BUT WHEN I DRIVE A CAR, I REALLY DON'T GIVE A CRAP WHAT'S UNDER THE HOOD.
OKAY, THEN IT'S ALL SET FOR A TEST JUMP ACROSS THE FACTORY FLOOR...
HOW ABOUT YOU DO THE HONORS AND BE OUR GUINEA PIG, ROSA.
WHAT IF SHE WORMHOLES OUT OF HERE?
NO, SHE WOULDN'T.
WOULD YOU NOW, ROSA?

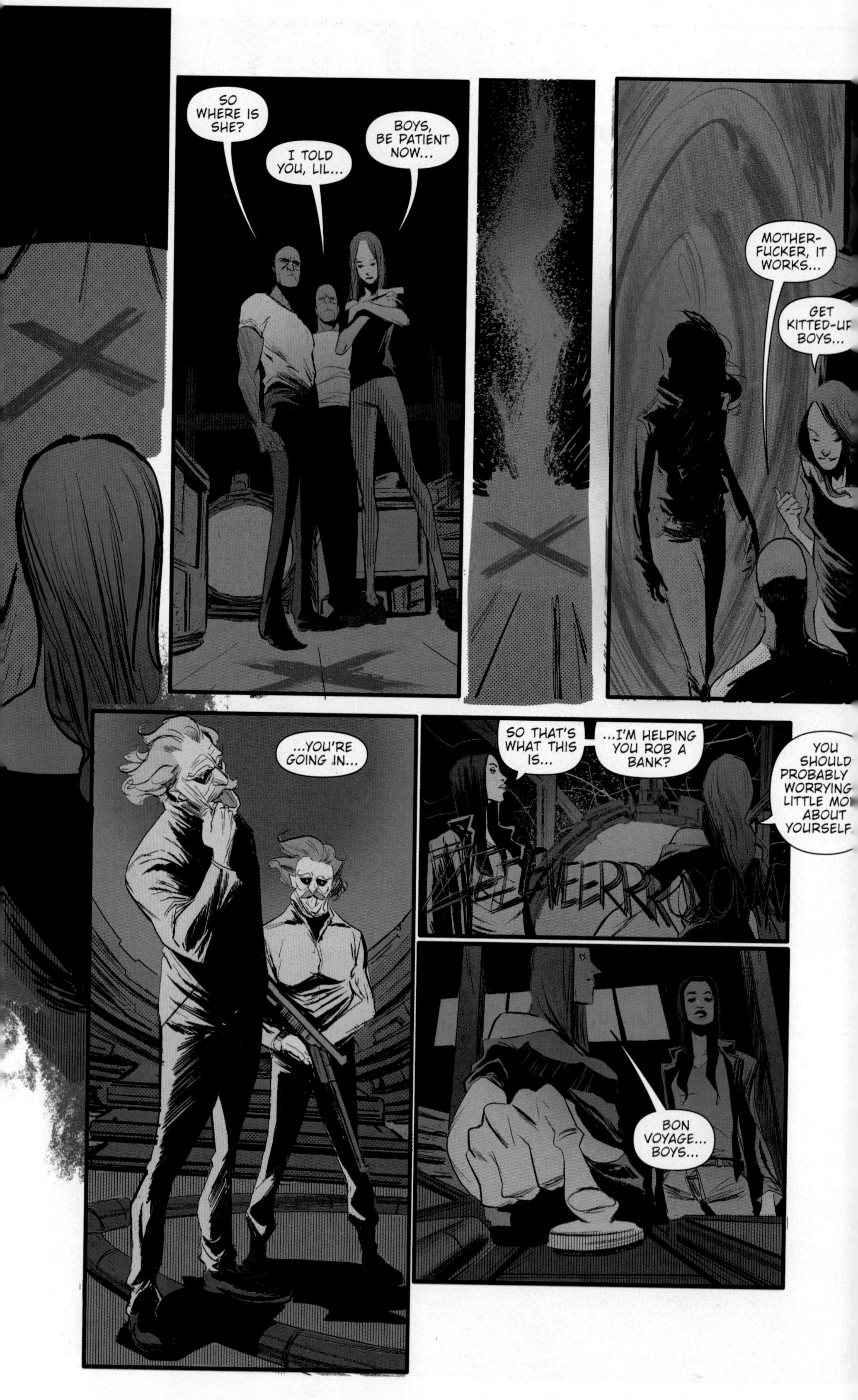
SO WHERE IS SHE?
I TOLD YOU, LIL...
BOYS, BE PATIENT NOW...
MOTHER-FUCKER, IT WORKS...
GET KITTED-UP BOYS...
...YOU'RE GOING IN...
SO THAT'S WHAT THIS IS...
...I'M HELPING YOU ROB A BANK?
YOU SHOULD PROBABLY WORRYING LITTLE MO ABOUT YOURSELF.
BON VOYAGE... BOYS...

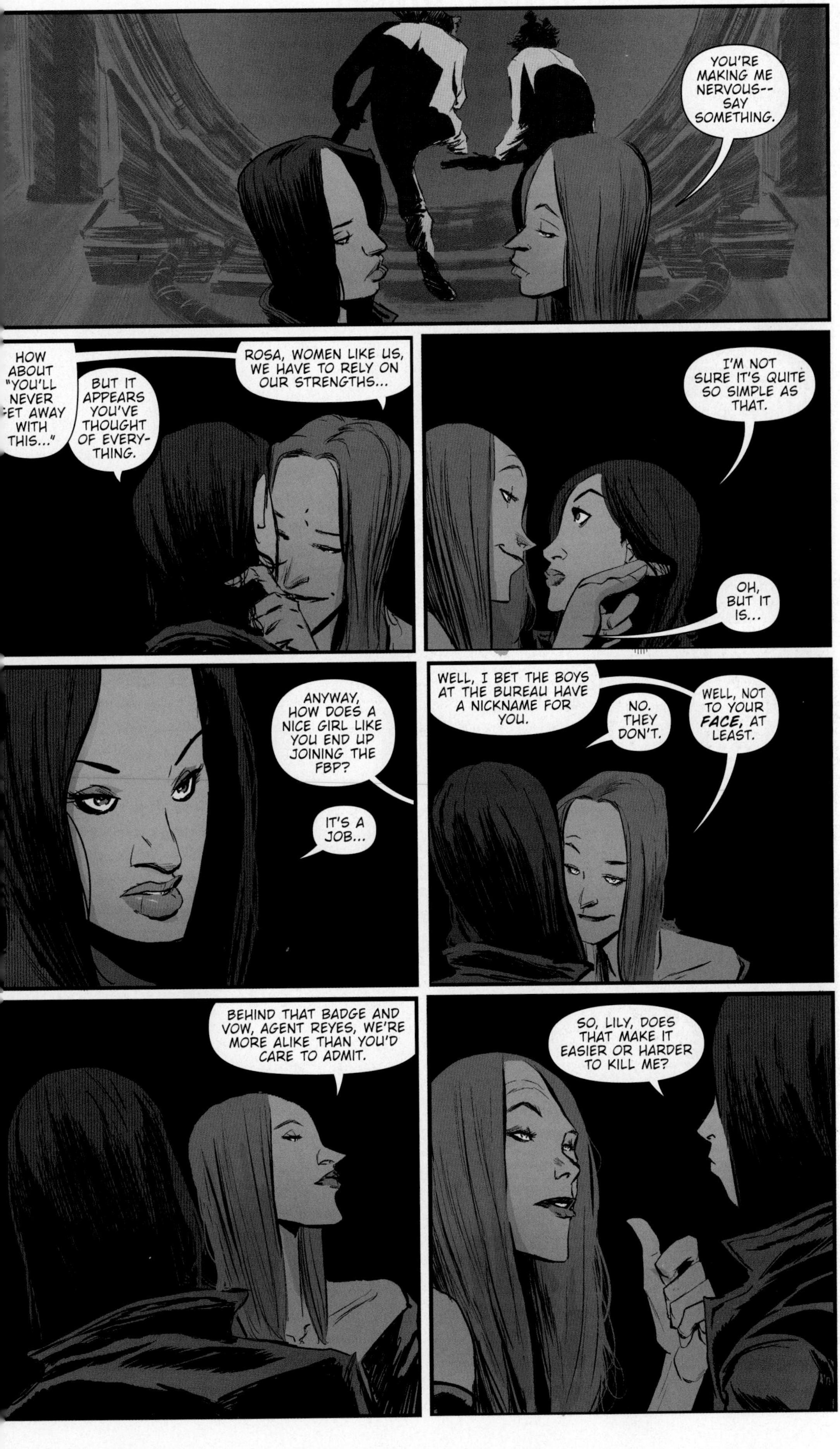
YOU'RE MAKING ME NERVOUS-- SAY SOMETHING.
ROSA, WOMEN LIKE US, WE HAVE TO RELY ON OUR STRENGTHS...
HOW ABOUT "YOU'LL NEVER GET AWAY WITH THIS..."
BUT IT APPEARS YOU'VE THOUGHT OF EVERYTHING.
I'M NOT SURE IT'S QUITE SO SIMPLE AS THAT.
OH, BUT IT IS...
ANYWAY, HOW DOES A NICE GIRL LIKE YOU END UP JOINING THE FBP?
IT'S A JOB...
WELL, I BET THE BOYS AT THE BUREAU HAVE A NICKNAME FOR YOU.
NO. THEY DON'T.
WELL, NOT TO YOUR *FACE,* AT LEAST.
BEHIND THAT BADGE AND VOW, AGENT REYES, WE'RE MORE ALIKE THAN YOU'D CARE TO ADMIT.
SO, LILY, DOES THAT MAKE IT EASIER OR HARDER TO KILL ME?

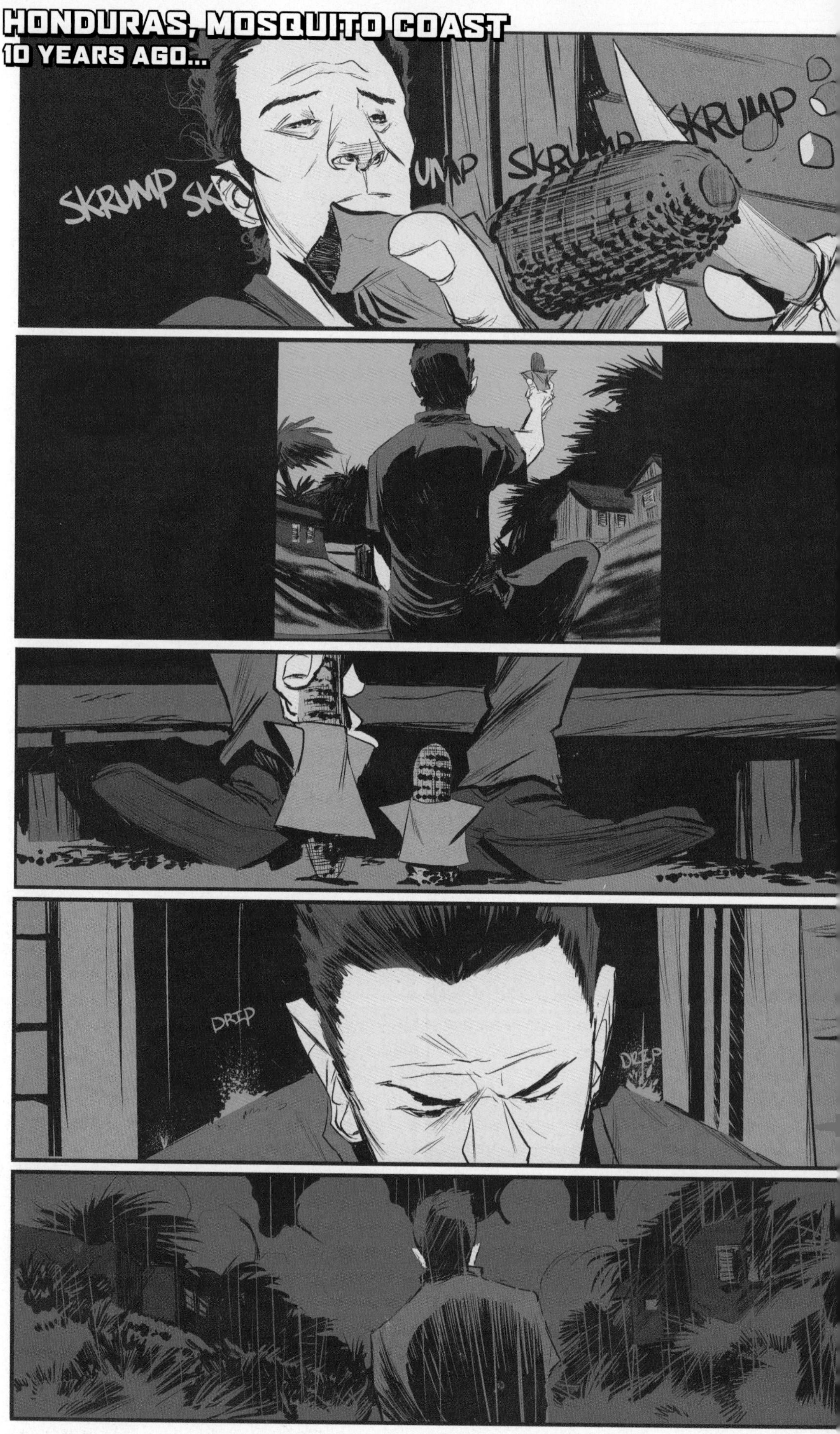
HONDURAS, MOSQUITO COAST
10 YEARS AGO...
SKRUMP
SKRUMP
DRIP

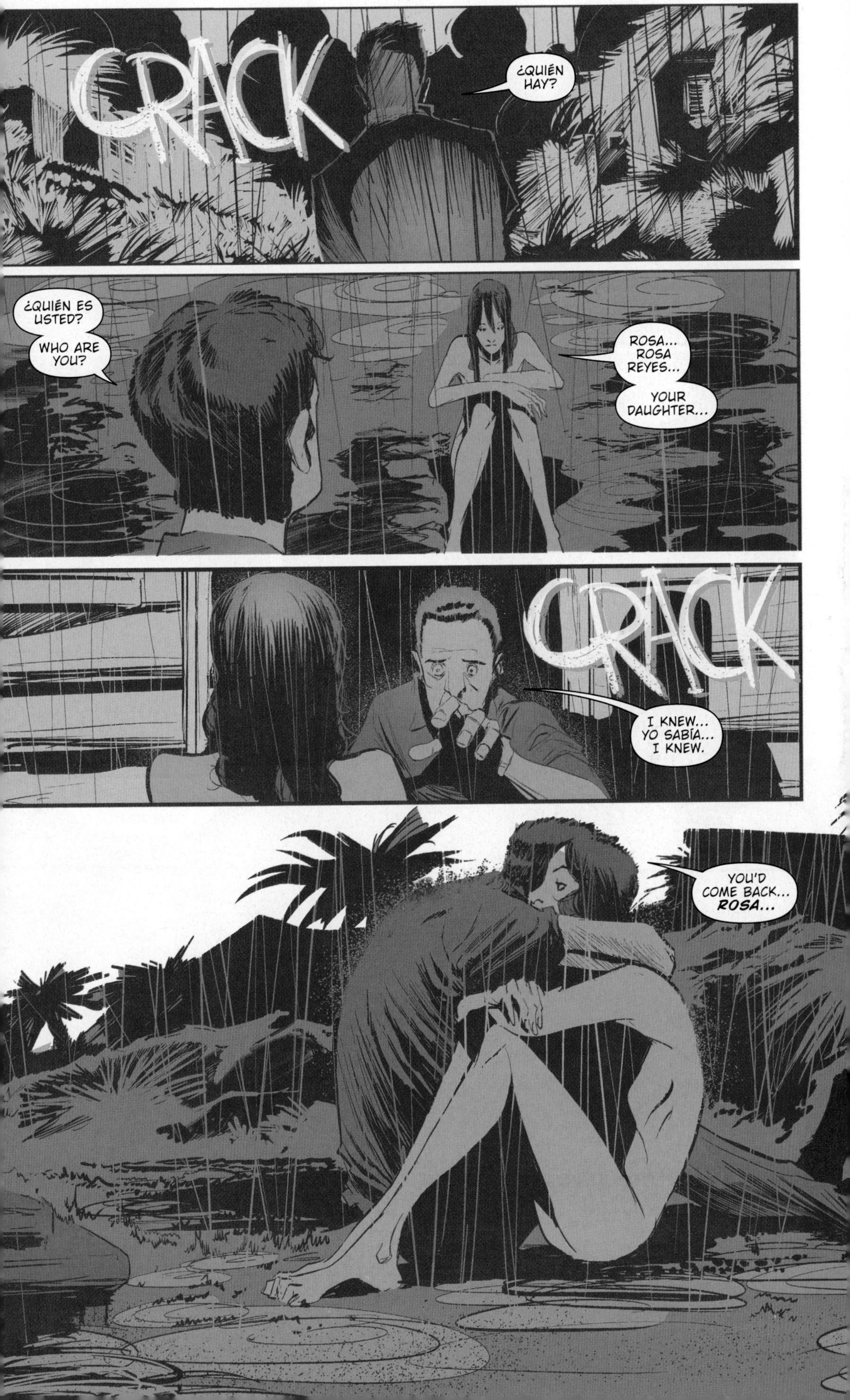
CRACK
¿QUIÉN HAY?
¿QUIÉN ES USTED?
WHO ARE YOU?
ROSA... ROSA REYES...
YOUR DAUGHTER...
CRACK
I KNEW... YO SABÍA... I KNEW.
YOU'D COME BACK... ROSA...

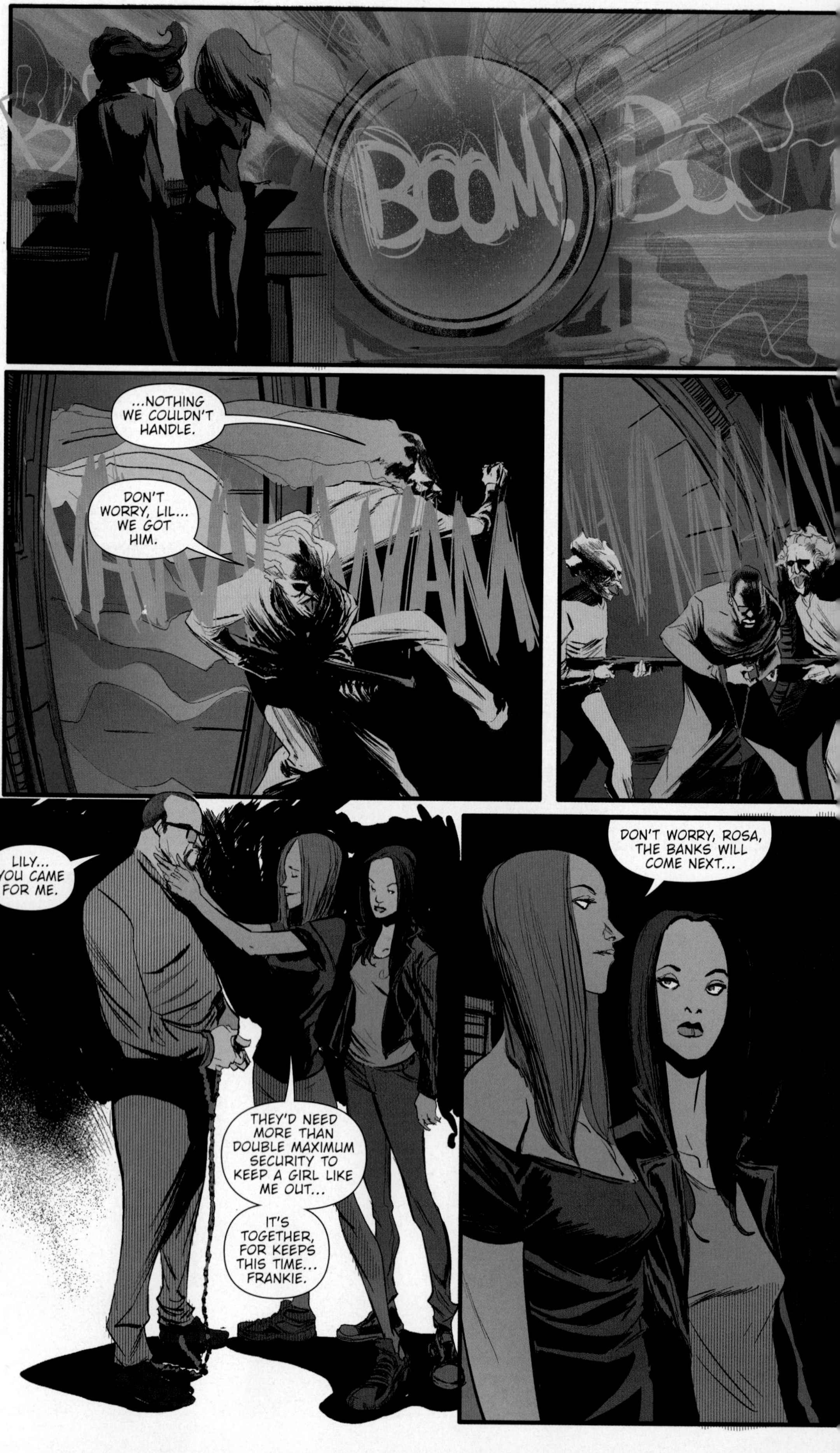
BOOM!
...NOTHING WE COULDN'T HANDLE.
DON'T WORRY, LIL... WE GOT HIM.
WAM
LILY... YOU CAME FOR ME.
THEY'D NEED MORE THAN DOUBLE MAXIMUM SECURITY TO KEEP A GIRL LIKE ME OUT...
IT'S TOGETHER, FOR KEEPS THIS TIME... FRANKIE.
DON'T WORRY, ROSA, THE BANKS WILL COME NEXT...

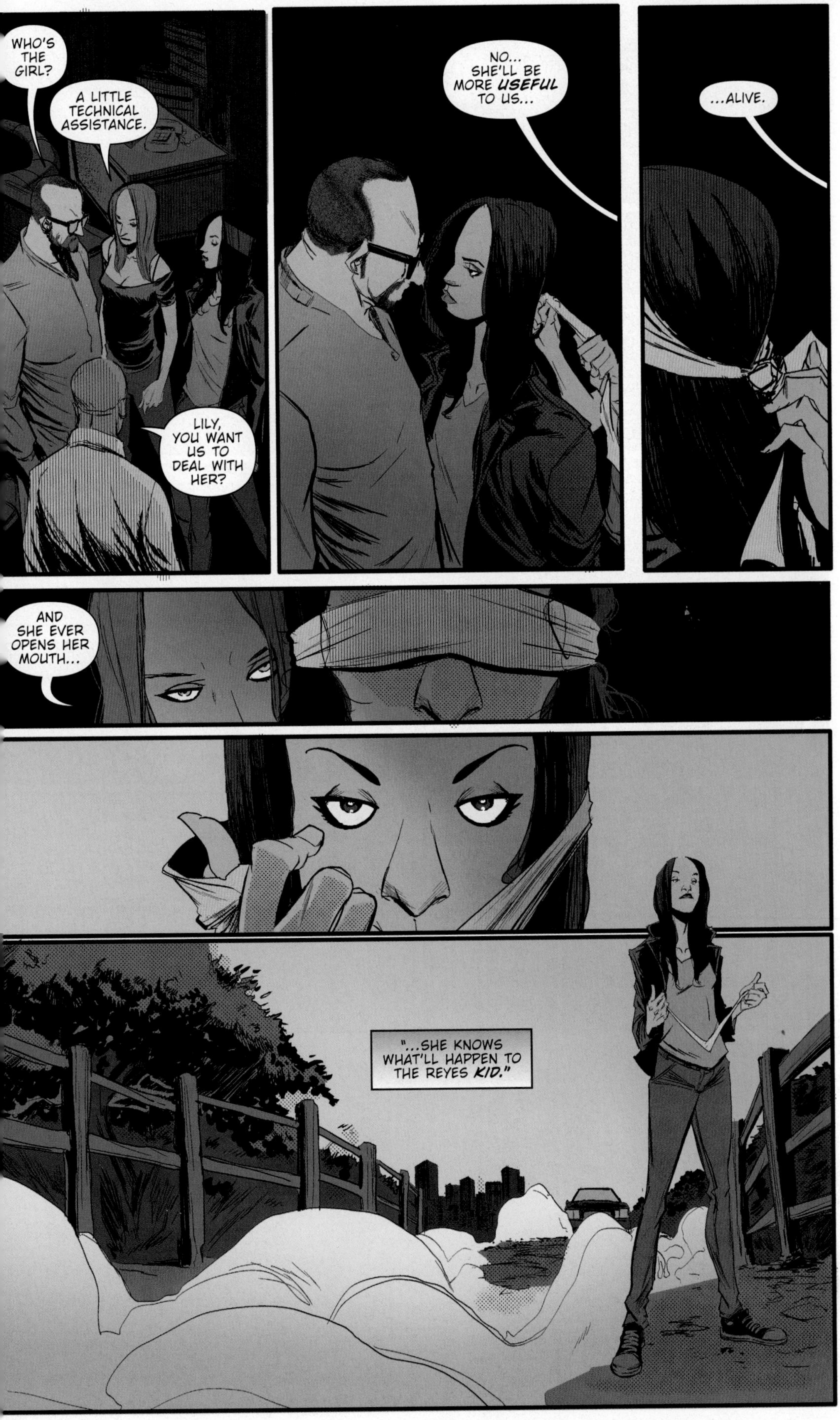
WHO'S THE GIRL?
A LITTLE TECHNICAL ASSISTANCE.
LILY, YOU WANT US TO DEAL WITH HER?
NO... SHE'LL BE MORE *USEFUL* TO US...
...ALIVE.
AND SHE EVER OPENS HER MOUTH...
"...SHE KNOWS WHAT'LL HAPPEN TO THE REYES *KID*."

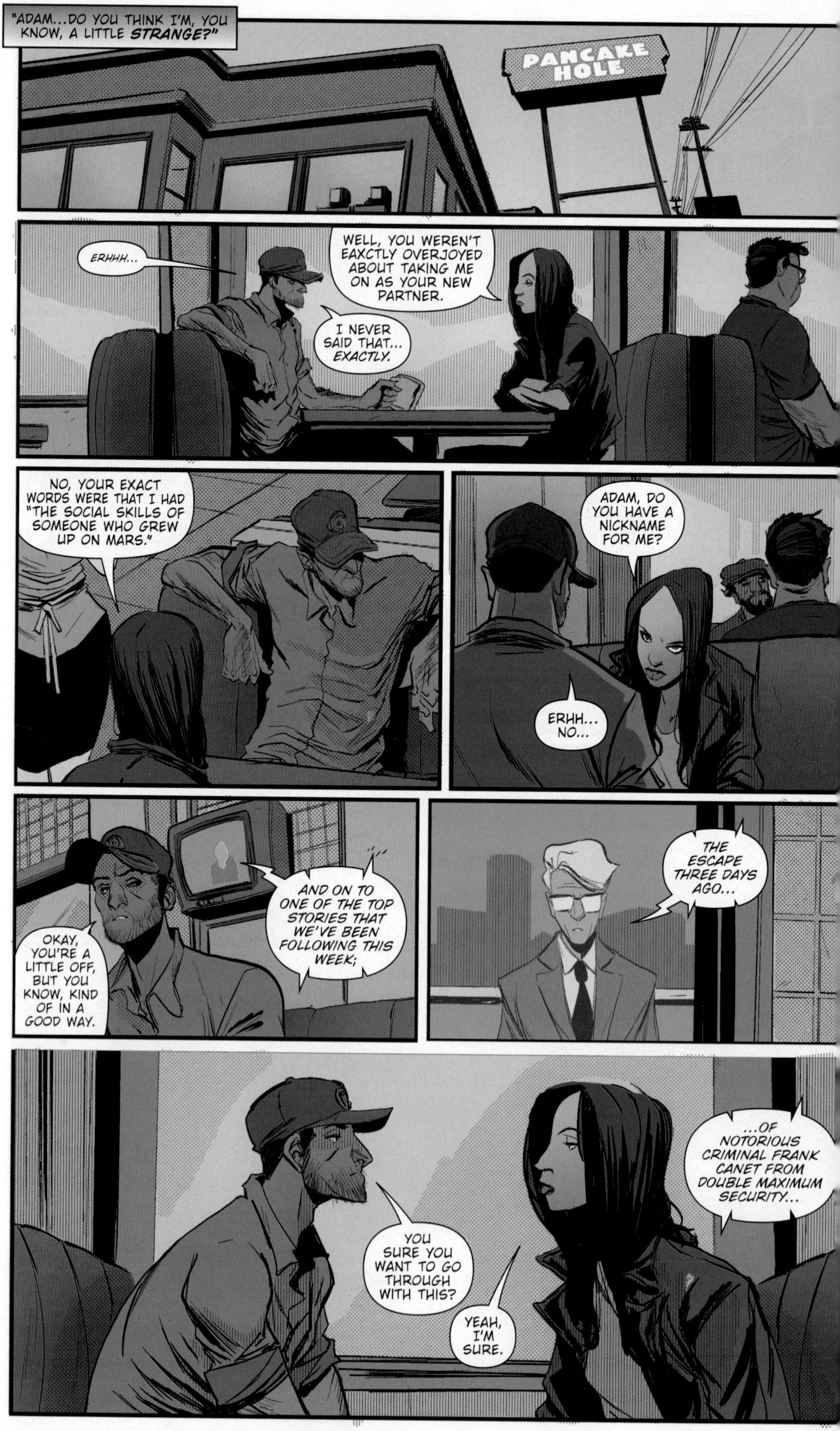
"ADAM...DO YOU THINK I'M, YOU KNOW, A LITTLE STRANGE?"
PANCAKE HOLE
ERHHH...
WELL, YOU WEREN'T EAXCTLY OVERJOYED ABOUT TAKING ME ON AS YOUR NEW PARTNER.
I NEVER SAID THAT... EXACTLY.
NO, YOUR EXACT WORDS WERE THAT I HAD "THE SOCIAL SKILLS OF SOMEONE WHO GREW UP ON MARS."
ADAM, DO YOU HAVE A NICKNAME FOR ME?
ERHH... NO...
AND ON TO ONE OF THE TOP STORIES THAT WE'VE BEEN FOLLOWING THIS WEEK;
OKAY, YOU'RE A LITTLE OFF, BUT YOU KNOW, KIND OF IN A GOOD WAY.
THE ESCAPE THREE DAYS AGO...
...OF NOTORIOUS CRIMINAL FRANK CANET FROM DOUBLE MAXIMUM SECURITY...
YOU SURE YOU WANT TO GO THROUGH WITH THIS?
YEAH, I'M SURE.

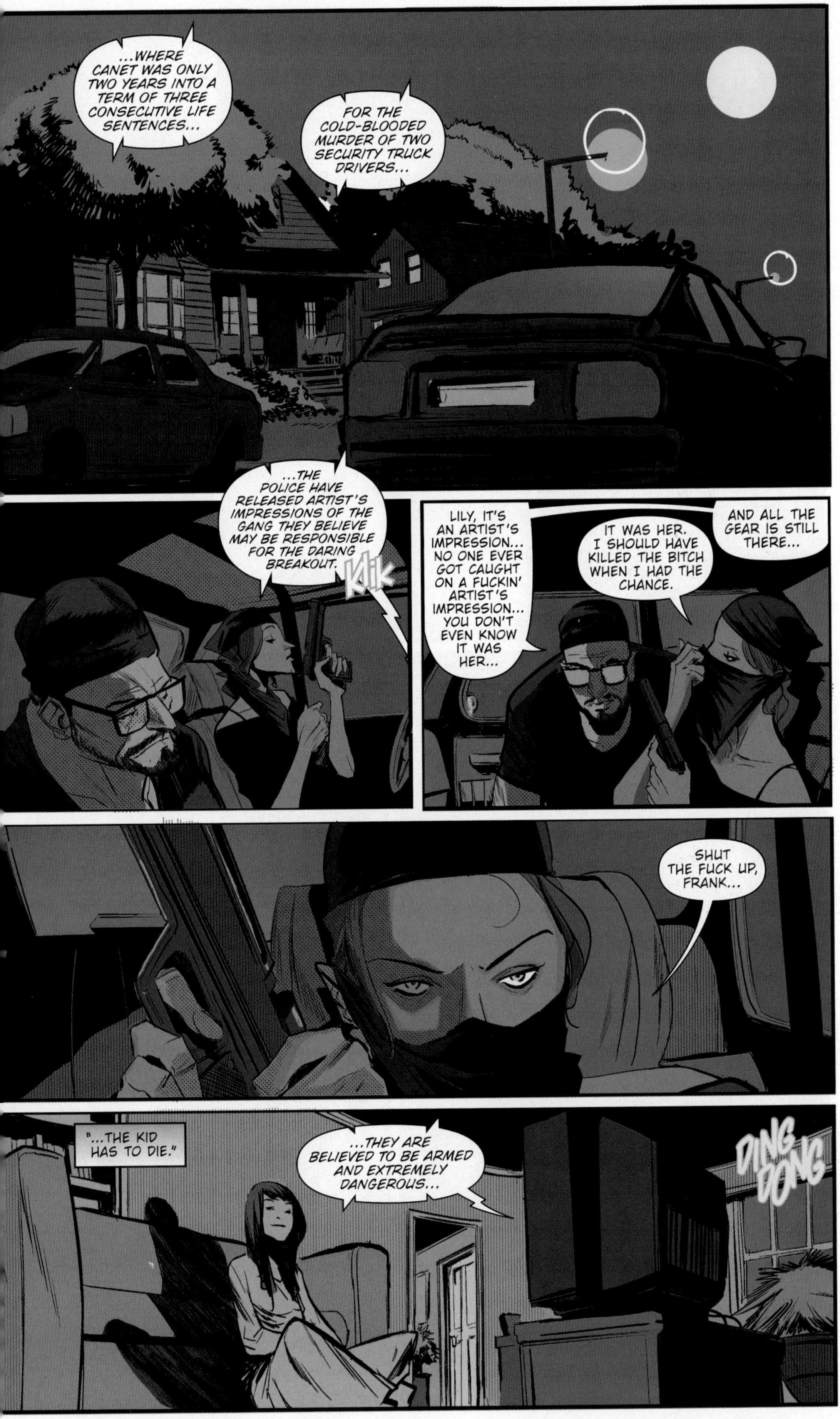
...WHERE CANET WAS ONLY TWO YEARS INTO A TERM OF THREE CONSECUTIVE LIFE SENTENCES...
FOR THE COLD-BLOODED MURDER OF TWO SECURITY TRUCK DRIVERS...
...THE POLICE HAVE RELEASED ARTIST'S IMPRESSIONS OF THE GANG THEY BELIEVE MAY BE RESPONSIBLE FOR THE DARING BREAKOUT.
KLIK
LILY, IT'S AN ARTIST'S IMPRESSION... NO ONE EVER GOT CAUGHT ON A FUCKIN' ARTIST'S IMPRESSION... YOU DON'T EVEN KNOW IT WAS HER...
IT WAS HER. I SHOULD HAVE KILLED THE BITCH WHEN I HAD THE CHANCE.
AND ALL THE GEAR IS STILL THERE...
SHUT THE FUCK UP, FRANK...
"...THE KID HAS TO DIE."
...THEY ARE BELIEVED TO BE ARMED AND EXTREMELY DANGEROUS...
DING DONG

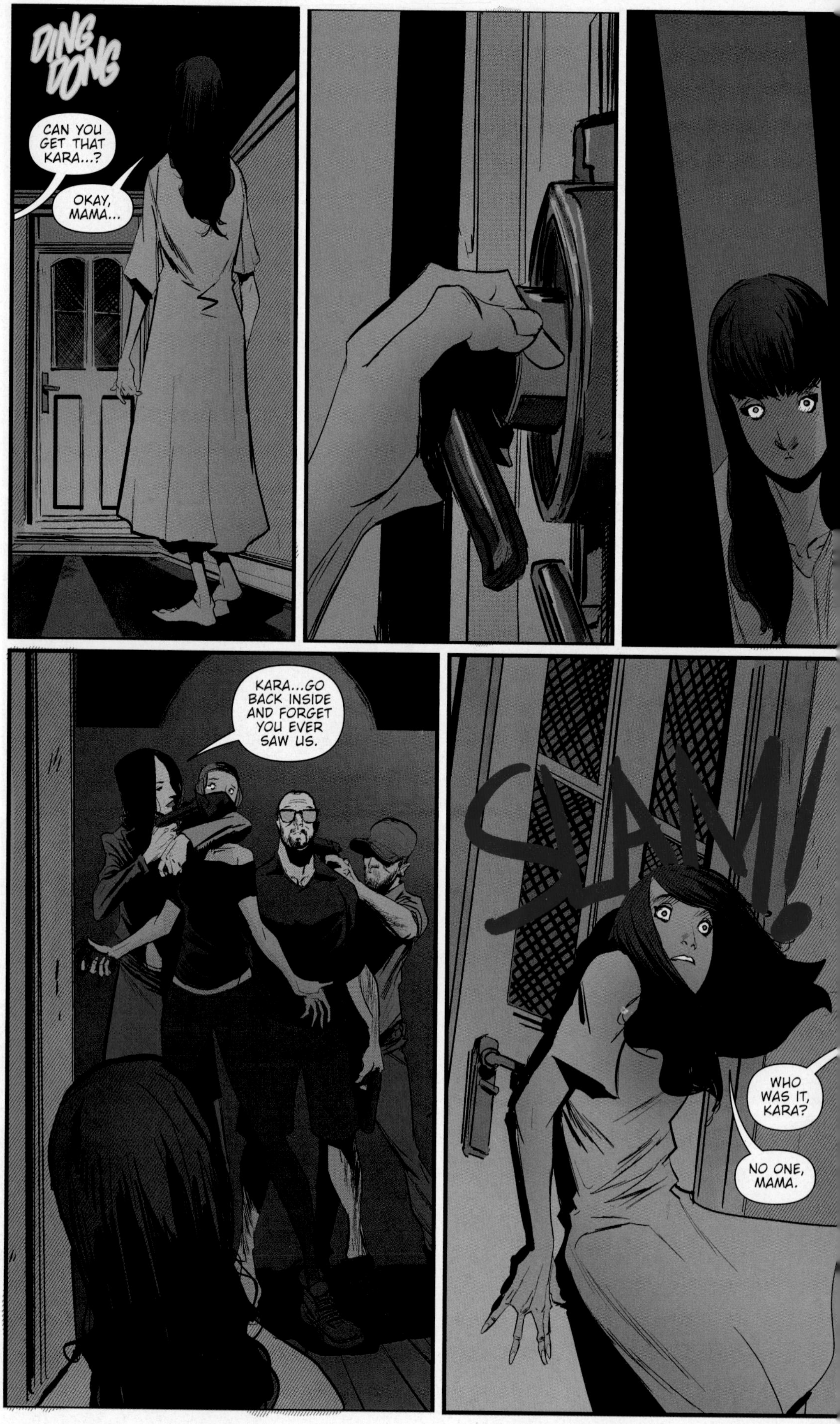
DING DONG
CAN YOU GET THAT KARA...?
OKAY, MAMA...
KARA...GO BACK INSIDE AND FORGET YOU EVER SAW US.
SLAM!
WHO WAS IT, KARA?
NO ONE, MAMA.

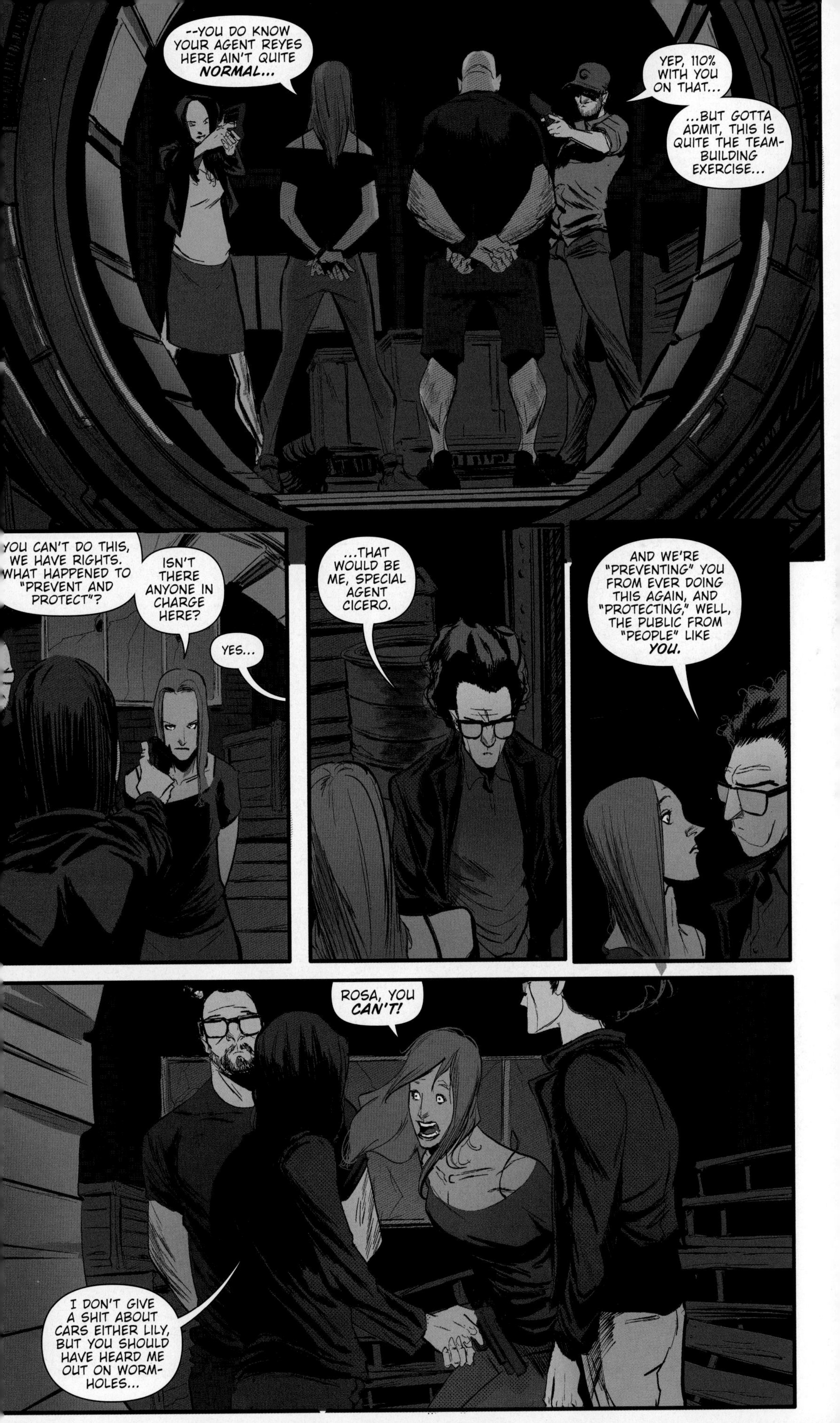
--YOU DO KNOW YOUR AGENT REYES HERE AIN'T QUITE NORMAL...
YEP, 110% WITH YOU ON THAT...
...BUT GOTTA ADMIT, THIS IS QUITE THE TEAM-BUILDING EXERCISE...
YOU CAN'T DO THIS, WE HAVE RIGHTS. WHAT HAPPENED TO "PREVENT AND PROTECT"?
ISN'T THERE ANYONE IN CHARGE HERE?
YES...
...THAT WOULD BE ME, SPECIAL AGENT CICERO.
AND WE'RE "PREVENTING" YOU FROM EVER DOING THIS AGAIN, AND "PROTECTING," WELL, THE PUBLIC FROM "PEOPLE" LIKE YOU.
ROSA, YOU CAN'T!
I DON'T GIVE A SHIT ABOUT CARS EITHER LILY, BUT YOU SHOULD HAVE HEARD ME OUT ON WORM-HOLES...

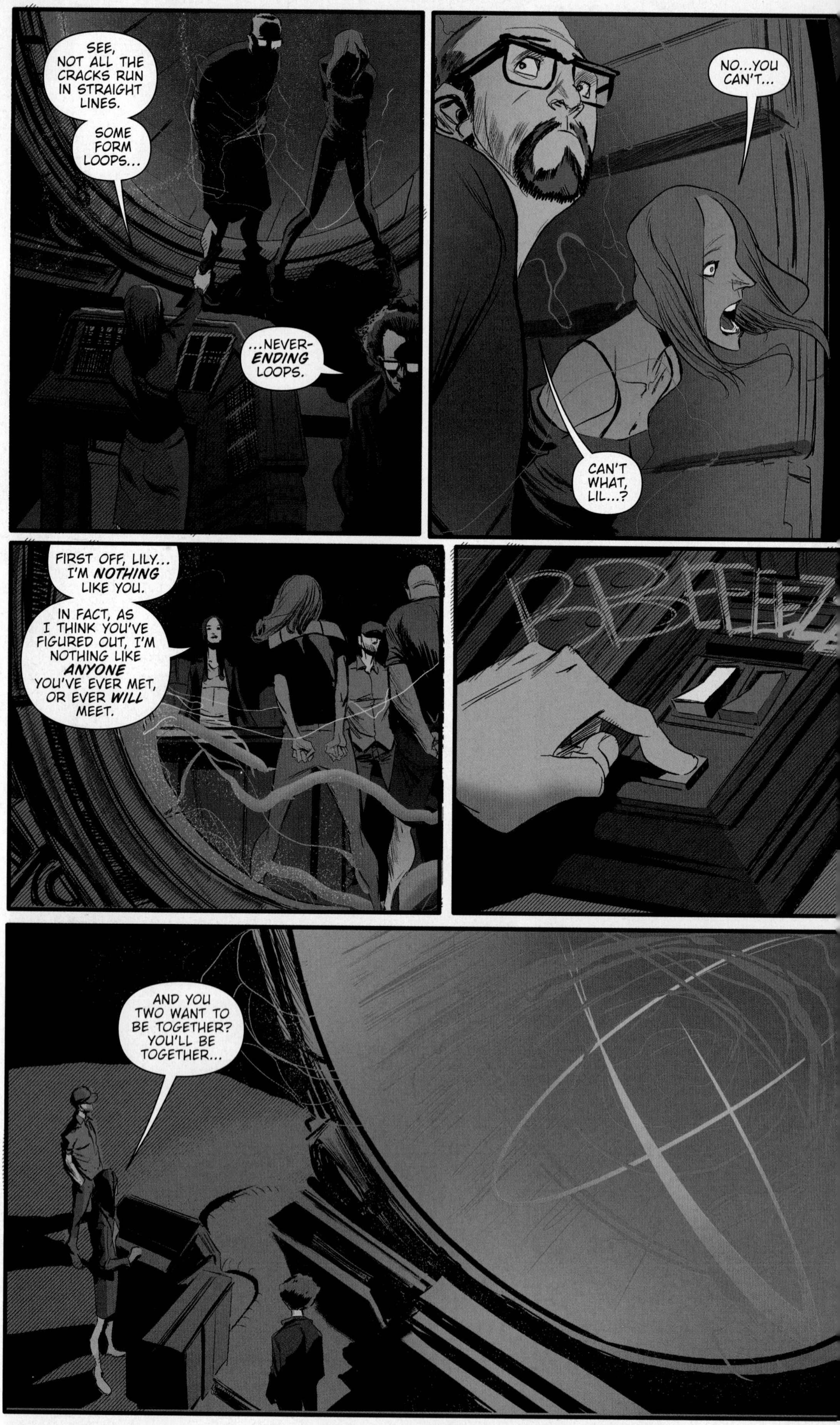
SEE, NOT ALL THE CRACKS RUN IN STRAIGHT LINES.
SOME FORM LOOPS...
...NEVER-*ENDING* LOOPS.
NO...YOU CAN'T...
CAN'T WHAT, LIL...?
FIRST OFF, LILY... I'M ***NOTHING*** LIKE YOU.
IN FACT, AS I THINK YOU'VE FIGURED OUT, I'M NOTHING LIKE ***ANYONE*** YOU'VE EVER MET, OR EVER ***WILL*** MEET.
AND YOU TWO WANT TO BE TOGETHER? YOU'LL BE TOGETHER...

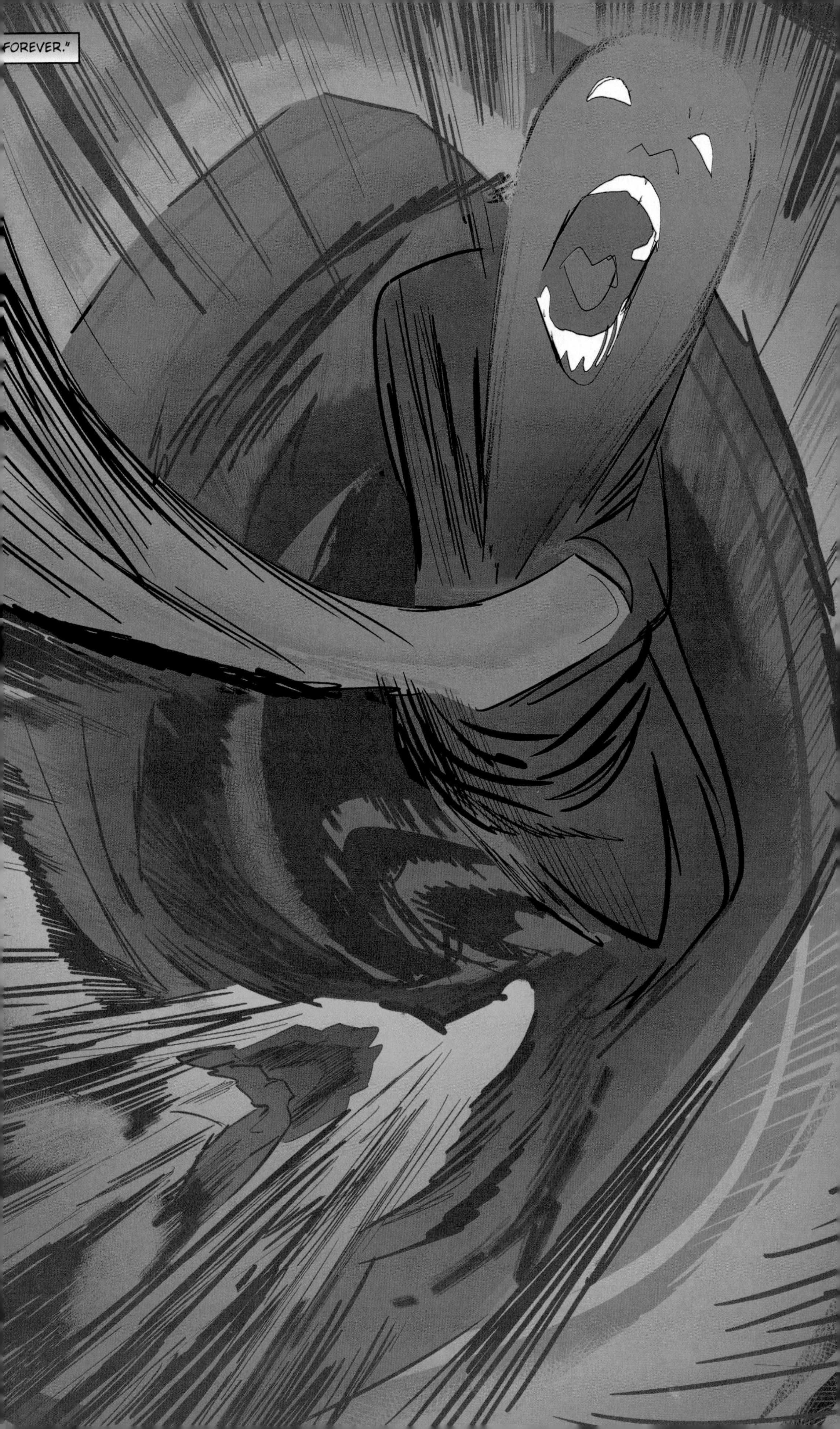
FOREVER."

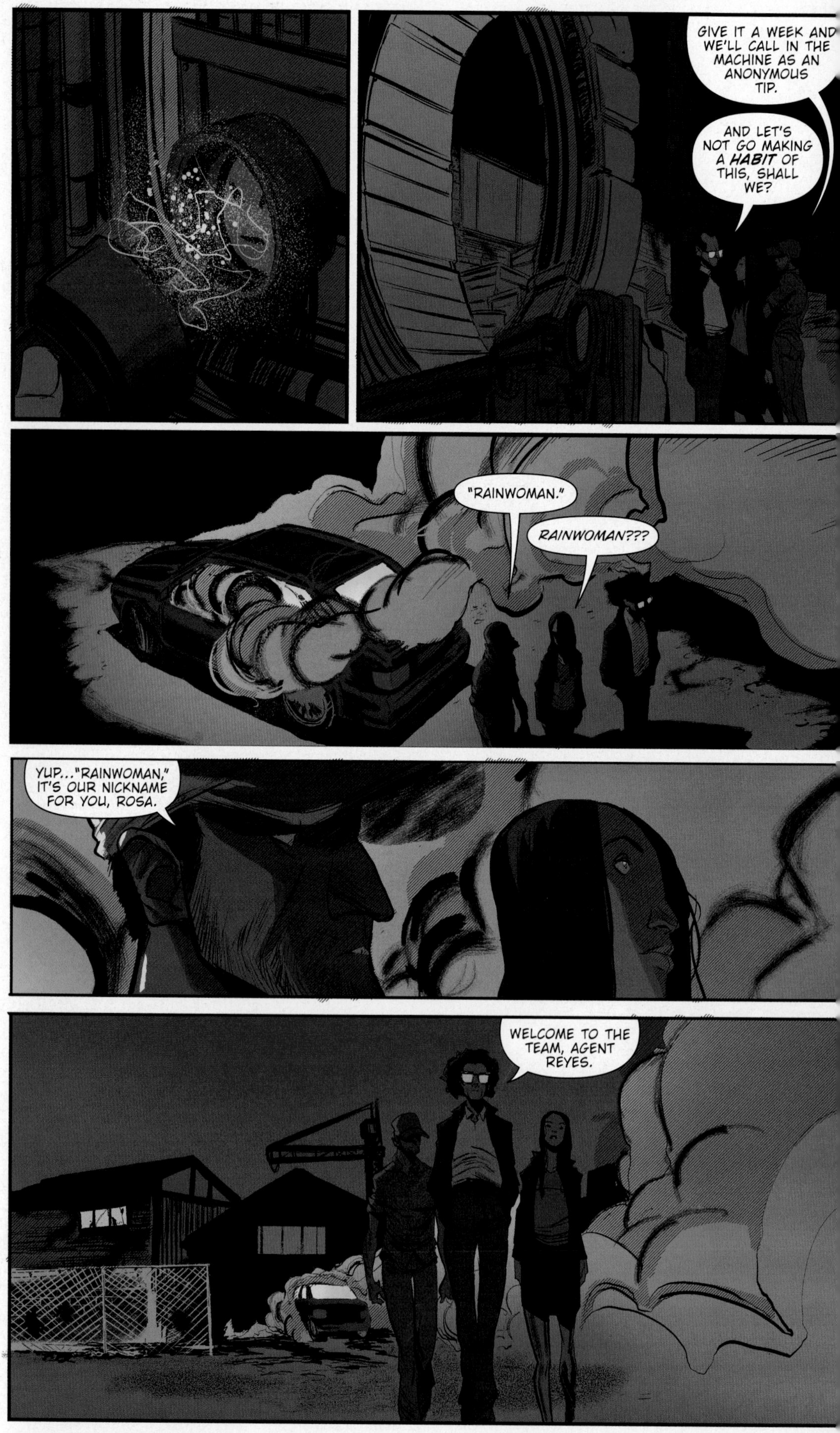
GIVE IT A WEEK AND WE'LL CALL IN THE MACHINE AS AN ANONYMOUS TIP.
AND LET'S NOT GO MAKING A *HABIT* OF THIS, SHALL WE?
"RAINWOMAN."
RAINWOMAN???
YUP..."RAINWOMAN," IT'S OUR NICKNAME FOR YOU, ROSA.
WELCOME TO THE TEAM, AGENT REYES.

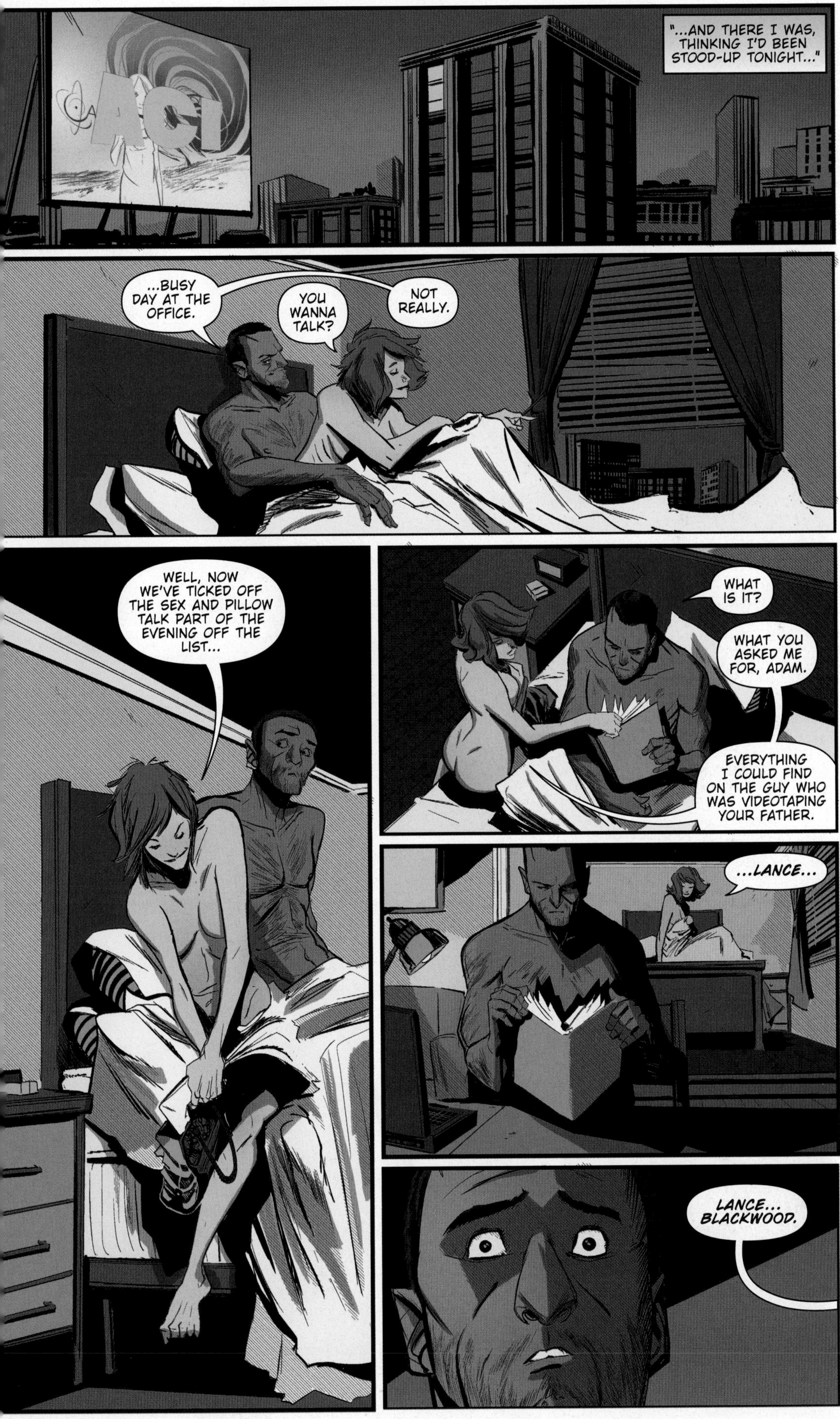
"...AND THERE I WAS, THINKING I'D BEEN STOOD-UP TONIGHT..."
...BUSY DAY AT THE OFFICE.
YOU WANNA TALK?
NOT REALLY.
WELL, NOW WE'VE TICKED OFF THE SEX AND PILLOW TALK PART OF THE EVENING OFF THE LIST...
WHAT IS IT?
WHAT YOU ASKED ME FOR, ADAM.
EVERYTHING I COULD FIND ON THE GUY WHO WAS VIDEOTAPING YOUR FATHER.
...LANCE...
LANCE... BLACKWOOD.

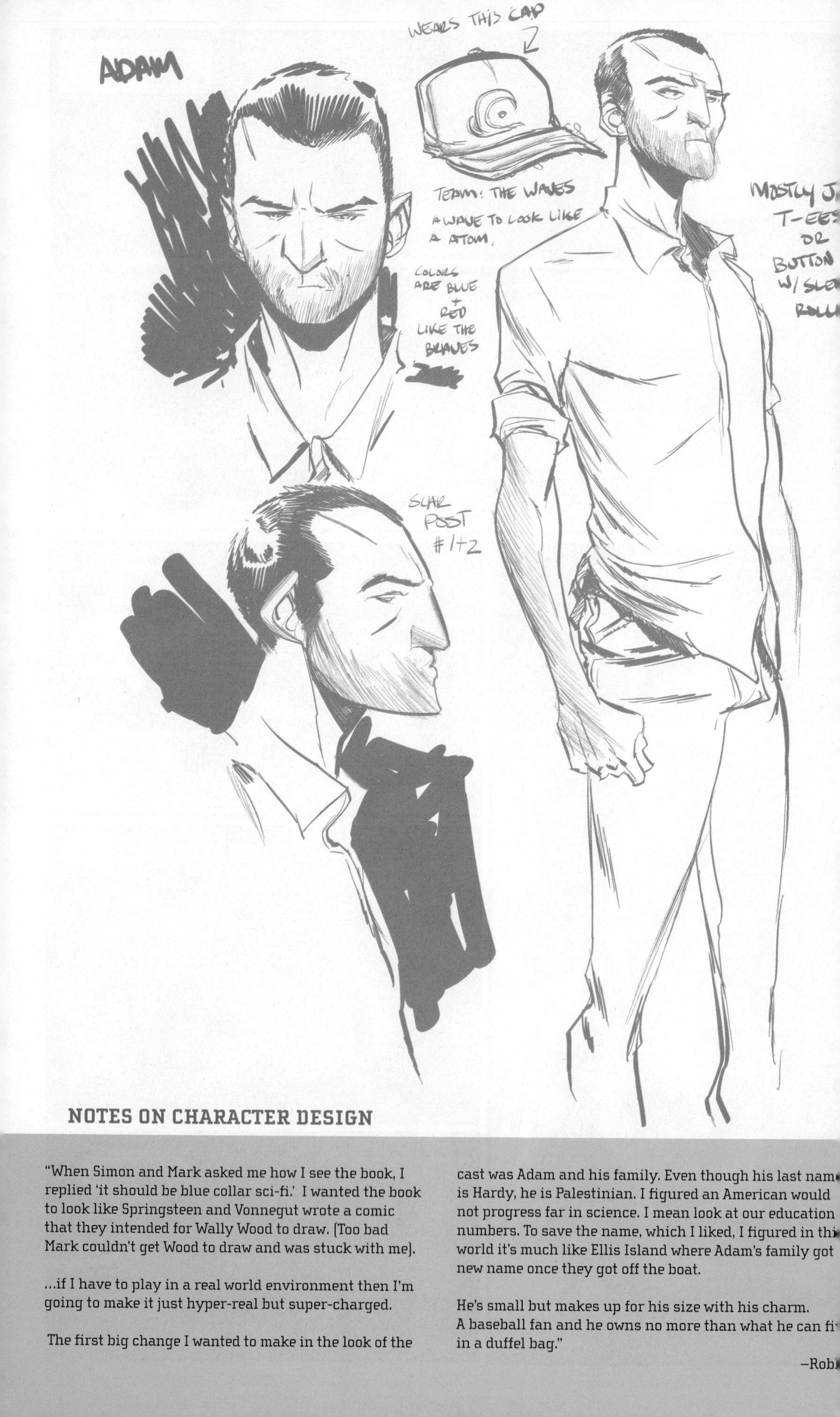
ADAM
WEARS THIS CAP
TEAM: THE WAVES
A WAVE TO LOOK LIKE A ATOM.
COLORS ARE BLUE + RED LIKE THE BRAVES
MOSTLY J
T-EES OR BUTTON W/SLE ROLL
SCAR POST #1+2

NOTES ON CHARACTER DESIGN

"When Simon and Mark asked me how I see the book, I replied 'it should be blue collar sci-fi.' I wanted the book to look like Springsteen and Vonnegut wrote a comic that they intended for Wally Wood to draw. (Too bad Mark couldn't get Wood to draw and was stuck with me).

...if I have to play in a real world environment then I'm going to make it just hyper-real but super-charged.

The first big change I wanted to make in the look of the cast was Adam and his family. Even though his last nam is Hardy, he is Palestinian. I figured an American would not progress far in science. I mean look at our education numbers. To save the name, which I liked, I figured in thi world it's much like Ellis Island where Adam's family got new name once they got off the boat.

He's small but makes up for his size with his charm. A baseball fan and he owns no more than what he can fi in a duffel bag."

—Robi

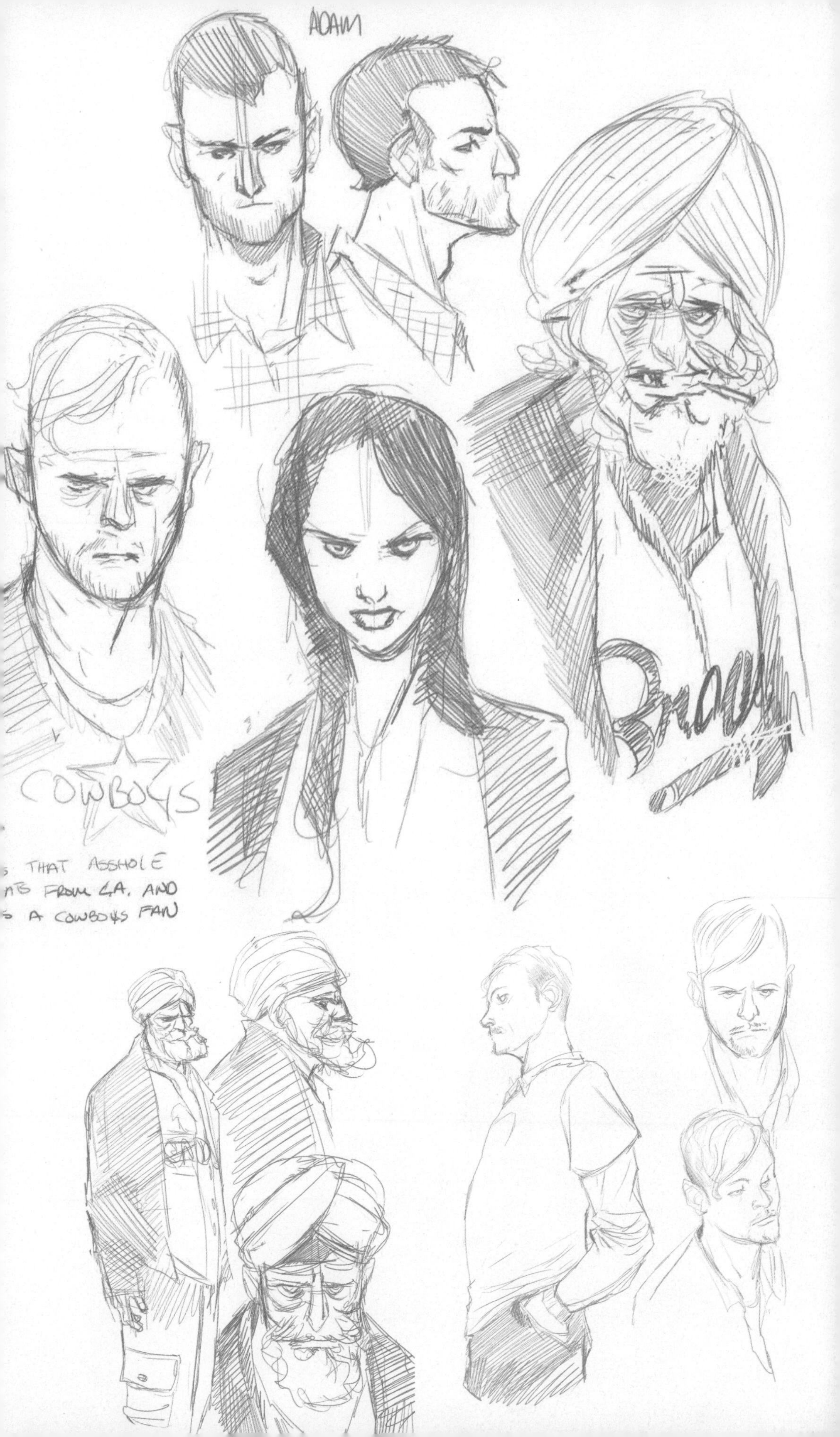
ADAM
COWBOYS
S THAT ASSHOLE
ATS FROM GA. AND
S A COWBOYS FAN

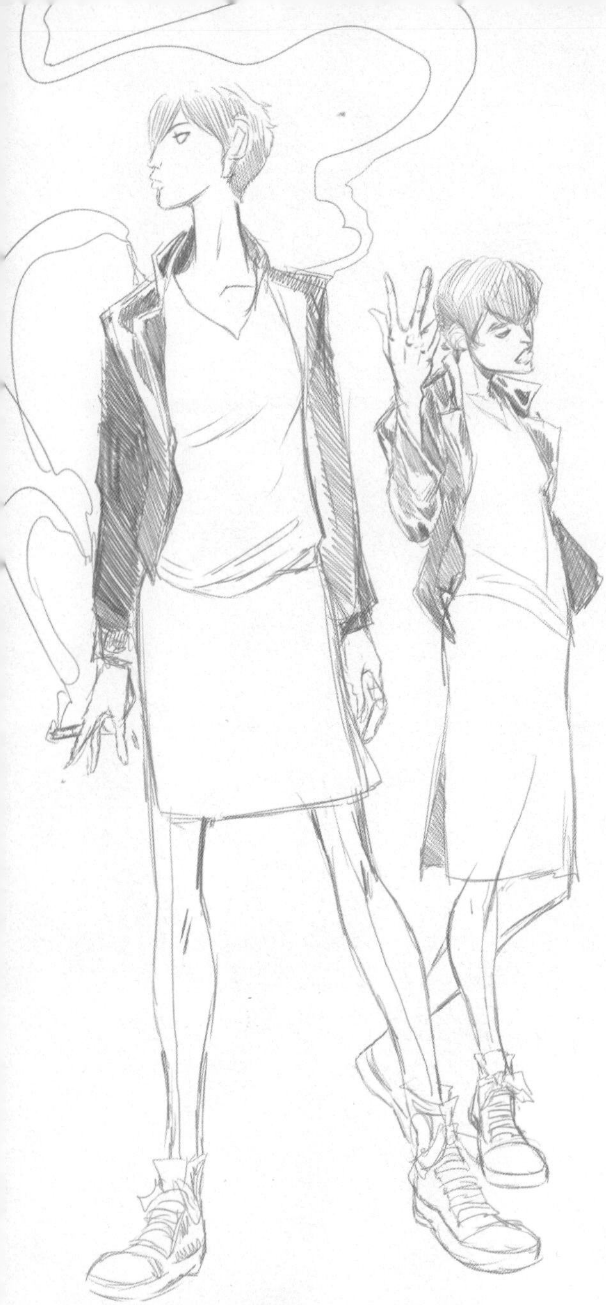

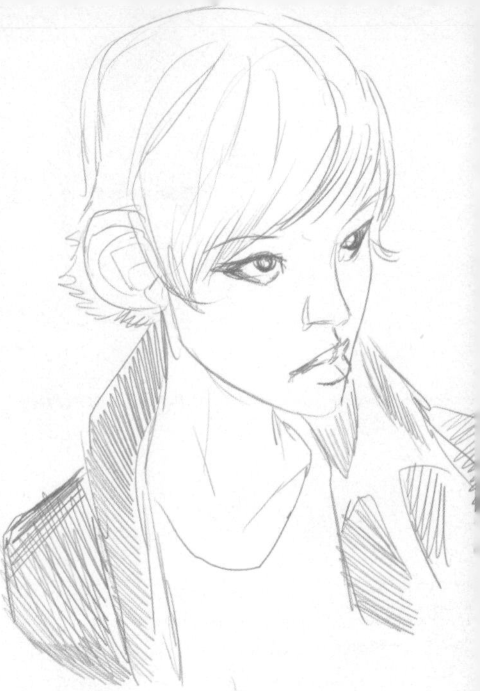

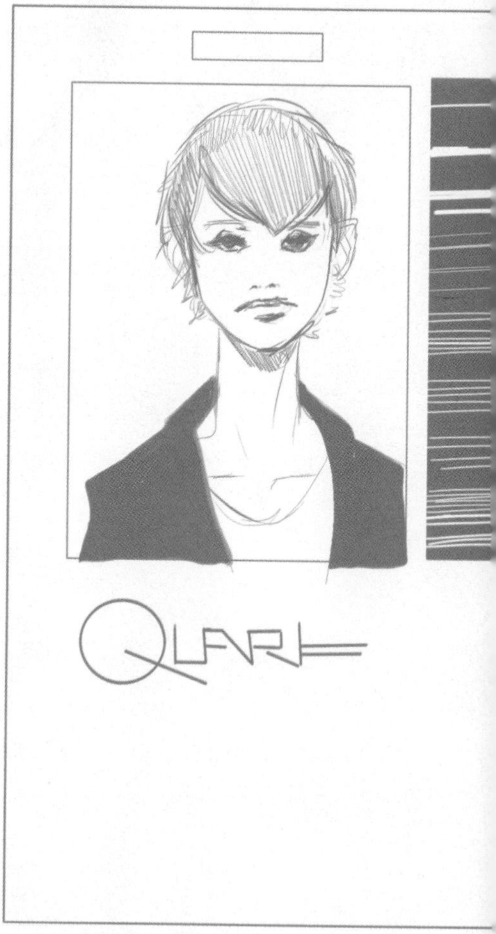
QUARK

Early design for Rosa.

Quark was an early working name for what became ACI, or Atom-Craft Industries.

BAND T-SHIRT OR
LOOSE TOP

PROFESSEONAL
TRUST.   BUTTON

JEANES
OR
SKIRT W/ TIGHTS OR STOCKINGS

ROSIA

Final Design for Rosa.

"That same thinking went in with all of the cast. I wish I could give you more here, but there is so much backstory in my head with each person we want to save it to play with down the road..."

—Robbi

CHUCKS
BUT MIXED MACHED

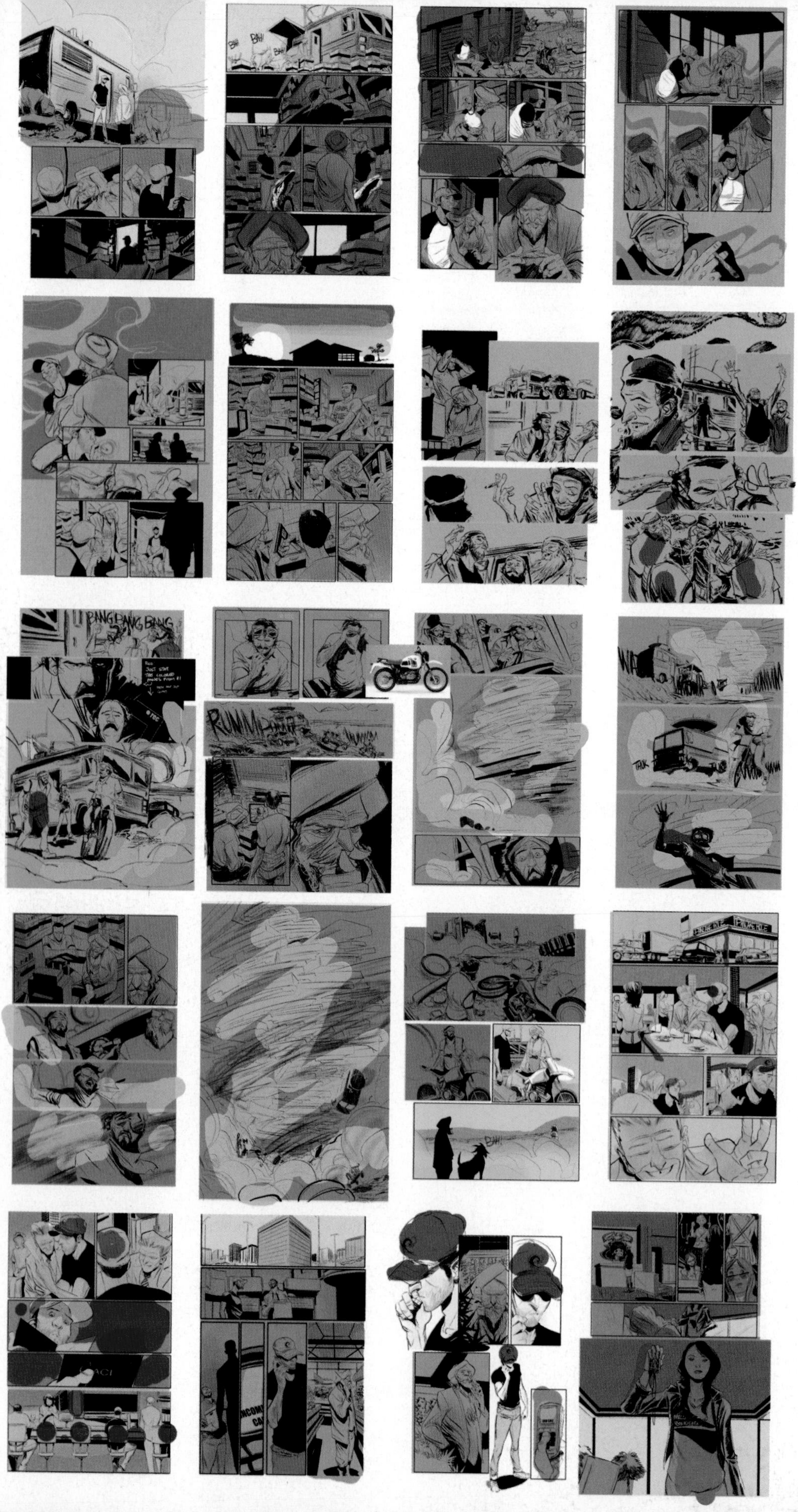
BAH!
BAH!
BAH!
BANG BANG BANG
THAK

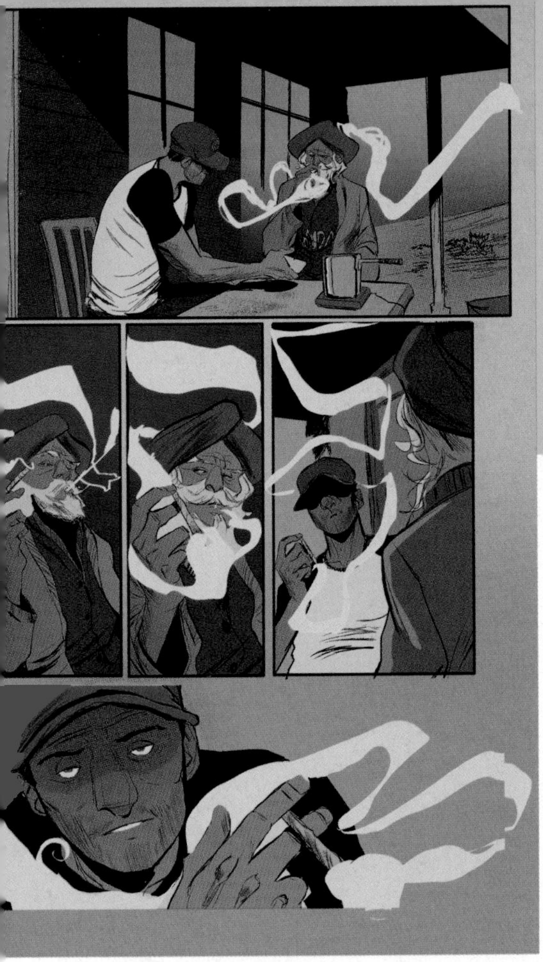

NOTES ON COLOR

"...A world where warm colors and lime green are king."

—Robbi

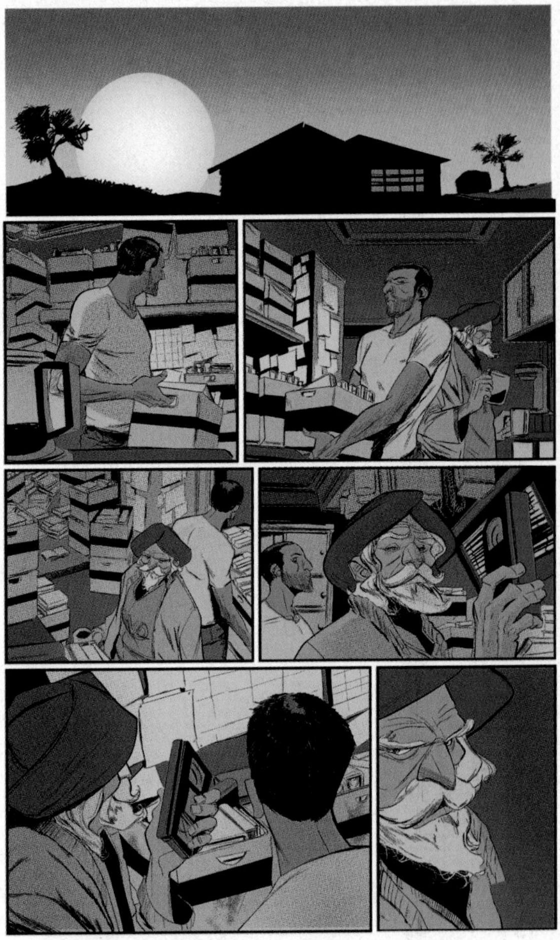

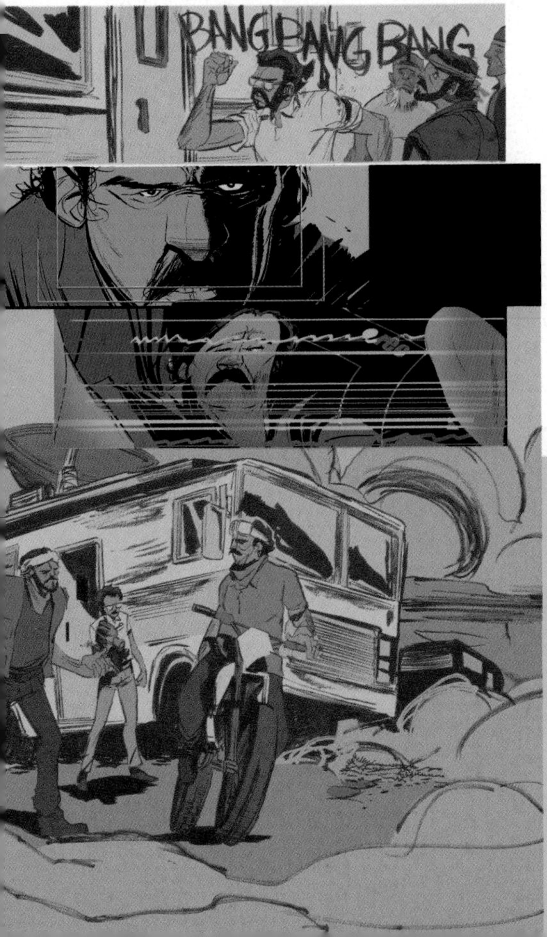
BANG BANG BANG

"I've wanted to work with Robbi for years. He's more than capable of coloring his own work so I definitely wanted to get his ideas and input before we started on this project. The key words I remember are 'AKIRA', 'Michael Mann', and 'no earth tones.' Since local color and I are not on good terms, I thought this would be a perfect book for me and it's been a blast so far!"

—Rico

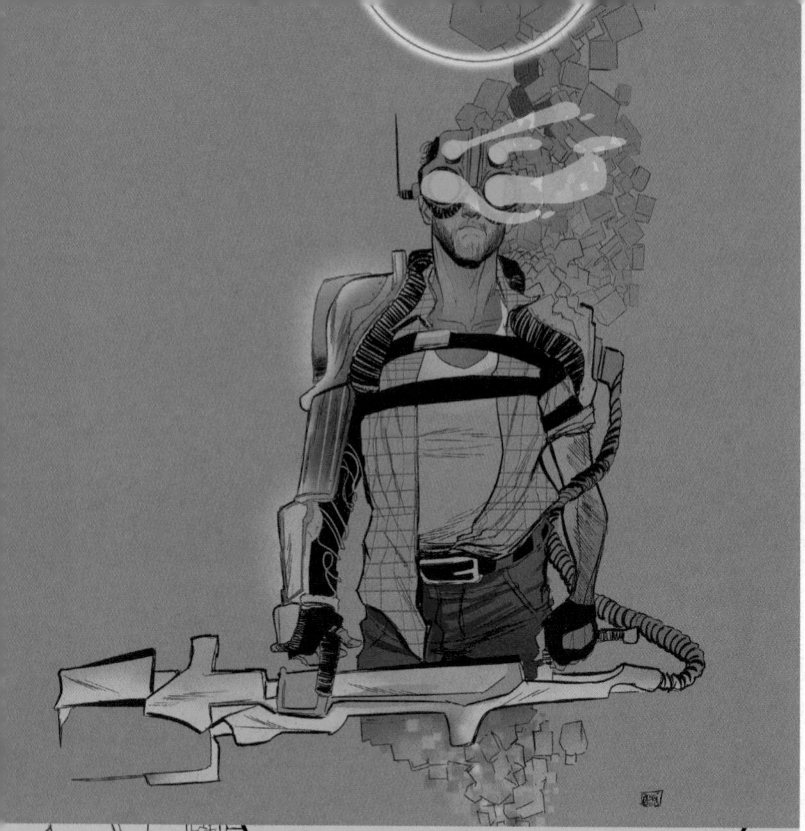

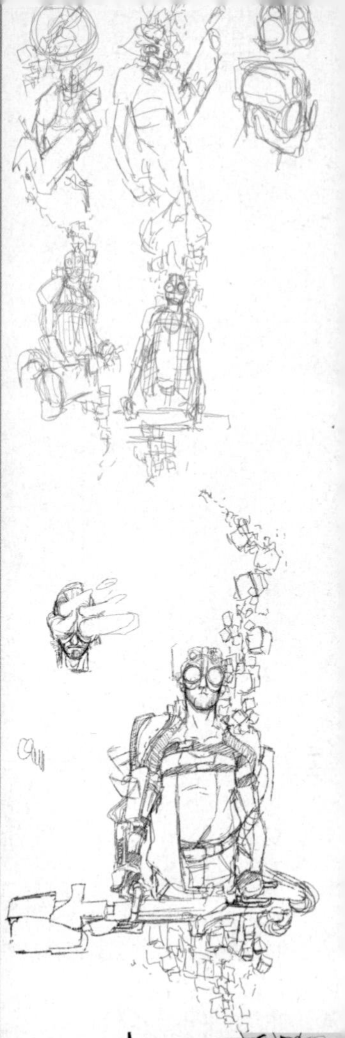

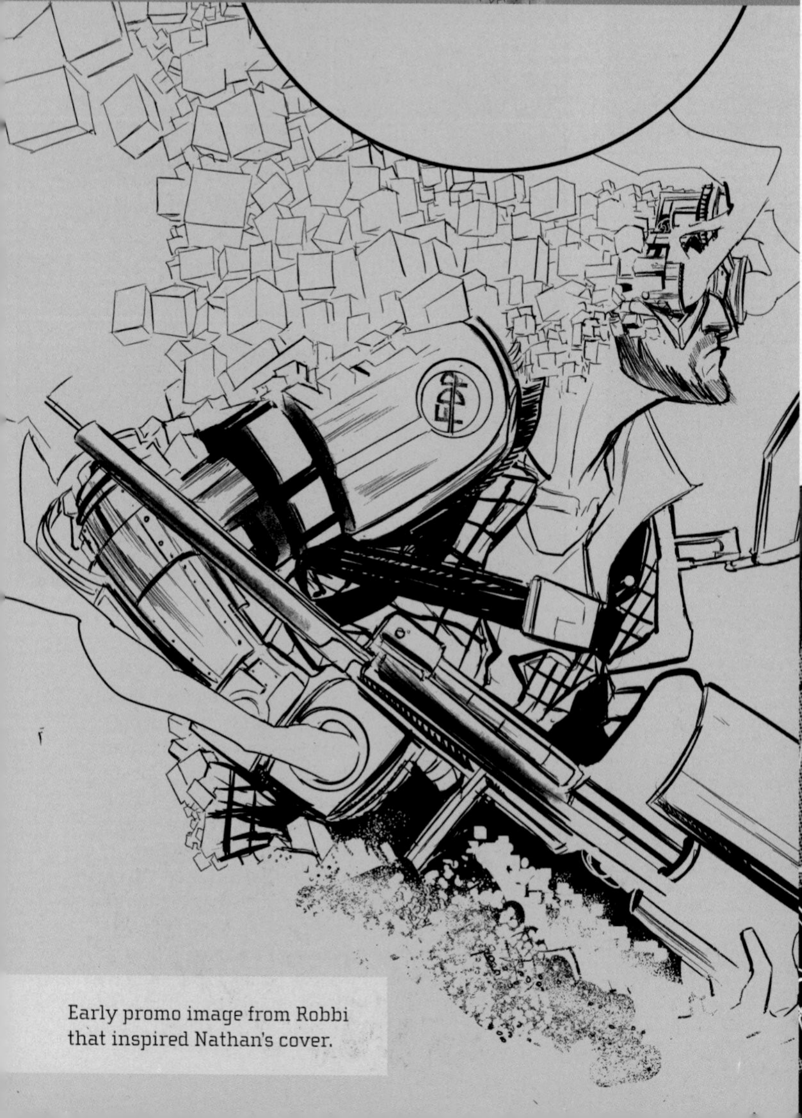

Early promo image from Robbi that inspired Nathan's cover.

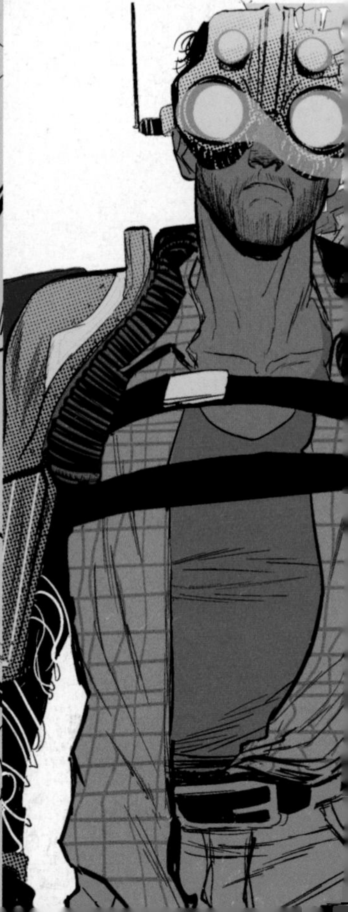

NOTES ON THE COVER

"Designing a cover for a first issue is hard. It has to grab you, has to say something about the book, has to tell a story — lots of pressure.

We knew NATHAN FOX was the man for the job. He's an incredible illustrator and his design-sense is top-notch. Nathan brought a lot of ideas to the first cover sketches (the badge, global phenomenon, vibrant color). We liked all of it, but when I took it to the rest of the Verti-gang to discuss Shelly [Bond, Executive Editor] and Will [Dennis, Group Editor] said, 'We love this line drawing of Adam and his crazy helmet. What if he just did that but kind of pushed in — gave it an interesting crop.'

I thought that could be cool, brought it back to Nathan and he said, 'yeah, cool, what if we just flipped him upside down?'

That was it. He nailed it."

—Mark

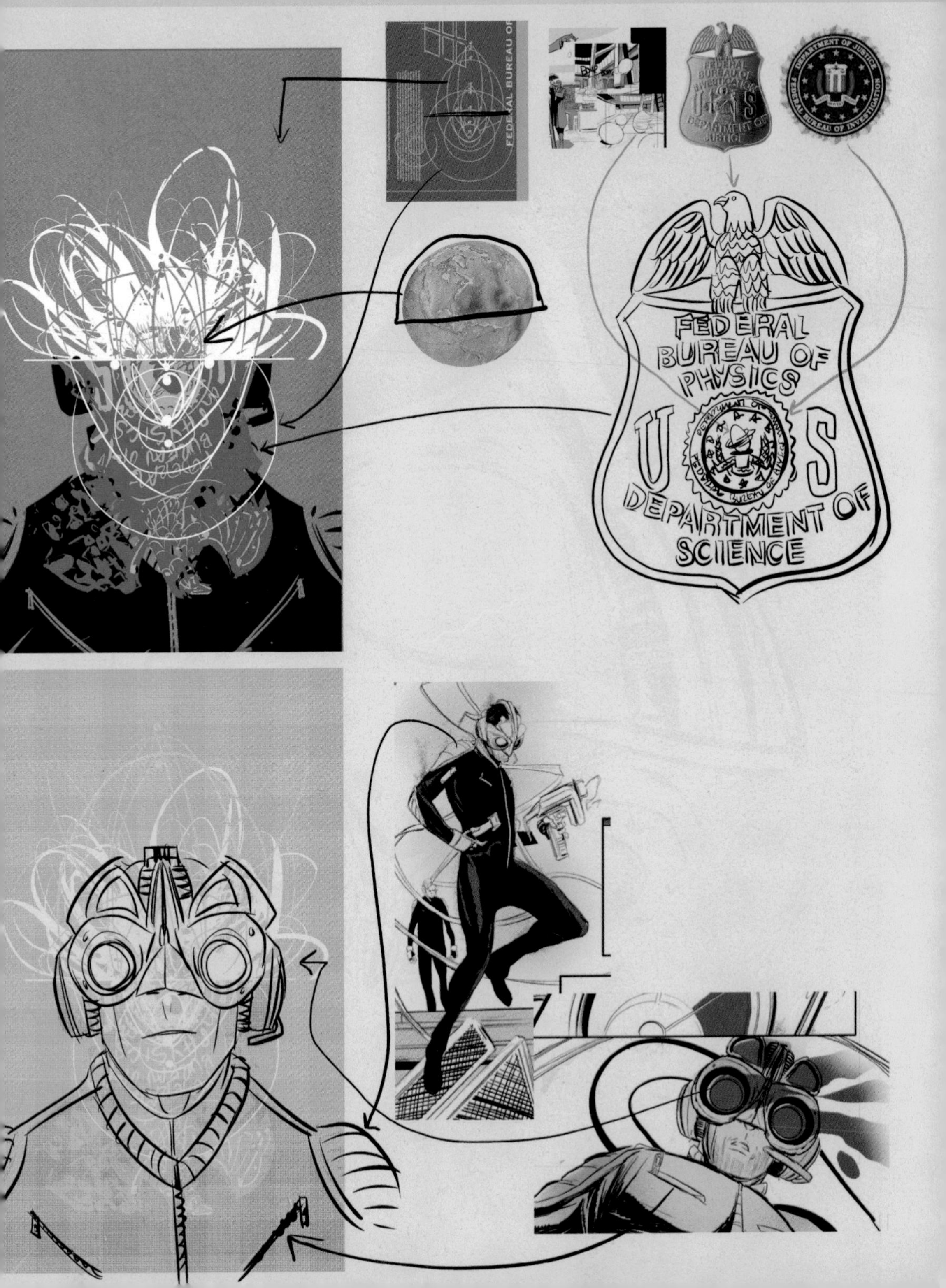
FEDERAL BUREAU OF
DEPARTMENT OF JUSTICE
FEDERAL BUREAU OF INVESTIGATION
FEDERAL BUREAU OF PHYSICS
U S
DEPARTMENT OF SCIENCE

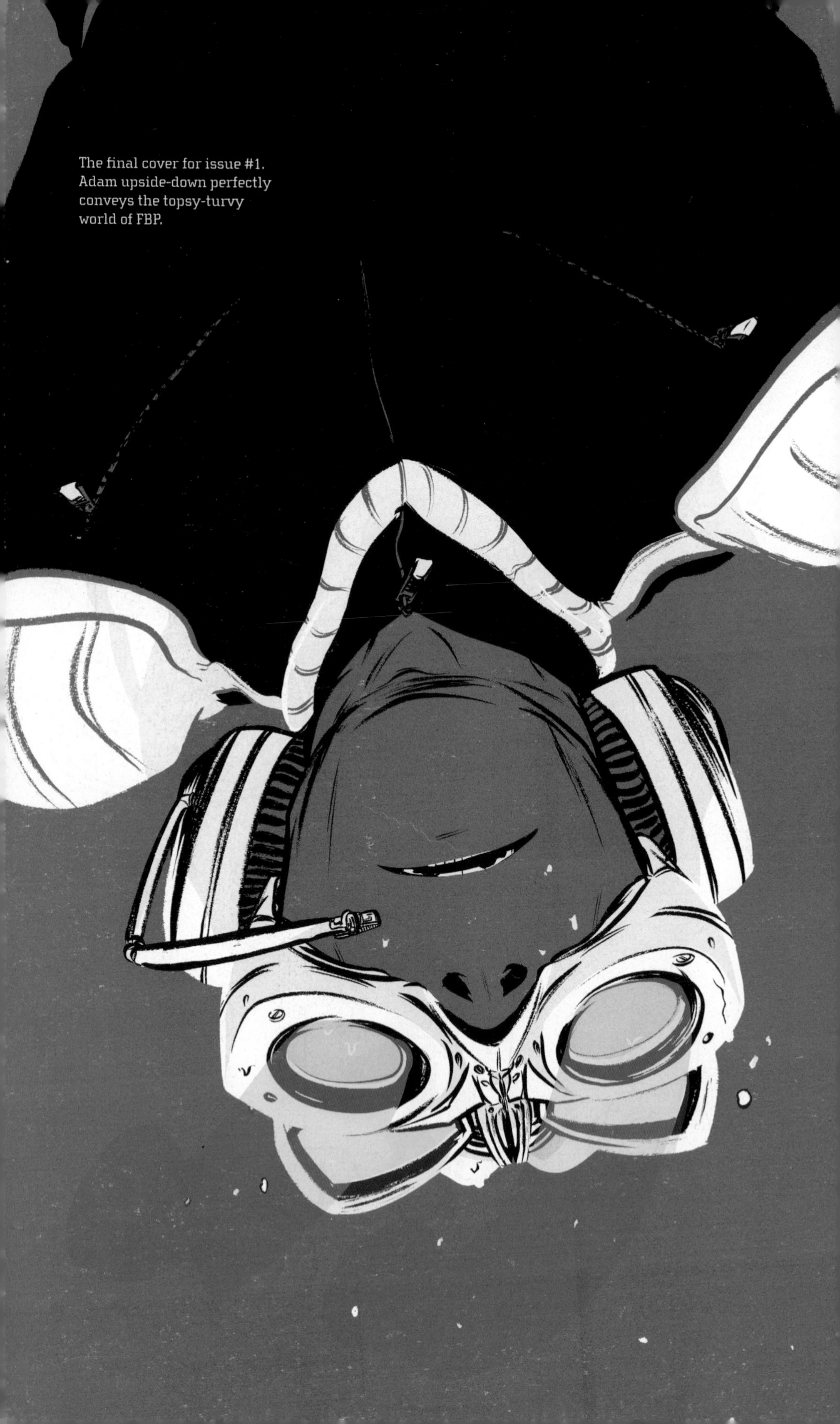

The final cover for issue #1. Adam upside-down perfectly conveys the topsy-turvy world of FBP.